Wheels Within Wheels

Wheels
Within Wheels

AN UNCONVENTIONAL LIFE

Lord Montagu of Beaulieu

Weidenfeld & Nicolson

LONDON

First published in Great Britain in 2000
by Weidenfeld & Nicolson

© 2000 Montagu Ventures Limited
The moral right of Lord Montagu to be identified as the author
of this work has been asserted in accordance with
the Copyright, Designs and Patents Act of 1988.

A CIP catalogue record for this book is available from the British Library.

ISBN 0 297 81739 6

Typeset by Selwood Systems, Midsomer Norton

Set in Adobe Garamond

Printed in Great Britain by
Butler & Tanner Ltd, Frome and London

Weidenfeld & Nicolson

The Orion Publishing Group Ltd
Orion House
5 Upper Saint Martin's Lane
London, WC2H 9EA

For my family and especially to Belinda
and our children, Ralph and Mary,
and to Fiona and our son, Jonathan,
for their constant love and support

CONTENTS

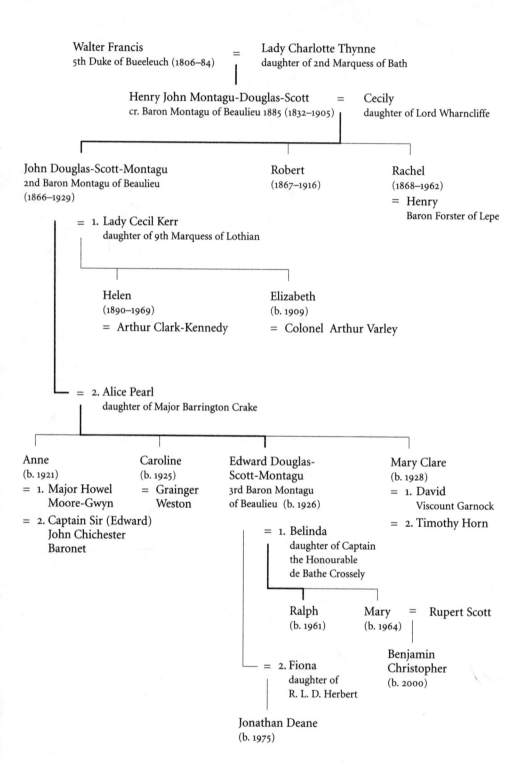

Walter Francis
5th Duke of Bueeleuch (1806–84)
=
Lady Charlotte Thynne
daughter of 2nd Marquess of Bath

Henry John Montagu-Douglas-Scott
cr. Baron Montagu of Beaulieu 1885 (1832–1905)
=
Cecily
daughter of Lord Wharncliffe

John Douglas-Scott-Montagu
2nd Baron Montagu of Beaulieu
(1866–1929)

Robert
(1867–1916)

Rachel
(1868–1962)
= Henry
Baron Forster of Lepe

= 1. Lady Cecil Kerr
daughter of 9th Marquess of Lothian

Helen
(1890–1969)
= Arthur Clark-Kennedy

Elizabeth
(b. 1909)
= Colonel Arthur Varley

= 2. Alice Pearl
daughter of Major Barrington Crake

Anne
(b. 1921)
= 1. Major Howel
Moore-Gwyn
= 2. Captain Sir (Edward)
John Chichester
Baronet

Caroline
(b. 1925)
= Grainger
Weston

Edward Douglas-
Scott-Montagu
3rd Baron Montagu
of Beaulieu (b. 1926)

Mary Clare
(b. 1928)
= 1. David
Viscount Garnock
= 2. Timothy Horn

= 1. Belinda
daughter of Captain
the Honourable
de Bathe Crossely

Ralph
(b. 1961)

Mary
(b. 1964)
= Rupert Scott

Benjamin
Christopher
(b. 2000)

= 2. Fiona
daughter of
R. L. D. Herbert

Jonathan Deane
(b. 1975)

ILLUSTRATIONS

Sections of illustrations appear between pp. 114 and 115; 146 and 147; and 210 and 211

The young Lord Montagu with his sisters and mother
His father, John Douglas-Scott Montagu, 2nd Baron Montagu of Beaulieu, with his son and heir, Edward
The family group in the grounds of Palace House
The young Edward outside Palace House
His stepfather, Ned Pleyell-Bouverie
Dressed up for the coronation of George VI & Queen Elizabeth
With his sister in South Africa
At Ridley College in Canada
At Eton
In Grenadier guard uniform
Refugees disembarking an illegal transport ship, Haifa, Palestine
At Oxford
The Oxford University Dramatic Society
Cast of the play 'Smoker'
Alan Clark as a student at Oxford
Lord Montagu under arrest, 1953 (*picture courtesy of Popperfoto*)
Peter Wildeblood (*picture courtesy of Popperfoto*)
Michael Pitt-Rivers (*picture courtesy of the Daily Mirror*)
The infamous *Daily Express* headline picture (*picture courtesy of the Daily Express*)
The beach hut exterior
The beach hut interior
Preparing for the opening of Palace House in 1952
Opening the Motor Museum
Edward, Prince of Wales, and his father in an 1899 Daimler
Two interior pictures of the Motor Museum as it was in the early days
London–Brighton rally with Jim Clark
With Sterling Moss admiring the W196 Mercedes Grand-Prix car
Showing the 1901 electric Columbia to HRH Prince of Wales & Earl Mountbatten

All pictures are from the author's collection unless otherwise stated

ACKNOWLEDGEMENTS

Many people have generously helped me with this book, particularly in jogging and rectifying my diminishing memory, and reminding me of many individuals and events, which in major or minor ways have moulded my life. My first debt of gratitude must go to my mother, who died aged 101 and whose diligent and splendid diary keeping since her early life allowed me to record, in such fascinating detail, my own formative years. In this, I would also like to acknowledge the great help my family in general have given me.

It was indeed fortunate that I possess the only known transcript of the trials of 1953 and 1954, so the accuracy of this period is guaranteed, although the newspaper cuttings of the time have proved too painful for me to have examined in detail, but others have done so. Lord Rawlinson of Ewell, Lord Hutchinson of Lullington and journalist Audrey Whiting gave helpful advice concerning this period, but of course, above all, Peter Wildeblood's book, *Against the Law*, was invaluable.

However very material were the volumes of books, cuttings and annual reports referring to other periods in my life, as a magazine publisher, President of the Historic Houses Association, President of the Museums Association and Chairman of English Heritage, but alas not much from my time in advertising with Voice and Vision, but compensated by splendid news cuttings of the Beaulieu Jazz Festivals.

I was keenly aware of my responsibility to record for the first time, in the fairest and most accurate way, the founding and early years of English Heritage. As its first Chairman, I considered it my duty to record its early history from 1983, and the substantial progress made in its first eight years of existence. My special thanks to Peter Rumble, Francis Golding, Jennie Page, and Jane Sharman for their contributions to the text, and to Lord Jenkin of Roding and Rt. Hon. Virginia Bottomley for their help.

Special thanks to Michael Webber of English Heritage and Christopher Raeburn for their musical advice; to my Grenadier batman, Jack

Brown, for the recollection of our time in Palestine; to Sally Moore for Canada; to Ken Robinson for memories of Beaulieu and to Valerie Home for introducing me to the poem *Wisdom from the East*.

Researching my life was never going to be easy and to collate it an even greater task. So my special thanks go to Tim Heald with whom I previously collaborated in 1967 in my book on the Stately Home Business, called *The Gilt and the Gingerbread*, for assisting me once again. I would like to thank him, most sincerely, for his dedication, patience, and tolerance over the past three years in the preparation of this book. Without his help, this book would never have seen the light of day, as my life is still too hectic, nor do I have the application to allow myself the time to contemplate my past years with the equanimity and objectiveness which the reader surely deserves.

M of B, Summer 2000

Two things are impossible:

To miss the happiness that fate had decreed for thee, and
To pass into the unknown before thine appointed time.

To lack energy to put an inspiration into execution
Is to fold up the carpet of pleasure for all time.
Every man's fate is decreed by his own constellation.
He who follows his star
Will have his heart purified from regret, like silver refined.
If in so doing, he lose a drachma
Fate will give him a jewel.
If chance deprive him of a silver apple
Fate will give him a golden orange.
If mishap take away his wax candle
Fate will give him an oil-lamp instead.
For he who is not a lover of adventure
Neither is he a man.

Wend now thy way, with brow serene,
Fear not thy humble tale to tell . . .

Wisdom from the East
Arab Traditional

PROLOGUE

Every word of that poem is a consolation and an encouragement to me but none more so than 'Fear not thy humble tale to tell'. For reasons that will become abundantly clear I have been apprehensive about telling the story of my life but it is a challenge that I have finally felt I had to face.

At times, sitting here in the library at Palace House overlooking my beautiful Beaulieu estate, I find it difficult to follow the path that took me here. Looking back from the high vantage point of my seventies I find it hard to believe that the mosaic of memories I have conjured up can really be my own personal history. Can I ever have been so young and so innocent? Was it I who did these things? Who felt such emotions? Who enjoyed such happiness? Who experienced such desolation? Much of the time I feel like an outsider looking in as I contemplate my earlier life. It is as if these events concern another person altogether; as if this world – these worlds – belong to another universe.

Yet I know that is not the case. Hard though it is for me to accept it, the character who advances across these pages from 1926 to the present day is unmistakably me. Goodness knows, I have changed and the world has changed even more. In those days we barely had typewriters; now I have to try to come to terms with the mysteries of e-commerce. In the Twenties and Thirties my family and I sailed abroad in stately ocean liners which took days to cross the Atlantic or travel to South Africa. Today I think nothing of taking Concorde to New York and arriving almost before I set out. I can leave Beaulieu in the morning and be trekking in the foothills of the Himalayas before sundown the next day.

In three-quarters of a century the world has changed almost beyond recognition and so have I. Yet the eternal paradox is that, as always, *plus ça change, plus c'est la même chose*. At one and the same time I find the Edward Montagu who attended George VI's coronation and the Edward Montagu who served as a young soldier in Palestine total strangers, yet I understand that it is me and me alone. Looking back I see, like a fly on the wall, an unbelievably naive young man who was sent to prison for a crime that he not only did not commit but which, thanks partly to him, is now not a crime at all. I see someone who married and had children, who made many friends and a few enemies, who won, mercifully, much more than he ever lost. I recognise someone who has been privileged to live through three-quarters of the twentieth century and to survive, fit and alert, into the first years of the twenty-first. At times I hardly know this person but at others I know him almost all too well.

By the same token I can barely remember what the beleaguered and ailing Beaulieu estate was like in the days of my youth and when I walk round the Motor Museum with its state-of-the-art technology, its modern buildings and its futuristic monorail I see a place which belongs entirely in the new millennium. Yet simultaneously I understand that there is a timelessness which makes it forever Beaulieu.

It is inevitable that I should muse like this as I contemplate a rich and varied life with a mixture of sadness and pleasure. Until now I have found little time or inclination for such introspection and contemplation of the past. Besides, it is not really in my nature. Now, however, as I think about my life I recognise that I have been lucky to enjoy such richness and diversity but the experience was sometimes difficult and salutary. It is partly because of this that I do now feel I owe it to myself and to others to share this life with them.

In doing so I have tried to remember the advice 'to thine own self be true'. I shall do so now throughout the pages that follow. Unbelievable though it may seem, this is a true story. Over the last seven and a half decades I have sometimes found it unbelievable myself. It has certainly been sad and happy, instructive and creative, entertaining and surprising. I hope that those who read about my life will be able to share it, however critically, and in doing so to experience something of the same.

It has been a great adventure and will be to the day I die.

1

'Born at His Granny's House'

He is born in a good hour who gets a good name.

Fifteenth century

Soon after dawn on Wednesday, 20 October 1926 the sleeping swans on the Beaulieu river suddenly took off, headed towards Palace House and slowly circled the walls three times. At least, that's the story. If true, that is how the news of my birth first reached the Hampshire home of my ancestors. I am not particularly superstitious but I like to believe that the birth of a male heir to the Montagu barony and the family estates was celebrated in this eerily symbolic fly-past. In fact, the swans and the Montagus of Beaulieu had enjoyed a symbiotic relationship for many years. Some who lived on the estate were quite unsurprised by the swans' salute, but they would have been more surprised if the birds had done nothing.

My father, the second Lord Montagu of Beaulieu, then in his sixtieth year, had waited thirty-six years for a son and heir. He had married his first wife in 1890 and she had borne him two daughters, Helen in 1890 and Elizabeth in 1909, nineteen years apart, before her death in 1919. When he married my mother in 1920 they also had two daughters, Anne (1921) and Caroline (1925), so that by the time the swans came to celebrate my arrival my father had already sired four daughters but no son. In addition to these four there had also been one stillborn daughter. It took time for him to realise that the dream for which he had prayed so long had finally come true.

My mother took a more prosaic view of the event: 'My baby', she wrote in her diary, 'was born at his Granny's house, 29 South Street, Thurloe Square, London. Brought into the world by Dr Bott and Nurse Spencer.' My father, apparently, was 'quite stunned' to find that, after four daughters and in his sixty-first year, he finally had a son to inherit his title and the family estate. I weighed eight pounds, exactly the same as my sister Anne. After the birth my mother ached 'all over as if I had rheumatic fever'. The event was duly recorded in the first editions of the London evening papers and 'Nanny Champ and all the Palace House staff sent congratulations, and are all excited'.

The excitement was understandable. The birth of a son and heir is a special event in any family but even more so when a title and a great estate are involved. In the case of my father, he had been trying for an heir without success for over a quarter of a century.

Years later I learned that my father also had one natural daughter from his long romantic affair with Eleanor Thornton, his personal assistant in London and the inspiration for the famous 'Spirit of Ecstasy' radiator mascot which adorns the bonnets of Rolls-Royce motor cars. Confronted with this regiment of daughters it was hardly surprising that he, along with practically everyone else, had given up all hope of an heir to the Beaulieu barony. The family had owned the estate for nearly four hundred years. My ancestors first acquired Beaulieu during the Dissolution of the Monasteries in 1538. Henry VIII sold the land and surviving buildings to Thomas Wriothesley, my great-grandfather ten times removed, for £1346 6s. 8d. I am the fourteenth member of the family to be Lord of the Manor, although I am only the third Baron Montagu of Beaulieu.

The monks whose abbey church and monastic buildings Thomas bought from the King had been on the site for over three centuries. However, the first mention of settled land on what is now the Beaulieu estate occurs in the Domesday Book of the eleventh century. There were four recorded settlements within the modern boundaries – Hartford, Otterwood, Througham and Wigarestun – but from the time of the Norman Conquest until the reign of King John it was part of the royal hunting forests. There was a royal lodge with the Latin name 'Bellus Locus Regis', meaning literally 'the king's beautiful place'. When the first Cistercians arrived from France in 1204 they translated this into French and dropped the king from the name so that it became simply 'Beaulieu' or 'Beautiful Place'.

There has always been puzzlement and controversy with regard to the pronunciation of 'Beaulieu', pronounced today 'Bewley'. French purists think we mispronounce the word, but in fact we are using the original French pronunciation of the thirteenth century. If you think how we pronounce 'beautiful' it becomes much easier to envisage saying 'Beaulieu' as 'Bewley' rather than 'Bowley'. More significant, the first time that Beaulieu appeared on a map was in the famous 1250 map of England by

Matthew Paris. Beaulieu was already important enough to be included but it was spelt 'Beuli', so I claim it is the French who have changed the pronunciation. This was confirmed to me by the mayor of Caen some years ago when he told me how delighted he was that we were still saying Beaulieu in the correct way.

The reasons for King John's uncharacteristically generous grants to the Cistercians are recorded in Dugdale's *Monasticon Anglicanum*. His relations with the order were generally poor and he had demanded money from the English Cistercian 'abbats' in 1200. This was refused. According to Dugdale, John was 'angry beyond measure'. When the Cistercians came to him in Parliament at Lincoln, hoping for a reconciliation, 'so cruel of mind was he, that he vilely ordered his servants to trample the said abbats under the feet of the horses'.

The servants refused; the abbats withdrew in haste and that night, according to Dugdale, John dreamed that the monks took their revenge by beating him with 'scourges and rods'. Next morning the King awoke contrite 'still feeling the blows on his back'! This time there was a reconciliation, part of which was the grant of his Bellus Locus to the Cistercian order. In 1204 thirty monks and an abbot arrived from the recently established community at Farringdon in Oxfordshire and set about building a new church with all the necessary support buildings – ecclesiastical, lay and agricultural. They were relieved to find themselves in the remote rural flat lands by the forest and sea. They had found Farringdon too metropolitan and hectic, and to them Beaulieu was a bucolic escape from the hurly-burly of Oxfordshire.

For the ensuing 334 years the Brothers prospered. They created fish ponds and a corn mill; farmed sheep at 'Bergerie' and cattle at 'Beufre', both of which names survive to this day, as does 'St Leonard's', their monastic grange. The abbey also became famous as a place of sanctuary where the king's writ did not run. Traditionally, any church in the kingdom was a safe haven but Beaulieu's rights and privileges were unique. Under certain conditions the abbot was entitled to offer a man sanctuary for life, provided he stayed within the 'Great Close'. This is believed to be an area bounded by the seashore, the river and the 'Great Manor Bank', much of which is still intact today. This peculiar dispensation meant that 'sanctuary men' at Beaulieu could lead as full and productive a life as any other estate workers. However, they were required to live on the other side of the river, isolated from the monastic community. In this way a village of lay people servicing the monastery was first established and this is the basis of the layout of today's village. Originally the monks used their lay brothers to carry out all the activities concerned with farming. These men were known as 'Conversi' because they had been converted from the service of man to the service of God. They lived in their own quarters on the opposite sides of the cloister and could be described in army terms as 'other ranks', compared with the monks who were the officers. They had a separate entrance to the church and independent rooms including the 'Domus Conversorum', or in other words a dormitory, which happily survived in the somewhat changed circumstances of the mid- to late- twentieth century and became an abbey museum, a cafeteria, a restaurant and a medieval banqueting hall. In the mid-fourteenth century, as a result of the Black Death, the Conversi were replaced by independent tenant farmers who paid rents and hired paid hands in much the same way as their successors do today.

By the fifteenth century most monasteries were run down, depleted and no longer prosperous. Nevertheless the estate which Thomas Wriothesley brought from Henry VIII had considerable potential, surrounded by the New Forest but strategically placed at the head of the navigable Beaulieu river, which flowed directly into the Solent.

As part of his purchase Wriothesley became the owner of the river bed, a unique privilege which has been passed on down the ages so that today I, too, own the whole of the Beaulieu river – banks, bed and all. My ancestor also acquired the abbey buildings and allowed thirty sanctuary men to stay at Beaulieu for the term of their natural life, but some were turned away as being 'hopeless men' whose crimes had been too severe. The survivors were the nucleus of Wriothesley's original workforce. One of their first tasks was to demolish the abbey church – a condition of the sale. The stones and the lead from the roof were sold and used in the construction of Calshot and Hurst Castles and the governor's house on the Island of Wight, which subsequently became the home of the Royal Yacht Squadron.

Only the foundations of the abbey church have survived, although some of the other buildings remain virtually intact – the monks' refectory, since the sixteenth century the parish church; the cloister; the Domus; and the Great Gatehouse, now Palace House, with its outer gatehouse.

The lay brothers' dormitory, which is what the Domus actually was, became a restaurant and cafeteria in the 1950s and 1960s, having previously served as the parsonage, a brewery, an agricultural store and a dance and concert hall. The Great Gatehouse, where the abbot received distinguished visitors, was never Wriothesley's principal home, for shortly before acquiring Beaulieu he had taken on the nearby abbey of Titchfield, where he constructed a great mansion which became his main house. He acquired several other Hampshire estates as a result of being chief henchman to Thomas Cromwell who was in charge of the Dissolution of the Monasteries. He certainly benefited from 'insider knowledge'.

Wriothesley's original name was, in fact, 'Wrythe'. In those days it was fashionable to lengthen one's name and so he became 'Wriothesley', almost certainly pronounced 'Roseley'.

The Wriothesleys owned Beaulieu for four generations. Sir Thomas, who became Lord Chancellor, was created first Earl of Southampton in 1547, but died only three years later. A protégé of Thomas Cromwell, his reputation is dubious and he only escaped Cromwell's fate by giving evidence against him during his trial. A notorious sadist, he is supposed personally to have tortured the Protestant martyr Anne Askew who was burned at Smithfield in 1546. Shortly after the accession of Edward VI he was deprived of the Great Seal for dereliction of duty. I have to confess that he is not an altogether admirable ancestor to have sitting on top of my family tree but he sits there nonetheless.

Henry, the second Earl, was a godson of Henry VIII but converted to Catholicism. He supported Mary Queen of Scots against Elizabeth and was imprisoned in the Tower. His was a short life and, compared with that of his father and son, a dull one.

His son, Henry, was an extrovert personality. Brought up by Lord Burleigh, he joined the Court at the early age of seventeen and soon gave evidence of his artistic temperament both by his 'long auburn locks' and by his willingness to throw his tennis racket at an exasperating opponent, or to scuffle in the presence chamber with the page on duty – a liberty at which Queen Elizabeth was as unamused as another great Queen hundreds of years later. She was even less amused when Henry eloped and married one of her waiting women, Elizabeth Vernon. As a result the bride and groom ended up in the Fleet prison and were never wholly restored to favour. More important, Henry is remembered as Shakespeare's famous patron and the dedicatee of *Venus and Adonis* and *The Rape of Lucrece*. The historian A. L. Rowse wrote extensively and controversially about the relationship between the two men, which he believed to be homosexual and crucial to our understanding of many of Shakespeare's best-known sonnets. Certainly Shakespeare's dedications are extraordinarily fulsome. 'Right Honourable,' he wrote about *Venus and Adonis*, 'I know not how I shall offend in dedicating my unpolished lines to your lordship, nor how the world will censure me for choosing so strong a prop to support so weak a burden.' In offering him *The Rape* he began, without equivocation, 'The love I dedicate to your lordship is without end.'

I contemplate the third Earl's memory with considerably less equivocation than that of his grandfather. His implication with the Essex rebellion led to attaintment and imprisonment in the Tower of London, together with his faithful black-and-white cat. Because of his 'youthful good looks', however, his death sentence was commuted. James I forgave him after his succession, removed the attaintment and gave his lands back to him. Henry finally died on an expedition to The Netherlands. He had previously been one of the founders of the Virginia Company and a 'Southampton' county still exists in the state.

His son, Thomas, was a good House of Commons Man who became one of Charles I's most trusted advisers, yet was well treated by Cromwell and survived to become Lord High Treasurer after the Restoration of the Monarchy in 1660. When he died in 1667, Bishop Burnett remarked, 'The Court was now delivered of a great man whom they did not much love and who they knew did not love them.'

The Beaulieu lands now passed to Thomas's youngest daughter, Elizabeth, after she and her two sisters drew lots to see which portion of his inheritance would be whose. One of the other girls got Bloomsbury, which was then just a sleepy village to the north of London. This is how it became part of the Bedford estates. Had the lots fallen differently, Beaulieu's and Woburn's entire histories could have been reversed.

Elizabeth's first husband was the Earl of Northumberland. When he died she married Ralph Montagu after whom, some three hundred years later, my own son and heir was named. The earlier Ralph was the third Baron Montagu of Boughton. Boughton, a great Northamptonshire house and estate, is still owned by my kinsman the Duke of Buccleuch.

The early Ralph was Charles II's ambassador to Louis XIV but fell from favour, only to have his fortunes revived under Queen Anne who, in 1705, created him first Duke of Montagu. Elizabeth, alas, died young, leaving Beaulieu to her husband who subsequently married the immensely rich but completely mad Duchess of Albemarle, widow of General Monk. The Duchess was determined that she would only marry royalty so Ralph disguised himself as the Emperor of China. Not only was the Duchess duped by this implausible subterfuge but she believed, to the very end, that she was the Empress of China, an understanding in which she was sustained by her servants who, until her dying day, served her only on bended knee.

Ralph's son John, the second Duke, married Mary, daughter of the great first Duke of Marlborough. John made some of the most important alterations at Beaulieu since monastic times. He fortified Palace House against possible invasion by the French and created a formal garden and the moat, together with a wilderness, a cascade and a serpentine. Even more important, he cleared woodland at Dungehill Copse on the banks of the Beaulieu river. This was the first step towards building a brand-new port, to be called Montagu Town. It was supposed to be a trading post dealing with sugar from the islands of St Lucia and St Vincent. George I had made the Duke governor of both these islands. The only drawback was that neither was yet under British rule. Accordingly the Duke mounted an expedition of seven ships with a hundred potential settlers on board. Their armoury included two state-of-the-art Puckle's machine-guns designed to fire round bullets at Christians and square ones at Turks. An example of such a gun still exists today and is on show in the Maritime Museum at Buckler's Hard. Alas, they proved of no avail and after a while the Montagu expedition was sent packing by a larger French fleet. The Duke lost £40,000 in the venture – the equivalent of more than a million modern pounds. There is still a Montagu Point in St Lucia to this day.

Although these West Indians plans came to nothing, the settlement on the Beaulieu river eventually prospered. Later, now named Buckler's Hard, it became an important shipbuilding centre for George III's navy. By the end of the Napoleonic Wars fifty-six men-of-war had been built there, including Nelson's personal favourite, *Agamemnon*. Today, Buckler's Hard is one of the most unspoilt eighteenth-century villages in the country, wholly owned by the estate, the only additions being a hotel, a small maritime museum, a chapel and one shop. Uniquely, the main street is a private road leading down to a privately owned river. There are no television aerials on the cottages. Nearby is now a flourishing marina and the river harbours over 200 moored yachts.

The second Duke was a notorious practical joker of whom his mother-in-law, Sarah Duchess of Marlborough, once wrote: 'All his interests lie in things only natural to a boy of fifteen, yet he is above two and fifty. To get people into his garden and wet them with squirts, put things into their beds to make them itch, and twenty other such pretty fancies.'

He eventually proved sufficiently sound to become Master of the Ordnance and Governor of the Tower of London. Apart from this he was a man of great, if whimsical, kindness and, like my other ancestor the third Earl of Southampton, a keen patron of the theatre. He introduced his own company of 'French Comedians' to the Theatre Royal in the Haymarket. Less than a year before his death he perpetrated his most infamous practical joke when, as a challenge to Lord Chesterfield, he placed a spoof advertisement in the London press. Chesterfield had said that there was a limit to what people would believe even if it appeared in the newspapers. Montagu disagreed. To prove his point he announced that on 16 January 1749 a magician would appear on the stage of the New Theatre, also in the Haymarket. This man would use a walking stick to imitate every known musical instrument; enter a quart wine bottle lying on a table and sing a song while inside; reveal the true identity of any member of the audience, however well disguised, and carry on a conversation with a departed spirit conjured up at the request of any member of the audience. Of course, no such magician appeared, but the theatre was sold out, even though the most expensive tickets cost 7s. 6d. Those unable to secure admission were locked out and formed an angry mob. Eventually there was a riot, the theatre was vandalised, a bonfire was set and several people were crushed to death in the mêlée.

Eccentric he undoubtedly was, but in other respects the second Duke of Montagu was far-sighted as well as being fundamentally well-disposed. Unfortunately he left no male heir and his estate was divided between his two daughters, Isabella and Mary. Mary, the younger, married the fourth Earl of Cardigan, a great favourite of George III and tutor to his children, who conferred the unusual favour of renewing the Montagu dukedom so that he assumed the title of his late father-in-law and became the third Duke of Montagu. Isabella was married first to the second Duke of Manchester and subsequently to Edward Hussey, who was created Earl of Beaulieu. Neither woman, however, bore a son, so the estate passed to Elizabeth, daughter of Mary and the newly created George, third Duke of Montagu.

Elizabeth continued the family tradition by contracting another spectacular dynastic marriage when she netted Henry, the third Duke of Buccleuch. After their death their elder son inherited the dukedom and the bulk of the family's huge estates. Beaulieu, however, passed to their younger son Henry James. He had no title but through a 'special remainder' was allowed to assume the style of Lord Montagu of Boughton, even though his title belonged to his mother's side of the family.

Sadly, he died without an immediate heir, so that Beaulieu reverted to his nephew, the fifth Duke of Buccleuch, widely known as the 'uncrowned King of Scotland' on account of the enormous tracts of land he owned north of the border. It was said of him, for instance, that he could ride sixty miles from Edinburgh to the Cheviot Hills without ever setting foot on anyone's land but his own.

The Buccleuch empire was such that the Hampshire lands scarcely rated. In 1867, therefore, the fifth Duke of Buccleuch felt able to give Beaulieu to his favourite second son, Lord Henry Montagu-Douglas-Scott, on the occasion of his marriage to Cicely, daughter of the Earl of Wharncliffe. Lord Henry was my grandfather.

It was he who studiously and with great dedication turned Beaulieu into the permanent family home which it remains to this day. The present Palace House retains most of the architectural features of the old abbey Great Gatehouse, but the new wing and interior rooms are essentially the Victorian residence created by him after he came to Hampshire with his bride in the late 1860s. The spirit of my grandparents still hovers benevolently over a house and estate which was, essentially, reborn in their image.

My grandfather was the very model of a Victorian landowner. He lived quietly and was never flashy, showy or ostentatious. He cared for his estates, his retainers and his tenants. He was a substantial figure in the locality and took his duties seriously. After serving as MP for the family seat of Selkirk he became MP for South Hampshire and subsequently for the New Forest. He was also, as Official Verderer, responsible for the governance of the New Forest. For relaxation he sailed, shot and painted. As a young man of twenty he sailed round the world, calling at South Africa, Australia, China and India, and such exotic locations as the New Hebrides, and developed a natural talent for watercolours. Later in life, delicate health led him to spend his winters in Egypt, where he painted many attractive watercolours, some of which are now on show in Palace House.

Compared with some of my ancestors he cut a quiet, almost insignificant figure and yet he, and men like him, were the very backbone of a traditional, ordered, hierarchical England in which everyone knew his place. In 1885 his quiet but solid virtues and his devotion to Disraeli and the Conservative Party were rewarded with a peerage and he became the first Baron Montagu of Beaulieu. Queen Victoria wrote personally to my great-grandmother, the Dowager Duchess of Buccleuch, to tell her the news. 'Dear Duchess,' she wrote, 'I am anxious to announce to you myself that with Lord Salisbury's entire concurrence I shall confer the Barony of Montagu on your son Henry. It gives me great pleasure to do this, and I am sure you will be glad that the name so long borne by your dear Husband's uncle should be revived again.' She was referring, of course, to Lord Montagu of Boughton.

My father succeeded in 1905 when he was almost forty years old. To the unspectacular Victorian virtues of my grandfather he added a *fin de siècle* panache and flair, exemplified most spectacularly by his passionate and visionary dedication to the motor car. Before inheriting his title he was a prominent Member of Parliament, specialising in everything to do with the newfangled invention of the motor car. He walked with kings – indeed also introduced them to motoring – yet kept a common touch. He was, after all, an active Member of Parliament, landowner, editor and journalist. He was the only member of the House of Lords to be a qualified railway engine driver and practised his skills in the General Strike of 1926, a few months before I was born, driving mainline locomotives on the Bournemouth line.

This, then, was my inheritance and my ancestry.

I was not yet a year old when Queen Mary herself came to visit my sisters and me in our nursery. In her diary my mother wrote: 'She gave Edward a silver mug with M. R. in blue enamel.' I still have the mug and I am told that upon receiving it I sank my teeth into it so hard that I marked it.

Of course I was unable to understand how privileged I was. To my parents and their friends and relations, to all who were connected with Beaulieu in any way, my arrival was a brilliant relief: a male heir at last. Ten thousand acres and almost a thousand years of history finally had an inheritor to guard and cherish them and, with luck, pass them on to subsequent generations.

When I first came to Beaulieu with my triumphant parents as an infant in a cradle we were met at Brockenhurst railway station by our chauffeur-driven Rolls-Royce with the family flag flying above the bonnet; the telegrams of congratulation kept coming in bundles of ten. Next day my father went to the private view of the Motor Show, where he fielded yet more congratulations before going on to the annual dinner of the Society of Motor Manufacturers and Traders, where the Minister of Transport, Wilfred Ashley, mentioned my birth in his speech and congratulated my father, and everyone clapped. Only then did my father allow himself a smile – his first since my birth. The realisation was just beginning to sink in. The Society even gave me a special silver dish – a precursor of the close relationship I was to enjoy with them many years later when I founded the museum to commemorate their achievements and products.

Soon afterwards he presented my mother with an emerald and diamond heart-shaped ring engraved with the words 'Our boy, October 20th'. I was put down for Eton and was christened on 28 November in 'an antique dress of cream satin', after which 200 people sat down to tea in the Domus and there was a three-tier christening cake with a cradle on top. The local schoolchildren saved up their pennies to buy me a life-size toy fox terrier. In return they each got a badge. The local gentry gave me a piece of silver and a testimonial list of the donors. The 264 tenants and employees of the estate presented me with a splendid silver tray engraved with their names – better than the proverbial 'silver spoon', people would now say.

Elsewhere Duke Ellington and Jelly Roll Morton cut their first ever discs; Trotsky was expelled from Moscow; there was a General Strike in which my father drove a steam train and was thanked by the regular driver for taking good care of his engine; and *Winnie the Pooh* was first published.

Of all this I knew no more than I did of the swans circling Palace House at 5.45 that October morning.

In her diary my mother wrote, 'One only wishes that little Edward could know what was going on, and hear all the good wishes people say.'

One member of the family felt slightly different. My half-sister Elizabeth, a teenager still at school, was given the news in the middle of a history lesson. Years later she told me how relieved she was. After years of being groomed as a sort of tomboy heir apparent, she looked forward to a happy release. Now perhaps she would be able to enjoy herself in London, rather than being pulled round by my father's labrador in the wild wet woods of the estate. That was what little boys were for. Especially when they were sons and heirs.

2

'What Is a Peer?'

They did nothing in particular
But did it very well.

W. S. Gilbert, *Iolanthe*

In March 1929 my father died aged sixty-two. I was just two and a half years old. The impact on Beaulieu was overwhelming as for over a quarter of a century he had been in charge of the running of the entire enterprise. A dynamic and vigorous character, he had managed to combine outstanding local leadership and administration while pursuing his distinguished public career. Had he lived on into his seventies or even eighties he would have been able to teach me something of the duties and responsibilities I was to inherit. Alas, this was not to be and with his relatively early death Beaulieu passed into the limited life tenancy and stewardship of my mother and a stalwart land agent, Captain H. E. Widnell. They were responsible to a board of trustees who were charged with safeguarding my interests until I succeeded at the age of twenty-five. For the family my father's death was naturally a bitter blow, but for Beaulieu, too, it was a tragic loss.

Unsurprisingly, I remember nothing about it. However, my mother's diaries note that in the months after he died I kept asking for him. So did my sisters. On 30 March, my mother wrote: 'Caroline would keep on asking for Daddy. So I took her and Edward along to my bedroom and took them on my knee, and told them as gently as I could, about gentle Jesus taking Daddy. I said poor Daddy had been very ill but God loved him so much, he'd taken him.'

It would be dishonest of me to say that this moment has left a conscious impression on my mind, although the subconscious and long-term impact on my character and life would be something else altogether. I am sure a psychiatrist would make much of it but although I later came to admire my father's many accomplishments, sadly I cannot honestly claim to have known or to remember him at all. He was often away and latterly he was seriously ill. In December 1915 he was on board the *S.S. Persia* when she was sunk by torpedoes from a German U-boat. It was an experience from which he never fully recovered.

We children led very semi-detatched lives. Much of the time we spent in the nursery under the supervision of Nanny Champ (who later departed to look after my friend Hugh, the late Marquess of Hertford). I was over a year old before I was allowed to join the grown-ups for breakfast; more than four before I attended church or sat down to a dining-room lunch. I adored Nanny Champ, who spoke broad Cockney, and was always with her. We often imitated her, much to my mother's concern, and ever since then I have continued to be attracted by the Cockney accent and slang. She used to refer to me as 'My precious little cargo'. Once a neighbour asked her whether she did not feel a heavy responsibility for such a precious cargo, to which Nanny Champ replied, memorably but not altogether reassuringly, 'What I say is if he dies, he dies.'

My mother doted on me too but she was, as so often in such circumstances, a more remote figure than Nanny. It was several months before I spent a day alone with my mother. In her diary she refers to me as 'my little sonny'. My half-sister Elizabeth (always 'Liza' to me), seventeen years my senior, was a glamorous but only occasional presence in my life at that time, although I sometimes felt she had a clearer understanding of what I was really like. Later she maintained that my mother never quite knew how to deal with me. Certainly her early diaries suggest that she found me adorable but rather perplexing. The entry on 20 October 1930 has a particular poignancy. 'My Edward's 4th birthday,' she wrote. 'I hate him growing up. He's such a sensible little chap on his own, but fights a bit with Mary Clare. She wants to do everything with him. He speaks very broken English at a great pace, with very long words and sentences which are very hard to understand. He's frightfully keen on trains and every morning he and I look at a train book together.'

My memories of early childhood, while sometimes vivid, are essentially jumbled. I remember the double prams in which my sisters and I were wheeled out. They seemed enormous then and would seem enormous still – limousines of the perambulator world. I recall games of hide and seek; playing on swings, see-saws and in a sandpit. There was a rocking horse in the nursery and a wind-up gramophone. One of my favourite records was Stanley Holloway's monologue 'The Lion and Albert', which I can still recite word-perfect. There were also records of Grace Moore, *Tannhäuser* and a military march called 'El Abanego'. So my musical taste was eclectic from the first. But of that more later.

Birthday parties were, of course, significant rituals. I was allowed, unusually, to visit my mother's bedroom before breakfast. There I would open my presents. On my second birthday my mother gave me a Noah's Ark and my grandmother animals to go with it. The high point was afternoon tea with cake, candles and balloons. Once the cake had sailing boats on it. There were usually three or four guests. At my first, for instance, there were 'four babies under a year: Mrs Christopher Heseltine's baby, Charles; Mrs Luxmore's baby, Peter; Mrs Bidhof's baby; and a tiny baby'. One's friends and acquaintances were, of course, carefully chosen. Not everyone was socially 'acceptable'. Later my favourite birthday tea included meringues, chocolate biscuits and chocolate cake with mint icing. To this day my favourite puddings still involve chocolate.

Encounters with the outside world tended to be formal, distant and hierarchical. 'The public', who years later were to enable me to remain in the home of my ancestors, had since the 1900s been allowed to wander around the Abbey ruins but for us in the nursery they might as well have been aliens from Mars. A guidebook, postcards and a few souvenirs were sold by an old man called Willis. Occasionally, the Wall's ice cream vendor used to sneak up the private drive on his tricycle and encourage the punters to 'Stop me and buy one'. When he did, my sisters and I would often go out, just as sneakily, and buy 'Sno-fruit' ice lollies, choc bars or vanilla tubs priced one or two pence each. When she realised what had happened my mother would issue forth and shoo him away. I remember that he had steel-rimmed spectacles and a moustache like Adolf Hitler. A 'Stop me and buy one' ice cream tricycle is now a prized exhibit in the Motor Museum.

Nanny Champ lasted four or five years, her stay prolonged because of the arrival of my younger sister, Mary Clare, in 1928. She was meant to be another boy and much to my father's disappointment was not. Nanny was eventually succeeded by a new governess, Miss Hoath (whom we called 'Hopey'). Hopey was very strict. She bullied me but eventually this was discovered and she was dismissed. Years later her sister entered my life, improbably, as the restaurant manageress at the House of Lords. (She always gave me very good service as if to compensate for the past misery to which I had been subjected by her sister.)

Miss Hoath was followed by Miss Strudwick. 'Struddie' was an altogether more sympathetic figure. In fact, she was chosen for precisely that reason. My mother realised that I needed a lot more carrot and a lot less stick. We remained on affectionate terms long after her retirement and we were in touch until her death in the 1990s.

She was 'PNEU' trained. The letters stood for Parents' National Educational Union. This involved a regular sort of correspondence course with set lessons and teaching aids, which arrived at regular intervals from PNEU headquarters.

Struddie was highly competent but traditional in her methods. I remember that the first book to which she introduced me was called *Our Island Story*, a fiercely patriotic history of Great Britain by Sir Henry Marten, the former vice-provost of Eton. I was mesmerised and have loved history ever since. I found the illustrations particularly inspiring and it was only years later, when I took my seat, that I realised the originals were the murals in the Houses of Parliament. We took the *Daily Express* and I soon became an avid fan of Rupert Bear, the famous anthropomorphically ursine hero of a daily comic strip. I was also precociously keen on news and current affairs, and listened to the six-o'clock news which always followed *Children's Hour.*

I did not think this early childhood was unusual. At that age one has very little on offer by way of comparison. Looking back on it, however, I am struck not so much by the rituals of the nursery – they were quite normal in those days – as by the lack of males. There were the chauffeur and butler, and at Christmas there was an invasion of male cousins when my mother's sister arrived with her four sons. But in retrospect I realise that I terribly missed male company. I remember once running down to the moat with a friend and he said, 'I'll show you my tummy if you show me yours.' I must have been four or five by then but I had never seen another boy's private parts. I always bathed with my sisters so I knew what they didn't have and wondered who else did. The only man in the house was the butler, Shepherd, who taught me carpentry. It was a rather unnatural state of affairs but the peculiarity of my situation only dawned on me slowly. I remember that one of the first times I realised that I was different in some way was when one of the servants called me 'My Lord'. It came as a shock.

I was a sickly child. It was not just that I had the usual diseases of childhood. In February 1932 I was very ill indeed. I recall little about it apart from the subsequent convalescence with Aunt Gladys in Hindhead. I vividly remember passing out in the bath and later being told that I had suffered a convulsive fit. It was only many years later, when I read my mother's diary, that I realised there was more to it than this and that my illness must have been really alarming.

On 3 February I woke with a temperature of 102. My mother said that I was like 'a little old man'. I lay on my back, not moving at all. Dr Maturin, our splendidly correct and proper family doctor, came and said it was flu. (I am intrigued to realise many years later that the author Patrick O'Brian named the ship's surgeon in his celebrated Royal Navy saga Maturin. I wonder if he too was a patient of the real-life Beaulieu doctor.) In any case, because the chauffeur also had flu my mother herself had to drive my sisters to a nearby fancy-dress party. She had no sooner arrived than the phone rang. It was Gravestock, her lady's maid, telling her that I had had a fit. Hopey had plunged me into a cold bath and sprayed me from head to toe with icy water. Dr Maturin could not be found. Eventually he turned up and said that Hopey had 'done everything right'. My mother was 'frightened to death' so the doctor stayed overnight by way of reassurance. I slept fitfully but next day still had a temperature of 102. I wasn't drinking enough, wasn't perspiring sufficiently and only took two teaspoons of Dr Maturin's personally concocted medicine.

It was a week before my temperature was back to normal. I managed warm milk and an occasional lightly boiled egg. The vicar called, and my mother went to my father's grave to pray and returned believing that my father knew of her terrible worry. I developed a cough that kept waking me but although I still refused to perspire I was, apparently, amused when the doctor shone a torch down my throat. Then, on the eighth, I ate jelly, sponge cake and chocolate blancmange, and a day later my temperature came down. 'It is too wonderful,' recorded my mother. By the following week I could cope with a 'huge breakfast of his beloved fishcakes'. But I was in the little night nursery for fifteen days and I had given serious cause for concern. 'We shall have to be very careful with Edward for a long time,' my mother told herself. 'He's been through such a lot.' And so to Hindhead to stay with Aunt Gladys Cubitt, where my mother thought 'the air will do Edward good'. I think it did, although I gave my grandmother and Hopey another terrible fright. I went out for a long walk over the heath and, having spent so much time in bed and confined to the house, I wasn't used to it. Next morning I could hardly walk and for weeks afterwards I was quite lame. Everyone naturally assumed that I had contracted polio but, according to my mother, it was simply stiffness due to overexertion.

So I was always thought to be a sickly child. In retrospect I wonder how much this was just the neurotic concern of a houseful of women for the health of their special infant charge. Shortly after this first serious scare I was taken for a general overhaul. Quite apart from my physical condition, my mother appears to have been anxious about my speech, which was very indistinct. People could not understand what I was saying. A team of doctors discussed this, passed X-rays to and fro, and pronounced my health generally excellent. There were no heart murmurs, no hip problems and nothing wrong with the brain. Even so my mother was instructed to keep me as quiet as possible and also fattened up. My appetite was adequate although my tastes, dictated by the fashionable nursery food of the day, were simple. I particularly favoured fried fish, mashed potatoes and roly-poly pudding. I didn't like bread-and-butter pudding. I can't have liked liver and spinach because I remember one awful day when it was served up cold at tea because I hadn't eaten it at lunch. Every day I was to have two hours' rest after meals and absolutely no parties. I do remember that I had started reading so I always looked forward to my rest. I also recollect being mortified about the ban on parties. Quite apart from the social deprivation it meant that I missed out on my favourite chocolate biscuits.

As I grew older there was a busy social calendar, especially during the summer months. Fixed, ritual events that stick in my mind include witnessing the Schneider Trophy – the most famous aeroplane race of the day – off Calshot Beach; the Beaulieu River Sailing Club Regatta (like my mother, I am now the Commodore of the Club); the Tidworth Tattoo – the great military parade at the army garrison on the edge of Salisbury Plain; and of course Cowes Week and the fireworks, which I watched with my uncle and aunt, Lord and Lady Forster, from their motor yacht *Mirama*. (My uncle had been Governor-General of Australia.) I learned to sail – taught by my father's old friend Sir Francis Dent, at one time the Managing Director of the Southern Railway, and by Mr Foster Pedley, a tenant of the Master Builder's House Hotel at Buckler's Hard. His wife had been my half-sister Helen's governess in the 1890s and he had been a colleague of my father on his weekly magazine, *Car Illustrated*. For my sixth birthday I was allowed a party with twelve children and twelve adults. A day earlier my mother took me to Harrods to buy my first ever watch. On the day itself I was given a Hornby clockwork train and my cake was decorated with another – sugar – train, as well as rose-hips and red candles.

'Such fun,' my mother wrote, 'but he's still a little chap and far from robust.' I had flu in January and Dr Maturin, correct as ever, was called. It was the time of the death of George V and even in those days I always had a radio playing within earshot. Dr Maturin came into the room while they were playing the National Anthem and he was so horrified at hearing it in such circumstances that he stood bolt upright to attention and refused to treat me or take my temperature until it had finished. A month later I missed my sister's birthday party because of a cold. I was to have gone as a Spaniard. Every time I was a page at a wedding I came out in a rash, although that was ascribed, rightly I think, to the fact that I was nervous of assuming such a prominent role in the ceremony.

Those childhood years were full of firsts. I was six when I flew in an aeroplane for the first time – a ten-minute circle of the Solent – piloted by a friend, Captain Luxmore, with my mother and my sister Mary Clare. A month or so later I made my first speech, a few faltering words at my sister Anne's birthday. I sometimes wonder if anyone understood what I was saying for my articulation was indistinct in those days.

But always there was the spectre of my ill health. Just before my seventh birthday my mother had yet another medical consultation, this time with a Dr Goodall. She described the news as grim, which was true, although in retrospect I cannot help feeling that Dr Goodall was being unduly alarmist. 'A long talk about my precious sonny,' she wrote in her diary.

He says there is nothing organically wrong with his heart and murmur, but his heart is on the small side and not a strong one for his energetic body. We must feed him with cane sugar and fats to give strength to the nervous system and the heart. We are not to try to shove him forward and to let him take his own speed. Riding is the best thing he can do. He must avoid excitement whenever possible. He's to do breathing exercises three times a day, to drive fresh blood through his heart.

It sounds primitive but apparently it worked.

Nevertheless it was, in most important respects, an enchanted child-hood in an idyllic home. It was an age of innocence; of conjurors at birthday parties; netting the Beaulieu river for fish, eels and crabs; handing out cigarettes after the Armistice Day parade and service; a Christmas entertainment with myself and other children dressed as ducks, chicks and elves; a visit to Southampton Docks to see the great Cunard liner *Queen Mary* dock for the first time; gallops in the forest on my pony Golden Farthing; turning on the tap for the new water supply for Beaulieu houses; winning the potato race at the Women's Institute Garden Party.

There were few real luxuries for money was short as death duties were paid by mortgaging the estate. This bit deep and in the years of depression meeting the annual premiums was a great burden. At peak periods Palace House itself was let to well-to-do Americans. There were certainly no foreign holidays. My mother was determined to hand the estate over to me intact. Some of the ancient and interesting books in the library were sold. From a very early age I was aware that I was inheriting responsibility as well as privilege. I remember sitting up on the stairs and listening with interest to a Trustees meeting below in the dining hall of Palace House. I also recall how Captain Widnell gently educated me in estate man-agement. 'Widdie' really ran Beaulieu. He took me to visit tenant farmers and taught me about mundane things like the importance of drains. I'm still mad about drains. To this day I can't see a blocked stream without feeling compelled to get down and unblock it there and then.

The top of the stairs is the one part of the house which frightened me and I still think it is haunted. But generally, cosseted by all those females, I seldom felt frightened. Elizabeth, my half-sister, the glamorous figure who came and went, took me to my first ever film, a boxing drama called *The Crowd Roars*, starring Robert Taylor. Going to it got us both into terrible trouble as I was supposed not to go to exciting adult films such as that. I was so overcome that at the Cadena café afterwards I consumed two whole plates of bacon and eggs, followed by two helpings of ice cream. My sister Anne was the leader; Caroline and I were close; poor Mary Clare was the one we all picked on – we called her 'Me too' because she was always struggling to keep up and asking to be included in our games and adventures.

Looking back, my growing up was a gradual process but there were watersheds, moments of transformation after which nothing was quite the same again. Gradually I learned I was different: a male among so many females; the heir to a great estate and title; a peer of the realm.

A month after my eighth birthday in 1934 I went to the House of Lords for the first time. It was the State Opening of Parliament and I stood with Struddie in the Royal Gallery and bowed as Their Majesties passed by. Afterwards my mother showed me the Chamber and I asked her, innocently, who sat on those grand leather benches.

'The peers,' she said.

'What is a peer?' I asked.

In her diary my mother wrote poignantly, 'Poor little chap. He didn't know he was one himself.'

3
First School

In 1935 I went abroad for the first time in a lifetime of travel. My health
was considered so fragile that it was felt I should spend winter somewhere
warmer than Hampshire. My mother, Caroline, Struddie and I sailed to
South Africa aboard the *Armadale Castle*. We travelled in some style, with
four cabins on the port side and forty-nine pieces of luggage. On the
third day out my mother and Struddie were seasick when we ran into
exceptional February gales off Finisterre. These continued for three days
and only abated when we anchored off Madeira eleven hours behind
schedule. Throughout the storms Caroline and I not only remained perfectly well but smugly consumed huge and unsuitable meals – in particular breakfast. For three days nobody was allowed on deck. Caroline
and I tore round in a state of great excitement. In fact, one of my abiding
memories of that trip was the pleasure of being allowed ice cream all day
and getting continual and devoted service from the few stewards still on
their feet.

When the weather calmed down we played deck golf, my mother
recording my performance as 'very slapdash' – it has never been a favourite
pastime as it's far too slow.

On 4 March my mother noted that as we crossed the Equator the
captain blew the ship's siren especially for my benefit. We then saw an
amusing charade called 'Shaving Neptune' put on by the crew. There were
races, several of which I won, and a cricket match between the officers
and passengers. I learned to swim in a canvas pool on deck. This was bliss
after early inundations in the chilly Solent in which it was far too cold for
me to learn to swim. On board ship I had daily swimming lessons which
were fun, even though I spent most of my time under water. It was a very

shallow pool – only four feet deep – which may explain why my mother remarked that 'Edward knows no fear'.

I shall never forget arriving in Cape Town at dawn and seeing Table Mountain looming ever larger as we came in. I count myself very lucky to have seen it from the sea that first time. Now that most visitors arrive by air they miss a great experience.

In South Africa we stayed with Sir Lionel and Lady Phillips in Vergelegen, their beautiful white Dutch colonial house built in 1703 and originally the governor's home. Sir Lionel had made a fortune from gold and was a famous figure in the public life of South Africa, as well as being an acquaintance of my grandfather, Lord Henry Scott, before the Boer War. As one of Cecil Rhodes's young men, he had come to prominence during the Jameson Raid when he was captured and imprisoned by the Boers in Johannesburg. Caroline, Struddie and I had our own separate guest house, a miniature mansion originally built as the slaves' quarters. We had our private sitting room and our black servants, 'Sixpence', 'Penny' and 'Pineapple'. They taught me how to crack a whip and Lady Phillips gave me lessons in water-divining, which was one of her hobbies. There were puppies and bantams everywhere, fruit trees on the hillsides where new dams were being built and pineapples on sale in the streets for a 'tiki', the South African slang for a threepenny bit.

We were away for almost two months, keeping up the routine of lessons with Struddie but otherwise enjoying what was for us a marvellous holiday. I loved the Cape and I have returned to South Africa many times, despite the old adage about never making return visits. On our way home we stopped at Madeira, where we had tea at Reid's Hotel and my mother bought us straw hats for a shilling apiece. I remember throwing silver coins off the ship and watching local boys expertly diving down and retrieving them from the depths.

It was all wonderfully exotic, especially for a small boy, and coming home to England was a definite anticlimax. As it was halfway through May we missed the Silver Jubilee celebrations of 1935, and it was rainy and cold. The faithful Captain Widnell came on board at 7.30 and joined us for breakfast, and our chauffeur drove to Beaulieu very slowly as the government had just introduced the 30mph speed limit in our absence. 'England', said my mother, 'looks so bleak, but so green.'

Caroline had acquired a new cocker spaniel called Jumbo and cook had cut out and kept for me all the Rupert Bear cartoon strips from the *Daily Express*.

It was at about this time that I first met 'Ned' Pleydell-Bouverie, who was to become my stepfather. He was the second son of the sixth Earl of Radnor who lived in Longford, a magnificent house near Salisbury just over the Wiltshire–Hampshire border. Ned was a serving officer with the rank of commander in the Royal Navy. He had gone to the Royal Naval College at Osborne as a cadet and been commissioned into the navy as a midshipman in 1914. He served throughout the Great War but only a few weeks after he joined up his ship, the *Hogue*, together with two other elderly cruisers, the *Crecy* and the *Aboukir*, was torpedoed off the Dutch coast. They were packed full of midshipment from Osborne. He was a mere thirteen years old at the time and was one of only twenty survivors. His father had the foresight to insist on him learning to swim before joining the navy – by no means a usual qualification among young naval officers. After being picked up he was taken to neutral Holland to be interned, but repatriated on account of his tender years. He made his own way back to England and to his home at Longford Castle. Arriving late at night and finding all the doors barred, he climbed into a window and put himself to bed. To the amazement and excitement of his family he came down to breakfast next morning, alive and well, as if nothing had happened. After a successful World War One career in the navy he continued to serve. In 1935, at the time of our meeting, Ned was the commander on the aircraft carrier HMS *Hermes*.

The stepfather–stepchild relationship is a notoriously difficult one but my three sisters and I got on well with Ned, although he and my half-sister Elizabeth did not hit it off as well. Elizabeth – intellectual, glamorous, bohemian, headstrong – was quite unlike Ned who was bluff, straightforward, typically naval and devoted to traditional country pursuits.

I revered my father's memory enormously but, tragically, my recollections of him remain, as I have already intimated, entirely vicarious. On my ninth birthday on 20 October 1935, for instance, my mother gave me a special present – 'a photograph of his daddy in uniform, which he had always asked for'. I treasure it to this day but it is the photo of a father I never knew. Ned, on the other hand, was flesh and blood, and very much alive. The next day, Trafalgar Day, Ned took me and my friend Dick Lewin (later Admiral of the Fleet Lord Lewin) to Portsmouth, showed us around HMS *Victory* and entertained us to tea in his cabin on board *Hermes.* I was impressed.

Shortly afterwards *Hermes* sailed for Hong Kong. My mother and Commander Pleydell-Bouverie conducted a courtship by cable. Their exchanges were cryptic and encoded but the following January they announced their engagement. My sister Caroline's immediate reaction was, 'Won't it be wonderful for Edward!' She meant, of course, 'Won't it be wonderful for Edward to have another man about the house.' She was right and although Ned could never be my father he certainly became a welcome father figure.

By no stretch of the imagination could Ned have been described as an academic or intellectual and in that sense perhaps Elizabeth had a point. He was not much use when it came to things like Latin, but there was our governess, Miss Hussey, to take care of things like that. ('Edward has worked so hard and loves his Latin. He is extra good at it.') But Ned was a real boon in other areas where I had suffered through being in an all-female household. He taught me to shoot – something I have loved ever since. He introduced me to the joys (and frustrations) of springer spaniels – a breed to which I am still devoted and two of which I own today – and he gave me my first shotgun, a Belgian 4.10. He threw me clay pigeons on the front lawn and taught me about gardening – especially how to use a billhook – another enduring passion. He 'ragged' with me in a way only a man could. It is quite true that when it came to art, music or literature Ned was not a kindred spirit but nevertheless he filled a gap. I became very fond of him and he, I think, of me.

My mother and Ned married on 2 May 1936. It was a sunny day and I was a page for the last time and wore my kilt. As a wedding gift the village commissioned a portrait of me. This has always seemed a little hard on Ned who would surely have preferred something else. The Hampshire artist was Cecil Vokes and I remember posing for hours, leaning nonchalantly on a golf club. This was rather inappropriate as golf has never been my game. Vokes was a very keen fencer so at intervals between my sittings we would fight duels with walking sticks. This struck me as greatly superior to golf and he did, in fact, teach me quite a lot about fencing.

My mother wrote:

Our Wedding Day. Ned and I cut the cake with his sword and the children were thrilled. Dear little sonny goes to London with Widdy on Monday, to Dor Pease (Lady Wardington) and goes to St Peter's Court, on Tuesday, for the first time. If only he keeps well. It is so odd not seeing him off to school as one has thought of it for so many years, but May 2nd was chosen for our wedding so that Edward could be there and feel the excitement of the wedding. (I hope) it will help in the final leaving of Beaulieu. Ned wrote him a sweet little letter yesterday and I wrote him today.

It was not, of course, 'the final leaving of Beaulieu' although at the time it did rather feel as if it were. Going away to one's preparatory school was, and to an extent probably still is, one of the great traumas in the life of an upper-or middle-class Englishman. I was prepared for it and had studied hard at such essential subjects as Latin. I had already met the headmaster, Mr Ridgway, and his wife for they had stayed at Beaulieu the previous year on their way to Devonshire. I had showed them round and my mother had been proud of me. She praised my 'simple good manners' and thought me 'utterly un-shy' and that 'I really wanted to show them everything. He couldn't have been better and I didn't prime him up at all.'

It was one thing, as Lord Montagu of Beaulieu, to show the Ridgways round my ancestral home but quite another to deal with them, as a homesick nine-year-old, on their own turf where they reigned supreme as master and mistress of a famous school in Broadstairs. However, when my mother telephoned to ask Mrs Ridgway how I was she was informed that I had arrived 'in great form'. A few days later I wrote to confirm this happy first impression. Prep school boarders learn to tell little white lies early in life, although, in fact, I only remember once 'blubbing' on the school train. 'Dear Mummy and Ned, I went round the school, am quite happy thank you, with very much love, from Montagu.'

At my first tea I sat next to and swore a lifetime friendship with Nicholas Holloway. Little was I aware that he was the stepson of Lord Tavistock, later Duke of Bedford. The friendship did not survive but I was desperately wanting a friend. No disrespect to Nicholas but at the time anyone would have fitted the bill. By week two I was able to report that I was top but one in Latin, fifth in French and eighth in Arithmetic. At cricket I had scored nine runs and taken nine wickets. I had invented an under-arm googly which for a time caused devastation to the batsmen.

It is probably impossible ever to prepare a small boy psychologically for the trauma of going away to boarding school. For instance, I had been immaculately trained in the basics of team games, but unfortunately they were girls' games. I was adept at rounders and netball, and was even an 'Honorary Brownie'.

When it came to academic work, however, Mr Ridgway, my mother and the indefatigable Struddie proved a formidable trio. My mother took great care over my education and both Struddie and St Peter's Court were wise choices. She had intended to send me to West Downs School near Winchester and rejected it. The question of expense may have entered into it, West Downs, at £70 a term, being £5 more expensive than St Peter's Court. She also felt that my supposedly feeble constitution would benefit from the bracing atmosphere of the north Kent coast.

St Peter's Court, although only established some fifty years earlier, was already one of the country's top prep schools and had been chosen by the royal family as an early school for Prince Henry of Gloucester and Prince George of Kent. Mr Ridgway was a Harrovian and St Peter's was well known as a successful 'feeder' for his old school and for Eton where, naturally, my name was already entered. (A very few St Peter's Court boys also went to Charterhouse, Radley and Rugby but anywhere else was considered below the salt.) Having decided on St Peter's, my mother very sensibly asked Mr Ridgway to write setting out the basic academic requirements he would expect on my arrival. His letter is, I think, a model of its kind. It is also a striking indication of the change in education in the last half-century or so:

First of all I like them to have a solid foundation of their own language for it helps so much when later on they are doing Latin. By that I mean really know their parts of speech, be able to analyse (to use a hateful word) simple sentences. To reproduce short stories in his own words, or write a letter with some idea of punctuation and stringing sentences together correctly.

When he can do this more or less, he should start Latin (new pronunciation). He cannot avoid the bottom form here unless he knows roughly his Ritchie's *First Steps in Latin* (the book we use) – the first twenty exercises. In passing, we use this in conjunction with Kennedy's *Shorter Latin Primer*, in which he should do the Grammar (apart from Ritchie) say the first three declensions (ordinary print, and not the words underneath the sample nouns).

This is a good deal, and possibly far too much, as he has been let off work, and it is better for him to know less thoroughly than all in a vague way.

In arithmetic, he should know his tables and do up to multiplication of money and I am a great believer (1) in plenty of simple mental work, five minutes at the beginning and end of each lesson, but not more as their brains won't stand it. (2) All sums to be kept short, i.e. not the ponderous multiplications and divisions I had to plough through.

History I gather from what you say we need not bother about, as he is enthusiastic and he had much better go ahead with it in the way he is used to and likes.

Geography. I like them to know their own country, plus some of the reasons for things such as ports and why they have grown trades, ditto such as coal, wool and so on.

French remains a problem. Strictly speaking at that age I think conversational French if it can be managed is best, if not some simple grammar and words. This all sounds rather hectic, but if he comes when he is nearly ten, he ought to avoid the bottom form as there are seven of them, and it takes, even with a move a term, which is unlikely, a long time to climb to the top! That is why I have stressed the question of Latin.

I only hope I have not frightened Miss Strudwick.

Lastly I am not the least keen about learning by heart. I never could do it myself and when that is so I rather think it destroys early on any likes for poetry.

Mr Ridgway had obviously not heard me recite 'The Lion and Albert' but Struddie was not in the least frightened and she taught me well.

My memories of private school are not exactly blurred but they are a mosaic. Certain moments and particular people are as clear as if they were part of my contemporary life and yet I would have trouble in composing an accurate chronology of my time in Broadstairs. I have an admirable crib, for my mother kept all my school reports, all Mr Ridgway's circular letters to parents, all the bills for such evocative extras as 'garters' (9d.), 'virol' (3s. 6d.), 'glucose and oranges' (£1 5s. 6d.). All my letters home have been preserved as well, but I never put the year in the date at the top so the only real indication of the passage of time is the trans-formation from spidery half-formed script and sentiments such as 'I arrived safely and eat two eggs for tea' to the relative sophistication of a fluent forward-sloping regular hand coupled with a keen interest in current affairs as in 'It is awful about this submarine only rescuing 4 out of 103. 99 were killed, of whom 93 were married.' I was referring to the sinking of the *Thetis* while undergoing trials in Liverpool Bay in 1938.

In most respects life, as exemplified by the handwritten end-of-term reports, seems to have remained much the same, day in, day out. Mademoiselle LeBrun, a Belgian teacher whom we all called 'Bun' and who signed her reports with a flourished 'Z de K L', seemed to be in a state of permanent Gallic exasperation. '*Il commence à mieux prononcer et à mieux comprendre. L'attention n'est pas toujours soutenue*,' she wrote in the summer of 1937. A year later she was writing about my '*grandes difficultés*' with her language, adding, a little unfairly, '*il n'a aucune idée de son*'. And still, in 1939, it was '*A toujours des difficultés a prononcer*'.

I definitely lacked patience, as an early Latin report says: 'He must learn not to be annoyed with himself or with me when he is corrected in work or behaviour.' Another teacher echoed this complaint, writing, 'I too find that he is rather argumentative under rebuke and very fidgety in form.' Even as late as 1940 Mr Ridgway himself acknowledged that 'we found him a trifle argumentative at the start [of term] though latterly this tendency vanished'.

On the whole, however, Mr Ridgway approved. His summing up, in almost unintelligible handwriting at the bottom of the regular report form, was almost always wholly favourable. His earliest verdict was 'he is a good keen person and takes an interest in everything' and on the verge of my departure he was saying that I had had 'an excellent term in every way and apart from work has grown up a great deal'.

I was reasonably good at games – always a help in a society such as this – and got my team colours at both soccer ('very plucky') and rugby (centre three-quarter). At cricket I eventually captained an unbeaten third Eleven, top-scoring with an unmatched twenty-one against Wellesley House and taking three for fifteen against Dumpton House. I belonged to the Meccano Club and teamed up with two other boys, Michael Bonsor and David Featherstonhaugh, to create a small garden. 'Our garden is looking very nice but the antirrhinums came out yellow instead of red which is a great nucance [my then spelling]' I wrote and, on another occasion, 'Please do not forget about my tennis racket and aeroplane. The garden is lovely. The white candituft is nearly out.' I very much enjoyed music and sang in the school choir, which came under the direction of a very good music teacher, Miss Kingsford.

Health was a major preoccupation and with good reason. Poor Mr Ridgway's school notes sometimes sound almost obsessively hypochondriac. 'We must definitely insist that no boy shall be sent back while suffering from either cold or cough, however slight, as these symptoms are often the prelude to measles and whooping cough, however innocuous they may appear to be in the early stages.'

He had good reason. At Easter 1938 he had to write morosely: 'Another term has been completely wrecked by an outbreak of measles which started the day we returned.' The disease effectively brought the entire school to a halt and also involved considerable extra expense. Each sickroom was provided with twenty-four-hour, round-the-clock nursing. I did not escape. My end-of-term report recorded my time in the sick bay: 'I can only say that he has been a very good invalid – patient in the literally adjectival sense of the word and was doing very well until he got ill.' In fact, I relapsed with pneumonia and developed a nasty discharge from the ear. A specialist consultant came from London and recommended that I should be given 'M and B', then only being prescribed on an experimental basis. This early antibiotic was powdered up and taken on a spoon of honey. In my case it worked brilliantly and I was one of the first people in England to benefit from this drug. Often, as the references to radio malt, linctus, quinine and glucose suggest, one was the victim of more minor ailments. I had trouble with teeth and occasional gumboils. 'I don't know if you know a man called Mr Thorn,' I wrote. 'If so he is one of the masters and he took the photograph of me. Why I have a bandage on my head is that I have one of those spots on my head, you know I had one for a wedding one day.' I still get spots today but now they are better known to be caused by too much sun.

The most popular masters were Patric Dickinson, who later became head of poetry for the BBC, and Mr Linford whom we all knew as 'Cork'. We used to greet Cork's jokes by wagging a finger at him, a secret gesture of recognition still practised among old St Peter's Court boys today – even in the hallowed precincts of Westminster.

We felt safe and secure at St Peter's Court. It was a regimental society with strict rules but it was not an unjust or unkind one. Jean Ridgway was a caring headmaster's wife who took trouble to assure my doting mother that her 'little sonny' was quite as content as he said he was in his weekly letters home. She and her husband and son, 'Mr Charlie', saw and heard more than we realised. In our dormitory, for instance, we assumed that we were unseen and unheard. Not so. In a letter to Palace House Mrs Ridgway wrote, 'Judging by the noise, chatter and laughter that goes on I think they must all be very happy together.' I think I *was* happy, although I was subject to a certain amount of teasing. I was very blond and delicate, and acquired the nickname 'white mouse', which I hated. But on the whole St Peter's Court was a friendly place and I felt comfortable and unthreatened. I enjoyed the all-male company, which came as such a change from home. Many of the boys I met there became friends who lasted all my life – Robin Leigh-Pemberton (now Lord Kingsdown, former Governor of the Bank of England), Sir Francis Dashwood (who died recently but was the proprietor of the Hell Fire Caves at West Wycombe), Michael Bonsor, Sir John Swire (of the famous Asian firm of Butterfield and Swire), Michael Alison, Mark Chinnery, Peter Talbot Wilcox, Sir Gerard Newman, Tony Royle (later a Tory minister ennobled as Lord Fanshawe), John Knatchbull (the film producer Lord Brabourne who married Patricia Mountbatten) and many members of the Cubitt family (the head of which was Lord Ashcombe whose eldest son had been engaged to my mother and who was killed in World War One).

I continued to read a daily paper – the *Daily Sketch* – and followed the rise to power of Franco, Hitler and Mussolini, so I was only too well aware that there was a world outside. Sometimes that world was benign, as when in 1937 I was summoned to attend the coronation of King George VI. I was the youngest peer present in my own right, known as a 'Minor Peer'. Minor Peers were those who had succeeded to their title but were not twenty-one. You also had to be ten years old by no later than 1 November 1936 so I just squeezed in by ten days. My mother said that I had a 'wonderful day'. I particularly recall getting a marvellous view of the King just as he was anointed – a gap between the massed peers in front of me opened up as if by magic.

I spent the night before with Lord and Lady Wardington, who took me to Westminster Abbey at an unearthly hour of the morning so as to be in our places on time. The press noted the special costume sported by the Minor Peers. We wore 'Black knee breeches with diamanté buckles, white satin waistcoat, white wing collar and bow tie, black pumps with silver buckles and an odd little hat with a Glengarry fold and stiffened sides'. I still have it today and it looks very Little Lord Fauntleroy-ish.

I particularly remember taking sandwiches in a special black velvet bag. This was important for we could not leave the Palace of Westminster until after the procession and then it took three hours to get away. This prolonged departure was an extraordinary mêlée of cars and taxis full of Indian maharajas dripping with diamonds and rubies, and peeresses with fabulous tiaras.

School was something of an anticlimax after that, although at least I was the only boy who could boast of such an experience. The sartorial requirements of school have almost as archaic a ring as those of Minor Peers at the coronation. 'Matron's list' for St Peter's Court, each item of which had to be marked 'with full surname', invariably printed in red on one of Mr Cash's name-tapes, included '2 knickerbocker suits ... four Eton collars ... twelve soft collars (from the school tailor, W. Stimson, 9 Hanover Square) ... House shoes from Daniel Neal ...' So the demands of the Lord Chamberlain on Coronation Day really had nothing – or not much – on those of St Peter's Court.

We basically only saw our parents once a term when they came down to Broadstairs for half-term, when they were allowed to take us out only for Saturday lunch and tea, and Sunday lunch. We all had to attend chapel on Sunday morning and were expressly forbidden to visit places like Dreamland in Margate, a popular pleasure park. The most vivid memory I have is of visiting Dover Castle and seeing a guide light a paraffin-soaked rag, and watching it descend down a very deep well. This is still done today. Little did I know that many years later, as Chairman of English Heritage, I would be in charge of Dover Castle and watch the children enjoy the same demonstration that I saw in the 1930s.

The most obvious collision between the outside world and the enclosed one of boarding school was the coming of World War Two. There was a horrid inevitability about this even in Broadstairs. In October 1938 we were already trying on gas masks and taping the windows to prevent flying glass following enemy attacks. Manston Aerodrome, later a key Battle of Britain flying field, was nearby and like most small boys I fell in love with fighter aircraft and especially the Spitfire almost as soon as it first appeared and hero-worshipped the daredevil pilots. Despite the proximity of Manston and the fact that if Hitler did invade Kent was likely to become a battleground, we were officially classified as being in a 'neutral area'. This meant that Mr Ridgway did not get any official grant towards the air-raid shelter he had to dig out. Nevertheless parents were invited to make voluntary contributions to the cost.

There was clearly agitation about what would happen at the school in the event of war. My mother was thinking of evacuation to Canada and approached Mr Ridgway on the subject. The headmaster was not enthusiastic. 'As to Canada,' he replied, 'I am not even considering it for I think the idea of taking a school over is quite hopeless.' Nonetheless he told parents that it was 'merely prudent to be prepared for any even-tualities' and 'in case of war we shall have to move the school'.

I am ashamed to confess that after the Munich agreement had been signed I looked up at a Spitfire and lamented the fact that war had not broken out. I was looking forward to watching the German planes being shot down by them.

Despite all this, school life went on. Cyril Fletcher recited his celebrated 'odes' at the school concert where Viscount Althorp (later Earl Spencer, the father of Diana Princess of Wales) and D. W. Featherstonhaugh sang 'De Ringtail'd Coon'. I was charged 1s. 9d. for a term's rhubarb, 3s. 6d. for radio malt and 1s. 6d. for nasal spray. My letters home remarked that 'instead of a walk next Sunday there are going to be physical jerks' and asked when Cows (sic) week was to be, whether a visit to Madame Tussaud's could be arranged and who was meeting me at the station. 'Will you send the *Illustrated London News* and not *Punch*,' I wrote. 'Please don't sent nasturtiums.' And then, feeling guilty, 'I am asking too many things.'

School holidays before the war were invariably spent at home. In the spring I often sailed and bird-watched with my friend Colin McDonald. I once even tried my hand at making perfume by boiling up spring leaves, which was not a success. In the summer there were tennis, sailing, trips to the beach, the Tidworth Tattoo and Cowes Week. The J–class racing yachts, including Sopwith's *Endeavour, Astra, Shamrock* and, before 1935, George V's *Britannia* were a great sight, whether becalmed off Beaulieu or bowling along the Solent with the spinnakers billowing before them. We always saw Cowes fireworks aboard the *Mirama* which, as I have already mentioned, belonged to my uncle and aunt, Lord and Lady Forster, who lived at Lepe at the mouth of the Beaulieu river. Winter holidays meant shooting, Christmas surrounded by Cubitt and Russell cousins and their resultant theatricals. Uncle Cyril Cubitt, a classy con-juror, always played Father Christmas, providing indoor fireworks. Nowadays we still have Father Christmas and fireworks but they are let off outdoors in a grand display.

The last peacetime summer holiday in 1939 saw my stepfather Ned Commander of the Royal Yacht *Victoria and Albert*. When moored off Cowes or elsewhere in the Solent area, Ned used to bring the royal family to our private beach so that they could have uninterrupted picnics. On other occasions they made informal visits to different places in the New Forest. I remember one day being hastily summoned to Buckler's Hard, where they were to re-embark for Cowes, to be presented to them. It was the first time I ever formally met the King and Queen, Princess Elizabeth and Princess Margaret. In August 1939, just two weeks before the outbreak of war, the reserve fleet of the Royal Navy was assembled at Portland and the King came down from London by train to board the Royal Yacht and review the fleet. This was, I believe, the King's last visit to his beloved yacht. My stepfather, I and the son of Admiral Sir Dudley North, the Flag Officer Royal Yacht, travelled two nights on board from Portsmouth to Weymouth and back to watch the proceedings. Today I have one of the *Victoria and Albert*'s old fire buckets in my drawing room. I use it as a waste-paper basket, which may sound like *lèse-majesté* but is actually a small gesture of homage to the past.

In September 1939 war was declared. Already St Peter's Court had left Broadstairs and moved, lock, stock and barrel, to Shobrooke Park, Sir John Shelley's house just outside Crediton in Devon. It was a tight squeeze and we were isolated from other schools so there was no one to play games against. My friend Mark Chinnery and I produced a play called *Shivering Shocks*. I knitted a navy-blue scarf for Ned, who was in Toulon as liaison officer to the French Navy. I had a camera called a 'Speedex-Clack' and made model aeroplanes, mostly, of course, Spitfires.

The summer term brought the fall of Paris and the evacuation from Dunkirk. Two of our masters from St Peter's Court, Mr Richardson and Mr McTurk, in different regiments coincidentally found themselves in the same slit trench waiting for evacuation from the beach.

The summer of 1940 – Battle of Britain summer – was extremely hot. For me it was to be my last term and I was preparing for common entrance to Eton. I remember that as dormitory captain I was kept up half the night giving fresh pyjamas to the boys who were sweating profusely.

I sat my common entrance exams and passed well into Eton. Then, just as I was looking forward to the last unexacting weeks at school, my mother decided that even Devon was too risky a place for her 'little sonny'. Her decision was very much influenced by the return to England of Ned after the fall of France and by his brother, Lord Radnor's, decision to send his children to America. At the end of June she received a cable from Ned's friend Grace Pitfield in Canada saying simply 'Delighted to have the children'. Immediately she got into the car and drove to Devon. 'Edward', she recorded,

> was busy playing cricket. He looked so well and brown. Whilst having tea in the garden I told him about the Canada idea. Poor Edward is very sad to be suddenly leaving his school at two hours' notice. We had a very hot journey back to London. Miss Hussey and the girls arrived at 5 at my club the Ladies' Carlton. Miss Hussey took them all to be photographed. Anne then took them back to Beaulieu, preparing to come up tomorrow with the luggage. I went to see Mr Holloway, the Passport Officer, to fill in many forms. All the children's names must be added to Miss Hussey's passport. I then went to the Canadian Pacific Railway and I was ushered up to see Mr Patterson at 1.30. He told me he had a 4-berth cabin, Deck D, 302. Just unbelievable at this short time.
>
> Wired Beaulieu for them all to come up at 3.20. Then I got £40 from the bank. £10 per head is all that is allowed out of England. Then went back to the CPR and got the tickets. Paid £199 8/4d. They are going to travel in a ship known as the 'Early July Special' [actually the *Monarch of Bermuda* which had just completed evacuating British troops from Narvik and had been renamed for security reasons]. They all arrived at my club at 5.20. I had a quiet 50 minutes with Miss Hussey then we went in two taxis for Euston at 7. The crowds were awful and real chaos reigned. The train left at 9.45. Anne and I felt dead beat. One wonders when the children will sail from Glasgow. No one knows. They may be days sitting in the Clyde.

Amid all the excitement I was bought my first suede jacket, a garment I treasured for many years.

In fact we sailed on 4 July. A day later Mr Ridgway wrote to my mother from Devon: 'I won't say I'm glad you got Edward off as I wanted him back!!' he said.

But I'm glad to put it another way – that your labours were not in vain and that you did what you thought was for the best. I am afraid it must have rather racked your heart to see them go but I am full of hope you will have them all back before long. I will write to him of course. It was sad about the confirmation and I know he will be sad too for he was keen and thoughtful, bless him. As for the rest, if and when he goes to Eton someone there will have to talk to him on moral subjects. It is a miserable world for all of us but I hope it will soon lead to a better if a very bouleversé one.

When saying goodbye I particularly remember the headmaster telling me how worried he was that Winston Churchill had become Prime Minister. He had known him well at Harrow and had a very low opinion of him. He thought him a cad.

For me this sudden evacuation was heart-rending. Leaving school friends abruptly, not knowing where or when we would ever meet again, leaving Beaulieu and the dogs, leaving my mother and Anne, who, because she was the eldest, was staying on – all this was extraordinarily traumatic.

Our last night at home had been rather overshadowed by the first bombing raid on Southampton. At least the sea voyage might be exciting and I might even see some action.

4

Education: Canada and Eton

Canadian football & peaches
versus
Early school & flying bombs

Unlike Mr Ridgway, I'm afraid I did not find wartime particularly miserable. It was certainly a world turned upside down but, as far as I was concerned, it was far from sad. Indeed it was, at times, exciting and even glamorous. I frequently listened to the daily radio news broadcast and often found myself dreaming that I was one of those Spitfire pilots.

During the Fall of France a few weeks before I sailed for Canada my half-sister Elizabeth incurred the family's wrath by refusing to return from France with her colleagues in the Mechanical Transport Corps. Her relationship with our stepfather was always a trifle strained and this episode did not improve it.

Ned, at the time the influential British Assistant Naval Attaché in France, had secured her a place on a British warship sailing from Bordeaux even as the Germans advanced towards the Channel. Elizabeth, who was enamoured of a very highly placed French government official, Roland de Margerie, decided to stay on the Continent. After a few months in unoccupied France and a number of perilous adventures, which included a narrow escape from the Gestapo, she made it to neutral Switzerland thanks to Mr Paravacini, whom we had known as Swiss Ambassador in London. Eventually she joined the American Intelligence Services and ended up working with Allen Dulles, later head of the CIA during the Cold War.

My mother was unamused: 'She's quite mad,' she wrote. 'But we can't do anything about it. She will probably be taken prisoner or find herself in a French Revolution. They are all furious with her, she is very naughty.'

I loved Elizabeth for her independence, her bravery and her disregard for convention. They were qualities which served me well later when I needed her most and she has always proved one of the most loyal of all my relations and friends. Like her, I was too caught up in the drama of events to worry about the effect the dangers might be having on my poor mother. As I sailed away across the Atlantic I felt brilliantly elated. Our ship's sister ship had already been torpedoed by U-boats. Five destroyers and a battle cruiser escorted us, and it was rumoured that our convoy was transporting the Norwegian and Dutch crown jewels to the safety of North America. RAF Coastal Command Sunderland Flying Boats roared overhead and we heard depth charges and were confronted, on a more mundane level, with an outbreak of mumps. I suspect the Deputy Head at prep school, Ridgway Junior, passed it on to me back in Devon; certainly he was one of the first of a Shobrooke Park epidemic. I got off lightly and suffered only a mild attack, which was lucky, because I was at the time going through puberty and mumps can be unpleasant for males not only causing severe testicular pain but also, sometimes, permanent sterility. Having to share a cabin with my two sisters and Miss Hussey also made me grumpy, but basically I was in a small boy's heaven. This was my boyish fantasy brought to life. As if to emphasise the point, one of our fellow passengers was the distinguished French writer André Maurois, inventor of an absurd British blimp called Colonel Bramble. He had to share his cabin with another boy put in Miss Hussey's charge and he was not amused. We eventually arrived at Halifax, Nova Scotia.

After the austerity of blitzed and beleaguered Britain, Canada was a revelation. Ward Pitfield, who had died only a few months earlier, had been a business friend of Ned's. His widow Grace lived with their seven children in a house called Saraguay on the banks of the Saraguay river at Cartierville just outside Montreal.

The intrusion of three strange English children and a governess was regarded with predictable apprehension but we soon paired off with those nearest our age. We led a very active outdoor life with the Pitfield children, riding, playing tennis and swimming. There was red meat, chicken, raspberries and ice cream; and I discovered something called 'Eskimo Pie' which was a Canadian choc ice. We were in the invidious position of sending food parcels to our family at home in Britain and the 1940 Beaulieu Christmas cake was made from the unrationed butter and sugar I sent from Canada. I sent preserved fruits, sweets and biscuits as well.

It was in Canada that I was first introduced to hot dogs, comics, Dick Tracy and Superman. Although, in the Province of Quebec, there was a comprehensive ban on anybody under sixteen attending a cinema, following a cinema fire where many children had been killed, there was no such legislation in Ontario and I always managed to see a regular three films of my choice in a day on my way to and from school. It was the night sleeper that made this possible, enabling me to arrive in Toronto in time to catch the 10 a.m. movie, snatch a quick lunch, take in the 1.30 session followed by the late-afternoon matinée, before catching the evening train to my destination. On my way home I could reverse the procedure.

Grace Pitfield, soon known as 'Aunt Grace', was a wise, generous but firm alternative mother who got on well with us but, unsurprisingly, soon fell out with Miss Hussey. She wasn't altogether thrilled when I tried my science class skills at manufacturing fireworks in my bedroom. That was quickly stopped, although she was more enthusiastic about the weekly magazine I produced for the household.

One distinguished family friend and neighbour of the Pitfields was General Vanier and his family, who had just returned from war-torn France where he was Canadian Ambassador. To my delight he told me that it was my stepfather Ned who had arranged his escape from Bordeaux in a sardine boat. They had endured an epic voyage crammed below deck with other diplomats escaping from France. After the war General Vanier became Governor-General of Canada, the first French-Canadian to do so.

Holidays could not go on for ever and schools had to be found for us. English governesses were alien to North America and Miss Hussey was hopelessly out of place and completely redundant. Grace Pitfield was full of remorse, for she could see that poor Miss Hussey meant well. After all, she had been sent over to look after us, but there was nothing for her to do and whatever she did do made the fact all the more painfully obvious. Luckily she had a sister in British Columbia and she was packed off there, albeit reluctantly. She asked to return to the Pitfield house for the summer holidays but poor Grace could not face the prospect. She wrote plaintively to my mother explaining that it was not that she did not like Miss Hussey – on no account must she let her think that – but she simply couldn't have her in the house as it was too disruptive. Reading the correspondence between my mother and Grace Pitfield after all these years, I wince at the emotions barely concealed between the lines.

As far as school was concerned there was little dispute about my sisters, who were sent to Netherwood at St John's, New Brunswick where the Pitfield girls went. In my case, however, there was argument. Grace Pitfield was keen that I should go to Bishop's College School in Montreal, where the Pitfield boys were educated; my mother, however, having consulted the Canadian High Commission in London, favoured Ridley in southern Ontario not far from Niagara Falls. It was a difficult decision for her, thousands of miles away on the other side of the Atlantic, and she felt, with my best interests at heart, that I should go to a different school from the Pitfield boys. After all, we had the long school holidays together. Ridley was a good school and one of only a handful of Canadian private boarding schools closely modelled on the public schools of England. Since at the time in England there were strict currency controls imposed on money leaving the country, it helped greatly that the school generously agreed to waive the payment of fees until after the war had ended. The question of money to support our Canadian exile had greatly exercised my mother and Ned, so this offer was thankfully received. It also helped several other English boys who were at Ridley, including my friends Henry and George Bathurst, Dick Kittermaster and Ray Nairn.

Ridley was an Anglican foundation named after the sixteenth-century Protestant martyr. The lower school was divided into sets named after Indian tribes: Huron, Algonquin, Iroquois and Mohawk. There was a school crest with a rather sedentary-looking beaver and a Latin motto. We played every type of team game, sang football songs, attended school chapel and had a school magazine called *Acta Ridleiana*. The school was one of the 'Little Big Four', a sort of Canadian Ivy League consisting of us, Trinity, St Andrews and Upper Canada Colleges.

As at Saraguay it was the lavishness of the food that made the greatest impression, although we British were also surprised by our Canadian counterparts' dedication to all things sporting. I particularly remember my first school tea which included corn on the cob and peaches in a barrel from which we could help ourselves to as many as we desired. I could have done without the peanut butter, which I dislike to this day; but generally speaking meals were a stunning contrast to food-rationed Britain.

Everyone was intensely patriotic and with the help of Dr Betts, the music master, I composed a song called 'Good Luck to the Boys in the RAF', which was played on the radio in Toronto. In my first term I cut out the front-page headlines from the *St Catharine's Standard* and hung them from five huge plastic boards in the fifth-form classroom: Our ambition was to be able to post a headline saying 'ARMISTICE SIGNED. GERMANY TOTALLY DEFEATED'. Ten per cent of the boys were American and I remember on 8 December, the day after Pearl Harbor, the whole school was assembled to listen to Roosevelt's speech about this 'Day of Infamy'. It reminded me of the day Britain declared war on Germany. I was at Beaulieu and stayed behind in Palace House to listen to Chamberlain's broadcast while everyone else went to church. I was the only member of the family actually to hear this broadcast. Shortly after, I crept into the family pew in church and whispered the dramatic news to them.

I founded a model aeroplane club and on the Monday before the Derby match against Upper Canada College I was made captain of the second Fifteen rugby team, playing to Canadian rules. Although I had never played the game before, I evidently 'improved with each day's experience' and I 'handled the team well'.

The squad consisted of eleven Canadians, six Americans, six English boys and one each from Bermuda, Cuba, Brazil, Venezuela and China. In the lower school 'notes' in the school magazine, my name and that of H. Bathurst appeared above an editorial that began,

A stroll through the Lower School dormitories this year will convince any visitors that, without question, 'there'll always be an England'. A considerable representation from that island has invaded Ridley and consolidated its forces. Should more follow, this peaceful invasion will already have done its work of improving further the understanding between Canada, England and the United States. The Lower School has a most cosmopolitan make-up as a boy from Rio sleeps next to a citizen of Bristol who flanks a native of Princeton, New Jersey and another from Maracaibo, Venezuela. A better example of the pos-sibilities of an English speaking union would be hard to find, as all groups appear to mix freely, make friends without regard to birthplace, and find a common interest in all matters pertaining to School life.

Naturally, Ned was concerned that I should be informed about the facts of life and accordingly wrote to the headmaster. I was duly summoned and questioned as to whether or not I knew the facts of life, which of course I did, and the interview ended rather unconventionally when, apparently for further explanation, I was also asked to drop my trousers. Of course, nothing untoward happened and I am sure he meant well as, after all, he was the headmaster, as well as a clergyman of a traditional, not to say reactionary, disposition. In any case, my morality was further improved by confirmation, which by rights should have taken place in England but in the end was conducted by the Bishop of Niagara, a splendidly exotic alternative to the Bishop of either Crediton or Exeter.

During the 1940 Christmas holidays I stayed at Ashanti, the Cartierville home of Mr and Mrs McDougall, the grandparents of the Pitfield children. Mr McDougall had been a noted ice hockey player and a star of the Montreal Maroons, precursors of the Canadiens. He was on the board of the latter and had box seats, so I became a devoted fan. While playing in the snow following a bout of flu, I strained my heart and developed mild rheumatic fever. On the advice of a specialist in Montreal I was therefore taken off games in school, much to my annoyance.

In Toronto, en route to the McDougalls, I was taken to see Gloria Swanson at the Royal Alexandra Theatre and afterwards I went to tea at the Royal York Hotel. I remember drinking grape juice or another uniquely Canadian drink called 'honeydew'. These exotic beverages were unheard of in England.

There was some concern at home and in Montreal that I had been taken to the theatre and to tea by a Ridley master, Mr Cronyn, a cousin of the famous actor Hume Cronyn, later married to the actress Jessica Tandy. Terence Cronyn was a dedicated schoolmaster but also a polio victim and a somewhat lonely and possibly disappointed man. The exiled British boys were grateful for his solicitude. I used to discuss the progress of the war with him every day and talked to him freely about the life I had left behind. He wrote to my mother often and at length, telling her about our conversations and reporting on my progress at school. Unfortunately he made the mistake of giving me extra pocket money and Grace Pitfield found out. She found this rather worrying and it is obvious, in retrospect, that she was afraid that Terence Cronyn's intentions were dishonourable. She did not see a friendly, solicitous schoolmaster but a predatory pederast and this view was shared by my stepfather. They tried to conceal it from my anxious mother who, however, was already worried about Terence Cronyn's attentions as evidenced in his long and rather fulsome letters to her. There was a confrontation and Mr Cronyn was upset. He was, he said, fond of me and of the other temporarily exiled and orphaned boys far away from their beleaguered home, and to act *in loco parentis* was natural and proper, but neither Grace Pitfield nor my mother was convinced. I can understand why, although they were mistaken, as Terence Cronyn never made any kind of improper advance towards me. He was kind and solicitous, and I liked him, learned from him and enjoyed his company to the day he died. After the war he came to England many times and visited me at Beaulieu. I remember once standing with him at the Henley Regatta watching the Ridley Eight rowing against the Eton team. I was obviously in a predicament as to which side I should support but nevertheless Ridley won handsomely; they were much bigger and better.

We spent our first Christmas and Easter vacations in Montreal, and in 1941 in Quebec. This was a most poignant moment as, in December 1941, just weeks after Pearl Harbor, the Japanese were besieging Hong Kong, which was being defended against attack by Allied troops. This defence force included the 1st Battalion of the Royal Rifles of Canada commanded by Colonel Bill Price, the husband of my hostess in Quebec who was the sister of Grace Pitfield. It was a very depressing time and I remember a great prayer service in the cathedral for the defenders, as there was no news about the final fall and surrender or the fate of 'our' troops. During this gloomy situation I had my first skiing lessons on the Heights of Abraham. It was very hard work for a beginner, not least because there were no ski lifts. The summer holidays were more pleasant and on our first long vacation Mary Clare and I went to Muskoka Lakes where we stayed on a remote island with Mr and Mrs Ted Brown, the headmaster of Lower School, Ridley. We learned to paddle canoes, cook the trout we caught and generally had a wonderful time in the simplest possible way.

Back at school, I continued to take keen interest in the school magazine. I still have copies of this with its clear, clean print, utilitarian typography and layout rather like an unreformed *Daily Telegraph*. It makes me realise, more than I did at the time, how privileged I was. There is my skiing report: 'I, similar to other English boys, was green to skiing ... I found one of the hardest things is going up hill.' There is the mock trial when a boy called Digby was accused of putting ground glass in someone's shredded wheat at breakfast. Henry Bathurst and I were the defence lawyers and we got him off. A page later there is a report of a school concert at which Henry and I were together again, this time singing such famous war songs as 'We're Gonna Hang Out the Washing on the Siegfried Line', 'Kiss Me Goodnight, Sergeant Major' and closing with, 'There'll Always

Be an England'. At the very end of the report there is a paragraph saying, 'In addition to joining Bathurst in singing, Montagu recited the immortal story of "Albert and the Lion".' (Goodness, Albert has stood me in good stead over the years!)

In the next issue of *Acta Ridleiana* I am sitting cross-legged at the front of the cricket team photograph and a few pages on I find myself playing Admiral Sir Joseph Porter KCB, in *HMS Pinafore* with Henry Bathurst as Captain Corcoran. Overleaf it was reported that I won the Speaking Contest with a talk on Winston Churchill's early life as a war correspondent and prisoner during the Boer War. On this heroic topic apparently Montagu 'held the interest of his audience throughout, spoke with perfect clarity and diction, and easy choice of words showed a marked familiarity with his subject'. Henry Bathurst came second, somewhat handicapped, I can't help feeling, by his subject matter, which was 'The Railways of Great Britain'. I also had a crystal radio set and began to listen to jazz. I discovered Artie Shaw, Henry James, Benny Goodman, and Glenn Miller ... unfortunately when I took the radio back to school it was confiscated.

In the summer of 1942 *Acta Ridleiana* reported that I played the part of Rosemary Farringdon in the school play, *Bachelor Born* by Ian Hay. Having to take the female parts was one of the curses of being a junior at an all-boys school. Then, the writer noted, 'Montagu will be back for another year', but sadly, this was not to be.

That summer I was sent to work for a local peach farmer called Goldring. I was paid $3 a week and I learned to milk a cow and hoe, prune, pick and grade peaches. I really enjoyed my time on the farm and have kept in touch with the family ever since. I certainly looked forward to my Saturday afternoons off when I went into St Catharine's and spent all my money on movies. I was, however, becoming a bit restless, because I knew that steps were under way to send me back to England. Already senior boys that I had known at Ridley had enlisted, gone to war and been killed. From Eton a friend wrote, in typically laconic Etonian style, that 'the black-out which you may have heard of is really an awful bore'. The reality was worse than that as Eton had taken a direct hit from the *Luftwaffe*, and although there were no casualties, one or two bombs had gone off a day after landing, destroying the headmaster's schoolroom, part of the Upper School and removing half the Chapel windows. There had been bombs, too, at Beaulieu – fourteen in a single night. At fifteen I felt I was old enough now to make up my own mind and the truth was that I was embarrassed about what others and I could only regard as 'funking the war'. For a time I pleaded in vain that it was time to go home.

This was easier said than done as the voyage was perilous and Drew, an Eton scholar, had died at sea when he, like me, decided he wanted to return to England from a North-American exile. His ship was torpedoed and after heroically helping survivors in the water he finally drowned in mid-Atlantic. The Pitfields and the Ridley authorities all advised against it and Mr Rowlatt, who should have been my housemaster at Eton, said his house was now full and could not take me.

Despite this my mother and Ned agreed that I should come back and fortunately a Beaulieu neighbour, Admiral Sir Geoffrey Blake, then the Fourth Sea Lord, managed to find me a berth, with a few other boys, on the aircraft carrier HMS *Dasher*, a recently converted merchant ship, which was due to escort a convoy to the Clyde from New York.

The news of my sudden return to England was sprung on me in much the same way as at Shobrooke Park two years previously, when I was told I was to be whisked off to Canada. Once again I realised I would lose contact with so many of my friends from all over the world who were at Ridley. Luckily, after the war, Ridley established an excellent international old boy network and currently I am chairman of the British branch, which has an amazingly large membership of about a hundred. One of our members, Michael Colston, very kindly gave the school a beautiful trophy for squash, a sport which, along with soccer, we introduced to Ridley during the war. Later, at the special celebrations for the centenary of Ridley, we British old boys presented the school with a special painting of Bishop Ridley, the Protestant martyr, to hang in the Chapel. We have always striven to express our great appreciation for the generosity of the welcome and care we received in those perilous days.

I kept a diary of my return voyage, which began, of course, with a tearful goodbye to Grace Pitfield and my two sisters who were remaining in Canada. 'A horrid ordeal,' I wrote. 'The grateful words I was going to say to Aunt Grace just fled from me and all I could say was "thank you" which perhaps is better in the long run. Of course C & MC were heartbroken seeing me going off. I tried to comfort them by saying that they too would soon be back. I boarded the train. Immigration officials came and fussed over papers and inspected baggage. All is well.'

I suppose this is why the British have a reputation for sang-froid. I was almost overcome with emotion and yet my way of dealing with it, even as a callow teenager, was to be tight-lipped and laconic. A French boy of the same age and in a similar situation would have wept and embraced. I remained dry-eyed and shook hands, although this did not mean that I was not churning with sadness and regret, not to mention gratitude. I do not know what Grace Pitfield and my sisters thought but I hope they realised that this was my way of containing feelings which I could scarcely bear. It certainly was not the way to behave, but it was the way I had been brought up to react.

Arriving at New York's Grand Central I had a mild altercation with a 'Redcap' over the correct tip and considered that 'New York is quite a fine sight – I say "quite" because there are not nearly as many skyscrapers as there are made out to be and otherwise it looks like any old town'.

I hurried to the New York Barbizon Plaza Hotel and brought a newspaper with the headlines 'LORD MONTAGU'S RUBBER-CHECK HOLIDAY', a story about a Lord Edward Montagu who was being sought by those whom he had conned right across the US. This character, a feckless ne'er-do-well, was the youngest son of the Duke of Manchester and had written to me claiming kinship. There I was in New York, called Lord Edward Montagu, with no money and no friends, waiting for an officer from the ship to pick me up. Needless to say, I lay very low. Some years later, in the early Fifties on a lecture tour of the States, his career caught up with me again when I received an anguished telephone call from one of his ex-wives demanding to know what had happened to her alimony. He died in Central America in 1954.

HMS *Dasher* took an age loading aeroplanes, mainly Grumman Martlets which I thought lovely. The seemingly endless delay was punctuated by visits to soda fountains and hot dog joints, as well as numerous films such as *Bambi*, *Tarzan*, *This Above All* and *Gunga Din*, with just a single disappointment: *King Kong*, which was 'very poor'. While in New York harbour, I saw the newly built *Queen Elizabeth* leave, 'Blighty'-bound, loaded up with troops, and return to reload all in the space of nine days. Eventually we sailed off on what promised to be an uneventful crossing. We stopped in Boston where I saw an eclipse of the moon, and Gary Cooper and Teresa Wright in the film *The Pride of the Yankees*: 'Very good – much better than I had expected,' I noted in my diary. Then our convoy, now numbering forty-two ships with an escort of four destroyers, lumbered at a stately five knots to Halifax and thence finally out into the open Atlantic.

In my diary I waxed quite lyrical about my last sight of North America:

I stood there on the deck gazing out upon a surly mass of green sea which seemed to fade into a blue towards the western sky. There was no moon but the water seemed to be alive and glittered like pewter as the wash from the ship met the Atlantic swell. I had watched for some time the last feeble efforts of the dying sun to light the world. The shores of Canada were disappearing into the night. I was having a final glimpse of the country in which I had lived for two years. I had stared long at that last outpost of the Western Hemisphere and now everything was fading. A mist was engulfing it and no longer was anything definite. Now had it sunk beneath the dark blue waters or could I still see it? But now it was gone, forever. No, not forever, for some day I will come again. These days have been happy ones.

I turned to go, but on the horizon I suddenly saw a light. It was a lighthouse sending forth its message from an outermost point. I stared at the light. I had not seen the last of that land after all. Here indeed was a symbol, I thought. This was the light of the New World, ever shining through the darkness, but I saw deep into it.

War and adolescence, exile and an Atlantic convoy were a heady brew.

As able-bodied young men we were required to keep watch, although we had the privilege of using the officers' wardroom. There was no laundry on board and I remember my cabin full of endless socks hanging up to dry.

It was a very cold September morning when we docked at Greenock. Apart from one submarine sighting and a barrage of depth charges in mid-Atlantic we had had a quiet time of it. I remember a breakfast of kippers – my first for two years – but there was no milk for either porridge or tea and after my Canadian cosseting this was almost as much of a culture shock as the kippers.

I had been away for two and a half crucial years. I was thirteen when I left and now I was little more than a month short of my sixteenth birthday. It would be a cliché to say that I had left as a boy and returned as a man, but I had certainly changed. My mother met my train ('only fourteen minutes late') at Euston. 'I found him very quickly,' she wrote in her diary.

'He's taller than me, and talks with a soft, low Canadian accent. Just too odd. Fearfully excited and looking tired and thin. He was really pent up with excitement and longed to go straight home.'

Forty years later she was still surprised by my Canadian accent and said she remembered that I had acquired Canadian figures of speech. She swore that almost my first words, confronted with the car that was to take us home from our local station, Brockenhurst, were: 'Say, where did you get that gas?' This sounds a little fanciful but it reminds me that when we first arrived in Canada Miss Hussey warned the three of us that we were not to 'become Canadian'. To some extent I suppose this was inevitable and it partly explains some of the problems I faced at Eton on my return from abroad.

After two years away I desperately wanted to be back. I enjoyed Canada but I missed 'home' in every sense.

Over the past sixty years I have always pondered how different my life and personality might have been if I had followed my contemporaries in that Battle of Britain year and pursued an Eton education, instead of going to Canada. There is no doubt that Canada taught me much. On the more academic level we learned Canadian and American history, the decimal system and coinage, science, public speaking and acting. They also taught us ice hockey, Canadian football, skiing and canoeing. As true and proud Englishmen we showed them how cricket should be played and introduced soccer and squash. Because pupils came from all over the world, we were exposed for the first time to a cosmopolitan atmosphere, and it certainly taught us that there was an outside world not like England. I learned to travel vast distances by myself, find and hold a paid job. I certainly returned to England no longer the 'Little White Mouse' that had left home in 1940.

The down side was being separated from my parents, family and friends, and from the mainstream education curriculum which I knew I would eventually need for Oxford. I was torn by guilt over not being in England for 'our finest hour' but I have no doubt that my time in Canada greatly enhanced my life and I do not regret the experience in any way. I still consider myself as half educated in Canada, as do my sisters. After the war my sister Caroline married Grainger Weston, scion of the great Canadian entrepreneurial dynasty of that name. After the war we also introduced one of the Pitfield girls, Sally, to a boy here whom she married and she has lived in Beaulieu ever since. I still love going to Canada and meeting my old Ridley contemporaries. Above all, I have an everlasting gratitude for the kindness and tolerance shown by the Pitfields and Ridley who welcomed and succoured us at such a difficult time.

Whereas Ridley had been a novel adventure, Eton was an ancient tradition. My cousin Harry Scott wrote from his home at Melrose in Scotland to congratulate my mother on having secured my entrance to the school at the unusually advanced age of sixteen and continued, 'We have a wonderful family record at Eton. Every male member of the Buccleuch family since the days of Monmouth's grandchildren has been at Eton, with three exceptions, my uncles Charles and brother John, who went into the Navy and my cousin Charles, who was a cripple. Two of Monmouth's grandchildren are buried there. Of course your John was "John Scott" at Eton.'

Apart from the difficulties imposed by the war itself, the school was split by an extraordinary clash between the Provost and the Headmaster. By tradition the Provost was a figurehead. The previous incumbent, M. R. James, had been a benign presence, happily writing his famous ghost stories in the Provost's lodgings while the Headmaster got on with running the school. The Provost in my day was the youngest son of the Marquess of Salisbury, Lord Hugh Cecil, universally known as 'Linky' because of his physical resemblance to that elusive evolutionary missing link between man and ape. Linky was determined to reassert the authority which he believed had been usurped by a succession of upstart headmasters. The Headmaster, Claude Elliott, was a kindly if sometimes ineffectual man, who nevertheless had helped me into Eton when the obstructive Rowlatt, whose house I should have been going to, refused to take me. Another housemaster, Nicholas Roe, who was married to a Beaulieu girl called Betty Poole, took pity on me and with the encouragement of the Headmaster ensured my acceptance.

Matters between Headmaster and Provost came to a head one Sunday morning in July 1944 when we were all assembled for morning Chapel and news came through that German 'doodle-bugs', or V1 self-propelled bombs, were headed in our direction. The Headmaster ordered us all out of the building but was not officially in charge of the choristers. They came under the authority of the Provost, who commanded them to sing on regardless.

I personally got off to a bad start because after a hectic three days of haircutting, suit fitting, the issuing of ration cards and clothing coupons, my mother and I somehow caught the wrong train and ended up in Weybridge. We finally made it to Eton just before six, hours after the appointed time, missing tea.

I was put in the Hon. George Lyttelton's class. Lyttelton was the brilliant and erudite father of Humphrey, the celebrated jazz musician later to become a friend and a star of the Beaulieu Jazz Festivals. I got to know Humphrey when he was convalescing at Eton, having been wounded in action with the Grenadiers. We became friends and held Sunday 'jamming' sessions with Francis Dashwood and Chris Hodder-Williams, members of his band. I later found a note in my diary which I had written after one of these sessions. It read: 'Went to jazz session in Humphrey Lyttelton's room. I have never seen such a talented man – trumpet, saxophone, clarinet and drums – a very good session.'

In Lyttelton's class I sat next to Nicholas Ridley, who went on to serve in Mrs Thatcher's cabinet. Nick was clever and I used to crib off him. Several friends from my prep school days also re-emerged: Robin Leigh-Pemberton, Michael Alison – later Mrs Thatcher's PPS when she was Prime Minister – and Mark Chinnery, a talented artist. The Bathursts also came back from Ridley but had to face the awful agony of the sudden death of their father. He had been on the way back from the Middle East to welcome them home and was killed en route. Poor Henry left Canada as Henry Bathurst and arrived home to find himself Lord Apsley in succession to his father. Julian Loyd was also in the same house at school. I remember him being immensely tall even then. He later became the Queen's land agent at Sandringham.

Several Ridley old boys came to visit us at Eton and I remember one of them telling an awful story about a French-Canadian soldier who was court-martialled. Apparently, he had hit a British army major who had called him a 'Canadian son of a bitch'. I blushed with shame on hearing this, as I had great affection for the Canadians and fond memories of my time there.

Despite my earlier prowess as a bowler of underarm googlies cricket had lost its appeal, so I chose instead to be a 'wet bob' and stroked the house Four unsuccessfully. I preferred to row my skiff gently up and down the Thames, which reminded me of home and the Beaulieu river. I remember one day, when I was rowing and another boy was cox, we had a terrible collision under the bridge, ramming into a pleasure boat and getting our 'bow bust off'. I got my house football colours and I ended up with distinctions in nine subjects in School Certificate but I wasn't altogether happy, as I was always being teased about running away to Canada and about my apparent Canadian accent. Oddly enough, this was quite the reverse in Canada where there were often comments about my English accent. I always seemed to be struggling to catch up but really never did until I left Eton and found myself on equal footing with my contemporaries. When I first arrived I was sixteen years old but I was made to 'fag' alongside the fourteen-year-old new boys. Coming back to Eton two years late meant I was put in the lower school and often teased. But the most awful experience was seeing boys leave and then hearing six months later that they had been killed. At the backs of our minds we all felt that we were just cannon fodder waiting for our turn to come as well. It did not always make for a happy atmosphere.

The war dominated everything from the profound to the trivial. The Eton Cadet Force was co-opted into the Home Guard, losing its traditional mulberry-coloured uniforms, which were thought, rightly, to make us unduly conspicuous. We had rather superior rifles and even our own Bren gun – a great rarity for any Home Guard Unit, especially a school one. I became an ARP messenger, which meant that I was allowed a bicycle and when on duty slept in Eton town hall immediately below the air-raid siren which, when sounded, felt like descending into hell. Most food was rationed but not sausages on the grounds that they contained offal. Occasionally my mother would send a pheasant and I remember that the birds came by post, unwrapped and unplucked, with just a label round their necks addressed to me at Eton. I was a very keen member of the Observer Corps and always had a pair of binoculars with me. I remember using them to watch the hundreds of gliders as they passed overhead on their way to D Day and Arnhem, and the thrill of seeing my first jet aeroplane, which must have come, I suppose, from RAF Northolt a few miles to the north.

Two days after D Day I noted in my diary that Allied forces had captured Bayeux, the first French town to be liberated. Soon afterwards I was sent by the school to the ordnance factory to help load up trucks for the second front. By coincidence the boxes of steel ropes we were loading had printed on them the words 'Made by McKinnons, St Catharine's, Ontario'. In my diary I noted my amazement that these consignments from my erstwhile place of exile would be in France by the next day.

In the holidays war work continued, and I fire-watched at Eton and worked on a farm at Beaulieu. I remember stacking wheatsheaves and doing factory work in Slough on Sundays. At home we made butter from the cream of a cow called Buttercup, which we kept on the lawn to mow the grass.

More exciting, since 1940 Beaulieu had become one of the principal training centres for the SOE. It was all very hush-hush and I had to have a permit to come home. We were never allowed to meet any of the brave trainees of the SOE, many of whom were captured by the Gestapo and met terrible deaths. (Kim Philby set up the school, years before becoming notorious as the leader of the spy ring which also included Burgess, Maclean and Blunt.) The instructors, however, were allowed to fraternise and we came to know several of them very well. They included such characters as Sir John Wedgwood of the china family, Paul Dehn the writer, Nobby Clarke, the King's head keeper from Sandringham who taught the recruits how to live off the land by blowing up our fish and poaching our pheasants, and Hardy Amies, later to become the Queen's couturier. Many of them came to dine, play tennis and pay court to my sisters.

However, it was not until VE Day that we finally discovered what it was they had been instructing and who their pupils were. Many years later I was able, after some initial objections, to obtain the support of the Special Forces Club to erect a memorial plaque in the Beaulieu cloisters. The words by Paul Dehn ask us to 'Remember before God those men and women of the European Resistance Movement who were secretly trained in Beaulieu to fight their lonely battle against Hitler's Germany and who, before entering Nazi-occupied territory, here found some measure of the peace for which they fought'.

In the summer of 2000 we celebrated the sixtieth anniversary of the arrival of the SOE at Beaulieu and hundreds of people came from all over the world to meet their wartime comrades.

Not knowing the nature of this wartime activity and being, after all, still an excitable teenager, I was more and more fascinated by the glamorous secrecy of it all as D Day approached. There were pillboxes hidden in dovecotes, troops everywhere, a strong naval presence on the river and, most important, houses that I had known since early childhood were now completely out of bounds. The friends who had once occupied them had disappeared and their places were taken by shadowy newcomers known to the rest of us as 'The Hush-Hush Troops'. At the time it was rather like being part of one of the action-packed black-and-white movies of which I was so fond. Only later did I realise how dangerous this activity had in fact been and how, had the fortunes of war taken a different turn, even the most innocent of us might have been under threat. As a result of interrogating some of our captured agents, the Nazis apparently had a thick file on the 'Finishing School' at Beaulieu. It was so thorough that they had even noted the name of my pet dog. I recall seeing a very large model aircraft flying off Needs Oar at the mouth of the Beaulieu river in 1943. It was one of Nevil Shute's pet projects that he was testing and it turned out to be a radio-controlled smoke-laying rocket plane. Shute was an aeronautical engineer and had also, since 1926, been a popular novelist. After the war he wrote a novel about his Beaulieu experiences called *Requiem for a Wren*.

Not everyone behaved well. One officer from a Welsh regiment not only demanded a field where he could place his caravan full of chickens to ensure that he had three eggs for breakfast each day but was also heard boasting that his batman had produced pheasant eggs for breakfast and he had then eaten 'the old girl' for dinner. My land agent who heard this story furiously reproached his colonel, who ordered the officer and his chickens to be left behind when his regiment departed for D Day. He was very cross about this but I have always felt it served him right.

A proximity to real life at its most dangerous and elemental helped to make the pettiness of school seem even more trivial and repressive. In due course I became a member of 'Library'. This is the equivalent of what other schools would have called a House Prefect although I was never elected to the famous 'Pop'. My house colours provided some consolation.

After Canada, I was never entirely at home with orthodox Eton, and my contemporaries and I were more impressed by the achievement of Carryll Cavendish, later Lord Waterpark, who was cited as co-respondent in a divorce case while still a pupil at the school, and by Charles Heseltine who conducted an affair with the woman who ran one of the tuck shops. Alas, the only piece of advice I remember from my Eton days was the famous dictum of the Headmaster, Claude Elliott, that whatever else one did one should never wear Old Etonian braces in a brothel.

The other day I found a diary that I kept during my last few months at school. Reading through it I was reminded once again of the opening words of L. P. Hartley's *The Go-Between* about the past being a foreign country. Could this familiar yet not quite finally formed handwriting really be mine? Can this uncertain, romantic, half-formed youth really be me? 'Went to *For Whom the Bell Tolls* with Gary Cooper and Ingrid Bergman,' I wrote in my first entry. 'Very good in every way. Also a good food film. Had late dinner and after stoking Church fire talked and went to bed. Something very sad about the New Year – 1944 (if we win the war this year) is a dawn of a new age and the epilogue of our present.'

I find it hard to believe that I spent so much time at the theatre. On Wednesday, 5 January, for example, having a day off from my fire-watching duties at Eton, I took a bus to Slough and got the ten o'clock train to Paddington. From the station I went straight to Irving Berlin's *This Is the Army.* I thought it 'perfect in every way' and particularly enjoyed the 'very good tunes' which included 'I Left My Heart at the Stage Door Canteen' and 'My British Buddy'. I was also impressed by the cast of hundreds and afterwards I had a quick lunch in what I described – even then – as a 'hamburger joint', before going to see Joan Fontaine as Jane Eyre. 'Excellent acting and directing,' I wrote. 'Superb job by O. Welles.' Bill Young then met me in Piccadilly Circus and we went to tea at the Albany which I described as 'very nice flats'. 'Later to *Ten Little Niggers* by Agatha Christie with Linden Travers and Terence de Mauney', which I enjoyed. Finally, 'Went to the Bagatelle – good dinner. Missed three trains. Arrived back at 12.'

The day after my sister Mary Clare finally returned from Canada I noted that 'the family had not sat down to a meal together since August 1939'. A day later I recorded:

Today I joined the Army. I went into Southampton and enlisted. Had 'Selection Test' which I did not finish and then, after many questions, had a medical which I passed A1. Had hours of time to learn sight test off by heart but there was no need! Medical was thorough in every way but no hitches. Then I took the oath. Everyone was very nice and helpful. How easy everything is once you come to it. Most people make too much fuss about things of that sort. Got a lesson from the whole thing. Helped M.C. unpack. A pouring wet day. Granny came over to lunch. So nice to have M.C. back.

Childhood was rapidly coming to an end and I was aware of this, confiding in my diary: 'This holidays has gone so quickly. I sense I am getting more grown up and less childish every day (I hope I am). An increased interest in the opposite sex too!' A day or so later I got my School Certificate results ('ten times better than I ever hoped') and dined and danced at the Swiss Restaurant with a girl called Patricia Manners (the daughter of Lord Manners). There were 'a lot of Yanks about, jitterbugging'.

At school I listened almost daily to classical music played on gramophone records and the wireless. A new discovery for me was the American Forces Network which I often tuned into and on hearing Frank Sinatra, probably for the first time, I wrote in my diary that 'he slobbered over his notes'. Despite the war our German master played us records of Act III of *The Mastersingers* and I decided: 'I think I do like some Wagner but not all by any means.' I also took part in countless conversations about everything from X-rays to 'things in general'. Occasionally there was an air raid and one night 'when practically all the noise was over the alarm bells went. Very pretty sight. Red and green balls of fire mingled with flares and A.A. bursts. Think I saw a plane shot down. No early school and all dead tired. Special Ash Wednesday service and the Provost broke down in the middle.'

Judging from the diary I seem to have been in love but it was not going well. 'I am having to face the awful situation of R drifting further and further away . . . oh how I long for R to be his old self towards me again.' I sound miserable about it and time has not dimmed the memory. There were other small unhappinesses: 'Corps parade absolute hell – rifle drill with Boer War rifles . . . Much contention about messing . . . Asparagus for tea. 9 out of 12 eggs smashed in the new box – very badly packed inside . . . It is rather a bore but it looks as if I will have to stroke the four through the races . . . How depressing it is getting bumped' (this happened four days in a row).

But not all was gloom: 'Had a good lecture by a major who was very interesting and dispelled the myth about how good fighters Japs are. Their grenades are also very small and one can be hit with one and not be killed . . . Took gooseberries down to Rowlands [the Eton tuck shop] and have had pie made of them. Very hot day. Could do no work. After prayers M'Tutor took us down to swim. Absolutely heavenly . . . Mummy brought down two lovely baskets of strawberries and some cream!'

On 6 June I wrote:

D-Day. Early this morning large forces of allied sea and airborne troops landed in France. At last this dramatic day has arrived. After hearing the German report at 9 at 9.30 came the dramatic announcement from SHAEF to the whole world (read by John Snagge). This was followed by announcements in all languages and a speech by General Dwight D. Eisenhower. It is now four years since we left France – Dunkirk and 1940 – going to Canada – and now at last European soil is being liberated. The King spoke at 9 this evening and Churchill made two announcements in the house. Very light casualties so far. Hundreds of planes going over including gliders. Tension terrific in the school but all relieved.

And the following day: 'Heard there is not going to be a dance at all which is a hell of a bore but perhaps it would not be too good in these terrific times.'

In 'Summer 1944' I first noted that the Germans had started to use the new pilotless bomb, later known as the V1, and one had hit the Bells of Ouzley pub. From then on Eton and Slough were under constant bombardment and we all had to spend more and more of our nights in the shelters; as a result some classes were cancelled. On June 19 I wrote: 'I saw two bombs come straight for the house but they must have gone over us and hit Slough. Eton had been very lucky – although there were 15 warnings in three days – so they must have hit Slough. . . . Terrible news, the chapel at Wellington barracks, in London, has been hit . . . and 150 people were killed.' One of the officers severely wounded was Major Howell Moore-Gwyn, who later married my sister Anne, but died within a few years as a result of the terrible injuries he had suffered.

They were strange times, a bizarre mixture of idyllic boating, sometimes in the Four, sometimes sculling on my own, of mother's fruit and flowers, of loading military trucks for France, of unloading asbestos at the Slough ordnance factory, of nights fire-watching or dozing in the shelters, of private tours of the Provost's pictures, of Myra Hess playing Grieg, of winning the annual cricket match against Harrow, of a 'not bad' Thucydides paper and a 'quite easy really' essay on Henry VIII, birdwatching at the Slough sewage farm with Hugo Money-Coutts.

Then, abruptly, without warning or valediction, the pages of my diary turned blank. In his final report M'Tutor – 'housemaster' in most other schools – Nicholas Roe, said that my 'Eton career has been a model combination of good sense and determination'. So far so good, but fulsome sentiments such as those invariably precede something less enthusiastic.

Sure enough, he went on to suggest that I could be 'ruthless and unfeeling in a clash of interests; generosity is more of the heart than of the head and it is here that I think he might fail'. I still feel that this was less than fair and my conditioning, like that of so many of my generation and class of Englishmen, was designed to repress or at least conceal my emotions. It was bad form and besides, it made one vulnerable and susceptible to bullying and betrayal. All my life I have, I think, been an emotional person, but all my life I have been nervous of revealing it. 'If he can cultivate that extra degree of generous humanity,' wrote M'Tutor, 'there's no reason why he should not become that greater thing, a leader.' I have never felt I needed to cultivate that sort of humanity. However, I do accept that I was bad at displaying it and like many of my friends from public school I was almost ashamed of showing emotion of any kind, as it could too easily be thought a sign of weakness. At least, that was what I had been taught.

Now, however, schooldays were over and I had to put away childish things and become a man. I was eighteen in October. On 5 January 1945, after a night out clubbing with my friend Tim Coats, I took the train to Sandown Park racecourse and joined the Brigade of Guards Training Battalion.

5

A British Grenadier

Some talk of Alexander, and some of Hercules;
Of Hector and Lysander, and such great names as these;
But of all the world's brave heroes, there's none that can compare
With a tow, row, row, row, row, row, for the British Grenadier.

Anon. 'The British Grenadiers'

The Grenadier Guards, originally titled The Royal Regiment of Guards, is the senior regiment of infantry in the British Army. The Grenadiers were not given their present title until after the Battle of Waterloo when, on 29 July 1815, the Prince Regent was 'pleased to approve of the First Regiment of Foot Guards being made a Regiment of Grenadiers'. Prior to this only the Senior Company were so styled. They were to be known as 'The First or Grenadier Regiment of Foot Guards', in commemoration of their having defeated the Grenadiers of the French Imperial Guard. It was also at this time that they adopted, as a regiment, their distinctive headdress, the bearskin cap. The regiment remains the only one to have taken its title as the result of action at Waterloo.

Since Waterloo the Grenadiers have won battle honours in almost every theatre of war. The Grenadiers' rivals, the Coldstream Guards, took as their motto the words '*Nulli Secundus*', which naturally we think vainglorious. The Grenadiers were, in the estimation of all who served with the regiment, not only the oldest but also the best. As the words of the regimental quick march above testifies.

Her Majesty the Queen has been the regiment's Colonel-in-Chief since her accession to the throne on 6 February 1952 and His Royal Highness Prince Philip our Colonel. Other members of the royal family filled similar positions in other regiments but I have always felt that the title means much more when applied to the Brigade of Guards. We are Her Majesty's household troops and our relationship with the royal family is genuinely personal. This was especially so in the years immediately after the war.

Such lofty loyal sentiments were far from my mind as I joined the motley crew of eighteen-year-olds, including many of my Eton friends, on the short walk from Esher station to the racecourse at Sandown Park, which had been turned into our officer training barracks. We slept in the Members' tote building and paraded in the car park. The grenade and gas training building was in the centre of the racecourse. It was a bitterly cold winter. The Battle of the Bulge, Germany's last counter-offensive, was raging in the Ardennes and at the same time we all came down with flu. Fortunately I was able to bribe the 'trained solder' who was in charge of our hut with a box of Cypriot cigarettes acquired from my stepfather's desk at Beaulieu. As a result I was moved nearer to the one and only stove in the hut. It was here that I heard on the news about the tragic fire at my prep school, St Peter's Court, where three young boys had died. I felt a great sense of loss.

After Sandown we went on to pre-OCTU (OCTU stands for Officer Cadet Training Unit) training at Pirbright. This was a very active and strenuous period. I remember one particularly tough five-mile run from the Hog's Back to base camp on the day of President Roosevelt's sudden death and also the happier occasion three weeks later when we were let out for the night to celebrate VE Day, when I remember swirling with the crowd in front of Buckingham Palace and recognising Princess Elizabeth and Princess Margaret also in the crowd, escorted by young Guards officers. That evening I spent the night sleeping in the St James's Park and before returning back to base, enjoyed the London night lights, which were lit up for the first time since 1939.

After Pirbright we progressed to OCTU itself at Mons Barracks, Aldershot for the final part of our training. We were kept in order by the famous RSM Britain whose stentorian voice would send a chill through any young cadet, not least myself. One day, unable to stop my motorised bicycle properly, I happened to drive through the punishment squad he was drilling. No one was hurt and I apologised profusely. Despite this I was called out in front of the whole battalion and made to shout out orders with my inadequate voice – a truly terrifying experience, but I managed it.

Having nearly killed myself on a motorbike and suffered and survived the food cooked by the Army Catering Corps cadets next door, I found myself on a training expedition in North Wales, near Snowdon, where in a pub one evening it was announced that Hiroshima had been destroyed using an atomic bomb. A few days later we were told the war was over by a shepherd high up on Mount Snowdon. Strange to reflect on one's whereabouts at moments of huge international importance. The most significant effect of the Japanese surrender for me personally was that training abruptly stopped and we went back to London to join in the celebrations for VJ Day.

As the time of our passing-out parade loomed closer we were allowed day visits to London to order our uniforms. I went with Hugh Stanley, son of Lord Derby, and in addition to collecting our new officer uniforms, Hugh managed to wheedle out of his father's club some gin and whisky, which we intended to drink at the passing-out party. On the way back to Aldershot Hugh ran straight into the back of a stationary car, parked at the side of the road. As a result most of the bottles broke and our uniforms were soaked in whisky and gin. Unfortunately it was not any ordinary car but a police car parked outside Bagshot police station. In spite of this Hugh was treated with considerable sympathy by the magistrate when he appeared in court, but it was not a good start to his army career.

The Princesses Elizabeth and Margaret were of the same generation as me. When the regiment was stationed at Victoria Barracks, Windsor, or Wellington Barracks, opposite Buckingham Palace, my contemporaries and I frequently found ourselves asked to make up numbers at meals, cards, dancing, charades or even singing madrigals under the guidance of the choirmaster of St George's Chapel Windsor, Dr Harris. On one such occasion I was invited to dine with the King and Queen and Princess Elizabeth in their private dining room at Buckingham Palace – an evening I remember fondly. It was a very relaxed affair and I was amused when a footman quietly brought in a small occasional table, placed a Roberts radio on it and tuned in to the BBC Light Programme. As we ate we all listened to *Much Binding in the Marsh*, a favourite comedy programme of the King's, starring Kenneth Horne and Richard Murdoch. It had a particularly catchy signature tune.

The ceremonial aspects of my soldiering were important. At various times I found myself mounting guard at Windsor Castle or Buckingham Palace, or accompanying the small pickets which performed similar duties at the Bank of England. The Bank picket was a most attractive option with a free bottle of port provided every evening. It was a great privilege to be able to entertain one's family and friends to lunch or dinner in the private quarters in St James's Palace where the officers on guard duty were quartered during their forty-eight hours on duty.

By the time I was commissioned in September of 1945 the wars in Europe and the Far East were over and I remained in Windsor and London until August 1946. The immediate post-war period was a very exciting time. The winter of 1945 and spring of 1946 saw the social life of London returning jubilantly with an enormous number of parties and the revival of the debutante season. The spring brought with it a very active London scene and I remember attending a succession of parties three days in a row, often held at number 23 Knightsbridge – a very popular venue owned by the still stylish Searcy's. The girls were often in their mothers' pre-war day dresses and evening gowns, and the men in uniform. Food was still being rationed and the popular main course tended to be pigeon, as it was one of the few types of meat that was not on coupons.

The highlight of the 1946 season was the Victory Parade held in London, with troops from all over the world marching down the Mall saluting the King and Queen. Since at the time I was stationed at Wellington Barracks, I was detailed to position myself beside the royal stand in case my services were required. In fact, I was not needed, but it did afford me a wonderful view of the parade. There was no doubt that I was overindulging the social side of life and as a result I was accused, quite wrongly in my view, of neglecting my duties as an officer. One day I was summoned by the regimental adjutant, reprimanded for my conduct and told that I was to be dispatched to join the 3rd Battalion in Palestine. Far from being appalled, I was rather excited at being given the opportunity to travel and serve my country abroad.

Palestine, though, was no picnic. The seeds of the Arab–Jewish conflict had already been sown. The 'Arab Revolt' had preceded the war and there was widespread resentment against the coalition of the victorious Allied powers who were perceived to be unloading their post-holocaust guilt by creating a Jewish Utopia far away from their own doorsteps. A difficult situation was being made steadily worse by the regular arrival of ships from Europe carrying alleged 'Jewish refugees' to Palestine. A number of those who sailed on these ships were not Jewish at all but claimed they were because it was their only means of escape. They were not entitled to settle in Israel and there were no formal checks on their identities. Many had no papers and the sheer numbers of displaced persons made it impossible for the authorities, already in chaos, to verify any entitlement to resettlement. It became a matter of verbal confirmation alone. Anyone could and did say he or she was Jewish.

It was the task of the British troops to monitor these immigrants and if necessary to perform the unpleasant task of sending them away again to Cyprus. At the same time we had to keep the peace between the Arabs, many of whom had been cruelly dispossessed of their land and houses, and the original Jewish settlers, a significant proportion of whom were not content with what they had been granted and were intent on pushing back their frontiers to include parts of Syria, Egypt, Lebanon and most particularly of what was then called Trans-Jordan. They coveted the west bank of the River Jordan. Shortly before I arrived the King David Hotel in Jerusalem was blown up by Zionist terrorists and there was considerable loss of life, mainly British. The railway station in Haifa was also bombed.

Like many peacekeeping forces, the British found themselves acting as pig-in-the-middle, taking flak from all sides. Life for a British soldier there was seldom dull. It was not a happy situation and I sensed that in time it could only get worse. It took an inordinately long time to reach Palestine and the journey provided an odd mixture of highs and lows. Europe was still a mess: Calais was in ruins, although there was plentiful *vin ordinaire*; the thirty-six hours on a German troop train were squalid ('no lighting, no water, no glass – only wooden windows and absolutely filthy') but despite this we were served with an excellent breakfast at a German-manned halt. Writing home, I remarked, 'One has to come to starving Europe to get hot rolls the colour of this paper. I had forgotten what white bread was like.'

Things really looked up in Toulon where we embarked on a requisitioned Italian liner of 6000 tons called the *Città di Tunisi*. In all we numbered seventeen officers in accommodation that would normally have housed 184. The ship was clean and the Italian cuisine 'marvellous'.

On arrival in Cairo we learned that there was a polio scare and we were effectively quarantined until it was deemed safe for us to continue to Palestine. There were worse fates ahead. For a start the town was full of familiar faces, quite apart from my travelling companions such as George Leeds, Nigel Robson and 'Rags' Courage, fellow officers bound for the 3rd Battalion. 'It is extraordinary,' I wrote at the time. 'I hear Christopher Petherick (my stepfather's nephew and later Managing Director of Searcy's) was down here, but only for a short time as the Life Guards are in Alex, so only come down for weekends. Last night who should I run into but that Indian woman Miss Bapsy Pavry who (she says) is just going to stay with her "great friend" King Farouk.' Bapsy Pavry later became, somewhat improbably, the Marchioness of Winchester, successfully wooing the geriatric Marquess so that she could fulfil her ambition of attending the coronation in 1953.

Once or twice I saw Farouk, fat and dissipated, on the terrace at Shepheards Hotel. My cousin Michael Cubitt, who was in Cairo with the British Military Mission and was rumoured to be having an affair with Farouk's sister Faiza, spoke fluent Arabic and had good contacts among the younger and more bohemian elements. On more than one occasion he took me to what I described in a letter home as 'the lower parts of Cairo' and in my bowdlerised version I also mentioned visiting a 'very amusing' fortune teller who was amazingly accurate. He forecast accurately the date of Michael's return to England to the day, a rationally impossible feat. There was another place, somewhat steamier, where the three of us found ourselves the lone spectators at a 'live sex' show in which three naked Arab girls writhed about on the floor without any evident sign of enthusiasm. Seeing that we were unimpressed by this display, the show's impresario asked us if we would rather watch what he described as 'donkey fuck woman'. After some haggling we agreed a price and were taken to a private house where, in front of a larger audience composed entirely of British army officers, the spectacle was enacted apparently as described. Neither participant seemed very enthusiastic and the woman appeared to be as bored as the donkey. The donkey had to be aroused from behind with an ostrich feather and, although unusual, the experience was rather dispiriting. On balance I preferred the historical sites of Cairo: the city museum, the pyramids and the Blue Mosque, more than the lurid nightlife. We spent most days at the Gezira Club and our Commanding Officer was Lord Bingham, later to become Lord Lucan, the father of the notorious disappearing Lord Lucan.

We finally arrived at the battalion headquarters about six weeks after sailing from Dover. The camp at Nahariyah was twenty-four miles north of Haifa, six from Acre, tented, although on concrete floors, with fine views of the sea and a valley behind. We had our own bathing beach and the nearby Jewish resort had shops and tennis courts. Best of all, 'the food is the best in Palestine because we have a special "wog" cook who is excellent'. We all referred to 'wogs', a racist habit which now makes me quiver with embarrassment but which at the time seemed entirely harmless.

I was a platoon commander with No. 2 Company and for most of the time we carried out 'routine' battalion duties, but in addition to our daily tasks we also mounted roadblocks and patrols, as well as investigating the frequent indiscriminate explosions. The Stern Gang and the Irgun Zvei Leumi were both active and to counterbalance this there were the Arab terrorist organisations too. So we were kept busy. It was interesting to reflect that some of the leaders whose pictures were displayed on our mess board as most wanted terrorists later became respected international politicians. Menachem Begin, the Israeli Prime Minister of the late Seventies and early Eighties, was the most obvious example. When I was in the Middle East, Begin was the commander of our enemy, the IZL. He was not someone I could ever warm to even in the years of his later acquired respectability.

After a few weeks the battalion travelled to Trans-Jordan for brigade exercises in which we 'fought' Glubb Pasha's Arab Legion and the Trans-Jordanian Frontier Force. We were in the desert surrounded by 'miles and miles of dry barren hills with no landmarks and complete aridity' and we collected water from a local oasis where there was even a large hedge of blackberries. I fell in love with the desert at first sight, entranced by the incredible light and space of the days, and the clear night skies littered with brilliant stars. The desert similarly captivated my grandfather and his paintings of it still adorn the walls at Beaulieu. I like to think this attraction is inherited.

When the battalion returned from the brigade exercises I was promoted to Motor Transport Officer. It not only meant that I was responsible for all the battalion's transport requirements, including the supervision and maintenance of the CO's vehicles, but I also had the responsibility of acquiring new vehicles from the division headquarters. When the battalion moved it was a major logistical exercise. I was very happy with my new appointment.

On the road we faced many hazards. The opentop vehicles had to be fitted with special wire cutters mounted on the bonnet so that the drivers and their passengers were not decapitated by the virtually invisible cheese wire stretched across the road. Animals, especially sheep and goats, also presented a danger and I shall never forget the day when a Guardsman returned to camp with a badly damaged Bedford truck. On enquiring what had caused such damage, the driver informed me that he had hit a camel that had cut across his path. Being well aware that had the camel been killed it would have led to an exaggerated and inflated claim from its owner, I dutifully asked the driver about the animal's fate. He told me it had got up and run away, apparently not badly injured.

My letters home now began a recurring request slightly reminiscent of days at my prep school, St Prep's Court. 'The one essential thing I didn't bring out was my gumboots,' I wrote. 'Could you post them out as we wear them the whole time when the rains begin?' Back in England it had never occurred to us that wet weather gear would be necessary.

While in Trans-Jordan I enjoyed the first of many happy days' recreational shooting. I had been told that the shooting in this part of the world was first-class and had, in fact, staggered out under the additional burden of 500 twelve-bore cartridges for my fellow officers. (In fairness I should admit that the bulk of this burden was carried on the back of my long-suffering batman, Guardsman Jack Brown.) The first shoot was at Lake Azraq. 'In the summer', I told my mother,

> the lake is a big swamp rather like our marsh in the winter. The sand grouse had gone back but we had a very good snipe shoot. We picked up about 30, but having no dog and it being very thick with tall reeds we lost about 20, which was very annoying. The whole marsh was alive with birds being the only water for 100 miles and there were lovely white heron and green bee catchers. There were also red and greenshank, godwits and sandpipers and lovely marsh harriers. We just wandered around up to our knees in water and had great fun. The other two guns were David Hill-Wood, whom I'd known at Eton, and Dick Birch-Reynardson.

Next day the Arab, aka wog, cook made a breakfast of scrambled eggs and snipe 'cooked better than I have ever known'.

Another highlight was a dramatic flag-waving exercise put on to impress the reigning monarch, Abdullah, grandfather of King Hussein and great-grandfather of the present King Abdullah. 'First,' I wrote, 'he saw the Welsh Guards fire every weapon they had and then we put on a Guard of Honour with Regimental Colours which were lowered to the strains of the Trans-Jordanian National Anthem which sounds like "Lili Marlene". In spite of a 60mph gale and sandstorm the day was a great success and he was thrilled. The COs are all expecting "Orders of the Camel's Hump". Two thirds of the battalion were 'booked' for having dusty rifles – scarcely fair, since the sandstorm was intense and unavoidable.

A little later we re-enacted the famous engagement involving the Guards Armoured Division at Nijmegen – purely as a training exercise. My former batman, Jack Brown, reminded me that I was pronounced dead after treading on a landmine, so I was glad it was only an exercise. Jack, a miner's son from Wigan, was a tower of strength. Forty-seven years later he got in touch with me and showed me the diary he kept throughout our time in Palestine. After the war he told me that he had had twenty-seven different jobs since leaving the army, driving cranes and lorries before finally settling 'on the buses' for London Transport, where he eventually became a training officer.

In 1994 Jack came to see me at my London flat and remarked perceptively, 'In those days when the difference in rank and status was strictly adhered to the chances of getting to know each other was very remote.' He added, a little disconcertingly, 'However, I did get to know you far better than you knew me.' I reflected that a man could pass himself off as a hero to many people but never to his batman.

Back at camp we found that an eight-minute tornado had wrought considerable havoc. I had bought three pairs of American nylons, one of which I had promised to my mother for Christmas although I said that if I were to give the others to my sisters I would appreciate some 'financial assistance'. (My finances were a shade problematical, mainly because of a misunderstanding between Coutts of London and Barclays of Haifa.) My gumboots had still not arrived and to the urgent request for them I added another for a book on classical music. I wanted to begin a series of classical concerts on gramophone records and was anxious to have some background knowledge in case of awkward questions.

Early in December I was able to report the eventual safe arrival of my gumboots, but unfortunately we had received news that my battalion was to be disbanded. Naturally the mood was of anger and we felt very strongly that this 'cut' was made in a spirit of vindictiveness by the Attlee government. 'Pure spite from the Socialists,' I ventured. It made no sense to disband good regular troops while maintaining a constant supply of bad irregular ones through the medium of National Service. Even though the war was over there was still work to be done.

This was demonstrated dramatically when we found ourselves in the thick of an ugly incident involving an 'illegal' ship, which docked in Haifa with 4000 men, women and children on board. I had already been on one of these ships and was appalled by what I saw. 'Unbelievable . . . the nearest thing to my imagined view of what Belsen was like,' I wrote.

On this occasion all was quiet until a boarding party from the Royal Artillery went in and announced that no one was going to be allowed to land. Almost immediately a group of would-be immigrants set upon the ill-prepared gunners and 'chased them off the ship with murderous gangster-like weapons'. The Grenadiers had been stationed outside the docks and it now fell to us to 'regain' the ship, but this was easier said than done.

Whenever anyone came near the ship they were met with a hail of full UNRAA (United Nations Refugee Aid Agency) food tins, bottles and bad meat which knocked several officers and men out causing bad cuts, which without exception turned septic owing to the filth in which the tins had been sitting for three weeks. Dick Birch-Reynardson and 'Rags' Courage were both hit by flying corned beef tins. They both had to go to hospital, one was concussed and the other had a broken arm.

In the end we tear-gassed them and armed with steel helmets and pick-handles, No. 2 Company managed to force themselves on board. The first five minutes produced a free fight but then they came down the gangplank slowly but surely. The first few off the ship soon came into the clutches of the Arab police, who proceeded to beat them up.

We soon stopped this, but blood was somewhat naturally up and the Arab policewomen thought they were making a popular move. It was but it obviously had to be stopped. One Guardsman who was reported drowned when he was pushed overboard in fact swam to shore but he had to go to hospital.

The trouble was all carried on by about a hundred agitators who disappeared into the crowd when we boarded. Down below were crammed three and a half thousand other people who were no trouble. There were hundreds of children and old people as well as about a hundred pregnant women.

It was a wretched affair. The press was largely hostile, alleging, for instance, that the refugees were starving. As they must have hurled at least 2000 full food cans at us, this was manifest nonsense. All the food was American and many of the cans contained pork. This was hardly tactful, but it was scarcely evidence of starvation.

Of course it looked bad. The men loathed having to carry out this sort of task, but they did it with commendable patience and discipline. Later, making my maiden speech in the House of Lords, I told my fellow peers, 'Our soldiers have always behaved with the most remarkable restraint in the face of every provocation.' One minute the Guardsmen were being attacked with axes and other steel weapons, the next they were 'good-humouredly and gently assisting the Jews to disembark, carrying their baggage off the ships'. As so often, the military were forced to clean up a mess made by politicians. It was unpleasant and disagreeable, and it was all too easy for hostile journalists to portray us as armed thugs.

It was a considerable relief to enjoy a day's duck shooting at Lake Huleh and, as Entertainments Officer, to immerse myself in the production of a Christmas show called *This Is the Show* – rivalled by a Coldstream effort called *Dick Whittington and his Kit*. The padre, who had been away for four months, was back in time to take the Christmas Day Communion service. There was a roast turkey dinner, the sergeants sang carols outside the officers' mess and some of my friends went down to Bethlehem. I did not relish a six-hour journey by jeep and went for a swim instead. The water reminded me of the Solent in September.

It was rough in the new year and we narrowly missed being blown up en route with my troop of entertainers. We were just a few yards from the police station in Haifa when a bomb went off. Four people died and at least sixty were injured. One of our men was killed when a truck of the 4th/7th Royal Dragoon Guards was blown up in Haifa and ran into a Grenadier foot patrol. Martial law was declared briefly. In the spring our division moved south around Lydda airport, now called Lod, to relieve the Airborne Division whose aggressive policy towards terrorists was criticised and resulted in many complaints from the Jewish population.

My friend David Hill-Wood and I managed to escape to Athens for a brief spell of rest and recreation. Once more I had occasion to exercise some self-censorship in my letter to Beaulieu. One evening David and I drank a great deal of a seductive local wine called Claris and found ourselves reflecting on questions of sex. It soon transpired that we were both virgins and before long we had persuaded each other that this was a state of affairs which should not be allowed to continue. We accordingly went out and found ourselves an amenable lady of the night who, after considerable haggling, took us back to her flat and duly initiated us. It seemed a sensible thing to do and we tossed a coin to see who should go first. Fortunately I won.

We had a wonderful time touring Athens, with the Parthenon almost entirely free of sightseers. We stayed in the King George Hotel for 2s. 6d. a night.

By now the end of my army career was in sight and I had to think seriously about my future. The regiment would be returning to England in October and there was no chance of leave before then. Once I was home, the army would allow me plenty of time off to prepare for my release.

It had always been assumed by the family that I would go up to Oxford and that I would take a place at New College where my father had been. I was very anxious that whatever I studied should have a practical application and I suggested Agriculture, Land Agency, Forestry, Law or Economics. I thought a year was the ideal amount of time to spend in Oxford. This meant that Agriculture was out of the question because the only available course lasted four whole years. If, as seemed probable, there were no appropriate short course at Oxford then I would have preferred to study elsewhere. In any event, I was adamant that I did not wish to read Modern History. It was not nearly practical enough and I was in a hurry.

I was determined not to be an absentee landlord for any longer than was absolutely necessary after I succeeded to the estate at the age of twenty-five. If the estate was to be managed properly, it might be appropriate to gain some experience elsewhere first. Above all, I felt it essential that in the year before I succeeded my contact with Beaulieu should be as close as possible. My absence in Canada and now in Palestine meant that I had not spent nearly as much time as I would have wished getting to know the 'nuts and bolts' of the estate's organisation. Whatever job I chose, I was anxious that it should not be in some business or industry that was about to be nationalised. (Mr Attlee's government seemed to be hell bent on nationalising as much as possible.)

In retrospect I see that I was ready to move on. I spent a fascinating Easter in Jerusalem and Bethlehem, although horrified by what I considered the kitsch excess of the religious ceremonies. The atmosphere grew even more tense with officers now required to carry pistols at all times, even at dinner in the mess. There was an increasing and alarming incidence of kidnappings. However, I complained that 'Life is still boring and hard work with no facilities for recreation'. I was not only in charge of Transport and Welfare for the battalion but I had also been ordered to run the mess. As always, the mess was heavily in debt and I was required to put it on a financially sound footing without compromising the standards of catering. The two were not, in my view, compatible.

The battalion next moved on to Nathanya, a thriving Jewish settlement north of Tel Aviv. This was a hazardous posting.

In June a party from our Brigade Camp got shot at while bathing on an unauthorised beach. Five were wounded. The following month two army sergeants were 'nabbed' at Nathanya. I wrote home: 'We put Nathanya under martial law and searched it. We have found about 20 terrorists and quite a lot of arms. The roads are mined day and night. An hour ago the Brigade Commanding Officer just missed a mine so a Company has gone out but I doubt if they will find anything.'

Shortly afterwards the bodies of the two sergeants were found. They had been hanged as a reprisal for an earlier execution of three Jewish terrorists in Acre gaol. At the time, of course, we regarded our action as entirely legitimate while the hanging of innocent men was considered a shocking outrage. Double standard? It did not seem like it then, but I do not believe that any other incident in the history of Palestine at this time caused such revulsion. I wrote home:

The two bodies of the Sergeants were found in a wood two miles away from here in a disgusting condition. The Sappers searched the place for mines but could not get the mine detector under the feet of the hanging men. An officer, now standing directly above, cut the rope and the body slumped to the ground setting off a mine. There was a stampede of pressmen out of the wood and they broke several cameras on the way. Luckily the officer was only slightly hurt because the two bodies, one of which was disintegrated, deadened the force of the explosion and all the shrapnel. They did manage to pick up a few remains of the other. There was a piece of paper on the bodies stating that they had been tried and convicted of many fantastic charges like murder, torture, illegal entry in the Jewish Homeland, being a member of an occupying army and so on . . .

Later, I was shocked when my neighbour at Beaulieu, Edmund de Roths-child, spoke of 'our boys' who were hanged at Acre. He meant the Jewish terrorists, not the British sergeants, but since he is a member of a leading Jewish family I forgave his natural sentiments although with difficulty. Nothing was straightforward in Palestine in those days. One senior officer from our brigade even had a mistress in Haifa called Ruth.

Shortly afterwards my cousin, Michael Pitt-Rivers, an officer in the Welsh Guards also stationed in Palestine, took me on a three-day trip to Damascus-Baalbec and Beirut in his new SS100 Jaguar. It was the first Jaguar I ever drove and every bit of the experience was fabulous. Beirut seemed as sophisticated as Paris. On our way home we stayed in a beautiful house built at Tiberias by Lord Melchett and then used by officers of the Welsh Guards for rest and recreation. At dinner we ate St Peter's fish – a local delicacy so called because each fish is supposed to bear the imprint of the apostle's thumb.

Years later I returned to the shores of Lake Galilee with my first wife Belinda. As we sat eating St Peter's fish, the first time I had done so since the visit to the Melchett house with Michael, artillery shells, launched from Arab positions situated in the Golan Heights, started to fall around us. Scampering for cover, I remember thinking balefully that here, call it Palestine or Israel, nothing ever changes.

In the end I did not have to wait until October for my return to England as I was suddenly ordered to take home leave that August. Then, after a few weeks at Beaulieu, I was told not to return to the Middle East, as I had expected, but to report instead to the Guards depot at Caterham. There I prepared for my demobilisation.

Shortly after my twenty-first birthday I left the Grenadiers and found myself back in civvy street, heading for the ivory towers of Oxford and the world of academe. As an undergraduate, in November 1947 I took my seat in the House of Lords and in January 1948 used the opportunity of my maiden speech to speak on the subject of Palestine. I told the House that during the past year we had witnessed in Palestine the enactment of a great tragedy. I said, 'Most fair-minded people would welcome the setting up of some form of Jewish State which would satisfy the longing of the Jewish peoples for national status.' With regard to the mass immi-gration of refugees, I warned that this influx would clearly be most detrimental to the social structure and to the development and prosperity of the young Jewish State. I warned that the Arab population was very perturbed at the prospect of the Holy Land being overrun by the most undesirable elements from Europe, mostly non-Jews. I warned that the Jewish people would not feel their statehood complete, as expressed by the revisionists in the *Jewish Standard* (5 December 1947): 'We proclaim today our faith that this first step forward is but the beginning of a march that will not end until Israel is ingathered within its ancient boundaries, stretching from the sea to beyond Jordan, and from the River of Egypt to the frontiers of Lebanon and Syria.'

During a later Palestinian debate after the Arab–Israeli war that followed independence and created a horrific Arab refugee problem, which still exists today, I suggested that the Jewish post-war refugee problem had been partly solved by creating an Arab one and that the world looked on Israel, I hoped not in vain, to make a contribution to the solution of this problem. I concluded by saying, 'The world must judge in the future whether the State of Israel has a heart, but let it never be said that the new State was born without a conscience.'

Looking back on these speeches, they seem sadly prophetic. Half a century later I sometimes reflect that, regrettably, little has really changed in this troubled part of the world.

I believe that the British Army that served in Palestine for several years had a genuine desire to be fair to all sides and found themselves in the unenviable position of holding the fort against both sides. We were keenly aware of the Jewish refugee problem and admired their bravery and aspirations to build a Jewish State in Palestine; equally we sympathised with the Arabs whose lands were being expropriated. To this day I am fascinated to follow the continuing saga. Fortunately, since that war I have twice been to Israel, first as a guest of Israel Sieff and second through the courtesy of Vivien Duffield, the daughter of Charles Clore and Director of the Clore Foundation. I was intrigued to see all the changes that the Jews have brought about and particularly admired the impressive improvements and their dedication to the archaeology of the Holy Land. I visited many of my old army sites and found that they were now non-existent, or only poignant remains.

In May 1948 the British Army left Palestine with a sense of relief but frustrated at not having handed over this troubled land in a more stable state. This was best illustrated by one retiring governor, who stopped the plane taking him off, got out and urinated, saying, 'I always swore that the last thing I would do is to piss on Palestine!'

Years later, when I was riding in a taxi in Tel Aviv and told the driver that I had been in Palestine during the British Mandate he revealed that he had been a member of the terrorist movement and had been imprisoned by us. He told me that he did not feel any bitterness, but was grateful that he had been fighting the British. They merely locked him up. Any other nationality would have shot him instead.

In 1947, for a young man such as myself it had been a fascinating and educational experience. For those who lived there it was not such fun. I was lucky to be able to move on.

6

Dreaming Spires and Spiralling Dreams

A University should be a place of light, of liberty, and of learning.
Benjamin Disraeli, House of Commons, 1873

My father had been at New College but his career had ended slightly ingloriously when he was sent down for blockading the dons, with huge snowballs, in their rooms after a heavy snowfall. He literally immured them, building impenetrable barriers of snow and ice around their doors and windows. I was keen to go to Oxford and to the College but I was not sure what I should study. I had already made it abundantly clear that I would have preferred a shorter vocational course but nothing suitable presented itself and so, with some reluctance, I opted for PPE (Politics, Philosophy and Economics). In those days demobilised commissioned officers were allowed to complete the course in two years – twice as long as I really wished, but a year shorter than the conventional requirement.

This compromise I reluctantly accepted, but when I actually embarked on PPE I found I loathed it and swiftly switched to Modern History. Particularly 'modern' it was not, but was described as such in order to distinguish it from Ancient History, which meant, more or less, that of Greece and Rome. I had specifically rejected the subject when it was first proposed to me in Palestine because although I loved history, it struck me at the time as hopelessly impractical. However, I was encouraged to change after attending lectures by one of the century's most distinguished historians, A. J. P. Taylor. Taylor always lectured at the uncivilised hour of 9 a.m. because he said that if he performed any later there was no room at the University large enough to accommodate those who wished to hear him. This sounds vain and probably was, but it was also true. He was a brilliant but erratic speaker and I shall always be glad that I took the trouble to struggle out of bed to attend his pyrotechnic tours de force. An even greater privilege was having another of the great twentieth-century historians as my tutor. This was Alan Bullock (later the author of authoritative works on Hitler, Stalin and the Labour foreign secretary of the day, Ernest Bevin). Bullock went on to be the founding Master of St Catherine's College. So although taking 'modern' history, from 'the beginning' as the University so quaintly put it, until the outbreak of the Great War was not the original plan, it was a stimulating discipline and I counted myself lucky to be able to study a subject at which Oxford excelled.

Looking back on my sojourn at university I wish, like so many other Oxford men, that I had been more diligent and made better use of my time there. At the time I certainly felt fully occupied socially, intellectually and academically, but I recognise now that I lacked the contemplative nature or concentration to take full advantage of the opportunities that academic study presented. Besides, my time in the Brigade and especially in Palestine had given me a taste of the adult life and real excitement. After the army, Oxford felt like a step backwards. It was like going back to school. Had I gone there straight from Eton I might have succumbed more compliantly to its seductive spell. As it was, I spent much of my time there hankering for the bright lights of London, longing to earn a living, and to get on with 'real life' and take up my work as owner of Beaulieu.

New College is not particularly new, even by Oxford standards. It was founded in 1379, almost sixty years before Eton. The founder, William Wykeham, had at the same time initiated his famous school at Winchester, with the idea that boys should move from the one to the other. This frequently happened and in the popular mind the College was often perceived as little more than an extension of the school.

The Wykhamists, assisted by a large number of 'closed' scholarships for which they alone were eligible, outnumbered the former pupils of any other school. Eton, however, came a respectable second. My school contemporary John Smith, later MP for the City of Westminster as well as founder of the Landmark Trust, was President of the Junior Common Room. My cousin Bill Pease, who had been at Eton and also served with me in the Grenadiers in Palestine, was at New College too, as was John Grigg, who later renounced his title of Lord Altrincham and caused a huge furore by writing critically about Her Majesty the Queen. Kenneth Rose, who became the distinguished founder of the 'Albany' column on the *Sunday Telegraph* as well as the official biographer of King George V, was a New College historian. While at Oxford, Grigg and I once organised a debate on the desirability of disestablishing the Church of England, and

Cyril Garbett, Archbishop of York and an old family friend, accepted our invitation to put forward the view of the Church. It was a splendid debate but the Archbishop did not entirely convince the sceptical youthful audience. As with any other Oxford college, the gates were locked at midnight and, like many students before me, we had to find a way back into our rooms without getting caught by the porter and placed on report. My preferred after-hours route was through the digs of Alan Clark whose rooms conveniently adjoined the gardens of New College. Perhaps mercifully, Alan had yet to take up his pen as one of the century's wittiest and most acerbic diarists.

Initially I shared rooms with Colin Tennant, a friend from Eton and now Lord Glenconner, latterly best known as a close companion of Princess Margaret and the man who placed the Caribbean island of Mustique firmly on the map, although my mother in her diaries describes him succinctly as 'Nancy Dugdale's great-nephew'. We shared a set of Victorian rooms up fifty-four steps in the 'New Buildings' and the views of dreaming spires from our windows were fabulous. I furnished our huge drawing room with carpets and Italian landscapes by Joli, taken from Beaulieu. We all arrived together from Hampshire in a Pickford's pantechnicon.

I entered into university life with enthusiasm, as there was much to do – lectures, concerts, parties and, above all, talk. We talked about everything, incessantly and often late into the night. I recognise, of course, that my lifestyle compared with some undergraduates' was a privileged one. For example, on my twenty-first birthday I became the proud owner of a new Hillman Minx, equipped with a green light to indicate that I was *in statu pupillari* and therefore subject to university regulations. I was only able to buy the car thanks to the co-operation of my friend Brian Rootes, son of the manufacturer's founding father, and pretending that I was still serving abroad in Palestine. This subterfuge meant that the car was officially an 'export model'. Nowadays even sixth-formers seem to drive their own cars but in my day there were very few student owner-drivers. I garaged my car in Holywell, in the original Morris Garage from which MG took its name. By happy coincidence, many years later when I was Chairman of English Heritage, the body responsible for recommending such designations, I saw to it that the building was formally listed as being of historical and architectural merit.

Not too keen on college food, Colin and I tended to eat in our elegant and enormous rooms. His father would send regular supplies of fresh milk from the family farms and we gave lavish Sunday breakfast parties. Colin always did the crossword while I scrambled the eggs and buttered the toast. We also threw two famous strawberry parties at the end of the summer term in New College cloisters. I was a keen photographer and achieved some success at it, becoming the official photographer for many theatrical and opera productions. One of my pictures, of Robin Leigh-Pemberton sitting on a wall in the Botanical Gardens reading a book, was the cover of *Cherwell*, the university newspaper.

I did not speak at the Union where the leading lights were Jeremy Thorpe, Edward Boyle and Anthony Wedgwood Benn. After all, I had already made my maiden speech in the House of Lords and I was given permission by the Warden to be absent to speak in the House whenever I wished. Perhaps it was truculent of me, but I thought the Union was a bit infra dig and adolescent by comparison.

Somehow I contrived to be part of the hearty world epitomised by the Bullingdon Club, as well as of the aesthetic one represented by the Oxford University Dramatic Society and the Film Club. The former was made up mainly of grand Etonians, the most memorable of whom was Ludovic Kennedy. Colin, who considered himself at least my social equal, was livid when he was not invited to join. The latter was the world of men who were later to become prominent in the arts. Michael Codron, for instance, was later to become a most influential impresario, John Schlesinger and Tony Richardson theatre and film producers of note, Robert Robinson a broadcaster. Above all I remember Kenneth Tynan, later the finest theatre critic of his time, sashaying down the High in green trousers and a purple cloak. The Bullingdon dined at the Bear in Woodstock. In earlier (or indeed later) times we would have worn royal-blue tailcoats with gold facings, but we were too close to the austerities of war to adopt such frivolous sartorial trappings. When we sat down at the table each member had a whole bottle of champagne in front of him and I shudder to recall how we drove back to College afterwards.

In 1948 I was invited to stay at Windsor Castle for Ascot week by the King and Queen. The mornings were taken up with tennis or riding and after an early lunch we were driven in horse-drawn carriages from Windsor Castle to the racecourse at Ascot, sitting in a different carriage every day. I will never forget the thrill of hearing the excited crowds, who lined the route, cheering on the arrival of the royal party. Not knowing much about horseracing at the time, I was delighted to be given a 'marked card' suggesting how I should place my bets by a member of the royal household. When we returned to Windsor, before dinner we usually played Racing Demon with the Queen Mother, then, of course, still the Queen. She was a very competitive player and always won hands down. I also remember the King noticing my Palestine campaign medal and questioning me closely about my service there. The King had an encyclopaedic knowledge when it came to military decorations and insignia. One of the guests at Windsor was Sharman Douglas, the glamorous socialite whose father was the American Ambassador. For a young impressionable, all this was very exhilarating.

I enjoyed being part of the aesthetic bohemian tendency, as well as a fully paid-up member of a more conventional society. However, this duality was echoed in a more fundamental personal dilemma. At Eton, although in a physical sense I was remarkably sexually innocent, I had definitely fallen in love with another boy and this was disquieting. Nothing 'happened' but I experienced all the emotions, high and low, usually associated with adult heterosexual love. This was not, I now realise, a unique or even an unusual experience. We were, after all, an all-male establishment and on reflection I decided that I was simply going through a normal healthy phase that would pass in due course. After all, one's teenage years are a time of sexual development, curiosity and turmoil. I knew I would sow the conventional wild oats, then marry, settle down and have a family, as I was aware, only too well, of the importance of fathering an heir.

To my surprise and, indeed, consternation, however, the phase did not pass when I left school. In many respects the all-male Grenadier Guards was much like Eton and homosexuality was a fact of life. There were a number of notoriously gay officers and I soon found myself being invited to all-male parties of an undeniably homosexual nature. I remember the first of these in the Hon. Ronnie Greville's London flat. Dinner was correct enough, served by stewards moonlighting from the Officers' Mess. Afterwards I was amazed when George Melly, then a young naval rating and not yet known in the world of music, arrived and proceeded to do an extremely suggestive striptease, after which some of the other guests followed his example. Another young officer and I, both embarrassed, made our excuses and left. As we were walking through the lobby we met a furious elderly gentleman in a dressing gown about to make his way upstairs and complain about the unseemly noise from the party.

Seconds later the doors opened to reveal our host, stark naked. 'Oh, father,' he said to Lord Greville, 'don't be such a bore. Can't you see we're just having a perfectly innocent party for a few friends?' My fellow officer from the Irish Guards, Tim Whidbourne, and I fled. We have never forgotten that bizarre evening. He later became a pupil of Pietro Annigoni, the Italian portrait painter who executed the picture of the Queen in Garter robes which hangs on the walls of every British embassy I have ever visited.

By the time I arrived at Oxford I was no longer so easily shocked. I had, after all, lost my virginity in Greece and had already enjoyed sex with members of both sexes. I could see this was by no means unusual and I realised I was not alone. I liked the company of girls and I enjoyed going to bed with them. Gratifyingly, they seemed to feel the same about me, but I could not deny that I sometimes felt much the same about men. Happily their reaction to this was usually as gratifying as the girls'.

Before Oxford I had thought that this bisexuality would pass, but this was not to be the case. I formed at least one deep relationship with another male undergraduate, but I continued to go out with girls. This seemed quite normal and, indeed, it still does. There is a lot of moralistic nonsense talked about 'normal' and 'deviant' behaviour, and although I have to acknowledge that my capacity for loving members of both sexes is still regarded by some as unorthodox it seems to me entirely natural and healthy. I often wonder whether, in a hundred or so years' time, the conventional heterosexuality of today's world might seem as repressed as the puritan hypocrisy of the Victorians does now.

I suppose I should have realised that sooner or later, in post-war Oxford, I would end up in trouble. In retrospect I do see that I was bound to be caught in a clash of cultures. Matters came to a head in the autumn of 1949. I had moved out of College digs and was sharing two floors at 12 Wellington Square with a friend, Roger Morgan, who later became the senior librarian in the House of Lords. Roger was the son of the famous author Charles Morgan. By now I was treasurer of the Bullingdon and also acting as co-opted photographer and public relations officer for such organisations as the Oxford University Dramatic Society and the Opera Society. These latter activities were so time-consuming that I actually employed a Trinity freshman called Martin Stevens as my informal private secretary. Stevens later became the Conservative Member of Parliament for Fulham and unfortunately died young. In those days he was immensely efficient and he loved organising my life: bills were paid on time, appointments were kept and he was quite invaluable.

Disaster finally struck in December 1949 when the Bullingdon chose the same date for their Christmas dinner as the OUDS did for their 'smoker' or end-of-term entertainment. The former involved prodigious quantities of food and drink while the latter took the form of a mildly risqué all-male cabaret. I was faced with a choice which, although awkward, was unavoidable. I had already agreed to be photographer at the smoker and did not want to miss it. So I told the Bullingdon that I had a prior engagement and opted for the OUDS.

The smoker was brilliant. The playwright Terence Rattigan was our guest of honour and Michael Codron, John Schlesinger and Brian Tesler, later chairman of London Weekend Television, were the star performers. The final act involved the entire cast each dressing up as Father Christmas. It seemed, at least at the time, extraordinarily funny and after the show Roger and I invited everyone back to our place for a party. There was, as usual, plenty to drink and I provided the music from my gramophone. Being rather warm in their Father Christmas outfits, some began to disrobe and remove their false beards. Before long there were more than a dozen Santa Clauses in various stages of undress and inebriation.

Then, suddenly there was the unmistakable noise of what Evelyn Waugh memorably described as 'the sound of the English county families baying for broken glass'.

It was the Bullingdon coming up the stairs. Most of them were as drunk as the Father Christmases and they were a lot more aggressive. They wanted their broken glass. A large bowl of tangerines was duly smashed and the fruit used as ammunition. My bicycle was thrown out of the window. Terence Rattigan took fright and fled into Martin Stevens's ground-floor room pursued by red-faced men in evening dress.

My rooms were wrecked through no fault of mine. Typically, however, the authorities took the view that in some curious and unexplained fashion I had only myself to blame and I was summoned to appear before the Dean who, obviously, wanted an explanation. He sent me to see my moral tutor, a very boring man, useless as a tutor of any kind and spectacularly so when it came to matters of morality. He told me that he thought it was time I considered my position – a curious phrase but it stuck in my mind. I duly considered my position and agreed that it was unsatisfactory. I had not really done enough work to be sure of a decent degree and in any case I was not certain that I needed one. I could not see that a degree in history would be hugely relevant to my future career and, to compound matters further, I now found myself at odds with some of my old friends from the Bullingdon, of which I was still treasurer. Many of them did come and apologise but the episode left a sour taste.

Taking everything into account, it seemed to me that it was time to go. Years before, the famous Warden Spooner was supposed to have sent down a New College undergraduate with the words, 'You have deliberately tasted two worms and you can leave Oxford by the town drain.' No one said or implied anything quite so drastic to me, but had they done so I would not have argued. Like many of my generation I probably came to Oxford too late. There were aspects of the place I much enjoyed but I was not sorry to leave. If nothing else I had been able, as a student, to begin to resolve the thorny question of my own sexuality. I felt my solution in that respect was the only honourable one open to me. I suppose that I should have realised that eventually it would lead to trouble; but at the time I was innocent and optimistic.

I might have felt a little apprehensive, but I was not fearful.

7

Public and Private Relations

He that puts on a public gown must put off a private person.

Proverb

Some landowners' eldest sons were sufficiently affluent to retreat to the family estates and lead a life entirely devoted to their management and enjoyment. This was not an option for me, nor did I want it. Instead, I was determined to seek employment.

At first I fancied myself as a publisher and saw a cousin who was in the business. Eventually contacts led me via Colin Tennant's father, Lord Glenconner, and the well-known advertising man Jack Beddington to advertising and public relations. I was taken on by Voice and Vision, a subsidiary of the famous advertising agency Colman, Prentice and Varley. They were the Saatchi and Saatchi of their day – prosperous and prestigious, with offices all round the world. The Chairman, the legendary Colonel Varley, later married my half-sister Elizabeth. Incidentally, in 1959 'CPV' were the first agency to be appointed by a political party – in this case the Conservatives – to mastermind its advertising. They helped Macmillan to win the election of that year.

So I moved to London, to a flat in an Edwardian block called Buckingham Palace Mansions opposite Victoria Station, which I shared with Robin Miller and Mark Chinnery, both of whom had been at school with me and one of whom also worked at CPV. Each morning we took it in turns to cook breakfast. There was no doubt that Mark and myself were much better cooks than Robin because he always got up last and it was invariably rather a botched job. We all then went to our office together, usually in my faithful Hillman Minx, which in those days one could park off Grosvenor Street without any problem.

Naturally, as young men about London, we gave lots of parties. The one I remember best was when Tennessee Williams came with his whole entourage of American friends. They were not aware that rationing was still in force and literally ate us out of house and home for a whole week. A friend of ours, who was also a gossip columnist on one of the national newspapers, kept on getting up and down during the meal and telephoning Tennessee's wittier remarks to his editor.

My first job at Voice and Vision was the launch of *The Eagle* which was due to be published by our client Hulton Press. They had accepted the brilliant idea of Marcus Morris, an improbable vicar from the north of England, to publish a respectable weekly comic for boys. Morris never wore a dog collar and had a distinctly unclerical sexual appetite, as he adored showgirls. In spite of this it was felt that this new comic, with its futuristic and moralistic editorial flavour, would not only rival such established but rather juvenile favourites as *The Beano* and *The Dandy*, but would also 'find favour with strait-laced parents and school teachers'. It was a new, exciting comic for the post-war age.

This was the first opportunity I had of employing my instinctive public relations skills professionally. My colleagues were gratifyingly impressed and I have to concede that my connections in society also came in more than useful in persuading the great and the good in youth organisations to endorse the new publication. People such as my good family friend Lady Stratheden, who was then head of the Girl Guide movement, proved invaluable. All sorts of Establishment figures accepted that *The Eagle* would be all that the Reverend Morris claimed, simply because I said so.

A few weeks before the launch date we hired a fleet of Daimler limousines, with enormous model golden eagles mounted on their roofs. These toured the country touting the forthcoming attractions of Dan Dare and the Mekon, Harris Tweed, PC 49 and other long-forgotten heroes. We gave away millions of vouchers for free first copies. Hulton ensured that their printers, Bemrose, were cranked up for a run of over one million copies of the first issue. It was a triumph – it sold out – and I like to feel that I played a small part in it. For millions of children it became *the* comic and was followed by *Girl*, *Robin* and many other imitators.

During my time at CPV it was made clear to me that I was expected to use my personal contacts to help obtain new clients and within a few weeks of joining the firm I managed to persuade my sister Caroline's new father-in-law, the Canadian entrepreneur Garfield Weston, owner of Associated Biscuits and Fortnum & Mason, to let CPV have the advertising account for Allied Bakeries. In spite of the ups and downs, the downs being mainly created by Varley's sometimes eccentric behaviour, CPV retained the Allied Bakeries account for many years. At my first Christmas with the company I was rather disappointed that I was given only £100 bonus for the introduction of an account that was to be worth millions in the years ahead.

After the pressure of academic life of Oxford, moving to London was a new adventure and the job itself was tremendously rewarding. The other day I came across the personal telephone book I used at the time. Turning the pages brought on an intoxicating fit of nostalgia. The London telephone exchanges, for example, still had names rather than numbers and you had to dial the first three letters: thus WHItehall, FLAxman, MAYfair, JUNiper, GULliver, GERrard, SLOane and so on.

The names of my contacts were even more of a reminder of those distant days. Here under 'A' is Gianni Agnelli, later the legendary head of the Fiat empire. I met him when we were employed to publicise the famous skiing resort Sestrières. This entailed flying journalists to Turin and showing them the delights of this Fiat-owned Italian resort. We used fashion models from *Queen* magazine, including Ingrid Wyndham, now Lady Channon, and Janet Stevenson, an American who married a Tory MP. In order to get the photographs into the Christmas issues, the pictures had to be ready to go to press not later than October. I remember taking the whole group of models and fashion designers to Sestrières in late September. When we actually got to the resort there was no snow. So we had to hunt high in the mountains, frantically trying to find some snow, and the poor girls nearly froze to death. I have never forgotten the scene of Marcus Morris in an Italian nightclub with a chorus girl on each knee. I drove up to Sestrières with Gianni Agnelli at breakneck speed around hairpin bends in one of the latest Fiat sports cars.

Tony Armstrong-Jones came under 'A' just under Gianni Agnelli. In those days he was an up-and-coming society photographer, who was once debagged at a deb dance and thrown into the Thames. He cropped up everywhere. Nobody would ever have believed he would one day be the Queen's brother-in-law.

Turning the pages of that dog-eared little book I see that 'C' was for Cadbury. I was responsible for the Cadbury account, with Adrian Cadbury in particular. The main objective was the 'social' promotion of drinking-chocolate. This entailed persuading large hotels, especially when hosting lavish dances, to make drinking-chocolate available as a late-night 'social' drink instead of coffee or tea. I suggested establishing Regency-style chocolate houses in Oxford, Cambridge and Regent Street. We persuaded Wedgwood, one of our other accounts, to design a special drinking-chocolate motif for mugs, which lasted many years. I remember going up to Bourneville for meetings with the directors and being impressed that they all ate in good democratic style in the same canteen as the workers. The only difference between the directors' table and the workers' was that the former got Kia-ora orange juice on theirs. Alcohol, of course, was strictly forbidden on the premises as the original founders of such firms as Cadbury, Rowntree and Fry were all Quakers. They went into chocolate as a missionary enterprise to woo the working classes away from the perils of alcohol. As a chocoholic myself I much enjoyed these visits and always came away with bags full of broken chocolate. Many years later I find myself the proprietor of my own chocolate factory in the Beaulieu village.

'C' also meant Francis Chichester and family, who were our neighbours and relations by marriage. Francis, of course, was to find fame sailing solo round the world and he kept *Gipsy Moth* on one of our moorings on the Beaulieu river, and we promoted his maps of London.

I used to lunch with another 'C', Norman Collins, then best known as a novelist. He and Lord Bessborough were planning the campaign to get independent commercial television accepted by the British public. Sadly, when it happened I was not in a position to benefit from all my previous work in establishing the principle of an independent advertising-financed service.

Alfred Esdaile, who had made a fortune during the war on girlie shows in London theatres, bought the Royal Court Theatre in Sloane Square, which was a wartime dance hall, and relaunched it as a theatre. I was very involved in its preparation and although it made a successful start there was a dispute among the directors, who included Sir Lewis Casson and his wife, Dame Sybil Thorndike, and the Playfair family who were running the theatre on a daily basis. Dramatically, one evening I had to announce to the press the Cassons' resignation from this venture, which was a rather crushing incident in the early days of the theatre. However, as the years went on the Royal Court became a most successful part of London's theatreland and was responsible for staging the first performance of *Look Back in Anger* and many other ground-breaking plays.

Much to my delight, Voice and Vision obtained several other theatrical accounts. One I was personally involved in was the publicising of the new Tarzan, Lex Barker, who came from a very good New York family and had served in the American Army in England during the war. Later he married Lana Turner and they both came down to Beaulieu for lunch. He told me that he enjoyed being Tarzan, with the exception of having to shave his chest, which made it permanently itchy. Anton Dolin, the ballet impresario, also asked us to publicise the career of the newly discovered John Gilpin, whose father was a Royal Navy petty officer in Portsmouth. Gilpin had a meteoric career in ballet, which was cruelly cut short by a serious injury to his knee, and later retired to Monaco, married the sister of Prince Rainier and died shortly afterwards.

My most glamorous theatrical experience was promoting the musical *South Pacific* when it first came to London. I got to know the producer of the show, the famous Hollywood director Joshua Logan, very well and discovered that he had been stationed near Beaulieu during the war and had a photograph to prove it. Josh and his wife Nedda became close friends and I always used to visit them in New York and see his latest shows.

What a treasure trove of memories that little contact book contained. Here, under 'H', is 'Hartnell, Norman' the Queen's dressmaker. He was also a fashion consultant to a Voice and Vision client called Berkertex, who were wholesale women's wear manufacturers. I helped organise fashion shows around the country at which Norman presented his collection.

So this was my world: the entertaining and exciting café society of the Fifties. Talking about cafés, 'Q' is for Quaglino's, which I also helped promote, as well as the Café Royal, but unfortunately during my time the owners destroyed the ornately decorated dining room where Oscar Wilde and his cronies, such as Lord Alfred Douglas and Frank Harris, used to dine frequently.

I hosted a lot of lunches every week although as I riffle through the pages of my little book I sometimes have difficulty remembering whom I lunched or wined and dined, and whom I didn't. Indeed, I sometimes wonder how well I knew the names. Some seem awfully hazy. Tommy Kinsman, the famous band leader, was hardly a friend; on the other hand Wolf Mankowitz, who wrote hugely successful musicals such as *A Kid for Two Farthings* and *Expresso Bongo*, was a good friend, as was Toby O'Brien, the Tory party's press officer; Searcy's the caterers were useful clients and contacts, and Barry Swaebe, the society photographer, was almost as ubiquitous as Tony Armstrong-Jones.

Ah, here under 'W' is the redoubtable David Williams who ran charter flights of pilgrims to Rome in Holy Year. I managed to persuade the Cardinal Archbishop of Westminster formally to bless the aeroplanes. That was arguably my greatest PR coup.

I could never have achieved what I did without my many friends in the press. They were legends in their day but, like Fleet Street, now little more than a fading memory: people like Anne Edwards, the *Daily Express* columnist; Don Edgar, of the William Hickey gossip column; Peter Dacre of the *Mail* (father of the present *Mail* supremo, Paul) and Noel Whitcombe of the *Mirror.*

In the evenings I began to explore London in a wider sense, particularly the more risqué piano bars, and was surprised how many of my friends were also to be seen there. In the summer of 1952 I was introduced at a London cocktail party to Benjamin Sonnenberg, doyen of American public relations, who ran a very successful consultancy in New York. Having arrived in America as a penniless emigrant from Lithuania, he rose to become one of the most respected people in New York society, with such blue-chip clients as Lever Brothers and Philip Morris. He was also responsible for the successful promotion of Pepperidge Farm from a small bakery to an international business. At that time he lived in Gramercy Park, in two adjoining houses that were full of valuable antiques, particularly historic brass, which he collected.

On being introduced to him I remarked that I gathered that we were both in the same racket. This apparently appealed to his sense of humour and before I knew what was happening he had invited me to come and stay with him in New York and work in his office to learn the trade. I immediately leapt at this opportunity, which was a necessary catalyst in carrying out another plan that I had been nursing for some while. This was to embark on a lecture tour from coast to coast of America to publicise Britain's historic houses in general and Beaulieu in particular. I could not really organise this properly from England, so I contacted the English Speaking Union to see whether they would be prepared to book me into some of their branches. Happily, as it turned out, they were able to provide most of the engagements for the tour and others came in as a result of Ben Sonnenberg's contacts or simply by word of mouth. The English Speaking Union engagements were a joy and at every one I received a warm reception and wonderful hospitality from its local branches.

To finance this trip I was able to persuade Sir William Rootes to lend me a Humber Hawk, which I drove all over the States as part of a drive to publicise British cars which at the time were in the midst of a big export push in America. Additionally, while I was touring the North American continent my coronation robes, which were due to be used at the Queen's coronation in June the following year, were also touring fashionable stores in America. They earned me much needed resources for the trip.

In September 1952 I sailed on the *Queen Elizabeth* from Southampton. Upon arrival in New York I was shown the magnificent separate apartment which Ben Sonnenberg had provided for my stay and on the very first night he gave a welcoming dinner party for me, which included as guests Alistair Cooke, Greta Garbo and her special friend George Schley. After dinner we went to the top floor of the house where Ben had a private cinema and saw a preview performance of Charlie Chaplin's *Limelight*. Ben's special contacts with the film industry enabled him to screen the latest Hollywood films before they were shown to the public. I was as impressed as I had been when my stepfather Ned gave me tea on HMS *Hermes*.

I arrived at a very dramatic time in American politics as the Presidential Elections were six weeks off and General Eisenhower and Adlai Stevenson were battling it out to succeed President Harry Truman. Ben Sonnenberg was very much a Democrat and many interesting people come to the house. One day he asked me to go and report on a lunch being given by Elizabeth Arden (also a client of CPV in London) for smart Republican ladies in New York. It took place in her large apartment and was called 'The Maine Chance Lunch', as that was the name of her health club in New England where ladies tried to lose weight. The lunch was carefully chosen so that there were virtually no calories at all and on leaving I was so hungry I had to get a hamburger. The main point of it was for her to tell her friends and clients that they just had to vote for 'that nice General Eisenhower' and not Adlai Stevenson, to whom she imputed every vice under the sun. None of which, of course, could have been repeated in public. I confess I was rather shocked although Ben Sonnenberg certainly wasn't. It was my first introduction to the ruthless politics that the Americans can sometimes practise. On election night I was invited by William Paley, the famous head of CBC, to watch the election results come through in the studio. This was fascinating, but what I liked best was having my first glimpse of the colour television with which they were experimenting at the time. I was amazed how each colour could be adjusted on the set to make it look as if people had red faces or dark hair. It was not long, of course, before colour television was introduced in America but it was unheard of back home in Britain.

I very much enjoyed my time in New York and, in addition to spending splendid fall weekends in New England and Pennsylvania, I saw lots of shows such as *Guys and Dolls, Wish You Were Here* and *New Faces*. During the evenings I explored New York with my ever-expanding group of friends. A particular favourite was a group of bars known as the Bird circuit, at one of which the young Eartha Kitt was making her name. Gore Vidal, who had just published his first big success *The City and the Pillar,* was also much in evidence.

In December I had to fly back to London for a charity ball which I had set up for Cadbury's. My Stratocruiser flew into heavy fog at Goose Bay and again in London. The London fog was different. Actually, it wasn't fog at all but smog. This was the last great fog, which claimed the lives of so many people, and because the Clean Air Act came into force shortly after it has, thankfully, never occurred again.

I stayed home for Christmas and returned to spend the New Year with the Raymond Masseys, whom I had met on the *Queen Elizabeth,* in their home in Connecticut, which was a converted farmhouse. I remarked to Raymond on the strange behaviour of his Alsatian who was apparently perfectly normal but refused to go near the main living room. One could see the hairs on his neck rise when he was called to do so. Raymond's explanation was that when it was a barn it burned down and two horses were burned to death. This confirmed my belief that animals are very psychic and can sense the paranormal as well as human beings.

Soon after New Year I set off in my Humber Hawk accompanied by Larry Skidmore Miles, who became my co-driver, navigator and general dogsbody. He was very useful but while I was giving my lectures he had a bad habit of disappearing to visit the less salubrious bars in town. Sometimes I did not see him until the following morning when I was due to leave for the next engagement. My first lecture dates were on the East Coast in Williamsburg, Washington, Richmond, Atlanta and so on, down to Miami. The lectures went well. In the Southern States when I told them that the last time a member of my family had been there was when my grandfather was attached as an observer to General Lee's staff in the Civil

War, I was greeted with a thunder of applause. I was not surprised to discover that schoolchildren in Atlanta were allowed two days off each year – one to see the Diorama of the Battle of Atlanta and the second to see the film *Gone with the Wind*.

In Washington I addressed the American Public Relations Institution and saw my old butler Shepherd, who had been butlering in Palace House before the war and who, on my sister Elizabeth's recommendation, was now working at the British Embassy. Almost invariably we stayed in private houses and the hosts and hostesses were as generous and caring as one would expect from Americans. These one-night visits all seemed to follow the same pattern: we would arrive in the late afternoon and find our hostess dressed in what they called tea gowns. Being an Englishman I was immediately invited to enjoy an English tea, which they had so thoughtfully arranged. The man of the house was invariably absent and would arrive hot and breathless from the office to be told by his wife to go and change immediately as guests were about to arrive. In the meantime I was also changing and came down to at least an hour-long cocktail party where I was expected to greet all the guests and carry on polite conversation, all the time worrying about my lecture. Very often I would be deluged with introductions for the next city in which I would be appearing.

I found the drinking at the parties before the lectures very difficult and discovered that a good trick was to drink ginger ale with lots of ice, which made it look exactly like Scotch. One could then not be accused of putting a damper on the party and as a result give a better lecture. Often on a spare day I would be given parties by friends of a different social standing. Twice – once in Washington and once in Miami – such parties were raided by the police for reasons which I have never discovered. The police claimed that it was for something trivial like the noise but we all thought they were operating to a different agenda.

One visit that gave me particular pleasure was to the home of Colonel and Mrs Robert Groves, in Beaulieu, Savannah in Georgia. The American Beaulieu had been so named by an early colonist from the Isle of Wight. He was so struck that the surrounding river and marshland looked like Beaulieu that he named the American site in its honour. I visited Beaulieu, Savannah several times and experienced there my first oyster bake.

Another highlight was my trip to New Orleans and being there for Mardi Gras. Since I was staying at the British Consulate I tried to behave circumspectly but I was virtually forced to go to the formal balls which took place in the theatres and at which outsiders like me could only watch from their seats while the members of various New Orleans societies danced on the stage with great formality in the most elaborate costumes. I tried to get away from these events as soon as I could and used to leave a bag with jeans and casual clothes in the cloakroom, then change and go on to the more amusing bars and jazz clubs in the city.

I also visited some of the great old cotton plantation mansions on the river, many of which were in bad condition, neglected and dilapidated like ghosts on the banks of the Mississippi. It struck me as strange that American tourists flock to England to see our historic houses but neglect the heritage buildings on their own doorstep.

From the Old South I drove the Humber to the West Coast via Texas, the Grand Canyon to San Diego, where there was an unfortunate incident. I was taken by friends across the border into Mexico to visit the bars in Tijuana. Getting into Mexico was of course no problem but coming back at four in the morning we were all asked by US immigration officials where we were born. My friends were allowed through, as they had been in America, but I, unwisely, mentioned that I had been born in London. As I did not have my passport with me I was arrested and my friends had to go miles back to my hotel in San Diego and get my passport before I was released.

I also went up to Los Angeles and in Malibu I stayed with Irving Rapper, well-known director of Bette Davis films, and met many people in Hollywood. After a week I moved up to Beverly Hills to stay with the famous film director John Ford, whom I had met in London, and he arranged tickets for me to attend the Oscars ceremony while he was himself in London. I was, of course, thrilled to be there when it was announced that he had won an Oscar for the film *The Quiet Man*, starring John Wayne. I remember ringing him at his London hotel, Claridge's, and waking him up to tell him the news. It was in Los Angeles that I appeared on my very first television show. It was about the time that both Stalin and Queen Mary died that I had to comment on the significance of their passing. Quite a challenge!

From there I went to San Francisco, where I made a point of visiting the Beaulieu Vineyard in Napa Valley, and back to the East Coast via Reno, Salt Lake City, Denver, Kansas, Chicago. Finally I spent the last three weeks in a friend's apartment on 8th Street in New York, passing many evenings in Greenwich Village listening to jazz and stars of the day like Mabel Mercer.

When I returned to London I found the preparations for the coronation were becoming more and more frantic, and I was asked by the British Information Service in New York to raise a question in the House of Lords about the lack of facilities being offered to American journalists covering it. I had a rather bland reply from Lord Fortescue and so I expressed the hope that Her Majesty's Government realised that foreign journalists need interpreters, telephones, typewriters and other facilities to do their job properly. I made a point of going to see the Earl Marshal, the Duke of Norfolk, who was in charge of the coronation, and I am afraid he was not very sympathetic, because I suspect he did not approve of the press anyway. However, I did my best.

So back to London for the coronation. Since I had been the youngest peer in his own right at the 1937 coronation, I was much in demand with the press to write about my memories and experiences of the previous event. This time there was no little Lord Fauntleroy suit or ham sand-wiches in a bag, but the full coronation robes of a peer. It was a wet and windy day, but all went well and from where I was seated I had a very good view of the ceremony. I knew most of the train-bearers, two of whom were my cousins, Lady Anne Coke, daughter of the Earl of Leicester and later wife of my old Oxford room-mate Lord Glenconner, and Lady Caroline Montagu Douglas Scott, daughter of the Duke of Buccleuch, who married Ian Gilmour. Many people I had met in America arrived in London. They came from all walks of life and my main memory is of constantly entertaining people who had been kind to me in the States. I particularly recall Elizabeth Arden coming down to Beaulieu for a visit. We also had John Wayne and his wife, and the head of Philip Morris.

By this time I had been appointed as a director of Voice and Vision. At weekends I was busy continuing the promotion of Beaulieu and the newly fledged car collection, now in its second year of opening and proving a successful draw with the public. In Washington at the annual conference of the Public Relations Institute I had been hailed as the most promising young PR man in England. I might have been . . . but fate decreed other-wise.

8

'Sensation en Angleterre'

We know no spectacle so ridiculous as the British public in one of
its periodical fits of morality.

Thomas Babington Macaulay

I suppose with the benefit of hindsight what became known, unfortunately for me, as the 'Montagu Case' was inevitable. At the time it was
a sensation and attracted more publicity than any event in my life. For a
while it made my name a household word not only in Britain but also
throughout much of the rest of the world. It was a wretched business and
caused me great distress, as it did to those nearest and dearest to me. This
I bitterly regretted. I still do regret it although I cannot in all conscience
say that I feel any guilt or shame for the actual 'crimes' I was supposed to
have committed and for which I was ultimately sent to prison.

For more than forty years I have made no public comment on what
happened in the early 1950s. Others, including those intimately involved,
pursued different policies and I respect what they did, but that was not
my way. After it was over I resolved that from the first day it would be
'business as usual'. I would not flinch from returning to Beaulieu, to
public life and, after an appropriate period of time, to the House of Lords,
determined to hold my head high in whatever company or situation I
might find myself. I decided to treat my prosecution, or what many felt
as 'persecution', for homosexual offences, the subsequent witch-hunt and
the prison sentence that followed it as past history. It was a searing episode
that taught me much about my fellow human beings and as a result
showed me who my real friends were. Even though much that had happened was deeply upsetting there was also a lot that was encouraging and
moments which were quite droll. The humour might have been a bit
black but it was sometimes there. Perhaps it helped to keep me sane. In
any event I was extremely relieved when it was all over. On balance, my
conclusion, once I was finally free, was that my trial and imprisonment

had been an ordeal that I had come through successfully, but had no wish to prolong.

My first action after my final release was to put all the verbatim transcripts of the court proceedings, my voluminous private correspondence and newspaper cuttings in an old leather cabin trunk. This I deposited in a London bank vault where it remained undisturbed until recently, when I had to refer to the papers while writing this book. Just looking at them has proved a very painful experience. Having consigned the archive and appointed a literary executor in case of my early death, I was determined to do my best to get on with my life. It is for others to judge how successful this policy has been. From time to time I have been asked to talk or write about my experiences, which I have always refused. In the rare instances when someone has been particularly insistent I have made it plain that I would not hesitate to take legal action, as quite apart from the libel laws I was also protected by legislation regarding the rehabilitation of offenders. However, I have not shrunk from publicity when I judged it to be either helpful or essential in promoting products or causes with which I was associated. If you were to play a word association game with the average person in the street today and started by saying Montagu, many people would recognise the name, but the most likely second response would be Beaulieu or motor cars or Heritage. It is important to remember that I was only twenty-seven then; so only those with long memories would remember the time of my troubles.

Family, friends and acquaintances have respected and assisted me in my vow of silence over the years and I am sure many of them have been grateful for it. Some may be shocked and upset that I should now be breaking it, so I feel that I owe them an explanation of why I should be doing this so late in the day. That it *is* so late is one good reason, for there are those who might at one time have been hurt by my raking over the past and the most important of these are my children. All this happened before their births but obviously throughout my life I have always been worried that either their schooling or business might be unfortunately touched by the consequences of those faraway events. Now that they are grown-up and beyond the reach of cruel school bullying or teasing, they are more than old enough to know the truth and I want them to hear it first-hand from me and not from a possible future unauthorised biographer or sensationalist. That, I believe, is the most important issue.

I am in my seventy-fifth year and must acknowledge the fact that I will not be around for ever to defend myself or to put my side of the story, much less be in the position to insist that the matter is not discussed inaccurately or irresponsibly in public. I accept the inevitability that historians and unauthorised biographers may minutely examine and expose my life when there is no one to correct their prejudices, theories and assumptions. I want to put the record straight before I die, as public memory is short and almost infinitely fallible. When, for instance, my fellow peer Lord Brocket went to gaol in the 1990s many people, including the media, seemed to think that this was the first occasion in modern times that a member of the House of Lords had been sent to prison – something that is totally untrue. (However, amazingly in the 1990s my name was never mentioned. By this time I was much more relaxed about this period in my life and would certainly not have objected to sensible comment about the past when contemporary peers were themselves being imprisoned.) The short span of public memory was further illustrated to me when Lord Brocket came to lunch with me a few days before he started his sentence. After the meal I asked him if there was anything I could do to help him. He thanked me but thought not. He asked me why I thought I could help. When I told him about my experiences of the 1950s he was frankly amazed, as he had never heard about my case. I wished him luck and hoped that public memory of his incarceration would almost entirely fade, as it has of mine.

It was never my intention to become a martyr for the 'gay' cause, any more than Oscar Wilde went to gaol to become a homosexual icon. Nevertheless, recently there are increasing signs – an essay in the pink press here, a university thesis there – that the Montagu case is beginning to take its place in homosexual lore and in the history of sexual legislation. It is now widely accepted that the public reaction to our trial and imprisonment was the single most important factor in the change of the law which decriminalised sexual acts between consenting male adults. In these circumstances I believe it is important for posterity to have my version of events, to represent the truth as I see it, as only I am in a position to tell it, although doubtless there will be other versions in the future.

The early Fifties were a dramatic period in our island's story. On the one hand it was a time of great optimism and excitement, with the Queen's coronation in 1953 and much talk of the 'new Elizabethan Age'. On the eve of the coronation itself it was reported that Everest had been conquered by

Edmund Hillary and Sherpa Tensing. There was a sense of gaiety epitomised by two musicals of considerable charm, Julian Slade's *Salad Days*
and Sandy Wilson's *The Boyfriend*, but a darker, more subversive note
was struck by the publication of Kingsley Amis's *Lucky Jim* and William
Golding's *Lord of the Flies*. In the world of opera, of which I had become
very fond, there were premières of Benjamin Britten's *Turn of the Screw*
and William Walton's *Troilus and Cressida*. In the world of international
politics the Cold War was at its most frigid, Nasser was coming to power
in Egypt, the Communists taking Dien Bien Phu and, most sinister,
Senator McCarthy was pursuing his anti-Communist witchhunts. The
world was still being ruled by dinosaurs left over from World War Two,
most notably for the West by Eisenhower and Churchill, but Stalinism
still reigned supreme in Eastern Europe.

Although it was a wonderful time to be young, the old guard was
still very much alive and they felt threatened. Not only did they see
reds under every bed; they saw them *in* every bed as well. This was not
helped by the defection to Moscow of the British Foreign Office spies
Burgess and Maclean and, even though Maclean was uncompromisingly
heterosexual, it was widely regarded as a conspiracy of left-wing 'queers'.
In the British Establishment there was a deep vein of anti-homosexual
prejudice, which went to the very top and included the notoriously
reactionary Home Secretary Sir David Maxwell Fyfe, later Lord Kilmuir,
the Lord Chief Justice Rayner Goddard, a keen hanger and flogger, and
the Commissioner of the Metropolitan Police, Sir John Nott-Bower,
who was convinced that the British way of life was threatened by a
homosexual conspiracy. Egged on by the national press, they believed
they had a mission to liberate British society from these 'evil' men.
Although such a policy was not overtly reported in the British press it
was widely publicised abroad. For example, in October 1953 the *Sydney
Daily Telegraph* reported that there was a Scotland Yard plan to smash
homosexuality in London:

> The plan originated under strong United States advice to Britain to
> weed out homosexuals – as hopeless security risks – from important
> government jobs. One of the Yard's top rankers, Commander E. A.
> Cole recently spent three months in America consulting with FBI
> officials about the plan, but the plan was extended as the war on all
> vice when Sir John Nott-Bower took over as the new Commissioner of

Scotland Yard in August. Sir John swore that he would rip the cover off all London's filth spots.

I was too innocent, naive or foolhardy to know much about this, much less to recognise that it constituted a risk to me personally. Something else also contributed to my undoing: I was regarded by the older generation of the Establishment as a traitor to my class and, although this notion looks ludicrous now, in those days the class system was rigid to an extent unbelievable today. My co-defendant Peter Wildeblood commented that I was one of the most completely unsnobbish persons that he had ever met. I have no reason to doubt him although I do not know why this should be. Even today I am flattered by his comment, but like to think I was 'doing what comes naturally' – a quote from a famous song from *Annie Get Your Gun*, a hit musical at that time. Perhaps my behaviour and attitude to others have something to do with the formative time I spent in North America. In any event it is true that I have always regarded snobbery as both incomprehensible and pathetic, and this may well have had some influence on my undoing. Of course, working in PR for four years exposed me to many people from all walks of life, from dukes to dustmen.

Wildeblood recognised the dangers of this far better than I did and later he wrote of me,

His guests, both at Beaulieu and in his London flat, formed an extraordinary assortment of conflicting types: businessmen and writers, Duchesses and model girls, restaurateurs and politicians and musical comedy actresses and Guards officers and Americans wearing handpainted ties. He was always intensely busy and often merely used to introduce his guests to each other and then disappear; a most disconcerting habit. I remember him doing this once in the middle of luncheon, leaving two big businessmen and a Canadian ice-hockey player staring at each other and wondering what on earth to talk about. Trivial though it may seem, this kind of behaviour enraged some people who took themselves extremely seriously and expected Lord Montagu to do the same. He made enemies, as well as friends.

This never occurred to me at the time, but in retrospect perhaps he was right. People did not expect this kind of lifestyle from 'someone like me'.

After my very successful lecture tour of America and all the excitement surrounding the coronation I got engaged to the beautiful and intelligent Anne Gage, whom I had met just two months before at, of all things, a Cadbury's chocolate party. The news even made the *New York Times* and *Le Monde*, where I was described (quite erroneously) as '*un des derniers prétendants à la main de la princesse Margaret*'.

Our happiness was, alas, short-lived. A few days after the announcement disaster struck. Some Boy Scouts who were camping on the estate spent August Bank Holiday helping out as guides in Palace House where coincidentally several friends, including the film director the late Kenneth Hume, were staying as my guests.

As it was rather hot, I decided to go down to my beach hut on the Solent for a swim. I thought the Scouts deserved a swim too and invited any who wished to join us. Two elected to come, so off we went, spending no more than twenty minutes on the beach as I had to run some of my guests to the railway station. As far as I can remember this now distant event, it was an entirely happy party that went to the beach, changed in the hut, went in and out of the sea several times and then returned to Beaulieu.

After this innocent episode I discovered that an expensive camera of mine was missing. I reported it to the police, who came to interview me. To my amazement they did not seem in the least interested in the camera, as one of the Scouts had countered my concern over the loss with an allegation that I had sexually assaulted him and the other Scout similarly accused Kenneth Hume. I adamantly denied the accusations but the police, it seemed, preferred the boys' word to mine.

The next three weeks were probably the most agonising of my life. Although no charges were preferred at this stage, rumours were rife and it was reported that Chelsea was covered by a cloud of smoke created by the burning of compromising letters and photographs. While the Director of Public Prosecutions was dithering about whether or not to bring a case his mind was made up for him by a threat of exposure from the Beaverbrook press. I was always led to believe that this came from the very top – from Lord Beaverbrook himself. He was certainly mischievous enough.

My lawyer, Eric Summer, was informed that I had to go to Winchester on a certain day to be officially charged. By this time I found the situation in England, waiting for something to happen in an atmosphere of increasingly rancorous gossip, debilitating and intolerable. I was on the verge of a mental breakdown. I felt physically sick almost all the time. I was assailed by friendly advice from all sides. The situation seemed unreal and quite ghastly.

I therefore decided to go abroad, especially to see Anne, who was staying with her grandmother in the South of France, in order to tell her the horrible position I was in. My decision to leave England was further influenced by the fact that my youngest sister Mary Clare was about to get married in October and it seemed intolerable for her wedding to be overshadowed by scandalous tittle-tattle about me. The South of France in August should be a place for sun and fun, but for me it was an agonising period, as telephone conversations with France were almost impossible and my lawyers had to fly down, very expensively, for conferences. Some people – including, I am sorry to say, my former assistant Martin Stevens – assuming I would never come back, embarked with others on Machiavellian plans to seize control of Beaulieu estate and presumably administer it for their own benefit. Just in time I saw through the plan and refused to sign the power of attorney, but this created even more distrust between myself and my friends back in England. I told who would listen that I was innocent and would definitely come back and face the unwarranted charge.

I broke out in a terrible nervous rash and travelled to Paris to consult doctors and to be nearer to my lawyers. Increasing press attention then persuaded me to go to America to stay with my sister who lived in Waco, Texas. An enterprising *Daily Express* reporter, Dick Killian, brilliantly tracked me down. Neither of us wanted to embarrass my sister further so we flew back together to New York on the same plane. By now British press interest in England in my whereabouts had reached the front pages and I decided to return to Paris in order to carry on to England to face the music as soon after my sister Mary Clare's wedding as possible.

My determination to return was not altogether welcomed by certain people, one of whom, a large client of Colman Prentice and Varley, offered me generous sums of money to stay abroad. On my arrival in Paris there was a swarm of pressmen and I was met by a young French lawyer who evaded the press by a dramatic car chase, a secret address and all manner of cloak-and-dagger episodes. I lived briefly in a quiet hotel off the Champs-Elysées but once again I was found by the press. This time the successful sleuth was the *Sunday Pictorial*'s redoubtable correspondent Audrey

Whiting, a close friend to this day. Her landlady had been in the French Resistance and was well aware of the wartime contribution Beaulieu made to SOE training, so she also insisted that Audrey should protect me, despite the possible damage to her career, until the time came when I could return to England. Although for her there was a clear conflict of interests we nevertheless did a deal. This involved my returning to England on a Saturday so that it became a good Sunday newspaper story. She found me a splendid small hotel in the Rambouillet forest where I waited impatiently for my return to England. I was not fleeing justice but escaping from unwanted smear, innuendo and publicity. When the time came I was determined to do the honourable thing. For me 'no wandering on a foreign strand'.

One puzzling incident happened to me in Paris when I was surprised by two men in my hotel bedroom who, using an introduction from an American I knew, suggested that I might like to take the route of Burgess and Maclean and go to Russia where I was promised a comfortable life. I sent them away without hesitation and later reported the incident to MI5 in London. I shall never know to this day whether it was a genuine approach or one that had been set up by Fleet Street. On telephoning Beaulieu to hear the news about my sister's wedding earlier that day, no sooner had I replaced the receiver when a reporter from an English tabloid newspaper called – I can only assume that the Beaulieu telephone lines had been tapped or wired – and I left the receiver off the hook for the rest of the night.

My return was arranged amicably with the British authorities and I finally flew back to London airport, where I was arrested and formally charged. I was then driven to Lymington Magistrates' Court, only a few miles from Beaulieu, where a crowd of 250 people had gathered to boo and jeer my arrival. They knew only what they had read in the papers, but nevertheless it was a disconcerting experience. Lymington had been our local shopping town since my childhood, and I knew many tradesmen and local people there. At the committal proceedings it was unnerving to hear a fourteen-year-old Boy Scout assert categorically that I had taken sexual advantage of him. It was even more shocking because it was described by the boy in graphic detail, smiling as he gave his verbal evidence. The transparency of the boy's claim was shown up in a letter from Dr Camps, the famous Home Office pathologist, in which he not only confirmed that there was no physical evidence to substantiate the accusation but also noted his general impression of the boy, which was that 'he enjoyed being in the limelight'. I still assumed at the time that he made the allegations in order to deflect attention from the missing camera – even if it was a rather extreme way of doing it. On further reflection, witnessing the extraordinary hostility of some of those involved in the prosecution, I began to think in terms of conspiracy and, although I am not naturally paranoid, I started to feel persecuted.

My lawyer tried, as did Kenneth Hume's, to challenge our accusers' evidence, but to no avail. We, of course, protested our innocence but the magistrates judged that there was a case to answer. In retrospect I can hardly blame them, as the situation looked bad, but essentially it was the word of a teenage Boy Scout against mine. In those days Scout's honour had an untarnished ring to it, not to be lightly questioned. We were duly committed for trial at Winchester Assizes.

Waiting on bail is a fascinating, agonising and revealing experience. Not only does one find out who one's true friends are, but every Tom, Dick and Harry feels he can benefit from the unfortunate position. When monthly account statements came in they were often accompanied by lawyers' letters, as they were doubtful whether they would receive their money. I remember a famous wine merchant in Bristol chasing me for a paltry amount. Other instances were more disturbing. For instance, my lawyers were approached by a young man from a racing stable near Newbury who swore that a friend of his had been accused by one of the two Boy Scouts of a similar offence a few months earlier. Although great efforts were made to trace the other man, including the use of private detectives, it was to no avail. Secondly an old drunk army friend of my half-sister Helen swore that he was a friend of Judge Ormerod's wife and with a little cash could have the verdict swayed. I quite clearly told this one to get lost and to drop this fanciful scheme. Finally and more disturbing were the activities in a certain pub in Portsmouth where no less than two members of the jury drank regularly in the company of the police. The police were apparently very active in rumour-mongering about me, telling all and sundry salacious stories, which were presumably designed to influence their final judgement. Michael Pitt-Rivers's brother Julian investigated the accusations, but by the time he had completed his research we were already convicted. I often wondered what the truth was.

Winchester is a dramatic and intimidating place to stand trial. The Great Hall had been drastically altered when I saw it as an accused prisoner so that we were, in effect, holding the trial in a room within a room. Nevertheless I could not help reflecting that it was here that Sir Walter Raleigh had once been sentenced to be beheaded. In fiction Thomas Hardy had chosen Winchester as the venue for *Tess of the d'Urbervilles'* conviction for murder. High on the wall, suspended like the sword of Damocles, was the Round Table said once to have belonged to King Arthur. And on a personal note I could see the name of my own grandfather on the list of those who had held the great office of High Sheriff of Hampshire. The sense of history was oppressive.

Nor did I like the look of prosecuting counsel Mr G. D. Roberts, otherwise known on account of his swarthy complexion as 'Khaki'. Khaki always conducted business with a glass of 'cough mixture' at his side. This actually contained a succession of stiff Scotches. A formidable six foot three, he had once played rugby for England and now, slightly gone to seed, he weighed in at eighteen and a half stone. A notorious hanger and flogger, he was known on the Western Circuit as 'a lawyer's lawyer'. Roberts had a history of high-profile trials. He had once unsuccessfully defended Ivor Novello for driving his Rolls-Royce without a petrol licence and managed to get Noël Coward off on a currency charge. His most notorious appearance had been at the Nuremberg trials, where he had made a fool of himself by asking such quintessentially English barrister's questions as: 'If an honourable German gives his word, he keeps it, does he not?' The culmination of this disaster was his cross-examination of Hermann Goering. Goering completely outwitted him and Khaki had to be replaced by the even more formidable Sir David Maxwell Fyfe, later, as Lord Kilmuir, Lord Chancellor. On home turf in an English courtroom, however, Roberts was a formidable opponent with a reactionary distaste for what he considered 'unnatural practices'. I did not fancy my chances of doing a Goering.

In his opening remarks at Winchester, prosecuting counsel Khaki remarked predictably that 'this is a very serious and sordid case; there is nothing pleasant about it from beginning to end'. I could only concur, although these were the only words he spoke with which I did agree. His account of what happened bore no relation to reality and I felt bemused and helpless, like the accused in a Kafka novel. The rest of the trial was, essentially, a rerun of the committal proceedings, with the single advantage that I was being judged by a jury rather than a bench of magistrates. It was they who reaffirmed my faith in my fellow man. Unlike the magistrates, they smelt a rat as they plainly preferred my word to that of the Boy Scout and the principal charges were therefore dismissed. During the trial my growing cynicism, and that of many others, about the police and their masters was confirmed. It became evident that my passport had been falsified to make it look as if during my self-imposed exile earlier that year I visited England but failed to surrender to the authorities. I had the judge, Mr Justice Lynskey, to thank for spotting this piece of forgery. Now at the very end of the trial the DPP, without informing me, my counsel or solicitors, introduced a brand-new minor charge. Understandably, the jury were thrown into a state of confusion and were unable to deliver a verdict. This charge would remain outstanding and it seemed that I would have to stand trial all over again at the next session, even though my alleged victim had been effectively discredited.

A few hundred yards from the beach hut the Hon. Ewen Montagu QC (no relation), the eminent Judge Advocate of the Navy, brother of Lord Swaythling and part of the team that devised the Man Who Never Was, one of the most successful intelligence coups of World War Two, was renting a house. Later it occurred to us that the beach hut could hardly have been a suitable venue for untoward behaviour, with such a distinguished watchdog so close. Indeed, he was in his house when it was alleged the offences were committed. Throughout both trials and afterwards he was enormously supportive, in particular in dealing with the peculiar tactics of the Hampshire Police.

I was able to spend a relatively peaceful and undisturbed Christmas at Beaulieu, confident the worst was over and that the minor charge would be countered satisfactorily and I would consequently be discharged. I was particularly touched when the film star Diana Dors, who was appearing in pantomime at Southampton, came specially to Beaulieu in order to wish me well. It quite restored my confidence but my optimism was soon confounded.

I totally underestimated the determination of the authorities to get me and prove themselves right. At 8 a.m. on 9 January 1954 the police arrived at Palace House, where they were let in by the butler and insisted on coming into my bedroom while I was still in bed. They told me that they wanted to take me down to the police station at once. I was not able to shave, have breakfast or contact my solicitor, which was actually done by my enterprising butler, who also hid the visitors' book the police were diligently searching for. They served a warrant for my arrest concerning two airmen. I was initially somewhat puzzled and did not know whom they were referring to. At the same time other police officers were arresting my cousin Michael Pitt-Rivers at his home in Dorset and my friend Peter Wildeblood, the *Daily Mail*'s diplomatic correspondent, at his house in Canonbury, North London – significantly, not by the ordinary police but by the Special Branch. They were not allowed to contact their lawyers either. For good measure the police also broke into my London flat in Mount Street. At no time in any of these operations were search warrants produced. Yet they still conducted detailed searches and removed whatever they took a fancy to – mainly personal correspondence. This was supposed to be England in the dawn of the new Elizabethan age, not Nazi Germany. I wasn't the only person to be astonished. '*Sensation en Angleterre*,' reported *Libération* in France. '*Lord Montagu of Beaulieu est arrêté pour la deuxième fois*.'

That evening, shortly after five, back at Lymington once more, I was formally charged. So were Michael Pitt-Rivers and Peter Wildeblood. The principal charges were that the three of us had 'on divers dates between April 1st and October 31st 1952 in the country of Southampton, London and elsewhere, conspired to incite certain male persons – namely John Reynolds and Edward McNally – to commit serious offences with male persons'.

The long-suffering Captain Widnell stood surety for me and Michael Pitt-Rivers, and Ken Tynan for Peter Wildeblood. Widnell, the ultra-conservative land agent, and Tynan, the prestigious *enfant terrible* of the avant-garde theatre, made an improbable pair, but this just added to the sense of the surreal. For me it was like a repeating nightmare – have I not been here before? My one overwhelming regret was involving my cousin Michael and my friend Peter in the proceedings, as I felt at the time, except for me and the determination of the authorities to continue to persecute me, they would not have found themselves in this situation.

In his opening remarks at the committal proceedings a fortnight later Khaki Roberts began by saying that this second prosecution was an 'entirely new matter'. In a sense he was right, as the new charges referred to events which were alleged to have taken place at least a year before those in my first case and the people involved were, with the notable exception of myself, quite different. On the other hand I was a notable and famous exception and it was, to say the least, interesting that investigations into this new case were instigated on the very day that the first case against me collapsed. Quite a coincidence!

After such a long time my feelings are inevitably less completely bound up in the two cases. The shadow I have endured for years has all but disappeared. In fact, I sometimes feel that all that happened not only took place in a distant time, in an alien country, but also to a total stranger. I almost feel now as if the Lord Montagu who appeared at the Winchester Assizes was another person altogether. There was also a growing confusion in my mind which was irretrievably bound up with my sexuality. On the one hand I was completely innocent of what was alleged and protested that the so-called charges against me were absolutely false. Therefore I had no qualms or hesitation about protesting my innocence. On the other hand I believe it was entirely wrong that such charges should have been levelled against anyone at all. The allegations were that grown adult men had indulged in homosexual relations with each other. In no circumstances could I bring myself to agree that this constituted an offence and therefore my plea should not have been confined to 'not guilty' but should have contained a caveat to the effect that I did not believe in the validity of the charges. In other words I was innocent, but had I been guilty I would insist that I had done nothing wrong, much less criminal.

Upon his release, Peter Wildeblood wrote a brilliant description of the trial and its aftermath, which attracted universal acclaim, and in his own way helped to change the law. The book *Against the Law*, published in 1955, contains a full description of the events which followed our arrest. I commend readers who wish a more detailed account to seek out this book, which was republished in 1999 with an introduction by the journalist and former Conservative MP Matthew Parris. Nevertheless I feel I must briefly describe the trial as I remember it and how it affected me.

Reynolds and McNally were orderlies at the then RAF hospital at Ely in Cambridgeshire. Both were confessed adult homosexuals so that, as Khaki Roberts was quick to acknowledge, there was no question, as in the case of the Boy Scouts, of 'any corruption of youth'. But no matter: the letter of the day was that homosexual acts between consenting adults were illegal and that was what was being alleged. Although it was not in itself a crime, it was clear from the outset that the difference of social class between myself and Reynolds and McNally disturbed the prosecution almost as much as the homosexuality, as I was a peer of the realm and a Guards officer. The words of Khaki Roberts were revealing: 'Under the seductive influence of lavish hospitality, loaded upon them by these persons, who were so infinitely the social superiors of these aircraftmen, Reynolds and this Corporal McNally responded perfectly cheerfully to the advances that were made, and were perfectly ready to gratify the desires of the three defendants.'

The proceedings in Lymington lasted three days and in the end there were minor changes to the twenty odd charges, but as seemed inevitable from the first, the three of us were committed for trial at Winchester Assizes. I could not help feeling that someone was out to get me, dragging poor Michael and Peter in my wake. I was not alone in this. For example, the junior prosecuting council in the first case was a brilliant young lawyer, Jeremy Hutchinson, at that time married to Peggy Ashcroft. I wondered, then, why he did not appear in the second case. Years later I came to know him well after he became a member of the House of Lords. He was never quite indiscreet enough categorically to state that he refused to accept the second brief, but he made no secret of the fact that he thought the second prosecution monstrously unfair and that he felt I was a victim of a witch-hunt being conducted in high places. In fact Roy Fox-Andrews, QC, who actually led for the prosecution in the first trial, also refused to accept the prosecution brief for the second trial. Fox-Andrews is dead now but his son, James, a New Forest neighbour, says that he recollects his father shared Jeremy Hutchinson's unhappiness and was particularly dissatisfied with the conduct of the police. James definitely remembers that his father's stance 'earned, for a considerable time, the ill-will of the Attorney-General.' As I still had a secondary charge hanging over my head, it was as though the Crown was itself committing contempt of court, since no jury could be unprejudiced after all the publicity that the first case created.

As the weeks went by I received more and more letters, not only from old friends but also from complete strangers. They ran decisively in my favour. Few expressed strong views on the question of homosexuality, but they were very concerned with the question of fair play. What upset people most was their fear that British justice was being undermined. The unpleasant smell of McCarthyite persecution, which the British people did not like, wafted across the Atlantic and there were many aspects of my case which people found disturbing. They were deeply suspicious of the fact that I was arrested for a second time so very soon after the authorities failed to get a conviction in the first case against me. It looked like pique and, as Khaki Roberts said, there was no question of corrupting innocent children, as Reynolds and McNally were consenting adults. What really stuck in people's throats was that the Crown had granted them immunity from prosecution provided they turned Queen's Evidence and became major witnesses to secure the conviction of Michael, Peter and myself. One law for the aircraftmen and another for us. It was gratifying that many people who wrote to me recognised this.

It was a ghastly period to live through and none of us was optimistic. Even if we were acquitted the publicity before and during the trial was singularly unpleasant and would eventually have long-term repercussions on our future lives. The whole business had, understandably, a disastrous effect on my relationship with Anne Gage. She and her parents were conventional and charming people who led a blameless and rather sheltered life in rural Shropshire, and were wonderfully loyal and supportive. Nevertheless there could be no question of our wedding taking place until matters were resolved. While waiting on bail for my second trial, we saw much of each other until I had a farewell lunch with her, as she was sailing to the United States to work there and stay with her grandmother. I fully supported this move, so that she could avoid any unpleasant publicity. We were still in love but the future looked bleak. February and March 1954 was a very cold time and there was snow on the ground on 15 March when I drove myself from Beaulieu to Winchester for the first day of what my mother in her dairy said 'was known in the papers as the "Montagu Trial", quite erroneously as Peter Wildeblood and Michael Pitt-Rivers are equally in this huge case'. It must have been a ghastly time for my mother and the rest of my family, but outwardly she was robust and utterly unwavering in her support.

The first few days were the worst because they consisted of the prosecution presenting their case and the charges themselves, with the constant repetition of 'conspiracy', 'gross indecency' and 'buggery' making them sound revolting. The references to 'aiding', 'abetting', 'counselling' and 'procuring' had an archaic ring which made them seem deeply sinister. Worst of all, under cross-examination by Peter Wildeblood's QC, Peter Rawlinson, later to be the Attorney-General and a colleague of mine in the House of Lords, Edward McNally was asked about his love for Peter Wildeblood and the letters they exchanged. The Court's invasion of privacy was obscene. As Peter wrote of this moment: 'It was horrible. I looked round the court. The jury and the people on the public benches sat with pinched mouths and clasped hands, looking at their shoes. The judge looked as though he had bitten a lemon. The Sheriff's eyes were closed; the Chaplain's popping. I wanted to get up and shout, "It was not I who made 'love' into a dirty word – it's you." '

Reynolds and McNally cut pathetic figures in the witness box. This was hardly surprising as they had been arrested on Christmas Eve, subjected to hours of pretty brutal questioning over the Christmas holiday, frightened out of their wits, threatened with dismissal from the RAF, with prosecution and with prison. Then, after the Christmas holiday behind bars, they were given the chance to save their skins by testifying against us. Now they had to face up to consequences they never reckoned on, in the glare of national publicity, before the full panoply of the law with a bewigged judge (Mr Justice Ormerod) sitting in Winchester's medieval hall under that enormous circular piece of wood which was reputed to be King Arthur's Round Table. There was the righteously indignant Khaki Roberts, fuelled from his bottle of cough-mixture, referring to them, without fear of contradiction, as 'perverts ... men of the lowest possible moral character ... men who were corrupted, who apparently cheerfully accepted corruption, long before they met the three defendants'. We almost felt sorry for them.

The prosecution case, simply put, was that Peter Wildeblood had met McNally by chance at Piccadilly Circus Underground Station, taken him back to his flat and begun an affair. Subsequently the two of them introduced me to McNally's friend, Reynolds. The four of us went to a production of *Dial M for Murder*. We had a meal together and evidence of a bottle of champagne assumed an extravagant significance in this repast – symbol, of course, of aristocratic, decadent corruption. In fact, it wasn't champagne, it was champagne cider, a very different matter. Although McNally and Reynolds genuinely didn't know the difference, Khaki Roberts did, but pretended not to. Then it was alleged that I lent Peter Wildeblood the Beaulieu beach hut for a short holiday and McNally and Reynolds came too. The two aircraftmen then produced a lurid tale of an all-male alfresco dance, which they said turned into some sort of orgy. This was nonsense, but I confess there was some mild dancing which in comparison to the modern discotheque was very tame and more resembled a school dancing class. In any case I only went down there for dinner, did not sleep there and returned to Palace House at once because very shortly I was due to leave for the United States on a lecture tour.

Subsequently, Michael Pitt-Rivers invited the other three to spend the next few days on his estate in the Larmer Tree Grounds near Shaftsbury in Dorset, where they helped him clear some of the area of nettles and weeds. I knew nothing about any of this and, in fact, as far as the case was concerned I ceased to feature once I left for the States. So much for the conspiracy charge.

Today all this seems incredibly trivial and would have seemed so at the time, except that much of the world's media and readers seemed to soak up every sordid detail with the utmost seriousness. On the fifth day of the trial I was finally called to give evidence and was examined by Bill Fearnley-Whittingstall, the QC who was leading my defence team. Unfortunately he was rather hampered through the trial with a serious chest infection. Eric Summer, my solicitor, whose partner, incidentally, was Bill Fearnley-Whittingstall's brother Bob, telephoned my mother during the lunch break and told her that I had been 'excellent' and 'was amazingly calm and unruffled', and speaking 'very clearly'. When I got back to Beaulieu that evening she thought I looked 'terribly tired'.

Basically Khaki Roberts simply kept repeating the allegations made by Reynolds and McNally, namely that I had engaged in sexual activity with Reynolds. Every time he made such a claim I denied it. As Peter Wildeblood later mentioned, one of the reliefs in being cross-examined by Roberts was that you could see his trick questions a mile off. Had he been a spin bowler he would have been quite incapable of disguising his googly. Sometimes he got hopelessly sidetracked. For example, I explained that one reason I was keen to attend *Dial M for Murder* at the Westminster Theatre was that I had been delegated by my employers, Voice and Vision, to monitor the serving of drinking-chocolate in the interval.

Voice and Vision, of course, had the Cadbury's account for the social promotion of chocolate. This led to prosecuting counsel reading out a letter from my staff to the manager of the theatre, Mr Pither. It went as follows: 'Dear Mr Pither, Here is a drum of chocolate. I hope it reaches you in good order. The wholesale price is 12s 8d. Cadbury's do not quote a retail price. The recipe for preparing iced drinking chocolate is as follows.' Roberts did not actually read the recipe, although he told the court that it involved using a single teaspoon and a pint of milk. 'Then,' he continued, 'in case this arrangement should prove complicated, or if you should have any queries about it, Lord Montagu will be in the theatre tomorrow night, Tuesday, and will make a point of looking you up. We are most grateful to you for your co-operation and look forward to hearing the results of the experiment.' At this point, even after all these years, I can still visualise Roberts reaching triumphantly for his cough mixture as he concluded, 'Well, there was obviously no need to go to the theatre on that?'

I disagreed. 'There was,' I said. 'My main objective in going to the theatre was not to see the manager; it was to see the actual chocolate being drunk by members of the public, in which case I had to attend the theatre in order to be with the public when they were drinking the chocolate.'

Roberts was quite truculent about this. 'Your staff work really broke down, because when you got there the public were not drinking chocolate?'

It seemed to me that Roberts was missing the point. The question was not whether the chocolate was being drunk but whether I was expecting it to be drunk. I replied, 'Mr Pither unfortunately had not laid the chocolate on at that stage. I was expecting it to be drunk. We had already sent the chocolate down.'

At which point Mr Roberts abandoned the 'chocolate line' of questioning and moved on to who paid for the seats, who sat next to whom and whether or not I enjoyed the play. The answers to this were straightforward and completely irrelevant: I paid; we happened to sit next to my friend the actor and writer Emlyn Williams and his wife; and I enjoyed the play very much.

Reading through the dusty transcripts of the trial I find myself quite incredulous. The remorseless questioning over trivial events of two years earlier was often boring but always invasive. Whatever happened, it really did not seem to me, then or now, to be anybody's business but our own. Wildeblood was, I suppose, 'incriminated' by letters of his to McNally, which were of an obviously intimate nature. Furthermore he admitted in court to being an 'invert', which was contemporary code for homosexual, and he also conceded that he and McNally had been in love. It did not follow from that that he and McNally had enjoyed sex together but I suppose, in the circumstances, you could not blame a jury for believing that the relationship was more than platonic. In the case of Michael Pitt-Rivers and myself, however, the evidence, apart from the allegations of the craven Reynolds, was entirely circumstantial. As my counsel, Bill Fearnley-Whittingstall, put it near the conclusion of his summing up, 'If you convict Lord Montagu, you convict him upon the evidence of this self-confessed pervert, and, in my submission, only upon that evidence.' Reynolds was, unsurprisingly, being threatened by the police. Basically he was told that if he did not give incriminating evidence against me he too was likely to end up in prison for at least five years. Nevertheless, much to the annoyance of the prosecuting counsel, he denied the two most serious charges, attempted buggery and buggery, which were duly struck off. At the time I wondered why and years later I found out.

Towards the end of the case the journalists covering it were laying odds of eleven to two on all three of us being acquitted. I wasn't so optimistic as it seemed to me that there was a pretty determined effort being made to have me convicted. 'Guilt' did not come into the matter as I was being persecuted *pour encourager les autres* and in the circumstances I did not see how the others could be acquitted if I were sent down. The 'evidence' against all of us was flimsy but the case against me was far the weakest, if only because it was unanimously agreed that I had been in the company of Reynolds for a total of seven hours in my entire life. It was, in the end, our word against their rehearsed lines, but I was in grave danger of being found guilty by association in relation to Peter's alleged sexual activities. The general consensus was that all three of us had made a good impression in the witness box whereas the aircraftmen had made a spectacularly bad one. Besides, there was the incontrovertible fact that they had been offered immunity from prosecution provided they testified against us. That alone should have contaminated their evidence and we further hoped that members of the jury would have refused to convict on those grounds alone.

Alas, none of us had reckoned with Mr Justice Ormerod. I was assured later – and our lawyers all reluctantly agreed – that nothing in his summing up was actually a misdirection in law. However, it was obvious from his manner and inflection, as well as the content of his speech, that he believed us guilty. When he presented the case for the prosecution he put it a great deal more persuasively than the often preposterous Khaki Roberts. On presenting the defence case he did so conscientiously, but after every point he went to great lengths to remind the jury of what it was that the prosecution had said and how it made nonsense of the opposing argument, although he was careful not to say this in so many words. There was no disguising his sympathies as he obviously found Peter's admitted sexual proclivities revolting, going so far as to describe his love letters as 'nauseating'. He also managed not to mention that the police had removed them from his flat without a warrant. In fact, he went out of his way to say that the legality of the police's action was nothing to do with the jury.

It was not just the question of homosexuality which so irked the judge but his obvious concern about the class differences and the dreadful social impropriety – as he saw it – of 'upper-class' people like us consorting with 'lower-class' men such as McNally and Reynolds. An example of this was a letter I had written to Reynolds to ask about plans for the weekend he and McNally were spending with Peter Wildeblood at my beach house. I started it 'Dear Johnny' and I had signed it 'Edward'. I suppose the judge would have preferred me to begin 'Dear Reynolds' and sign it 'Montagu of Beaulieu', but I was not so pompous. These people were friends of my friend and it seemed not just polite but normal to use Christian names.

The judge did not agree. 'Well,' he said, 'a great deal has been said here – and it may be perfectly right – that Christian names are common property in these days and there is nothing unusual in somebody like Lord Montagu calling himself 'Edward' and allowing himself to be called 'Edward' by a man in the position of Reynolds. It may or may not be so. It is a matter for you to judge.'

That phrase 'It is a matter for you to judge' recurred frequently in Mr Justice Ormerod's summing up. It never meant what it said. What he was actually saying was that even though the verdicts were for the jury to decide he was demonstrating that the only possible verdict was 'guilty'.

And so it turned out. For eight days the Court had examined the significance of Christian names, whether champagne was the same as champagne cider, whether a loaf of bread and a slice of ham constituted 'lavish hospitality', whether or not photographs were 'suggestive' or merely 'chummy', but, above all, whether or not my friends and I were to be convicted on the evidence of proven liars conspiring with the Crown. At half past four on 24 March the jury filed back and delivered their verdicts, and all three of us were pronounced guilty on almost every charge. However, almost as if to highlight the error of the judgement the jury found that Peter Wildeblood was innocent of one of the 'offences' alleged by McNally. In other words the jury had rejected the evidence given on oath by McNally, the Crown's principal witness.

It could not have mattered less. With marked relish Mr Justice Ormerod told us that all three of us had been found guilty of 'serious offences'.

The traditional family group in the grounds of Palace House. (*Left to right*) My sisters, Mary-Clare, Anne, my Mother, myself and Caroline.

At last my Father holds his long awaited son and heir in his arms: age, one month. November 1926.

Nannies, sisters, cousins and dog, with me looking grumpy in a pram.

Left:
Unaware of things to come, my first car, outside Palace House.

Below left:
My stepfather, Ned Pleyell-Bouverie, who married my Mother in 1936.

Below right:
Myself in the black velvet suit ordained for minor peers for the coronation of George VI and Queen Elizabeth, May 1937.

Caroline and myself at Vergelegan, the Cape home of Sir Lionel & Lady Philips.

Proudly wearing my school blazer at Ridley College in Canada, May 1941.

In my last half as an Eton schoolboy, 1944.

The recently commissioned ensign in the Grenadier guards – a so-called Debs delight!

Jewish refugees disembarking from an illegal transport ship at Haifa, (Palestine) 1946.

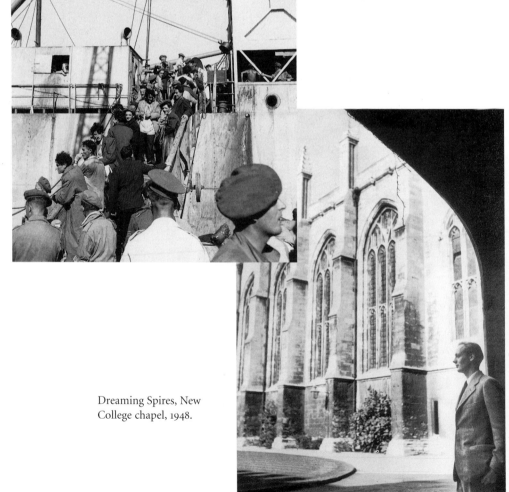

Dreaming Spires, New College chapel, 1948.

Sketch performed by members of the Oxford University Dramatic Society. (*Left to right*) Jack May, Michael Codron and John Schlesinger.

Cast of a 'Smoker', including Oxford friends such as John Schlesinger, John Mayer, Christopher Raeburn and Charles Hodgson.

Oxford Days. My friend Alan Clark, the budding historian and politician, through whose rooms I achieved late night entry into College.

Under arrest.

Below left:
Peter Wildeblood

Below right:
Michael Pitt-Rivers.

Montagu is driven to jail in Rolls

● *A prison warder held the door open and into the car that was to take them to jail stepped Lord Montagu, Pitt-Rivers, Wildeblood. .. Lord Montagu is partly hidden here, with Pitt-Rivers on his right and Wildeblood on his left.*

Our troops

The infamous 'doctored' picture featured on the lead page of the *Daily Express* the day after the trial.

Beach hut exterior and interior photos from police files. Hardly luxurious accommodation!

On my knees, scrubbing the floor and hanging the pictures prior to the
first opening of Palace House, April 1952.

The first Motor Museum was established in the front hall of Palace House and
made the whole house smell of oil.

However, my offences were considered slightly less serious than those of the others. They were guilty of 'felonies' whereas I was considered to have committed merely 'a misdemeanour'. He claimed to have taken everything said on our behalf into consideration but he was forced to conclude, 'Of course, it is quite impossible for these offences to be passed over. I am dealing with you in the most lenient way that I possibly can. You, Wildeblood, will go to prison for 18 months; you, Montagu, for 12 months; and you, Pitt-Rivers, for 18 months.'

The shock of the sentence was slightly mitigated by the fact that I thought it might have been more, although I was embarrassed that both Michael and Peter got six months longer than I did. I remember, when walking out of the court down to the cells, that I had worked out that I would be home for Christmas, with the customary one-third remission.

As we were led away in a state of considerable shock there was a momentary flash of humour which, not for the first time, did much to restore my sense of perspective and of sanity. As we were led away Michael's brother, Julian Pitt-Rivers, said in a very loud stage whisper: 'I think I better get mine cut off!' I couldn't help smiling – if only to myself.

After a three-hour wait in the cells below we were driven to Winchester gaol in the Sheriff's huge Rolls-Royce. The reason for the unusual delay was that a crowd of 200 was waiting and the authorities were afraid there might be trouble. There was, but it was not me or my friends they were after. When McNally and Reynolds emerged, in tears, there was a chorus of booing and hissing, and their car was attacked – a rather British touch this – with rolled umbrellas and newspapers. It was felt that after all we had gone through to subject us to further humiliation would be gratuitously cruel.

So when, finally, it was judged safe for us to emerge there was still a small crowd, mainly female, but to our surprise there was no booing or hissing. Instead, there was clapping, backslapping, cries of 'good luck' and 'keep smiling'. As we were driven away in the dark to prison, the crowd went on waving and one or two gave rather forlorn thumbs-up signs. I wish that Khaki Roberts and Mr Justice Ormerod could have witnessed these scenes. I wonder what they would have made of them. Long experience taught me to lie flat on the floor in front of the back seat to avoid the photographers and the following day the *Express*, frustrated at not getting my photograph, carried a doctored photograph in which my head had been superimposed on Peter Wildeblood's body. It seemed an apt comment on the whole ghastly business.

9

Through the Nights of Doubt and Sorrow

If you walk through a storm keep your head up high
And don't be afraid of the dark.

Oscar Hammerstein II

from *Carousel*

Naturally, the other inmates anticipated the arrival of three such notorious 'VIP' prisoners at Winchester prison with curiosity. We were to stay there six weeks before being dispersed to more permanent places of residence. Our arrival at the prison late in the day and after experiencing all the laborious reception formalities meant that we were 'banged up' in our cells long after the other prisoners had been locked up for the night. At least we all had single cells, but this was customary for sex offenders. Michael and Peter always teased me, saying that I put my shoes outside my cell to be cleaned; it was a good joke, but if anything, I was treated more strictly than the others. However, for the first few days we felt very much like rare new acquisitions at a zoo and we were stared at by warders and prisoners alike.

The first morning gave us our first experience of 'slopping out', which literally meant inmates queuing up at a drain point, each holding a chamber pot containing solid and liquid excretions from the night before. This disgusting and humiliating procedure continued for many decades and has only recently been discontinued. We were then subjected to the usual new boy regimes, visiting the doctor for body examination, having our hair cut and visiting the padre. By mid-morning we were sent to sew mailbags, which I confess I did very badly and this provoked many jokes about ability to sew 'male-bags'. During the lunch break a friendly prison officer, colloquially a 'screw', showed me some of the daily newspapers, which reported my imprisonment with glee. In some ways it was a relief to be away from all the drama and, having lived in a state of acute mental agitation for so long, to have some private time to oneself. Above all, it was a relief to be cut off from the intrusive media.

Easter occurred soon after our arrival and I arranged for a whole mass of daffodils to be brought from Beaulieu to decorate the chapel, and a warder brought me a cake made by his mother – so I was not entirely *persona non grata* in my home county of Hampshire.

All three of us were in a state of shock and disbelief at our conviction and imprisonment. I must be careful not to assume that others took the same view of these events as we did in thinking that the judge's summing up was biased against us. Reading my mother's diary, for instance, I see that she wrote of Mr Justice Ormerod's performance on the last day of the trial 'he was so wonderfully fair'. That was not how it seemed to me. Yet my mother would have been at least as sensitive to any lack of objectivity as I was myself.

In some ways it was worse for her than it was for me. She had to go back to Beaulieu to face the residents and employees. I could only be fatalistic, make the best of a rotten job, behave well and thereby qualify for the automatic remission of a third off my formal sentence, which would get me home in time for Christmas. At an otherwise low moment in my life this was a sort of solace. I was now cut off from the outside world and while, naturally, this was a deprivation, it was also an escape; I did not have to deal with the press, nor did I have to earn a living. I could use this time to reflect and plan for the future.

I had taken the precaution of leaving signed letters with my solicitors to my clubs and other organisations, mainly charities, submitting my resignation, should the worst occur. I also left sufficient resources behind to cover any outstanding bills.

I knew nothing at the time about the reactions of people further afield, many of them completely unknown to me, and was not aware of them until after my release. In the Southern United States, for example, a young Conservative MP, William Deedes, was on a lecture tour. The Foreign Office had given him an itinerary almost identical to mine of the previous year. In his memoirs, published forty years on, he recalled the reaction of his hosts – old Southern families who, such a short time before, had played host to me too. 'My hosts', wrote Lord Deedes, as he has now become, 'could hardly bring themselves to mention the subject. They were profoundly shocked, in a way that is inconceivable today, which illustrates how swiftly social attitudes can change within half a century.'

Attitudes in the Deep South were probably even more antediluvian than in a certain kind of middle-class England. There must have been many like Sir David Maxwell Fyfe and Sir John Nott-Bower who rejoiced that we 'evil men' had got our just deserts. It was consoling, however, that I was not aware of them. Mail to prisoners was strictly rationed and censored. Other correspondence was channelled through my solicitor who dealt accordingly. If there was hate mail I never saw it. I recall with amusement one of the screws, a languid Yorkshire man, handing me a letter from Texas with the remark, 'Your mother writes very interesting letters, doesn't she?' Obviously her letters were a welcome relief in comparison to the others he had to read.

I had half expected the press to be on the side of Sir David, Sir John and the judge, but I suppose it helped our cause in this respect that Peter Wildeblood was a respected journalist and that I myself worked in public relations and had many good friends in Fleet Street. This would not, on its own, have affected editorial policy. On the whole I would have expected proprietors and editors to be members of the Maxwell Fyfe tendency, but even newspapers not known for their liberal or progressive disposition surprised me. Hannen Swaffer, a famous columnist on the *People*, wrote a piece which at first glance looked characteristically crypto-fascist and homophobic. Swaffer made no secret of his hope that the verdict in our case might have a deterrent effect and 'frighten into a less repulsive way of life scores of well-known men, some famous and highly placed, who for years have flaunted their vices and, indeed, almost publicly paraded them'.

Along with what I have to admit in those days must have been a majority among 'straight' members of society, Swaffer did not condone homosexuality. He regarded it as an aberration. But, unlike the law, he did not regard it as a crime. In this he represented what had hitherto, I believe, been a silent majority. Now, thanks in part to men like him, it was about to become vocal. Unfortunately poor old Swaffer, despite being a legend in his own lunchtime, was several drops short of a pint. He rather spoiled the effect of his plea by concluding with the ringing peroration: 'Montagu and his two associates may have earned our condemnation. But they are also entitled to pity. They should be treated by psychopaths, not isolated by warders.'

Oh, well. At least I think we knew that he meant 'psychiatrists' not 'psychopaths', although if it was a slip it was probably a Freudian one.

Other public voices were more articulate. The *Sunday Times*, also inherently conservative, had already aired the problem of homosexuality and the law in an article headed 'A SOCIAL PROBLEM'. They grasped the nettle by pointing out that although our case has excited such enormous publicity it was only one in hundreds. In 1952, the most recent year for which statistics were available, there had been 654 convictions in the higher Courts for 'acts of indecency with males'. As the paper pointed out, 'This is not a momentary scandal but a deep-rooted malady.'

As with the more populist Swaffer in the *People*, the *Sunday Times's* sexual sympathies were clear enough and, even if restrained, essentially homophobic. The leader writer and his masters were not in sympathy. 'Let it be admitted', were the words, 'that the offences are to most of us disgusting.'

'Let it be admitted.' Nevertheless the paper felt obliged to concede that 'one may well ask whether in regard to consenting acts between adult males, the truth is not that the real offence is to be found out. Notorious inverts occupy eminent places, and few people of wide acquaintance would be prepared to say that they know one whom they could suspect of conduct which – if found out – would bring legal punishment and social disgrace. In all this matter, our society is riddled with hypocrisy.'

The basic problem, ran the argument, was that the law was out of kilter with the facts of life and for this reason alone 'the case for a reform of the law as to acts committed in private between adults is very strong. The case for authoritative inquiry into it is overwhelming.'

There was another issue which many commentators found as disquieting as the central one of whether private behaviour between consenting adults could ever be a criminal matter. In this respect it is instructive to quote the words of John Gordon, the editor of the *Sunday Express*. Man and paper were, if possible, to the right of Hannen Swaffer and the *People* – possibly even to the right of Attila the Hun – yet, as a leading homophobe, even Gordon was concerned:

A rather disquieting episode disclosed at the Montagu trial demands urgent consideration.

A detective sergeant admitted that on the morning Pitt-Rivers was arrested in the country he entered Pitt-Rivers's flat in London and searched it without permission and without a warrant.

Now I have always assumed – in common with most people – that in Britain a policeman has no right to enter any citizen's house and examine his property without the authority of a search warrant issued by a magistrate.

We have been encouraged to believe that to be the vital difference between a Police State and a democracy.

Have we been deluding ourselves? Do policemen really have the right to enter a house and rummage without a search warrant?

If they do, it seems to me a most alarming development.

If the Establishment had lost control of John Gordon they were in serious trouble. In fact, of course, the Establishment itself was divided. At the time I heard – although I have never been able to prove – that at one of her weekly audiences with the Prime Minister the Queen referred to my case and asked if the prosecution was really necessary. Constitutionally Her Majesty would never have requested that the case be dropped but her interest was implied. Churchill, I was told, shook his head more in sorrow than in anger and said words to the effect that he was afraid that, distasteful though it might be, the prosecution was essential if the national interest was to be served. It would have been impossible for the Queen to disagree with Winston Churchill of all prime ministers, but the mere fact that she is reported to have raised the matter at all strikes me as extremely significant.

Swaffer and the *People*, Gordon and the *Express* were unlikely and unexpected press supporters. Others were more predictable. The *New Statesman*, for instance, was liberal with a small 'l' and 'Labour' with a large one. On 27 March the *Staggers* withheld comment on the sexual aspects of the case but expressed outrage about the way in which the authorities had proceeded: 'The methods of the police in getting the evidence will have shocked public opinion more than in any case since the affair of Irene Savidge in 1927,' they wrote, predicting a Royal Commission on police powers and procedure. Royal Commissions were a popular device in those days providing, as they did, the best possible excuse for government inaction at least until they had finished their deliberations. 'It is hard', continued the *Statesman*,

to decide which is the more repugnant, to have the police breaking into private houses, without even a search warrant from a magistrate, and reading men's private letters in order to prosecute them for incidents in their sex life (which an increasing number of people and newspapers are coming to feel ought not to be the concern of the law) or to see that evidence supported by the 'confessions' of accomplices obtained by a promise of immunity. The whole wretched case which has, of course, won far more public interest than its intrinsic importance warrants, may nevertheless have far-reaching consequences.

This sense of outrage was characteristic of the many personal letters of support I received. Some came from known or admitted homosexuals but at least as many came from heterosexuals. Hardly anyone commented on the sexual side of the business, indeed some, like John Gordon and Hannen Swaffer, obviously found the idea of relations between members of the same sex repugnant. There was, for instance, an almost incomprehensible letter from old Ridgway, my former prep school headmaster at St Peter's Court. 'My dear Edward,' he wrote. 'I'm not thinking of the rights or wrongs of this trouble, but I want just to write you a line to say I hope and pray you may be given all the courage you must need in your ordeal whatever eventuates. This needs and expects no answer of course, but I should be heartless if I did not write.' It was decent of him to write and I sense it cost him some effort.

Others were less equivocal and they ranged from anonymous strangers to the great and the good such as Cyril Garbett, our old friend the Archbishop of York, and Bernard Miles, the actor and impresario whose Mermaid Theatre I had helped to publicise. John Gielgud, who had recently been prosecuted for 'cottaging', but who managed to avoid prison but not the publicity, wrote poignantly to say, more or less, 'There but for the Grace of God go I.' All this was a consolation and much appreciated.

It is perhaps invidious to single out individual letters but nevertheless I have culled three from my archives. They give some sense of the sentiments expressed by so many. The first is a short note from B. A. ('Freddie') Young, assistant editor of *Punch* and later a distinguished theatre critic for the *Financial Times*. Freddie wrote after my second arrest, 'It made me grind my teeth with fury to read about this monstrous persecution. The whole thing is an absolute caricature of justice, and the way it was handled was a disgrace.' Two others came from fellow members of the Brigade. Of all the institutions with which I have been connected, the Guards have always been the most conspicuously loyal. As with all 'family regiments', the sense of solidarity was extraordinary. It is, of course, what makes them such an effective fighting force.

The first was from the late Patrick Forbes, author of one of the finest books on champagne and a famous London Director of the House of Moët et Chandon:

> I feel there must be times in one's life when a word of encouragement from – for want of a better term – an 'ex-brother officer' cannot be entirely unwelcome. I never got round to it though, and then it no longer seemed necessary. But this latest bombshell you've been presented with strikes me as so totally childish and uncalled for that I wanted you to know, for what it's worth, that I'm plugging for you. Hitting a man when he's down has never been an action that appeals to the English; yet that, it seems to me, is precisely what is being inflicted on your goodself. I can't imagine any worse ordeal and I certainly hope you've developed a spiritual elephant hide to cope with it. My own reaction to your business at Winchester was that the only people who lost their name – and how – were the Boy Scouts.

The second was from Freddie Mutesa, the Kabaka of Buganda, who was living, exiled from his Central African kingdom, in Eaton Place. Freddie eventually died in exile in London but his son has had his lands restored and, by a strange twist of fate, I am now a trustee of his Kabaka Foundation. I did not know Freddie personally at the time. Nevertheless he wrote as follows:

> My excuse for writing is really that I was in your Regiment about the same time as you were, and that we have several mutual friends. This letter is to tell how much I feel for you in your undeserved ordeal. I, too, happen to be in a somewhat unfortunate position, but to a lesser degree and a different one to yourself. Much consolation, I feel, can be derived from the knowledge that because of the treatment to which you have been subjected, there are many whose sympathies are entirely with you.
>
> Forgive me if I have spoken out of turn but I feel very strongly about it.

Such letters were enormously fortifying, even though I was unable to read quite a few of them until I was eventually released. Certainly the knowledge that there were so many people on my side would have made the rigours of prison much easier to bear. Moreover, that support was not confined to those who were still enjoying their freedom. I had a strong sense that a majority of those who were incarcerated with me in Winchester and later Wakefield prisons felt that it was unfair that I ended up 'inside'. This was the feeling not only among my fellow prisoners. A number of my warders seemed to think the same and it helped, too, that several of them had formerly been non-commissioned officers in the Brigade.

There was no doubt that there was widespread concern in the country that the law should be reviewed. Within weeks of our incarceration there was a debate in the House of Commons led by Bob Boothby, Conservative, and Leo Abse, Labour, resulting in a committee of inquiry, chaired by Sir John Wolfenden. The inquiry, officially known as 'The Departmental Committee on Homosexual Offences and Prostitution' – a title which in itself was an astonishing admission of prejudice – was set up to investigate the problems of female prostitution in London, the clearing of vice from the streets and also the reform of homosexual law, which currently made any relations between consenting males illegal. I have often been told and I am now proud to accept the fact that the so-called Montagu case had more effect on changing the laws than any other factor. Public opinion was, I felt, particularly influenced by the police's unscrupulous methods in invading private property, the vindictive and relentless prosecution by the DPP and the Chief Constable of Hampshire, and most of all by the dignified way we behaved during the trial and upon our release.

And prison itself? I can honestly say that it was not as bad as expected. It is a cliché that English boarding schools or officer training for the Brigade of Guards are a thoroughgoing preparation for prison but there is an element of truth in this as far as I was concerned. I was educated as a child to being away from home, cut off from family and close friends; I was used to an all-male society disciplined by routine and the clock; I was already hardened by indifferent food and a degree of physical discomfort. After about three weeks in prison one physically gets used to the situation, hard as the beds are. Then it becomes a mental battle and here I could draw little comfort from my fellow prisoners. It was rare to find intellectual companionship, so it was certainly very lonely at times. Not being used to the North, I found Wakefield very cold, even in the summer, usually sleeping in my prison trousers. I frequently experienced the strong feeling, reportedly shared by others, that I was outside the prison looking down on myself from the sky with a voice telling me: 'What the hell are you doing here? Don't worry, this is not really you.'

From the start I was sensible enough not to try to pull rank. Many other inmates would automatically assume that I was not one of them, despite the fact that I was a convicted criminal, so I was extremely careful, for example, to stand in line for food. Peter Wildeblood reminded me of our first lunch in Winchester prison. I had forgotten the incident but apparently I was lining up with my plate, into which the cook ladled some gristly meat, a 'wedge of washed-out cabbage' and three potatoes. The man next to Peter nudged him and said in a loud stage whisper, 'Cor, look at Monty getting his dinner!' Even as he spoke, one of the potatoes rolled off the server's spoon and on to the table. I picked it up and put it back with the other two. It seemed the natural thing to do, but according to Peter, 'The incident caused as much of a consternation as if a General Amnesty had been declared. All the other prisoners nudged each other, pointed and beamed. After that, Edward was "Monty" to everyone in the prison.'

This seems to have made more of an impact on Peter than it did on me but the basic principle was one that stood me in good stead. Peer of the realm I was, but in prison I was no more and no less than the equal of my fellow inmates, and it was not only prudent but also realistic to behave accordingly. I never asked to be a 'Blue Band' – a prisoner who has a special privileges rather like a non-commissioned officer and often finds himself in cushy jobs like working in the library or the kitchen. Nor did I request such privileges. In fact, the authorities fell over backwards to treat me, if anything, worse than the other.

At least for the time being I would not have to confront the problems of my confused sexuality. Of course there was sex in prison and for all the wrong reasons. I found myself frequently propositioned. I knew perfectly well that one of the main reasons for this was that men regarded the idea of having sex with me as a sort of trophy. The case had given me that kind of notoriety. However, this posed no problem. I resolved from the first that my time behind bars would be a period of complete celibacy. It is important to add that I was still very much in love with Anne and kept her photograph in my cell throughout my incarceration. It was taken by Anthony Armstrong-Jones and it was a hauntingly beautiful study.

Naturally, I would have given anything to have been in her comforting and supporting arms. I still adored her and we exchanged letters regularly. Nevertheless, if I am absolutely honest, I have to confess that prison was, in the circumstances, almost the easier option. I had problems enough explaining myself to myself. I wasn't sure that I was really ready to explain to Anne. I was sure of my feelings about her but at the same time I could not deny that I was sometimes tempted by members of my own sex. This ambivalence was difficult enough for me; I recognised that it was ten times more difficult for her.

There was no such escape for my mother. She telephoned Anne in New York at 6.45 in the morning after the trial's conclusion. 'Three minutes for two pounds fifteen shillings,' she noted. 'She had already got the cable from her father. I did all the talking – poor girl, she was in a terrible state. It's all such an unbelievable tragedy. They should have been happily married on October 15th – and all this happened 14 months before that.'

After our time at Winchester we were officially and deliberately separated because, as I was told by one warder, we were a 'dangerous conspiratorial gang of homosexuals'. Consequently I was posted to Wakefield in Yorkshire, Michael to Maidstone and Peter to Wormwood Scrubs. The night before we left the governor sent for me and gave me a long lecture about how I had disgraced my class and would be despised and rejected for ever, just as the working-class men of London rejected Edward VIII and spat on pub floors on hearing the abdication speech.

The next day we travelled by coach, dropping off prisoners in various places and since we could not get to Wakefield in one day I spent the night in Winson Green prison in Birmingham. We were all handcuffed to each other and I was poignantly reminded of Oscar Wilde's experience of waiting for a train at Paddington Station to go to Reading. At least we were not jeered at. Wakefield was altogether a more modern prison compared with Winchester; quite apart from its layout of more up-to-date buildings, it was also the site of the Imperial College to train prison officers from the Commonwealth. It was certainly an improvement on Winchester's Victorian layout and architecture. At Wakefield there were movies, sports facilities and other recreational activities, and we were assigned to a mess table where more permanent friendships were struck up over meals. We still had to slop out every morning.

I was put to work in the tailor shop on a pedal-powered sewing machine making shirts and trousers for the other prisoners. To begin with I was rather bad at this and I pitied any prisoner who eventually ended up wearing the results of my early tailoring efforts. Fortunately the two prison officers in charge of the tailor shop were both ex-Grenadier Guards non-commissioned officers, who were as kind to me as discipline allowed and certainly helped me to become a more proficient tailor. Later on I was incensed at having been denied an opportunity to be sent out to the prison farm. The authorities claimed they feared journalistic intrusions, but finally I was allowed to work in the gardens for the last six weeks, planting wallflowers for the spring. Even though, fortunately, I was not going to see the fruits of my labour, I trust that they were enjoyed by the other inmates come spring.

During my time at Wakefield I refused to allow any close member of my family to visit me, but one surprise visitor who caused great consternation was the Archbishop of York, Cyril Garbett. I was treated like a schoolboy and told to have a haircut and clean my shoes. The Archbishop was splendidly supportive, as was Lord Calverly, a Labour peer who started life as Mr Muff and who after the war chaired a Labour government-appointed committee of inquiry into Britain's public schools. He reported that they were a good thing, much to the annoyance of fellow members of the Labour party.

On the whole I had good relations with my fellow inmates and before I was released I used my hard-earned prison allowances – which I normally spent on jars of molasses to go on my breakfast porridge (in fact, Canadian Pig Food: Grade 2) – on gifts of cigarettes and jam as a farewell to my table mess. At the same time, without being patronising, it seemed to me that someone with my education could actually be of help. I was astonished to find out how little some of my fellow prisoners actually knew. Much of their schooling seemed to have been scandalously inadequate. Before long I established a regular current affairs group in which I talked about my foreign travels, the army, music, automobiles and anything else I knew about. Inmates were allowed to receive books but not to take them out after release. Consequently I bequeathed a number of esoteric and perhaps inappropriate titles to the Wakefield prison library. Many were concerned with peculiarly obscure areas of estate management.

I also found myself acting sometimes as a sort of informal counsellor. Habitual crime seemed to me a terrible waste of life and without, I hope, being priggish, let alone censorious, I did tell my fellow prisoners what I thought. Sometimes this worked. Forty years later, out of the blue, I received a letter from a man who had been in Wakefield with me serving a term for Grievous Bodily Harm. He was a hard man; it was not his first offence or his first conviction. He admitted as much. We talked and I told him I thought he was mistaken. He listened to what I had to say but I had no idea whether he was convinced or whether he thought I was a condescending bleeding heart. The best part of a lifetime later he wrote to thank me. Since our conversations he had never once been in trouble with the law. He said it was due to me and he wanted a chance to thank me in person: 'I sat next to you,' he wrote,

> at the big wooden table for our meals. I was only 22 at the time, doing three years for GBH. And after taking your advice on altering my ways I became a 'Blue Band', the youngest ever in Wakefield – quite an honour. But only you made it possible through your advice. Also I was on a bricklaying course in there. When I passed the course you offered me a job on your estate which I declined. After my release in January 1956, I moved to Essex with my mother. Put my bricklaying to good use. Married a lovely Essex girl, Pauline. We had three girls, all happily married. Three grandchildren – two girls, one boy. But it all started through you all them years ago. I've kept on the straight and narrow ever since.

I asked him round to my London flat. He and his wife came to tea. He was still a hard man – big, barrel-chested and heavily tattooed. He sat on the end of my sofa, patted me on the knee and, turning to his wife, told her – rather embarrassingly – 'If it hadn't been for Eddie here I'd never have gone straight.' So prison had its compensations.

Two of the most famous prisoners at Wakefield during my time were Klaus Fuchs, the notorious atom bomb spy, and Christopher Craig who, because of his age, was not hanged after the murder of a London police-man, although his accomplice, Bentley, who was at the time in police custody, was hanged instead. I was delighted that after many years of struggle by Bentley's sister a posthumous pardon was granted. Fuchs was extremely reserved and his main complaint was that he missed female company. Craig was rather brash and cocky. Another celebrity was the Union Castle steward James Camb, who murdered Gay Gibson, a ship's passenger, by pushing her through the cabin porthole as they were disturbed during a moment of intimacy.

Prison had its funny moments and retaining a sense of humour in gaol was essential to maintaining one's sanity. In a sense the two were indistinguishable and in my case it was vital to have a sense of humour and proportion about myself. My love of theatre resulted in my helping to produce a concert party, which was excellent therapy. I suggested singing Noël Coward's famous song about the stately homes of England, which has almost become my signature tune. Later in my life I sang the same song with the Duke of Bedford and Lord Bath on the television programme *Tonight* with Cliff Michelmore, and again on the *Bernard Braden Show* with Esther Rantzen, and finally with fellow members of the House of Lords at the 'End of the Peer Show' to mark the reform of the House of Lords. At Wakefield my singing partners included the Duke of Sutherland's former butler, who stole the family silver from Sutton Place, and we were accompanied on the piano by an ex-organist from Norwich cathedral. The show was a great success and I very much enjoyed being involved with it.

So my eight months passed. Towards the end, inevitably, came the collapse of my relationship with Anne. This was the saddest aspect of the whole affair. From her American exile she continued to write and offer her support throughout my imprisonment. At the time I noticed no change in tone but looking back all these years later I see clearly now between the lines. Gradually the letters became more distant and less passionate. Then one day, shortly before I was released, a last letter came. It had been sent to my solicitor, Eric Summer, who was privy to her thoughts. Eric consulted my mother. It was the ultimate 'Dear Edward'. No one could blame her, least of all myself. She had done more than anyone could reasonably expect but now she had decided that her future could not and would not lie with me. At last and finally she wanted me to know that we were finished. Later she married – happily I am pleased to say – and we have managed to remain good friends throughout our lives. This is a huge tribute to her generous and forgiving nature, and I'm grateful.

At the time, of course, the rift came as a shock, inevitable though it had become. My mother got Eric's call in the middle of my nephew Jamie's third birthday. He asked my mother whether he should send it on to me or should it wait until I was released? Was I to confront this before I faced the outside world? The decision was my mother's. 'All so awful,' she confided to herself, 'yet it has to be faced. I decided sooner the better!

So he could get over the initial shock before his release. But such things are never the right moment, poor old boy!' This was the day before my twenty-eighth birthday. 'So many thoughts keep crowding in,' she wrote. 'I keep mine on a very level keel. He has been through such tribulation, such fire since August 7th 1953 and through such mental strain since March 24th. Never must another birthday be anything else but happy!'

Although I was sentenced to a year I got the customary four months' remission for good behaviour. Knowing that the press would be waiting for me at dawn, the governor, a decent man, agreed I could be smuggled out at one minute past midnight before the vultures assembled. I hoped that they would not recognise me as I had lost a lot of weight and grown a moustache.

When I first went inside, everything I surrendered – all my clothes and personal effects – was confiscated, including a signet ring which had belonged to my father. This was the usual practice. I was told, of course, that it would be returned on my release. It never was and I sometimes wonder who is wearing it now. Or if – more likely – it was melted down to make someone a modest sum bearing no relation to its previous financial, let alone sentimental, worth.

Two memories stand out from the immediate prelude and aftermath of my release. One was a plea from another young prisoner at Wakefield who had also been convicted of homosexual offences. His was one of those sad, half-ludicrous, half-pathetic stories characteristic of the era. He lived quietly in Leamington Spa with a friend and he was a homosexual. They were raided at dawn one day and arrested. This was unusual in that genteel, old-fashioned Regency town and there were very few men of a similar disposition. Every week, on Friday night, Leamington's homosexuals would go out to one or other of the local pubs, along with many of the town's predominantly heterosexual population. The only way in which the homosexuals indicated their persuasion was by wearing yellow ankle socks. This became known in the town as the 'Yellow Sock Club'. After closing time they would all go back to the home of one of their number and hold a party.

His plea was simple: 'If you aren't brave enough to go to Beaulieu after this is over,' he said, 'how can I possibly go back to Leamington?' I vowed more than ever to do so in order to help him and others like him.

The other moment that remains etched in my subconscious was lunch at the Mirabelle, then one of the smartest London restaurants. It was in

Mayfair, very plush, very expensive and very 1950s – now resuscitated by Marco Pierre White. Lovely Barbara Goalen had assembled a few old friends to join us for lunch there. It was a friendly and much appreciated gesture, and my first lunch out in the capital since my release from prison. As the meal progressed it was clear that one or two of the neighbouring tables disapproved. The atmosphere became unpleasant and remarks were made which were obviously meant to be overheard with the intent to wound.

A few tables away Hugh Gaitskell was having lunch. We did not know each other but he clearly recognised me. At the time he was Leader of the Opposition and of the Labour Party – a considerable figure in the land and widely expected to be Prime Minister in the foreseeable future. He could see perfectly well what was going on. After a while, he laid down his napkin and crossed the room to our table. 'How nice to see you back,' he said, holding out his hand, which I shook with surprise and gratitude. The action silenced the surrounding hostility. I was grateful for and reassured by this generous gesture.

My fellow Brigade officers, led by Robin Leigh-Pemberton and others who had known me since prep school, gave a lunch for me in Soho; a friendly gesture which boosted my ego and confidence.

A few months later, in March 1955, Peter Wildeblood and Michael Pitt-Rivers were released. I was staying with friends in Rome and it was there that Peter wrote me a poignant letter: 'The last few months have been so fiendishly cold at the Scrubs that I had to sew myself up in mailbags at night and having lost 17lbs, my poor bones were practically exposed to the winds. Anyhow since 8 am yesterday it has been Moët et Chandon all the way.' Evidently there had been a celebration breakfast with Frank and Elizabeth Longford, their daughter Antonia and a dozen others. Now Peter was staying with his parents and seeing the dentist (five teeth to be extracted) and the optician 'just to make sure I am ready for battle'.

For Peter the battle was to change the law. I was naturally all in favour and in any case the Wolfenden Committee had already started its work. I had been in touch with Frank Longford myself about prison conditions, but I was not prepared to become a high-profile public campaigner. Upon release all prisoners are always warned to be aware of having too much contact with ex-prisoners. However, together with Frank and the publisher Victor Gollancz we formed a prisoners' help organisation and I suggested the name the 'New Bridge'. I happily add that it is still going successfully. Representations were made to the Home Office and I'd like to think it resulted in more variety in breakfast menus other than the Canadian Grade 2 Pig Food they had been serving during my detention. Peter recognised my reason and was generous enough to remark that my full rehabilitation and reacceptance in society and business would do as much good as being a crusader. 'I think', he wrote,

> that you've behaved quite impeccably all through and must have given courage to a lot of others by your example. I know your problems are different to mine and I do not suggest that you should do what I am going to do myself, which is, briefly, to do anything I can to get the law changed and a fair deal given to (a) homosexuals and (b) other discharged prisoners about whose plight I feel very strongly. Both these things to be done with the utmost possible candour and dignity and at the highest possible level, which is the only one that counts.

I admire this attitude but I was not going to meet the challenge in the same way. Peter was right. I had different problems and while I felt no shame about them, I did not, at the time, feel that they were anyone's business but mine. It was, after all, the invasion of my privacy which had been one of the most repugnant aspects of my prosecution. I was not about to court more publicity and so I resolved to keep quiet. I hoped that I could do this with dignity and that I would be able to return as well as possible to my previous life and become a respected member of society. I recognised that this would involve many challenges and hurdles, but I was determined not to flinch from them.

My only other behind the scenes effort was when Lord Mountbatten asked me to go to Broadlands one day to meet members of his committee set up to investigate the security of prisons. Respecting Lord Mountbatten, as I did, I had no hesitation in accepting and I was keenly quizzed about life inside. I think I rather surprised my audience, by admitting that after three weeks one became used to the physical conditions and the food. The great battle was the mental side, and not the physical one: indeed, sometimes overweight prisoners come out of prison a great deal healthier physically – even I lost some puppy fat!

Whenever I was tempted to do so I thought of the sad persecuted man with the yellow socks. If I did not go back to Beaulieu, how could he possibly return to life in Leamington Spa? The first few weeks after my release were rather difficult. Having hidden for a few days in my sister, Mary Clare's house in Yorkshire, the worst experience was actually going home and coming face to face with one's neighbours and employees. I deliberately set about meeting them, although some of them found eye contact very difficult. But we all tried to have as happy a Christmas as possible, bearing in mind that poor Michael and Peter was still incarcerated for a further three months. I was, of course, besieged by the press with all sorts of lucrative offers to write for the Sunday newspapers and, bearing in mind the costs of paying for the defence of Kenneth Hume and myself, funded by loans from my bank, the money from Fleet Street would have been very beneficial to me financially at that moment. However, I vowed never to discuss this matter with the media and have not done so. I did, though, allow one old colleague from Voice and Vision to visit me and he reported the following Sunday that I had grown a moustache. I shaved it off that morning.

Over the years more and more facts have come to light concerning the prosecution's behaviour in both cases. Many other protagonists have, of course, disappeared. Sadly both Peter and Michael died in the last months of 1999. Before he died, Peter Wildeblood told me that McNally went to Australia and when his identity was revealed the gay community of Australia gave him a bad time for turning Queen's Evidence. A year or so after our release Peter saw Reynolds, who told him of the bullying and terrible pressure put on them by the police to learn and stick to their 'script'. If they did not, they were threatened with many years of imprisonment. Reynolds confirmed to Peter that he had done his best to change his evidence against me as much as he could by denying that there was ever any question of sodomy or attempted sodomy. I was vaguely aware of his intentions as I was listening to his evidence. To this day I am grateful to him and hold no bitterness towards him.

There were three major problems confronting me on my return to freedom. The first was finding somewhere to live in London during the week. I found a basement flat in Neville Street off the Fulham Road and discovered it was owned by the Chester Beatty Hospital (the Royal Marsden). The hospital's director told the house agents that they were not prepared to let it to me as I was considered an 'unsuitable' tenant. Fortunately several powerful and influential friends, including the Hon. Michael Astor, a trustee of the hospital, and Sir Ian Gilmour vehemently protested on my behalf and in due course I was allowed to take up the lease where I lived until I got married in 1959.

Another problem was being inundated by requests from unknown young men who wanted to come and live with me, or at least to meet me – so much for the deterrent effect of my sentence. One even went so far as to turn up on my doorstep complete with a dinner jacket, which he said he would need for social occasions. Fearing that some of these young men could well have been sent by the police or the press, I got my lawyers to write fierce letters to them all to prevent further harassment.

The third was, of course, meeting up with old lags who came to Beaulieu for work on the pretence that I had made promises to them during my internment. The most dramatic and ironic incident occurred at Beaulieu while Lord Longford and his daughter Antonia were staying as guests. Antonia was working on her new book and her father, showing his characteristic humanity and concern, came to offer his solidarity and boost my standing locally. We were enjoying Sunday morning breakfast when the doorbell rang. There on the doorstep was not only an ex-fellow inmate, but one who had escaped from prison and was on the run (he was known as 'the thin man', as he was always escaping). This put me in something of a panic. I could not shelter him, nor was I inclined to turn him in to the police. Since he particularly asked for Peter Wildeblood's address in London I gave it to him and sent him off with a bacon sandwich. I then rang and warned Peter, who after a few days persuaded him to give himself up. Lord Longford, who always had great sympathy for the condition of offenders and their plight, never knew how close he was to meeting a convict on the run. I wonder how he would have dealt with that situation?

However, by far the most significant and final paragraph in this chapter of my life occurred in South Africa, during a Veteran Car Rally touring the Garden Route from Cape Town to Durban. My wife Belinda and I stopped for rest day over a weekend in Port Elizabeth and left our cars in an underground car park in the town. When I returned on the Monday morning to retrieve mine there was a young man standing by it who told me that he had been waiting since dawn to speak to me. He revealed that he was one of the Scout party, but not one of the two accusers who went swimming in the Solent with us. He wanted to tell me what really happened. I was dumbfounded. There I was, servicing the car and trying to get it started so that I arrived at the control on time, while he related the truth of the situation as he remembered it. Most important, he wanted to stress that the camera was not involved at all and as far as he knew the theft was not perpetrated by any of the Scouts' party.

What really happened was that while I was swimming with Scout A, Kenneth Hume was behaving mildly indecently towards Scout B and I had later walked into the room and disturbed them. When the two Scouts returned to camp there was some jealousy from the others who had not been invited to swim, and they began teasing the two Scouts and asking them to tell what had been going on. Scout A had apparently told the others what had happened between himself and Kenneth Hume, provoking Scout B to say that he too had had a similar experience with myself. This good-natured though stupid boasting was unfortunately overheard by the Scoutmaster, who thought it was his duty to investigate the matter further. The Scouts, not wishing to admit they lied and then lose face, got deeper into the mud and the accusations became exaggerated. Then all hell broke loose in the camp; the police were called and the two boys were sent to hospital for examination. The rest of the Scouts were apparently completely indifferent to the so-called events at the beach house which had ruined their holiday, as they enjoyed their annual stay at Beaulieu and working with the cars. This information naturally amazed but did not surprise me, as it was also obvious to me from the demeanour of the boys during the trial in the witness stand that they were aware of the difficulties they had got themselves into.

I was in a great quandary; I would have liked very much to talk further. Important as this information was to me, as I had been acquitted of the main charges, in many ways it was only relevant because it sparked the second case of which I was convicted. It was frustrating that I was not in a position to continue the discussion at the time and he left, telling me how sorry he was about the events of 1953. I eventually arrived at the control station completely shocked and dazed. Up to now I have never told anyone, let alone family or friends, of this conversation but to me it was the closing chapter on the first Montagu case. I felt finally vindicated and it is not until now that I have felt disposed to reveal it. After all, this horrible experience occurred over forty-five years ago.

If my experience in Port Elizabeth was a vindication, the gloomy spell that had hung over me for so long was finally broken in the 1970s when Shirley Bassey – whose husband, Kenneth Hume, had recently died – was recording one of her shows at Beaulieu. The final number required me to drive her down sun-dappled leafy lanes down to the beach in my 1909 Rolls-Royce while she sang 'Just the Way we Were'. As the sun set the final shots took place next to the site of the beach hut – little did she know the full significance of this. I recalled the famous song she sang from *Carousel* which seemed pointed and apt: 'If you walk through a storm, keep your head up high and don't be afraid of the dark'.

10

Interlude – Rebalancing the Wheels

There is a tide in the affairs of men
Which, taken at the flood, leads on to fortune;
Omitted, all the voyage of their life
Is bound in shallows and in miseries.
On such a full sea are we now afloat,
And we must take the current when it serves,
Or lose our ventures.

William Shakespeare

After the jury announced its verdict on 24 March 1954 my counsel Bill Fearnley-Whittingstall addressed the judge on my behalf. His words were measured and sombre, and I shall always remember them:

Whatever the future may hold, in the past he was a useful member of the House of Lords and a kindly landowner who had done much good and hoped to do much better. He is faced with a bitter future.

After such a horrific and eventful period it was time for reflection and, hopefully, even for calm. When I did reflect I found those words of Fearnley-Whittingstall's constantly echoing in my mind. In particular, I was haunted by that final sentence, worse in its way than anything uttered by the judge: 'He is faced with a bitter future.' True or false? I had no way of knowing whether my future was predestined or whether I could take control of it myself and whether I had the spirit, determination and patience to make it sweet. Whatever happened I was determined that it would not be bitter.

To promote Beaulieu effectively I could not shy away from all forms of publicity but nor was I prepared to become a walking 'gay cause célèbre'. While in no way ashamed of my sexuality, I did not regard it as a matter of public concern. It was essentially a private matter, and I was determined not to share it further with the press and public. I had done my share of that. However, my personality would never allow me simply to vegetate and to bide 'quiet and simple'. It is true that I am never happier than when walking through the Beaulieu woods or standing on the wooden deck of my beach house as the moon shines on the blue-black waters of the ever-changing Solent. On the other hand, sooner or later the lights of London, New York, Paris or Sydney would always beckon, for I enjoyed and needed the buzz of the big city. I had many friends in show business, journalism and what is called high society, and I relished their company. I am a restless person and sitting still does not come naturally; I craved action and excitement and diversity. I like to build businesses, make contacts, create publicity and, above all, live life to the full in the fast-moving contemporary world.

Until now, I reflected, my life had been reactive rather than proactive. I had danced to the music of time and floated where the tide took me. Events had taught me that this would have to change. What had hitherto seemed a basically benign landscape, populated by friendly smiling faces, was now revealed as a dangerous jungle. Life was not all threat, but I had been deeply wounded and had certainly lost my innocence. For the first time I realised that there were dangerous snakes in the grass. I had never previously felt so much the need for ruthlessly planning to control my future and take charge of my own destiny. My early life had seemed charmed. I had always worked and played hard, and had held the view that the future would take care of itself, but from now on it was in my own hands and it might well be tough going.

So my plan for recuperation and the restoration of my life, and the blueprint for the future, was simple. I had to accept that in 1954 I was a notorious figure whose name was synonymous with young men and indecency. Somehow I had to change that impression, but it would take time, patience and skill. In conceiving the plan I was much helped by my public relations training, knowing that folk memory can be very short, especially if one can replace it with another image to blot out its pre-decessor. What was needed was a positive public relations campaign of which I would be the 'account executive' and there would be only one client: myself.

My first task was to promote Beaulieu as a popular tourist destination and expand the museum, adding on the world's first ever motorcycle museum in 1956 and calling the collection the Montagu Motor Museum.

This led me to get involved with the TT in the Isle of Man and sponsor some of the leading riders like Jack Brett. Then there were the jazz festivals, which I describe in a later chapter. Between 1956 and 1961 they established Beaulieu in the contemporary world with as much publicity as my case in 1954. Finally, after a suitable period, I retook my seat in the House of Lords and went back to speaking in debates. So gradually over the years my unfortunate reputation began to be forgotten and replaced with another much more positive one. Today there must be very few people who can recall in much detail the events of 1953 which caused my friends and me to become so infamous.

Peter Wildeblood and Michael Pitt-Rivers, confronted with similar problems of readjustment, reacted differently. Peter wrote his courageous account of the case in the much-admired book *Against the Law*, published in 1955, and became an early champion of gay rights. Of course, the publication of the book prolonged my agony, but I could not in all conscience object. In fact, I felt that if Peter wanted to write it, it was his privilege to report his involvement with the Montagu Case in his own words. I hoped that it would be a good book, and a significant one, and it was, with far-reaching effects on the change of the law in 1967. The book was republished in 1999, with a special preface by Matthew Parris, in which he wrote,

> ... this book is not a breast-beating appeal, nor a confession, nor a pathology, it is simply a story, one man's story: remarkable for its picture of a police state in 1950s Britain; remarkable for the author's self-knowledge in a world which offered him no template; and remarkable for his confidence and courage in publishing. As a fellow-journalist who never faced, and could not have stood, a fraction of the ignominy heaped upon Peter Wildeblood, I salute him.

After its publication Peter continued to write more books, produce musical and theatrical shows, and later became a television producer, spending most of his career in Toronto before retiring to Vancouver, where he lived until a severe stroke incapacitated him. He died in 1999, but not before he had read Matthew Parris's introduction and taken pride in being saluted for the contribution that his book made in changing the law. In my own personal copy from 1955 Peter wrote, 'For Edward, in the hope that he will not take umbrage at this final "slopping out" and with the wish that no one will ever need to write a book like this again. PETER.'

Michael Pitt-Rivers retreated into the relative obscurity of rural life, a much-admired landowner and farmer who bred Arab horses, eventually becoming a judge of the breed who was in great demand worldwide. He was ten years older than I and always a very private person, so the publicity surrounding the case affected him more than it did Peter or myself. He, too, died, after a long and sad illness, at the end of 1999, admired for his stewardship of his estate which, of course, includes the famous Cranborne Chase. After 1954 we never all got together to discuss the Montagu Case, but occasionally, in passing, we would remember the humorous moments, although not the miserable ones.

The year 1954 was certainly a watershed in my life. In this book my previous chapters are chronological, because that is how the years developed. One episode followed another neatly and inexorably, each self-contained, an item in its own right. Its components can easily be isolated, each having a strongly defined character: home; school; Canada; the Army; Oxford; public relations and finally gaol. Other people's lives are similarly composed in boxes and they move from one episode to another, rather like Shakespeare's Seven Ages of Man, with almost inexorable predictability. Most people can chart their careers as neat steps up the ladder of life. Field marshals have no trouble in cutting up their past from the time they were a subaltern to commanding a battalion and reaching the top; so can the Cabinet minister, an archbishop or even a successful businessman. Such lives reveal themselves much as history is taught at Oxford, with the past reduced to well-packaged parcels tied up by famous dates such as 1066 or 1815 and whole chunks of it being defined as the Renaissance, the Industrial Revolution or even the Swinging Sixties.

Looking back on my own life since 1954 I find such divisions artificial. Instead of being episodic and chronological, I think of my later life as a series of themes conducted concurrently across a broad front. I have been variously but simultaneously a country landowner, an historic house entrepreneur, heritage campaigner and museum founder; a motoring lobbyist, journalist, author and rally driver; tourism promoter and lecturer; a parliamentarian and civil servant; a gastronome and wine lover; an environmentalist and traveller – and much else besides. At times, one or other of my interests has taken precedence over the others nearly to the exclusion of all else, but such times have been brief indeed. Instead, I have always tried to live on a broad front, mixing town and country, business and pleasure, and being many things to many people.

So, reflecting on my life since 1954, I prefer to think in terms of interests and occupations rather than in decades. Obviously my thirties were not the same as my seventies. But on the whole the similarities are greater than the differences. My life has been composed of portfolios and periods, which coexist as a rich and colourful mosaic rather than a chronological photo album of separate black and white pages. The chapters to come therefore do not follow each other in neat chronological order, but instead advance together in parallel. Thus I shall write about my remaining years not so much as the passing of time, but as the pursuit of dreams, successes and failures. These chapters represent the things that have mattered to me in my life and have forged my career. They have always been with me and will remain with me until the day I die, as together they have moulded my life in a way the years themselves have not.

11

The Whole House Smelt of Oil

The Stately Homes of England, how beautiful they stand
To prove the upper classes still have the upper hand
Though the fact that they have to be rebuilt
and frequently mortgaged to the hilt
is inclined to take the gilt
off the gingerbread
and certainly damps the fun of the eldest son.

Noël Coward

Unlike many so-called 'stately homes' Palace House, because of its relatively modest size, has never presented insuperable problems for its owners. It is still a sensible house for twenty-first-century living and my grandfather spent a lot of family money to create what was a practical home in the nineteenth century. It remains so today, helped by various conversions and additions. This is a great credit to various architects because it was never originally built as a domestic home.

The name 'Palace' itself is misleading, for it is smaller than even the most modest palace while at the same time larger and grander than 'the house in the street'. It was originally the Great Gatehouse of the abbey. As it only contained two large central halls with two chapels above and no other rooms it was little used after the dissolution. In the early eighteenth century John, Duke of Montagu created living accommodation, dug a moat and built turrets to protect himself from the French. The most important subsequent alterations were carried out by the Victorian architect Sir Reginald Blomfield under the direction of my grandfather Lord Henry Scott. He restored the south front as closely as possible to its original Gothic glory and pulled down some rather undistinguished post-dissolution additions, while adding what is virtually a Victorian wing in the style of the day. He had, after all, been born at Drumlanrig Castle, the family seat in Dumfries, so he knew a thing or two about Scots Baronial!

The result is a mixture of the thirteenth and nineteenth centuries: a characteristic British blend of ancient and modern which I love. However I must confess that, as an historic house, Palace House falls between two stools – too small to house an institution, yet too imposing to be a cosy home for the twenty-first century.

When I left Oxford and joined Voice and Vision early in 1950 I was aware that I had less than two years to plan for the great day I had looked forward to for so long: my twenty-fifth birthday on 20 October, when I was to succeed to the estate. My father had deliberately and sensibly suggested my twenty-fifth birthday rather than my twenty-first, as it would to give me an opportunity to attend university or face other problems like conscription and war. As my succession loomed I was faced with the gloomy news from my financial advisers that I could expect no more than £1500 a year from my inheritance and no capital. What little there was remained under the strict control of the trustees.

The house was the first problem for since my father's death in 1929 it had continued as the family home of my mother, my sisters and myself. My succession would have far-reaching effects on many people's lives, particularly that of my mother. My stepfather had bought a house thirty miles away, near Stockbridge, and my mother agreed to leave her beloved Beaulieu and move there in order to ease my task, particularly when I got married. It was obvious that it would be impractical for me to live in Palace House alone and I wondered whether I should move to the other family house in the village, The Lodge, where my father had lived when he first married and his father was still living in Palace House.

One solution to the problem could have been the Bishop of Winchester, whose diocese needed a home for distressed or redundant clergy. Beaulieu seemed ideal as it had a suitably religious provenance, was conveniently situated and could have accommodated a reasonable number of former vicars in conditions not so far removed from what they were used to. They could also be relied upon to look after the place and I suggested that I might retain a small portion of the house as a private apartment. After some consideration the Bishop fortunately decided that it wouldn't do and looked elsewhere.

I asked Captain Widnell, my agent, to see if he could find a school or college that might be prepared to take on the greater part of the building under a similar arrangement to the one we had proposed to the Church. One of my sisters suggested opening an hotel but this was no more practical than turning it into a school or an old clergymen's home. In any case, while I did not mind having a flat in either of those, I really could not face the thought of living as a permanent guest in my own home. It became obvious that we had to find a solution that would release me from the onerous burden of the house as it was inevitably going to involve large and unending maintenance and repair bills. The running costs would be prohibitive for a mere public relations executive, no matter how generous his salary, as it would cost a fortune to heat and would require staff. In 1951, to any sensible, rational being the house was a white elephant. The wise solution was to get rid of it.

For me, however – neither entirely sensible nor rational – that was unthinkable. Beaulieu was my ancestral family home and I therefore not only loved it but felt a sense of duty, trust and obligation towards it. To have relinquished Palace House would have been seen not only as a loss but also a slap in the face to my mother and the trustees. After all, my mother and the trustees had made great efforts and sacrifices to keep the estate intact for twenty-five years so that I could succeed to it as my father had left it. It would have been a churlish betrayal if I had spurned their efforts on my behalf. Come what may, I was determined that my home would continue to be my home throughout my life and that I would pass my inheritance on to my heirs just as my ancestors and my father had passed it on to me. Sacrificing one's privacy was the price I was prepared to pay to keep a roof on the house. I accepted that whereas most people possess their belongings I, paradoxically, belonged to my possessions. I determined to make a last-ditch stand to fight for survival.

A solution that became increasingly attractive was that of opening the house to a paying public. The Marquess of Bath had pioneered the post-war 'Stately Home Business' by opening Longleat in 1949 and it was doing well. Since the 1890s Beaulieu Abbey Ruins had been open and the year before I succeeded no fewer than 40,000 people visited and paid a shilling each. That meant £1500 a year after costs, which was not exactly riches beyond compare but was better than nothing. I reckoned that if 40,000 people paid a shilling each to look round some monastic ruins then most of them would be prepared to pay 2s. 6d. to be allowed inside an historic home full of family heirlooms. Public access would be restricted to the rooms in the old part of the house so that the privacy of my personal apartments in the Victorian wing would be preserved. It sounded practical, manageable and even rather exciting.

By October I was ready to embark on the risky venture of opening to the public. By doing so I had hoped that I would be able to keep the remainder of the estate intact and in good order. There were many essential repairs and refurbishments to be carried out, especially with the farms and woods. The costs were estimated at £150,000 which, midway through the twentieth century, was a prodigious amount of money. The only way to raise such a sum was to sell off portions of the estate. Over the next ten years I had to sell about fifteen per cent of the land I had inherited. I bitterly regretted this, then and now, but it was the only solution. People mock the owners of great houses for 'selling off the family silver' to maintain them, but they fail to understand what a huge and constraint drain on one's finances even relatively modest stately homes can be.

The opening was complicated by the fact that I was also converting the Victorian part of the house into flats for myself and others. This would provide additional income. In fact, I was still letting out flats there until 1959. In the months before the opening, therefore, I was still living on the ground floor – very much in the line of fire. The flat conversions, difficult anyway, were complicated by government regulations which specified that no more than £500 could be spent on converting a single 'unit'. In spite of this we somehow managed to do five flats.

Although the custom of displaying the country's great houses to interested outsiders was two centuries old, the idea of opening in a professional and businesslike manner was unheard of until Lord Bath's efforts at Longleat. He had already achieved some fame as the first of the century's showmen peers. I did not approach him for advice, however, but instead went to the agent of Lord St Levan at St Michael's Mount, that romantic island castle off the Cornish coast, which had been open to the public successfully but with little fanfare for the previous five years.

In my previous book *The Gilt and the Gingerbread* I quoted the agent's advice with a certain wry amusement. Fifteen years after it was first offered, in June 1950, it seemed impossibly primitive. As I write now, almost half a century has elapsed and the words from St Michael's Mount have assumed an almost prehistoric quality. The agent wrote:

It was suggested to me that the charge for admission by the public, which at present is 1s. od. should be increased to 2s. od. if the Palace House were thrown open. I am rather opposed to this for two reasons: (a) there might be a certain amount of resentment against the increased charge and (b) I cannot see any corresponding advantage would be likely to accrue to Lord Montagu if the charge was increased ... if an increased charge was made then tax would be payable on it, and Lord Montagu would not, in my opinion, benefit to any appreciable extent. If Palace House residence is to be thrown open to the public it should be restricted to not more than three days per week during the months of May to September or October.

The laying down of some coconut matting in some of the principal rooms should be considered ...

You might also consider allowing the public to walk along that part of the grounds which leads down to the river, with express instructions that no bathing is to be allowed. In other words, try and ensure that the public see as much as you possibly can without interference with Lord Montagu's privacy.

Even then I was sophisticated enough to realise that this advice was primitive. It had a certain charm but it was scarcely helpful.

The first point I accepted was that Palace House was not an architectural masterpiece like Blenheim or Chatsworth. Such houses virtually sell themselves and I was well aware that we were not in that class. Our situation in the middle of the New Forest – one of southern England's most popular tourist destinations – was a huge plus. We had a beautiful setting and a particularly attractive spring garden but apart from the Abbey and the former shipbuilding village of Buckler's Hard we were thin on artefacts to display.

Many of my attempts to make the house more attractive to the general public were, looking back on it, amateurish and low-key. I assembled the portraits of the more significant of my ancestors and grouped them together in a display that formed the centre of a 'Beaulieu Museum', which also included maps, family trees and other items of historical interest. They were fine but I did not have the sort of pictures that were attractions in their own right. I possessed nothing like Woburn's Canalettos or Wilton's Van Dycks.

As we were opening a year before the Queen's coronation we created an exhibition of documents from previous coronations in which members of the family had participated and displayed the family robes, originally made for the coronation of William IV. Another room contained a selection of rare birds which had been shot on the estate over the years. And

Edward, Prince of Wales, seated with my Father in an 1899 Daimler, in front of Highcliffe Castle, at Christchurch, Hampshire, at the end of the Prince's first major motorcar journey, 1900.

Interiors of the Motor Museum as it was in the early days.

London – Brighton car rally with Jim Clark.

Stirling Moss and myself admiring the W196 Mercedes Grand-Prix car.

Showing Her Majesty, Queen Alexandria's, 1901 electric Columbia to HRH Prince of Wales and Earl Mountbatten – she used to drive the car in the grounds of Sandringham.

Dancing on the lawn in 1958.

Beaulieu's last Jazz Festival in 1961, with a specially built stage.

Jazz greats, Johnny Dankworth with his wife, Cleo Lane.

The riots inside the grounds, 1961.

Hippy invasion of the village, which brought the festival to an end.

Handing over a petition of 1.5 million signatures against the proposed imposition of a wealth tax to Labour MP, Ted Graham, (later Lord Graham of Edmonton), who presented it to the House of Commons on behalf of the Historic Houses Association.

Attending my second coronation in 1953, this time as a full Peer of the Realm.

Cartoon of myself as Chairman of English Heritage, with Stonehenge in the background – the most intractable problem of our national heritage.

My first wife, Belinda, taken in 1959.

Ralph with his father and mother, March 1961.

In 1976 I celebrated my 50th birthday, the theme of which was World War II. Here is our guest of honour, Dame Vera Lynn with my second wife, Fiona. I was just able to squeeze into my army belt!

In 1969 I celebrated 100 years of estate ownership. Here I am as my ancestor, Charles I, dancing with Diana Dors as the Prince of Denmark.

The wedding of my sister, Caroline to Grainger Weston, February 1950.

The wedding of my sister Anne to Major Howel Moore-Gwyn, March 1946.

The wedding of my sister Marie-Clare to David, Viscount Garnock, October 1953.

then there was a Buckler's Hard room with full-scale models of men-of-war and a portrait of its founder John, Duke of Montagu.

This was all very charming and I am sure the agent from St Michael's Mount would have approved, but it was not the stuff of a major tourist attraction. I found it difficult to envisage a great crowd of visitors forking out 2s. a head. In the event we actually charged 2s. 6d. a head, to include the Abbey Ruins – a quantum increase which would have greatly upset the agent at St Michael's Mount. Compared with the Marquess of Bath and others, I had to concede that I was more of a cottage industry than a stately home business.

What catapulted me permanently into the major league for the future was the idea of exhibiting old cars. This was a notion that came to me, almost fully fledged, as I lay awake in bed one night. Like most of the best ideas it was very simple – so much so that in retrospect it seems extraordinary that no one else had already thought of it. Without it my life would have been very different and I doubt whether I would have been able to remain as the owner and occupier of my ancestral home.

I have always tried to avoid being too pigeon-holed or to have had a one-dimensional career of life, but I think it is fair to claim that the Motor Museum and all that flowed from it has been absolutely central.

My experience of public relations taught me that I needed some attraction to make a visit to Beaulieu special and unique. At first glance, automobiles might not seem special or unique but on reflection I reasoned that the average British male was irresistibly interested in cars. It is a common male obsession and in 1952 there were no motor museums open in Britain.

However, my main object was to pay homage to my father. He had been one of the great pioneers of British motoring with an impressive list of 'firsts' to his credit. He had been the first Englishman to race a British-made car on the Continent and the first to take a British monarch for a drive in a motor car. As an MP he had introduced many of his fellow members to the delights of motoring and had even managed to persuade Arthur Balfour, then Leader of the House, to go out and buy one. His 1899 Daimler was the first automobile to be driven into Palace Yard, Westminster. He formed and chaired Parliament's first all-party Motorists' Committee and he introduced the 1903 Motor Car Bill, which he then steered through all its stages. The bill made number plates compulsory and raised the speed limit from twelve to twenty miles per hour.

Perhaps most significant of all, in 1902 he started one of the country's first weekly motoring magazines, *Car Illustrated*, and was its editor until the outbreak of the Great War. He was recognised as the unofficial public relations officer and political lobbyist for the embryonic motor industry of Great Britain.

A collection of early cars shown together with his pictures, trophies and other motoring memorabilia was 'a fitting epitaph' and was a tribute I wanted to pay as I was intensely proud of my father's achievements. I always felt a sense of deprivation because he had died when I was young and I had never had the chance of knowing him, so the Motor Museum was a modest recompense. For the post-war period it was a novel idea, although Dick Shuttleworth had started a motor collection before the war but was tragically killed, so it was moribund. I did not dare to try to dignify my small display of cars with such a grand title as 'Motor Museum'. That came much later.

The main drawback was that when I first conceived the idea I only had one veteran car. This was my father's 1903 6hp De Dion Bouton, which had remained at Beaulieu since his death and had originally been surrendered to him by one of the farm tenants in lieu of a bad debt. Subsequently it was used by the estate electrician, before passing into the care of another pioneer motorist and Beaulieu resident, Captain Jack Holder. He had not done a great deal with the car so that when he generously returned it to me before my succession it was in poor shape. I personally rubbed it down and painted it in brighter green than its original colour. As a result it looked better than it had done but I was under no illusion: the improvements were cosmetic and when it broke down on my first Brighton Run I realised that it really was in need of a complete overhaul. Luckily Air Vice-Marshal Sir Alec Coryton of the British Aeroplane Company also owned a similar De Dion and kindly agreed to submit my own car to the necessary restoration, so at least I would have one genuine veteran car in mint condition.

That represented a good beginning but it did not exactly constitute a worthwhile display. I needed more, so my next port of call was the Society of Motor Manufacturers and Traders. The Secretary, Roger Gresham Cooke, was sympathetic and agreed to approach its members on my behalf. The results exceeded my wildest dreams. Daimler immediately offered me an 1899 model similar to the one in which my father had taken Edward VII on his early excursion in the New Forest. Rootes went even better and lent three items from 1896 – a Beeston Forecar, a Beeston Quad and a motorised tricycle. They also lent me a 1901 Sunbeam Mabley designed for back-seat drivers as the driver sat in the back and his passengers went in front. Vauxhall sent a 1905 two-seater and David Brown, the owner of Aston Martin, a 1906 Lagonda. Finally, two private enthusiasts made valuable contributions: the local Ford dealer Percy Hendy lent me an 1899 Benz and Commander Woollard of Parkstone, Dorset let me have an 1896 Leon Bollee, which was originally owned by Captain Widnell.

My father had left a large collection of books, photographs and other relics of the early days of motoring. Most significant were the works of Charles Sykes who was not only art editor of *Car Illustrated* but a cartoonist and sculptor of distinction. It was he, of course, who created the beautiful mascot Spirit of Ecstasy which still adorns every Rolls-Royce and which was modelled on my father's secretary and lover, Miss Thornton. I also still had the framed originals of his front covers, which I hung in the front hall of Palace House. Indeed, the front hall was the only room large enough to house the cars so to provide access we had to make a hole in the wall and winch them in.

Among other interesting exhibits, pride of place went to the summons issued against my father by the Basingstoke magistrates in 1902. This accused him of exceeding the 12mph speed limit and he was eventually found guilty and fined £5 'to mark the seriousness of this breach of the law'! No wonder he introduced the Motor Car Bill the following year and got the limit raised. I should imagine the Basingstoke magistrates were distinctly unamused. At that time the Abbey Ruins were attracting 40,000 visitors a year and I hoped that with luck we would be able to entice a similar number into the house. I also, naturally, wished the motoring exhibits to prove popular but I did not think that my motoring section was more than the icing on the cake. It gave me great personal satisfaction but, at the time, I did not believe that it would prove central to our appeal and be the major attraction it turned out to be. One thing was only too apparent – it made the whole house smell of Castrol oil.

The opening was scheduled for 6 April 1952 and the preceding winter was chaos and confusion. There had been no such cleaning in the house for sixty or seventy years. Now everything was changed and my mother's furniture and effects were moved to her new home, The Lodge, at the far end of the village. (Ned had died that previous spring, sadly young, and the move to Stockbridge had consequently been abandoned.) Pictures and furniture selected for my personal use were taken to my flat upstairs, carved out by my architect, John E. M. MacGregor. Mercifully my old Oxford friend Christopher Raeburn, later head of classical recording at Decca, spent a few months helping me out and together we threw away a lot of Victorian objects, which I now deeply regret. Stuffed birds in cases and copper cooking utensils seemed perfectly ghastly at the time but have since become very valuable.

I realised how important good publicity would be in attracting people to the house. Through Voice and Vision I had good contacts in the press and I planned to make the most of a good story. A stroke of luck occurred while I was staying at Wilton House, the home of the Earl and Countess of Pembroke, early in 1951. They told me they were opening their great house, Wilton, to the public that year and, knowing that I was in public relations, asked me to assist.

I leapt at the chance because I realised that it would be a very good dry run for me and would get me just the right contacts, which I could use myself later. Fortunately, the opening of Wilton went very well and the experience stood me in very good stead when I opened my own doors to the public.

I decided to keep the car collection secret until the actual opening day so that there would be something special for the journalists present to report. However, the announcement that I was going to open to the public was enough in itself to generate paragraphs in the local and national newspapers. I also managed to come up with what would now be referred to as a 'sound bite' but which in those days was simply a good quote. My words were: 'I would rather keep my home and surrender my privacy than have things the other way round.' I was also quoted as saying that deep down the owners of historic houses absolutely hated having busloads of complete strangers coming into their homes. As soon as this was quoted I denied having said any such thing. Various other owners were asked about it and all vociferously denied it, although I suspect some at least were lying through their teeth. Given the option, surely anyone in his right mind would like to retain his home *and* his privacy. Unfortunately, for myself and my fellow owners it was hardly ever an option.

I also contrived some excellent 'photo opportunities', which were not difficult to arrange – in fact, they were not really arranged at all. I simply asked one or two well-disposed press photographers to come down to

Beaulieu while we were preparing for the opening. Amid the inevitable confusion they got some telling snaps. One popular number was the picture of me on the floor with a scrubbing brush. The *Sunday Pictorial* captioned this 'It's enough to bring a peer to his knees'. The foreign press were just as intrigued, even though their writers were less imaginative. The *Schweizer Illustrierte* ran the same picture with the very literal description '*Seine Lordschaft schrubbt die Boden*'. I was obviously not very experienced when it came to scrubbing as several correspondents wrote to point out that I was holding my brush in quite the wrong way. A photograph of me polishing some pewter proved even more popular and failed to excite similarly adverse comment.

Looking back now, I confess the whole procedure of opening up was wonderfully, charmingly amateurish. We had no proper box office or souvenir shop and although the afternoon teas in the Domus were excellent it could only accommodate forty guests at a time. We had no turnstiles, only a primitive admission system involving ropes and cords to prevent unauthorised and unpaid access. I thought I had pulled off a beneficial coup with the guidebooks as by doubling the original print order I had managed to achieve a saving of a halfpenny per copy. This economic wizardry was undone, however, when two lorries turned up at the back door shortly before opening. I had simply not realised how much space 50,000 books took up and as there was no room available they were squeezed into the cellar store. Alas, we experienced a record high tide, which flooded the cellar. The water came into the moat, up the drains and into the bookstore and for days afterwards every room in the house was festooned with clothes lines supporting drying books. I believe we were the only stately home to offer a choice of two guidebooks – pristine dry at 2s. 6d. and wet watermarked at half price.

On opening day I told my house guests that if we had more than a hundred visitors by 6 p.m. we would have champagne with dinner. The doors opened at 11 a.m. and by 12.30 the hundredth visitor had arrived. We had champagne with lunch. My publicity efforts really paid off.

That Easter we had 7000 visitors over the weekend. In those days the *Daily Express* published a regular league table of stately home attendances. On the Easter Monday the Duke of Devonshire was the clear winner with 5763 visitors at Chatsworth House. Second was the Duke of Marlborough with 4207 at Blenheim Palace. And third was Lord Montagu of Beaulieu with 2700. Within a week of opening we had gone ahead of such established favourites as the Marquis of Salisbury's Hatfield, the Duke of Rutland's Belvoir and Haddon, and even the Marquis of Bath's Longleat which, unaccountably, was not even mentioned. On 17 May Godfrey Winn wrote an article about Beaulieu for *Women's Illustrated* – the equivalent, in those days, of a cover story in *Hello!*.

No wonder I was euphoric. At the end of the year another newspaper poll put Beaulieu in fourth place with 70,000 visitors – almost double my most optimistic prediction. Publicity continued to roll in from all round the world.

In the very first year Beaulieu, with the historic motor cars, had become a major tourist attraction. The future looked set, but I have to admit I had no idea that my car collection would one day become the National Motor Museum, one of the country's top tourist attractions and a crucial record of Britain's motoring heritage. So that little green De Dion – like a single acorn – certainly grew into a sterling oak.

By 1959 that stripling tree had outgrown my front hall and moved outdoors. Gradually, after that, the house reverted to being a home once more and I shared it every year with ever-growing thousands of visitors, the income from whom enabled me to start a programme of much-needed repairs.

Almost half a century after that original, modest, heart-stopping opening I am still *in situ* and hundreds of fellow house owners large and small have followed suit. My home is still my castle, my castle is still my home; my house is your house, as I firmly believe that places like this, originally built for the pleasure of the few, should now be enjoyed by the many.

12

A Poor Man in His Castle

By uniting we stand, by dividing we fall.
John Dickinson

For years I tried to persuade my fellow historic house owners to co-operate with each other in order to present a common front to the government. This was not easy as one of the strengths of the landed aristocracy and gentry is that they are, virtually by definition, fully paid-up members of the 'awkward squad'. It was frustrating to find them so averse to discipline, co-ordination, mutual self-interest and everything else that might have turned them into a coherent, effective fighting force. At the same time I could not but take pride and satisfaction in their collective bloody-mindedness.

As early as 1952 even before Beaulieu had opened, I convened a small gathering of these fellow owners to discuss the possibility of what the press, with a fine sense of irony, referred to as a 'trades union'. Only the British Travel Association and Sir Harold Wernher, owner of Luton Hoo in Bedfordshire, enthusiastically supported me. In *The Gilt and the Gingerbread* I nominated him as captain of a notional gentleman's team as distinct from more professional and possibly vulgarian owners such as myself. I categorised Sir Harold and his team as 'owners of essentially amateur status, usually the occupiers of naturally attractive properties, but with no inclination for the cruder aspects of professionalism'.

Perhaps I was unkind. Certainly I must have been a bit naive, in 1952, if I seriously thought that someone like Sir Harold was going to treat the exploitation of his historic home as some kind of team game. His house was not a massive palace on the scale of Chatsworth or Longleat, but nor was mine. In truth, his contents were superior to mine as he owned some fabulous treasures including Rembrandts, Titians and most notably Fabergé objets – a legacy of his Russian wife, Zia, who was a Romanov.

Yet his attendance figures never exceeded about 40,000, whereas after only a few years of operation Beaulieu was attracting more than half a million visitors a year. This had little to do with the inherent attractions of our relative homes but it spoke volumes about the philosophy, and the business and marketing acumen of the owners.

At our original meeting at the Dorchester Hotel I proposed an annual subscription of £25, with a sliding scale of reduced fees for smaller houses with fewer visitors. Shock, horror! Owners were not prepared to pay, nor did they see the advantages of a joint advertising scheme. They wanted to do their own thing in their own way, so the meeting ended in disarray and disillusion.

It was more than twenty years before an independent Historic Houses Association was finally formed, although in fairness I should say that we were not all idle during the interim. In the 1950s some fifty of us who did believe in the value of co-operation joined the British Travel Association (later to become the British Tourist Authority). We believed that in the absence of our own independent organisation the BTA would provide the best umbrella, as they appreciated the attraction of historic houses to overseas visitors. By the end of the Fifties there were a hundred historic house owners in the Association. Five years later we met for a formal conference and as a result, in 1966, the BTA's 'Historic Houses Committee' was formed.

In 1971 Sir Alexander Glen, the BTA's chairman, proposed a Standing Conference for Historic Houses. His idea was that this should be a quasi-independent body, which would speak on behalf of all of us. Although in many respects an archetypal Establishment man, Sir Alexander had a fiercely maverick streak, which worked greatly to our advantage. Years later he remarked: 'Strictly speaking our remit was marketing overseas – but I do not over-heed remits and prefer a David Stirling type of SAS approach if there is a job to be done.' It was encouraging to have a maverick at the helm.

Despite their highly individual, not to say idiosyncratic, approach, historic house owners had many interests in common, especially when it came to finance and taxation, and to planning controls. The Duke of Grafton, a lifelong conservationist, was the first chairman and although it seemed politic to channel our representations through the BTA it was already clear that if all went well we would soon come out from under the umbrella. Governments were increasingly understanding the importance of tourism and therefore listened to the BTA. They did not yet properly understand the contribution that historic houses could make to the tourist industry as a whole but that would soon change.

My personal contribution was to introduce a series of Historic Property Management courses at Beaulieu. This was an essential initiative as many of our owners had only the most rudimentary ideas about how to run a business and it was no use applying the techniques they had traditionally used on their estates. We were now inevitably in the tourism business and we were appealing to government to help our efforts on behalf of the national economy by not only letting us have better signposting but by giving us more substantial grants and tax breaks. No government was going to do that unless we could demonstrate that we were conducting our affairs according to sound business principles and encouraging tourism, especially from overseas.

In the 1960s the press enjoyed building up a great rivalry between the Duke of Bedford, the Marquess of Bath and myself. All sorts of challenges were thrown about – in particular, the Duke of Bedford calling Beaulieu 'just a garage' and my accusing him of running a nudist camp. However, I thought it would be a good idea for us to work together. More so, we surprised the press by announcing in a London restaurant that Woburn and Longleat were going to give away vouchers at our own houses which would enable visitors to go to the houses of the others at advantageous admission rates.

In 1975 after the Duke of Bedford had gone abroad his son, Lord Tavistock, and I decided to enlarge the group and were joined by George Howard (Castle Howard); the Marquess of Bath (Longleat); the Duke of Marlborough (Blenheim Palace); the Earl of Harewood (Harewood House) and Lord Brooke (Warwick Castle). We called ourselves 'The Magnificent Seven'. The group was a great success and other historic houses were anxious to join. We eventually decided to form a group of ten, the criteria being that each house must have at least 100,000 visitors. There was a slight hiccup when Madame Tussaud's bought Warwick Castle and Lord Bath objected to being part of a group which included a commercial organisation, even though it was headed by Lord Cowdray. So he resigned – to the advantage of Broadlands, which had just opened and was enjoying enormous attendance figures following the tragic death of its previous owner Lord Mountbatten.

The great advantage of membership of such a group is that our managers meet regularly to discuss common problems and once a year the owners visit one of the houses in the group and, when possible, our sons and heirs are also present. The group, now renamed 'The Treasure Houses of England', consists of Beaulieu, Blenheim Palace, Castle Howard, Chatsworth, Harewood House, Leeds Castle, Longleat House, Warwick Castle, Wilton House and Woburn Abbey.

The preservation of English historic houses was a cause that needed to be supported by economic arguments. Many years later the conference celebrating the tenth anniversary of English Heritage was entitled 'The Great Opportunity: Making the heritage work harder'. We were asked to consider how 'this asset can make a greater contribution to the economic and social problems confronting Government and the country'. I have spent much of my life trying to make the heritage work to do just that. Even so, I do sometimes wish that such a beautiful and historic part of British civilisation could be valued for what it is rather than as a sort of economic asset. These houses are worth preserving for their own sake, not just to make money.

A key player in those early days was George Howard the owner of Castle Howard, that great Vanbrugh house in North Yorkshire which featured in the famous TV adaptation of *Brideshead Revisited*. Big, burly George, famous for hosting dinner parties in a voluminous kaftan, later became an unlikely chairman of the BBC governors and was a consummate political operator. He chaired the HHA's taxation sub-committee and was determined to make people understand that we were asking for concession for the house and not the owner. It was, and is, a vital distinction as critics and the public often only saw us living in beautiful houses, surrounded by beautiful objects, works of art, parks and gardens, and considered us privileged. I could not deny that such an image existed. At the same time we were now sharing these privileges with the public and the nation had an interest in preserving this unique part of its heritage. Of course we are lucky, but we are merely the unpaid temporary custodians. We inherit the past, and owners may come and owners may go but houses go on for ever – sometimes with new custodians.

In 1972 the BTA Historic Houses Committee commissioned the architectural historian John Cornforth to conduct an independent study on the future of country houses. Two years later he reported his gloomy findings, which confirmed our view that new and punitive financial measures were inevitable. This was the Heath–Wilson period of British politics and there was precious little sympathy in either the Labour or Conservative parties for hereditary principles or the heritage. That prejudice was, obviously, sharper on the Labour side but the Conservatives were still smarting from the way in which the aristocratic leadership of Alec Douglas-Home had been so derided. Labour's chancellor boasted that he was going to squeeze the wealthy 'until the pips squeaked'. It was not a good time to be an hereditary peer, to own a family estate or live in an ancestral home.

Cornforth was pessimistic but he also sought to introduce some reason into the debate about the future of the historic house. If the hereditary owners were ejected, he argued,

> they would not be the only losers. Just as they are holding their houses as trustees for the future, the nation must consider its own responsibility to posterity, as well as to the present. And a great many people now, and in the future, will bitterly regret the results of such a negative and destructive policy that conflicts with the general and non-party concern for the environment. What could be more short-sighted than to pursue one policy that is supposed to enhance the environment and improve the general quality of life of the whole nation, and another that only succeeds in wiping out one of the most effective guarantees for maintaining and contributing to that quality of life.

These were sentiments with which I strongly agree.

It was clear at this time that the Standing Conference was outgrowing its usefulness. The third annual meeting was attended by eighty people, so meaningful, detailed debate was impossible. I now argued for the creation of a completely independent Association with its own executive committee and secretariat. The BTA had already offered to lend a senior executive as our first secretary. I thought we should accept and, at last, a majority agreed. George Howard invited the Duke of Grafton to be our first president and at the initial meeting of the executive committee on 5 December 1973 I was elected its first chairman, with George Howard as my vice-chairman. Subsequently the Duke of Grafton was elevated to patron and I became president. More than two decades after that abortive meeting at the Dorchester, the Historic Houses Association was finally in business.

Our original committee carried impressive clout. We included two dukes – Argyll and Marlborough – as well as the heir to another dukedom, the Earl of March, son of the Duke of Richmond and Gordon, a qualified accountant and our first treasurer; Robin Cooke of Athelhampton House in Dorset, who was about to become the Conservative Member of Parliament for one of the British constituencies; and the Hon. David Lytton Cobbold, who was the son of the Governor of the Bank of England as well as being a banker in his own right. So quite apart from our joint experience of running such famous properties as Blenheim Palace, Goodwood and Warwick Castle, not to mention Beaulieu, we brought together many disparate talents and qualifications. To enhance this we were joined by representatives of the National Trust and the Department of the Environment. We were not only able to speak for all our members but also to do so with skill and authority.

Although my work at Beaulieu had made me a prominent and widely recognised figure in the heritage world, this was the first time I had been appointed to a position with any national body. I welcomed the challenge for I believed that I brought an expertise to the job which would benefit my fellow owners and contribute to the preservation of our great houses, large and small. There were some who questioned this. Because I preached that marketing was a vital and invaluable tool of our trade they thought that I was too populist and a vulgariser who would commit acts of cultural vandalism around or against our ancient buildings.

I was to encounter some of the same prejudices when I was later appointed the first chairman of English Heritage but the fears were groundless. I recognised that the only way forward was to make our properties more accessible to the general public. I think that all but the most conservative already understood this even if a significant number did not like the idea. I was committed to quality and to presenting what we had to offer with style and taste. There was a quid pro quo involved here and it was a doctrine I had preached all my life. The equation was a simple one: more access equals more grants and concessions, and vice versa. It was straightforward, reasonable and honourable and, contrary to what was sometimes alleged, I was never tempted by stunts and fast bucks. That is a short-term approach which nearly always, in my experience, ends in tears.

It seemed to me vital that visitors to any of the houses owned by our members should enjoy their day, be made welcome and therefore feel inspired to visit other such houses. This was my philosophy at Beaulieu and I now hoped to apply it on a wider canvas. Opportunities came swiftly. In April 1974 I was approached by the architectural historian and conservationist Marcus Binney. Binney was planning an exhibition for Roy Strong's Victoria and Albert Museum. Its title was 'The Destruction of the Country House, 1875–1975' and it told a depressing story. Since 1920 no less than 1400 historic houses had been demolished. In 1955, the worst year of all, it was estimated that one house was being lost every five days. It was heart-rending.

Oddly enough, the early to mid Fifties were 'the worst of times and the best of times'. It was a period of unparalleled loss but it was also the beginning of the fight back. The Gowers report of 1953, for example, led to better protection of historic houses, recommending the establishment of the Historic Buildings Council, and to the institution of grants for preservation. It was during the late Sixties that some owners had at least begun to band together as a significant lobby. Nevertheless, in the early Seventies we were faced with an antagonistic Parliament and government. The Labour government produced a green paper on wealth tax and a white paper on capital transfer tax.

In our 1974 seminar, 'The Historic House – Planning to Survive', George Howard quoted an apt parody of 'All Things Bright and Beautiful' first delivered by the Bishop of Leicester during an earlier debate in the House of Lords:

> The poor man in his castle
> the tourist at his gate
> the Chancellor and his wealth tax
> broke up the whole estate.

In conclusion George told us, 'If we are not able to achieve anything, Henry VIII's dissolution of the monasteries will have nothing on Healey's disposal of country houses and their collections, and the actions of this Government will be remembered much as those of a previous Commonwealth, that of Cromwell. Does this Government really want to be remembered for its vandalism, its philistinism and its destruction of so much of the history of Britain?'

Support came, mercifully, from some unexpected quarters. The guest speaker at our first annual meeting was Lord Goodman, the legal *éminence grise* who was a close friend and adviser of Harold Wilson. Goodman told us that our work was 'of massive importance'. He continued: 'There are many forces at work which are engaged either innocently or otherwise, unconsciously or deliberately, in destroying the things for which you stand that any effort by people who believe in their preservation is to be welcomed and should receive the greatest possible support. What we are seeking to preserve are the human values that we need, increasingly, to permit our society to live in a civilised world.'

Despite much despondency, the HHA had made a solid start. Already we had 162 members; we were planning a first ever international conference in Oxford and York for the following year; we were making forceful and coherent representations on taxation and other matters, and we had established a sound administration. We faced an uphill struggle but at least we had marshalled our strength and established an effective fighting force. The Victoria and Albert exhibition had demonstrated the staggering losses of the past and that the Government's taxation plans were a threat to the future. But at least historic house owners had, for the first time in their history, formed an effective lobby.

Combat was swiftly engaged. While on a lecture tour to the States I received a letter from Denis Healey, the Chancellor of the Exchequer. It said that the Government was now considering the position of historic houses in relation to capital taxation as a matter of urgency – he was referring to a wealth tax. This was because of encouraging undertakings given during the committee stage of the Financial Bill and it was fine as far as it went. Nevertheless, I had seen enough of government and bureaucracy to know that 'urgent consideration' was usually a meaningless platitude. Whatever the Government was proposing was unlikely to be either 'urgent' or 'considered'.

Our response was to launch a national campaign and petition. On 11 June I led an HHA deputation to give evidence before the Select Committee on the wealth tax. There were only four of us – George Howard; Commander Michael Saunders Watson, a stalwart of the Association whose family had been at Rockingham Castle since it was given to them by Elizabeth I; and Mrs Oddie of Heath Hall in Yorkshire: 'True Yorkshire if anyone was,' remarked Sir Alexander Glen. She was there to speak for the owners of the smaller houses and although there were just the four of us I was able to tell them that we spoke for 500 members. Moreover, although houses such as Mrs Oddie's only attracted a few hundred visitors each year, the giants of the industry were significant tourist attractions by any standards. At Beaulieu, for instance, at that time we were catering for 600,000 people every year – about the same number as watched the whole of the Six Nations rugby tournament in a year and six times the capacity of Wembley Stadium.

I put forward two main arguments. The first was aesthetic, cultural and historical. This was the heritage argument, pure, simple and unrefined. I was not optimistic about carrying the day on this with a committee of Members of Parliament but the point needed to be made. I trusted that politicians couldn't all be materialist philistines. Besides, in my view the principal reason for preserving historic houses is that they were – and are – part of the nation's soul.

My second argument, inevitably, was economic. In 1974 Britain's historic buildings had attracted almost fifty million visitors. This was an increase of approximately 300 per cent over the preceding ten years but the increase in the private sector was double that percentage. Four million people visited private properties ten years earlier. In 1974 that number had risen to a staggering twenty-six million. I knew from my experiences abroad that our great country houses were an increasingly important plank in Britain's tourist platform. These statistics proved it and it was quite false to think of them simply as the private possessions of the privileged. They were a national asset.

It was a huge help to have the finely honed intelligence of George Howard and Arnold Goodman on our side. We were also careful, in the face of depressing ignorance and prejudice, to remain courteous and even friendly. Most of the politicians ranged against us were products of the politics of envy. They had no idea of the downside involved in owning, managing and paying for the maintenance of our homes. They only saw privilege and inequality. I shall never know how much effect our arguments had. However, by the time the petition was presented to Parliament – by a Labour MP, Ted Graham, now Lord Graham – it had attracted no less than one and a quarter million signatures; one of the largest petitions ever sent to Parliament. Politicians are impressed by such numbers as at election time they become votes. Governments are elected by voters such as these and the careers and lives of politicians are similarly determined. Support in such numbers was a salutary salvo for our political opponents.

It was vital for us to be pragmatic and rational at all times. With this in mind we engaged the agents, Strutt and Parker, to prepare a sort of user's manual for house owners opening to the public. Brian Hubbard of Strutt and Parker was a trusty lieutenant at Beaulieu and between us we were able to draw extensively on our own experience and that of other pioneers. A lot of the advice may now look naive but at the time it was necessary. Newcomers and even those who had been open to the public for some time were effectively hopeless in many important areas. They still ran their properties, vis-à-vis the public, as if they were opening for one day a year in aid of the local church or the Red Cross. This was not good enough and would not work or lead to success. One had to have modern, well-maintained toilets, not just corrugated iron and drainpipes in a field; we needed proper quality in the tearoom or restaurant, charming though the ad hoc methods of ladies from the Women's Institute might have been. Much of our claim for special treatment was based on being an important part of the tourist industry and if this was so there was no room for amateurism.

I always recognised that we should give as much as we received. First and foremost we had to give satisfaction and pleasure to our millions of visitors, but there were other ways in which we could contribute to the nation. At Beaulieu in 1970, for instance, we instituted a pilot educational scheme which, with the help of local Education Authorities, produced packs for schools based on many different aspects of historic houses. This was such a success that we appointed a full-time education officer and were the first historic house to do so. The next stage was a separate educational trust and in 1977 the HHA staged a special Heritage Education Year for Historic Houses, launched at our AGM by the estimable Jennifer Jenkins. She was, incidentally, the wife of Roy Jenkins, newly appointed as Chairman of the Historic Buildings Council and one of the most remarkable conservationists of her time. It was a great mark in her favour that, when it came to conservation, she was immaculately apolitical. Education remains to this day an important plank in the HHA's platform and at Beaulieu it plays an important role in our operations, as indeed it does in many other historic houses.

Gradually, in the Seventies, the tide began to turn. Our greatest victory was in 1976 when the wealth tax was dropped.

I continued to come up with initiatives of my own, not all of which were adopted. I was concerned, for instance, that with the exception of a few very rich and enlightened owners, such as Andrew Devonshire at Chatsworth, the idea of patronage of the Arts had slipped off the agenda. I wanted to encourage the use of historic houses as galleries for contemporary artists. I also proposed an annual award for the owner who did the most in any given year to attract visitors or improve the quality of his display. Although both these ideas fell on effectively deaf ears, my enthusiasm for a good house magazine was easily accepted.

Sometimes I met with opposition from within the organisation as well as without. Once even George Howard was tetchy. 'I know', he wrote to me, 'that the way in which you occasionally spring things on us arises entirely from your commendable enthusiasm and anxiety to get things done, but your lack of consultation does make a sensible working of an organisation such as ours much less easy.'

I felt duly chastened.

We also set up a 'Friends' organisation. The executive and I felt it was important to have a popular base of support and so we decided to recruit as many members as possible. They were charged £6 a head and in return they were granted free admission to members' houses. Not all members were happy about this and one who complained was Lord de L'Isle VC, KG, owner of Penshurst, who was not a good person to antagonise. To my intense regret he felt it necessary to resign from the Association. The most publicised case, predictably, was that of Althorp House where the recently installed chatelaine, Raine, formerly Countess Dartmouth and later to become stepmother to Diana, Princess of Wales, decided to charge half price to 'Friends' and instructed them to claim the balance back from the HHA. She also refused to allow fellow house owners in free. The press had a field day and Althorp's membership of the HHA was terminated.

Despite these minor setbacks the organisation flourished. We grew to 1500 members with a formal constitution of governing council, executive committee and sub-committees to match. We produced a thirty-two-page quarterly magazine and we had twelve English branches, as well as national branches for Scotland and Wales. We even went international, advising similar organisations in a number of other European countries and forging beneficial relationships with owners groups in Italy, France, Austria and many other countries. Later we took the initiative in forming a union of Historic House Associations on the Continent (of which I was afterwards president) that still exists and has annual meetings at which we discuss problems of mutual interest.

During my time as president of the HHA I did much work around the world for the BTA making press and television appearances, and in particular promoting the 'Open to View' ticket which I did on three separate occasions in the United States. However, the most important tour was in 1976 when I led a delegation of historic house owners from the private, National Trust and government sectors to celebrate the American Bicentenary, stressing that the history of America since 1776 was merely a continuation of all that is best in the English-speaking world.

My delegation included, among others, the Duke of Marlborough, Lord Tavistock, Sir Hugo Boothby and several other members of the National Trusts. We had a splendid time visiting New York and Boston, where we were greeted with a parade of soldiers in eighteenth-century uniform. We then went to Washington where we were presented on the floor of the Senate by Edward Kennedy and had a splendid dinner in the Governor's House at Williamsburg at which Lord Dunmore, a direct descendant of the last Governor of Williamsburg, was present.

We had all been asked to bring a special symbol from our houses – I took a Rolls-Royce mascot – and the Duke of Argyll, because of his American ancestry, took a lock of George Washington's hair. Not wishing to leave it in plain view in his hotel room he put it in a refrigerator overnight. However, he failed to retrieve it before he left and unfortunately it must have been cleared up by a hotel maid and thrown away. Despite countrywide appeals he was unable to find it.

Our delegation then travelled down to the south-west and up to Los Angeles. It was a truly remarkable trip, which the BTA confirmed was one of the most successful they have ever organised in North America.

During this period we made a film at Beaulieu called 'One Pair of Eyes'. Produced in 1970 for a BBC series, the idea was that I would make my own film, having been provided with a director, cameraman and sound recordist. We spent three weeks making the film and its main theme was to compare the philosophy of the British towards the stately homes 'business' with that of the French. I highlighted that whereas the British public love their stately homes, the French are not so 'chateaux-minded' and probably would not even bother to look out of the window if told that a French Duke was having tea in the garden below. Quite different from the attitudes one comes to associate with the British public!

By the time I retired as president in October 1978 the HHA was well established. Half a century ago, at the dawn of the new Elizabethan

Age, the stately homes of England were in what seemed then a state of irreversible decline. Those that were not destroyed altogether seemed destined to become government offices or roofless ruins. The climate of opening had changed but there was still a threat and that threat will probably continue until the end of time. But at least we had learned to band together and fight for our nation's heritage.

The tide had turned and for that I feel I can take some modest credit. There were plenty more battles to fight and I continued to be in the vanguard, but I felt I could now pass on the HHA's baton with a clear conscience. My successor was my vice-chairman, George Howard.

In 1999 the HHA celebrated its twenty-fifth anniversary by staging a wonderful exhibition at the Tate Gallery of some of its best pictures, most of which might well have been sold had it not been for the HHA's efforts over the years. Now, in the year 2000, there are new threats as the Government intends to disallow setting off losses on the house against income from the estate. I am confident that the HHA will do all it can to fight this proposal.

I consider that the foundation of the HHA was one of my better achievements from the time when I was almost alone in trying to unite owners in a sound and effective organisation. Thanks to the support of many successive past presidents, like George Howard, Michael Saunders Watson, Lord Shelburne and Richard Proby and, presently, the Earl of Leicester, we have a strong and effective organisation to protect our interests.

13

'Early Sun on Beaulieu River'

Early sun on Beaulieu river
Lights the undersides of oaks,
Clumps of leaves it floods and blanches,
All transparent glow the branches
Which the double sunlight soaks;
To her craft on Beaulieu water
Clemency the General's daughter
Pulls across with even strokes.

Sir John Betjeman

An Englishman's home may be his castle, but no house is complete without a garden and no *great* house is complete, or indeed viable, without an estate. The old stones and mortar of Palace House and the Abbey mean a great deal to me, but they would be much less pleasurable if they were not surrounded by the glorious farms and woodland that make up much of what is best in the English landscape and countryside. In addition, owning the bed and banks of one of England's most beautiful and historic rivers is a privilege unique in the world where all navigable waterways are invariably state-owned.

Early on in a varied and prolific career as a journalist and author, Trevor Fishlock wrote a four-part series on Beaulieu for the local county magazine, *Hampshire*. Fishlock had a shrewd eye for 'the story behind the story', and saw beyond the razzmatazz that characterised the Beaulieu of the Sixties. Despite the images recorded by the world's press he wrote: 'For miles in all directions the real life of Beaulieu continues, largely unobserved, following a centuries-old pattern – albeit at a brisker pace – through the seasons. Ironically it is likely that the showmanship which has enabled the historical reality to continue in style and dimension will itself be outlived by that which is older and more enduring.'

While I sympathise and agree with all this, I find myself suppressing a wry smile – the 'historical reality' of running an estate can be a pretty prosaic business. I value the timelessness, the beauty, the traditions and all that goes to make Beaulieu the magical place that it is but, nevertheless, at the end of the day I am forced to concede that estate management is a twenty-four-hour-a-day job. All sorts of problems face the owner, like the regular maintenance of buildings, road repairs, storm damage on the seashore and, above all, drains. Waste disposal and effluence flooding on the river has been a never-ending source of worry and complaint, requiring energy, improvisation and, above all, expense. We had a major flood of the river during Christmas 1999, when the cellars of Palace House and the village houses were flooded by up to two feet of water. It may seem distasteful and unromantic, but estate management without a proper maintenance and drainage policy is effectively useless.

In some ways I am an urban creature, completely at ease in the city. Indeed, I love London life partly because, unlike most people, London is where I go to relax and be anonymous. The country is where my life has to be most public and where, for the most part, I earn my living. In a sense I am the complete reverse of the Englishman with his town base and his country cottage. My country cottage is in the West End of London; my office is in rural Hampshire where I live over the shop. Yet there is a part of me which is as romantic and lyrical about the country as John Betjeman and Stanley Baldwin, two quintessentially English heroes of mine who loved town and country in almost equal measure. I believe, with Baldwin, that the essentials of our country life 'strike down into the very depths of our nature and touch chords that go back to the beginning of time and the human race, but they are chords that with every year of our life sound a deeper note in our innermost being'.

My land has an ageless quality like that evoked by Baldwin but Beaulieu is doubly blessed for it has water too and even a famous poem to celebrate our luck. I love John Betjeman's elegiac 'Youth and Age on Beaulieu River'. He wrote it for Clemency Buckland whom I knew well as a child. Her father, Brigadier Buckland, was responsible for the Special Operations Executive's training school coming to Beaulieu in 1940. I think Betjeman's poem is too good and apposite not to quote in this context. The first stanza appears as the opener for this chapter:

> Schoolboy-sure she is this morning;
> Soon her sharpie's rigg'd and free.

Cool beneath a garden awning
Mrs. Fairclough, sipping tea
And raising large long-distance glasses
As the little sharpie passes,
Sighs our sailor girl to see:

Tulip figure, so appealing,
Oval face, so serious-eyed,
Tree-roots pass'd and muddy beaches.
On to huge and lake-like reaches,
Soft and sun-warm, see her glide –
Slacks the slim young limbs revealing,
Sun-brown arm the tiller feeling –
With the wind and with the tide.

Evening light will bring the water,
Day-long sun will burst the bud,
Clemency, the General's daughter,
Will return upon the flood.
But the older woman only
Knows the ebb-tide leaves her lonely
With the shining fields of mud.

Very John Betjeman and very Beaulieu too.

For my first two years in the saddle Captain Widnell was my right-hand man. Widdie had been Steward of the Manor since the end of the Great War and he had served my family for thirty-four years. He had been wounded in Mesopotamia. My father interviewed him for the job in London and was immediately certain that he was the man he wanted. Over the years he had become almost as much a part of Beaulieu as my father, my mother or my sisters. His had been an admirable and conscientious stewardship, characterised by an unswerving devotion to my mother. At the end of his career Beaulieu was in as good a position as anyone could reasonably expect, and I was glad to be able to offer him a retirement job sorting out our historic archives and writing a history of the estate and parish church.

In 1952, however, the world was against people like Captain Widnell and myself. When I succeeded, traditional hereditary estates throughout Britain had been in decline for years – most of all in the period during which my mother, Captain Widnell and the trustees were struggling to maintain Beaulieu. There were numerous reasons for this – changes in agricultural practice and in land management, the war, crippling death duties, a dislike of inherited wealth and possession, and possibly of titles themselves – all effectively institutionalised under successive governments, especially Labour ones. Some estates were subsidised by wealthy owners who were fortunate enough also to have inherited lucrative urban property. The Dukes of Westminster and Bedford and Lords Cadogan and Portman, who between them owned much of fashionable London, were some of the more obvious examples. Beaulieu, however, had no such advantages. Moreover, Captain Widnell was handicapped because my mother and the trustees were determined to hand me an intact estate when I inherited on my twenty-fifth birthday. Elsewhere struggling owners could 'sell off some family silver', either in the form of land or other possessions, but this was a limited option at Beaulieu, as there was no free land and few possessions. It was all they could do slowly to pay off the mortgage on the estate that had been raised to cope with death duties.

Together Widdie and my mother performed miracles and, against all the odds, the 10,000 acres bequeathed by my father on his death in 1929 survived intact into the 1950s. The land had been as well maintained as a shoestring budget would allow, but there was not the money to make essential capital improvements to the infrastructure. In the 1930s Palace House was occasionally let out to rich Americans and it was around this time that a young Duncan Sandys, Churchill's son-in-law, and Anthony Head, later also a Conservative Cabinet minister ennobled as Viscount Head, borrowed a piece of statuary from Palace House as a wager. They were young army officers in training on Salisbury Plain at the time and it was the sort of escapade which went down well in the officers' mess. However, it was the kind of joke my mother could have done without.

The war period brought the estate new and peculiar difficulties, with land, houses and even the river requisitioned by the government for training SOE secret agents and other war purposes. By and large the inexpensive day-to-day maintenance had been well carried out, but no amount of assiduous repairs and painting could disguise the fact that the estate had not kept pace with the times and that, effectively, we were running a Victorian operation in a new Elizabethan Age. In its way it was an efficient and effective operation, but it was at least half a century behind the times.

At the end of the summer of coronation year Captain Widnell retired to the agreeable nominal duties of Warden of the Abbey, which he loved. I also put him in charge of the house and of the fledgling motor collection. I was very grateful to him, but it was time for change and it seemed to me that the best first step towards modernisation was to appoint a leading estate agency to manage the estate (as distinct from Palace House and the Motor Museum). Strutt and Parker were an obvious option, for they were pre-eminent in this field, but the final choice rested in personal interviews I conducted in London. One leading agency's nominee for resident agent casually mentioned he would like to continue to hunt at least three times a week. Strutt and Parker, however, shrewdly suggested Brian Hubbard who, at thirty-three, had all the qualities of an enterprising manager. I was very impressed with Brian – he was efficient, entrepreneurial and modern-thinking, with a keen sense of humour. He quickly involved himself and became one of the most important architects of modern Beaulieu.

The essential problem was simple, but how to progress was complex. Neither Brian nor I was going to rush in blindfold, so I commissioned him to make a thorough study of the situation before we committed ourselves to a plan of action. The Hubbard Report took a year to produce and the end result was a sort of twentieth-century Beaulieu Domesday Book.

On first reading, 'Domesday' seemed an appropriate word. I had hoped that I would not have to sell off any part of the existing land, but it became clear that if the patient were to survive, some form of surgery was essential. I would have to sell about a tenth of my heritage in order to conserve the rest and raise money to invest in it. Despite everyone's best efforts the estate was only worth about half a million pounds and Brian Hubbard argued that it was vital to increase that value. There was no point in managing for income, most of which would be taxed at 19s. 6d. in the pound, so any profit had to be ploughed back into the estate. Modernisation was essential and increased income for me just had to wait.

The report advocated a five-year plan starting in 1955 and to implement it we re-established the old Beaulieu Development Company, first started by my father in the 1920s. Brian Hubbard became Managing Director as well as Resident Agent.

The first priority was to deal with the twenty-six estate farms. They alone needed £70,000 spent on new milking parlours and barns; so muddy yards were concreted, electricity and water supplies were provided for everyone, and new cottages were constructed for workers. This all contributed to greater efficiency – fewer workers doing more work – and dramatically increased rents. The report predicted a rise from £1 to £3 per acre, but in the event the increase was still greater.

To help pay for these improvements we initiated a policy of conversion, from ninety-nine-year leasehold to freehold, of almost fifty large houses. These were comparatively grand properties which my father had originally allowed his friends to build on the Estate on long leases. They were superfluous to its working and nothing save modest ground rents would be lost by the change. Essentially, a ground rent of £150 a year was translated into £15,000 in cash. The owners could then, of course, raise a mortgage if they wished. All this was carried out under very strict conditions and the conveyances stipulated that the owner would not be able to alter the essential appearance and character of the existing houses. Today these fine properties continue to be an adornment to Beaulieu. Sadly, none of the original owners remains, but today's are, as always, a diverse and interesting group of people who contribute much to the social life of the place. Some of the properties now change hands for over two million pounds each which, I have to confess, does sometimes give me pause for thought.

In addition, to raise further capital, we sold a number of building plots. These were selected and sited with great care, just as were those of the ninety-nine-year leases chosen by my father. All of them were surrounded by trees, so that little or no change to the countryside would be apparent. Twenty-two were sold in 1956 and twenty-one in the following year, and from then on further development of that type was discontinued.

One or two of the tenant farmers resisted change, but when they saw what was happening on neighbouring farms they quickly changed their minds. Trevor Fishlock interviewed twenty-seven-year-old Gordon Hiscock, who farmed 335 acres at Beufre on the road to Buckler's Hard. Gordon had just moved into a brand-new cottage; a new Dutch barn replaced an old one; a new milking parlour and feed shed were installed and the old mud yard was replaced by well-drained concrete. As a result of this they were increasing their herd from forty-five Ayrshires to a hundred. The improvements to their farm alone cost £4000 and the rent had risen accordingly, but Gordon was happy. 'It's worth it,' he said. 'A higher rent has given us greater incentive to do well. Instead of an old-fashioned, clumsy place, we have a clean, efficient, more productive farm – a farm we're proud of.' Sadly, Gordon later left Beaulieu to take on the senior job of looking after the sacred turf at Ascot racecourse.

With growing inflation our original assessments inevitably turned out to be too low. More money had to be found and, very reluctantly, I agreed to sell off six farms at Sowley, on the south-western corner of the estate, and a little later some of the surrounding woodland.

Woodland covered 2500 acres of the estate, so forestry played an important part in the overall strategy. I knew that conifers were a sounder economic proposition than hardwoods, but oak and beech were indigenous and traditional – Nelson's great warships from Buckler's Hard were 'men of oak'. Beaulieu's ancient woodlands were very beautiful, they had been there since time immemorial and I resolved that most should stay.

Our head forester for fifty-seven years was David Kitcher, from a very old and respected village family, and friend and companion as boy and man to my father in his shooting and fishing expeditions. He and his sons after him gave a lifetime of devoted service to the estate. When he retired I was lucky enough to secure the services of Bob Rowland who, after war service with the Yorkshire Dragoons, had joined the Duke of Devonshire at Chatsworth where he had risen to the position of deputy head forester. There are four principal woods. Ashenwood has 616 acres, Hartford 452, Moonhills Keeping 509 and Abbots Standing (so called because it was where the monks hunted wild deer) 224. All had been carefully maintained, but there had been insufficient replanting and consequently there were not enough young trees and polewoods, or middle-aged trees. Although the visible peripheries of the woods, particularly the river banks, were still stocked with traditional trees, we planted new conifers in the interiors. Part of the clearances involved hazel coppices which had been used for pea sticks, thatching spars and hurdles, as well as fuel for two old-fashioned bakeries. Hazel was redundant and so we introduced new Douglas fir, larch, Scots pine, and even small numbers of Sitka spruce and poplar. Gradually we created a programme of felling and replanting sixty acres a year, and slowly Bob Rowland's eighteen-strong little army of foresters transformed the Beaulieu woodlands. We also established a sawmill and joinery at Exbury on the Rothschild estate, which we hoped would prove an effective economic operation. Unfortunately, this was short-lived. I would not want to pretend that everything we tried was successful. We had our failures and this was one. Bob Rowland, incidentally, was succeeded by another Chatsworth man, Neil Edmundson.

Ever since I was a boy I have loved to shoot and, thanks to Ned Pleydell-Bouverie's tuition and a certain natural talent, I have always been a fair shot. From the beginning of October to the end of January I regularly shoot once or twice a week. I participate in two of the four shoots, which cover 4500 acres and although there is an excitement in the actual shooting of game birds and wildfowl there are other aspects I love – the pleasure in my two springer spaniels' expert retrieving and the beauty of the flat frosty forest in the middle of an English winter. It is strange that I am profoundly happy out shooting whether in the woods or on the Scottish moors, even if nothing is happening, yet fishing bores me rigid. Standing up to my thighs in water with a rod is of no interest whatsoever to me, no matter how beautiful the surroundings. It is a paradox I cannot explain, but possibly it is the fact that the odds of getting a successful shot are better than those of getting a bite.

Trevor Fishlock caught something of the flavour of the shoot when he described old Herbert Earp, who joined me, briefly, as head keeper in the early Sixties. He was fifty-six then and had been a Hampshire gamekeeper for forty years.

Jaunty Herbert Earp is a seven-day-a-week worker and chuckles when you mention holidays. Who wants a holiday, he says. I'm right out here with the old sun and the wind and the rain. I'm all right. And off he strides in his old balloon breeches and thick tweed coat, his favourite slouch hat pulled down on his lined brown brow, his gun tucked under his arm, his thick brown brogues snapping the bone-dry sticks. There's a swing and gusto about him as he marches off to the wooded glades he loves. His springers, Pip and Jet, scamper and scuffle behind him.

I'm pleased that, like me, he favoured springers as well as labradors. They perform their role with boisterous and undisciplined charm – tremendous workers, but also rewarding friends.

So the Fifties and early Sixties saw much change in Beaulieu, which had progressed from being an enterprise predominantly rooted in agriculture and forestry to one which relied on tourism, museums, historic buildings and yachts in the river for the income which keeps it going.

I re-established the annual Estate Dinner in 1955. It was an old custom originating as an 'audit' dinner, given by the Lord of the Manor to mark the occasion of the payment of rents. It was a sort of 'thank you', combined with a sigh of relief and a glass of port. It certainly helped to soften the blow on those rare occasions when a rent increase was imposed. Some owners of large estates had discontinued these occasions and thought them archaic and anachronistic, but I thought they had charm and usefulness. It is an opportunity for a family get-together, a sort of end-of-term report and presentation of future plans. I feel like a headmaster as I stand to tell everyone about our disagreement with the Ramblers Association, about hurricane damage, the sale of a village antique shop, the silver medal for our Beaulieu wine, a new hide overlooking Blackwater, toilet facilities at the yacht club, births, marriages, deaths, a new management at the Master Builder's House Hotel, a Fire Engine Rally in aid of the Fire Services Benevolent Fund – all this in a single speech, filmed, incidentally, by Turner TV from Atlanta, Georgia who were making a programme about the 'English Way of Life'. My annual speech is not only a post-mortem, but a forecast too. Just as the Queen's Speech in Parliament sets out the agenda for the forthcoming parliamentary session, so my speech at the Estate Dinner describes the plan for the next year at Beaulieu and is usually followed by one from a distinguished guest of honour, who has several times been a Cabinet minister.

As I riffle through those old speeches I feel as if I am walking through autumn leaves, turning up a forgotten memory at every step. For instance, in 1974 I remembered four deaths, including our oldest resident, Rosemary Dilke, whose maiden name was Troubridge and who was an old family friend through her father, my father's best friend, Sir Thomas Troubridge. Then I recalled the marriage of tenant farmer Arthur Rolf's two daughters, both weddings celebrated on the same day. That year we lost a thousand trees, blown down in spring gales. A further thousand were damaged and then in the summer we lost six acres of forest at Hartford in a fire which burned for three weeks. Two woodmen, the Lovell brothers, retired after forty-five and forty-six years respectively. At the vineyard we harvested a good crop – four tons.

In 1974, Brian Hubbard's twenty-first year at Beaulieu, he told me that he felt his job was done and the estate was now on an even keel. As his involvement with other Strutt and Parker clients was also increasing, he said he would like to give up the day-to-day running. Reluctantly I agreed, but asked if he would continue as a consultant, retaining his handsome house on the estate. Tragically, not long after his retirement the TB he had suffered from years before began to reassert itself. Against this he battled with predictable fortitude, but eventually he succumbed without ever enjoying the leisure and reflection he so richly deserved. He made an enormous contribution to modern Beaulieu.

I have been enormously fortunate with my employees in Montagu Ventures Ltd. At that time Ken Robinson had already been with me as Manager for four years. Ken was to continue as Managing Director for more than two more decades, until eventually he was asked by Peter Mandelson to become the first Director of Operations at the Millennium Dome at Greenwich. Beaulieu, my family and I, and the Museum owe him an incalculable debt, as he was a brilliant Manager and tourism expert, and it is thanks to him that the National Motor Museum Trust grew and flourished at Beaulieu, and the whole structure of the enterprise was modernised and rationalised. By the end of the century we had become a model of our kind, and that was largely due to the vision, foresight and hard-working competence of Brian and Ken, ably supported by Roger Snell, the Accountant, John Phipps, the Agent, and Michael Ware, the Curator of the Museum. Now others are bearing the burdens.

Looking back on the past forty-eight years it is difficult for me to remember in detail the estate as it was then and to recall the dramatic improvements which I initiated for the benefit of all who lived and worked here. On the agricultural side, for example, twenty-six farms have been amalgamated and now only number five. They are fully modernised and tenant Arthur Rolf milks a herd of 400 Friesians daily with only two men. He, like others, has transformed the land on his rented farm. Other tenant farmers, John Boyd and the Dolbear brothers, have flourishing pick-your-own and farm shop businesses. Originally all our efforts on the estate were designed to grow more food. Now, however, we have 'set aside', which means growing less. Today's farming industry is under threat as never before.

The woods have been subjected to massive felling and replanting, and are well positioned to make a major contribution not only to the income, but also to the environment of the estate. The shoots have flourished and we now have two large and two small commercially run shoots. The sport is greatly in demand.

The river continues to be the jewel in the crown, and the building of the marina and the laying of extra swinging moorings and private piers for house owners will ensure it has a prosperous future. The Royal South-ampton Yacht Club has a clubhouse on the river and, in order to save Gull Island, one of the largest concentrations of nesting black-headed gulls and rare terns in England, from being swept away a special Act of Parliament had to be introduced to enable us to close the 'swatchway' at the mouth of the river. This was done in six days and we were delighted when the area at the mouth of the river was designated as a National Nature Reserve Grade 1. We work closely with English Nature to conserve the site as a Site of Special Scientific Interest. In 1972 the village was transformed by the building of a bypass to relieve congestion and now-adays the shops are not those one would normally associate with village life. They include a chocolate and ice cream factory, a jam and chutney factory, a patisserie, dried-flower shop and an art gallery. Unfortunately the village butcher now only makes cane furniture. Only the great Beau-lieu family of Norris have their traditional shop.

After waiting many years to have a sewerage system installed we were at last able to begin building new houses, a project in which my son Ralph took a particular interest, and these greatly enhance the look of the village. Luckily Beaulieu still has its own Fire Brigade, on call night and day, and largely staffed by estate employees. We are very proud of them and we feel much more secure in the knowledge that they are close by.

The main business, tourism, has expanded in an overwhelming fashion and will continue to be vital for the life-blood of the estate. Although, no doubt, it will have its ups and downs in years to come, I am sure that Beaulieu will continue to attract visitors. Meanwhile, many new resi-dential houses have been built and they, together with those built before the war, now command prices which would have been difficult to con-template some years ago. Houses selling after the war for £5000 are now going for several million pounds, which I feel is a tribute to the sustained efforts of the estate in ensuring that, as the name Beaulieu suggests, it will always be a beautiful place in the future.

So after years of hectic evolution the estate and company have settled down to a period of consolidation. Some years ago I began to pass ownership to my elder son Ralph, to ease the impact of death duties. This was done in regular tranches to ensure a painless transition, especially if I died early. By the beginning of the 1990s Ralph was beginning to assume more and more responsibility for day-to-day management and now it has become customary at the annual dinner for his speech to follow mine. Almost imperceptibly and without realising it, I began to feel relaxed enough to absent myself for weeks at a time, knowing that things were in safe hands in the care of a devoted, energetic and able team of professionals. Gradually the old regime was fading away and a new generation was taking its place. In 1997, for instance, Bill Grindey, the harbourmaster, retired, after joining us in 1957. He supervised the building of our marina and all the many improvements at Buckler's Hard. He helped Sir Francis Chichester prepare and victual his yachts – the Gipsy Moths – for his round-the-world voyages. Bill's departure was the end of yet another era in Beaulieu life. Yet life goes on and I am confident my successors, like all the other successors have, will become as much a part of Beaulieu's fabric as myself and my contemporaries. Estates such as Beaulieu are a vital part of the English way of life and I am proud that I am able to pass it on in much better shape than when I inherited it in 1951. I believe that fine traditions have been maintained, while vital improvements have been made. It has been a tricky balancing act, but I think it has been successful.

I take pride in my possessions but, more important, joy in managing all I own. It is a shared responsibility and a shared pleasure. The hereditary duties and joys of Beaulieu are embodied in the person of the current Lord Montagu of Beaulieu, but they have never been and never will be discharged selfishly or savoured in isolation. Beaulieu is a family business and the family encompasses all who live and work here.

I believe the estate is a fine advertisement for sound management and the hereditary principle. It survives and it survives with style. The sacrifice of privacy is relative. At night, even the heart of the estate is quiet and secluded, and if the crowds became too oppressive I can always retreat to my enchanting beach house on the shores of the Solent. Hugh Casson, that most charming and puckish of artists and architects, designed it for me. In 1953, while staying with the famous Hollywood director Irving Rapper at Malibu on the Pacific coast of California, I was much attracted by the open plan of his house and thought how suitable the concept would be on the Beaulieu foreshore. In 1956 I invited Hugh Casson, who rented one of our cottages, to a cocktail party in Palace House and asked if he would be interested in creating such a house for me. He accepted enthusiastically, especially since he had designed very few houses, having been preoccupied mainly by the Festival of Britain in 1951 and then new offices. The site was very important, as I had loved and known it since I was a child, but it was at that moment polluted in my mind by the presence of the old beach hut which had brought so much grief to so many. Indeed, I found it difficult to visit the place. I could not wait to have it pulled down, but had to get the necessary planning permission for its replacement and was confident that Hugh Casson's name on the plans would work wonders. It did just that and within a year or so my new beach house, no longer a hut, was constructed. The house was open plan with a living room, dining room and bedroom all giving onto each other and a vista of sea and sky. I got especially teased by having no door on my bedroom, but a large window facing the sea and the sunrise. We filled the house with trendy new Scandinavian tables and chairs, and to satisfy my rather eccentric musical tastes I had half of one whole side of the house filled up by an enormous speaker, six feet square, containing twelve smaller speakers. It was the last monument to mono sound and passing yachtsmen used to tell me they could hear it right across the Solent.

Stereo sound was to appear very soon, so this great horn became redundant; indeed, it was riddled with rot as it faced the prevailing wind and sea. Since 1957 I have extended the beach house, and today it is where I can enjoy my greatest moments of peace and relaxation. It is now part of a National Nature Reserve, so the bird life and flora are wonderful, never the same from one week to the next. The ever-changing scene of the Solent and the Isle of Wight is a joy twenty-four hours of the day. Here I enjoy cooking for my friends, using our own fish and game, and living off the land with seagull eggs, samphire, sea beet and sea kale, and picking myself some of the best blackberries you can find anywhere. The beach house is my very private spiritual home, where I have spent some of my happiest moments. It has fully exorcised and eliminated memories of its predecessor, and I am enormously grateful to the late Hugh and Rita Casson who, as architect and interior designer, interpreted my dream house with such skill and sympathy.

Later another friend, Alan Clark, in his entertaining diaries, was less than gracious. Quite apart from being gratuitously rude about Hugh Casson, his verdict on the beach house, where I may say we enjoyed an exceptionally relaxed and entertaining weekend, was characteristically dyspeptic: 'Bleakly isolated amid dunes and scrub heath of the Solent shore, beach house is a big wooden bungalow with transom windows and thin walls through which you can hear the other occupants conversing (and indeed farting).' We shared a passion for vintage cars and in September 1999 he and Jane were due to come and stay at Beaulieu the very weekend he died. I miss him. He was always such good company, but so often wrong about facts. Not least the farting!

14

Historic Motoring – Home and Abroad

What Englishman will give his mind to politics as long as he can afford to keep a motor car?

George Bernard Shaw

I have already written about my father's love affair with the motor car and how it inspired the original modest display of automobiles in the front hall in his memory. However, my own passion for motoring is much more than just an act of homage to my father. I could not have given so much of my time and energy to motors and motoring if I had not inherited his own enthusiasm and built on the foundations he laid. I supposed that my motormania must have something to do with genes, but it is more than simply an inheritance. It is a bond stronger than words that comes from within myself and which I would feel even if my father had never been the slightest bit interested in the motor car.

'The motor car', he wrote, 'is a jealous animal and wants your whole attention.' He did not write in jest. The words appeared in the weekly 'Editorial Jottings' that he contributed to *Car Illustrated* under the jolly pseudonym 'Jack'. In this case he was explaining to male motorists that it was unwise to allow oneself to be distracted by a female passenger. 'However fond you may be of the lady, disaster will result if you endeavour to steer with one hand and entrance your lady with the other,' he warned.

Despite a lifelong attachment to the motor car my father's interests were too disparate for him ever to take his own advice entirely to heart. I too have inherited his enthusiasm for all aspects of motoring, but never to the exclusion of other loves, interests, hobbies and pastimes. I have enjoyed a lifelong affair with the motor car. I have never managed to be scrupulously faithful, even after an accident. The honeymoon may be over, but the love affair goes on.

Obviously its greatest expression has come in the form of the National Motor Museum. Looking back on its development since the 1950s it seems fantastic that my faltering, amateurish first attempts at starting a motor collection should have turned into a truly national and international institution.

Although my father never contemplated a museum at Beaulieu, he did, in fact, donate his second car, the famous 1899 12hp Daimler, to the Science Museum and the Beaulieu horse-drawn fire engine to Hull Museum. The Daimler has been restored and is now back at Beaulieu on display, courtesy of a permanent loan from the Science Museum.

My father and I lived in vastly different epochs in the history of motoring. He was a pioneer at a time when the automobile was in its infancy. The car was still comparatively primitive and controversial, its future lay in the balance and few, with the exception of my father, could have foreseen the many ways in which it would transform society. He was a considerable prophet, but he was not omniscient. In 1906 he wrote:

What is the future of automobilism? That it will to a great extent replace nearly every other kind of traction upon the surface of the earth, I have but little doubt. That it will help to solve political and social problems but at the same time create others, is equally obvious. It will affect values of land, towns and houses by a redistribution of values. Town houses and sites of all kinds, whether for business or pleasure, are going to become less valuable because they largely depend for their value on concentrated humanity, in other words, on inferior transit facilities. On the other hand, land in the country and on the outskirts of towns and in villages remote from railways will become more valuable because of the greater ease of access.

Population will gradually tend to become less concentrated and be diffused over wider areas. Travelling in the broad sense will increase enormously, and dustless motor ways will be constructed between principal towns to carry the ceaseless traffic which will use them by night and day. The workmen employed by the new method of transit will in twenty years overshadow in numbers and importance those employed by railways and tramways added together.

Large towns will have special arterial roads to connect their centres with main roads outside. There will be but little noise, no smell, and, with dustless roads, no dust in the traction of the future. No bacteria will breed in fermenting horse-manure, and the water-cart will be unknown. Produce will come direct from the country to the consumer, and the necessities and luxuries of life will be alike cheapened.

The cultivation of farming in all countries in which the motor-car eventually prevails will gradually alter; the foods raised for the horse, partly or exclusively, will tend to disappear, for oats, for instance, will not be wanted to feed horses, and more foodstuffs for cattle will be grown, and a greater amount of land will be devoted to the raising of foodstuffs for mankind.

Another great change which the motor-car will bring about will be the creation of a new kind of internationalism. To this influence the one preliminary condition will be the existence of passable roads. Europe in a few years' time will become for the motorist one vast holiday area, whether he is seeking health, change of scenery, a warmer or a colder climate, as the case may be. Hotels, even in anti-motorist countries such as Switzerland, will find the motorist not only the most profitable but also the most common source of revenue.

The country which has the best roads will in future tend to become more and more prosperous, given that its natural advantages are not inferior to the countries which surround it. New countries which are being opened up will no longer build railways, but roads – as was the custom till seventy years ago, before the coming of the railway, and roads will be justly regarded as the necessary hallmark of civilisation. Enormous sums will be invested in new road-making and new vehicles all over the world.

Is this an exaggerated picture, the result of a vivid imagination only, or a prophecy to be fulfilled? Time alone can show.

One of his principal missions was to demonstrate that motor cars were durable and practical. This was a time when there were only 1500 cars on British roads and the jury was still out on such fundamental issues as to whether or not engines should be cooled by air or water, whether power should be transmitted to the wheels by belt or chain, or even whether the cars should be driven by petrol, electric batteries or steam. If the automobile was to grow up, pioneers such as my father had to demonstrate its worth and trumpet their belief, especially in Parliament and in the press.

In 1899, for instance, *The Autocar* reported that 'Mr Montagu came to town recently on a motor car. He left his father's place at Beaulieu on the outskirts of the New Forest at 5.40 a.m. and reached Clapham at 10.30, doing the distance of 105 miles in less than five hours. This, says the *Daily News*, beats the record so far as it has been set up in the House of Commons.'

As my father revealed: 'I cannot describe the joy this first car gave me. I began to realise at once that the mechanical vehicle was going in time to produce a wonderful revolution in our transport methods. Often I waxed eloquent before older men about its possibilities but was generally laughed at and severely snubbed. Later on, when some of my prophecies came true, I became more disliked by my "horsey" friends. Such is the fate of most prophets.'

The joy of that first car, a four-seater, six-horse-power Daimler, lay largely in its very primitiveness. 'One of the anxieties of those early cars was that if there was strong wind the ignition lamps blew out. When they had to be re-lit it was a risky job, for the petrol which had not been consumed after the lamp had been blown out occasionally exploded. As to the steering, if one struck even a small obstacle on the road the tiller was nearly wrenched out of one's hand. The springing was primitive and the bumping severe on any except a really good road.'

In 1900 he, along with sixty-four other 'automobilists', took part in a famous Thousand Miles Trial from London to Edinburgh and back. My father drove his 1899 12hp Daimler and won a bronze medal. The gold went to Charles Rolls, driving a 12hp Panhard. Thirty-five of the entrants completed the course under their own power, which was considered a formidable achievement. In June 2000, the hundredth anniversary of the Run, a re-enactment was organised by the Veteran Car Club of Great Britain. I was very proud to enter once again the actual 1899 Daimler which my father drove on the original Trial.

It is difficult to single out all the events in what has been nearly fifty years of continual progress at the Museum. It may be dedicated to the past, but it never fails to look to the future, and we are always acquiring new exhibits, adding new dimensions, improving facilities and trying to keep one step ahead.

In the years after the opening in 1952 the offers of new vehicles came in far faster than we were prepared for or had space for display. We were not then as selective as we should have been in the face of this embarrassment of riches. Nowadays the value and importance of historic cars is universally appreciated, but in those days many treasures were hidden away in barns, yet to be discovered and restored. One of my most important acquisitions came in 1954 when I brought a 1909 Rolls-Royce Silver Ghost, chassis no. 939, to Beaulieu. It had been doing service in Northumberland, ignominiously, as a farm tow truck. After scrupulous restoration this magnificent car is now one of my favourites and our most popular exhibit; with it I have rallied around Europe, behind the Iron Curtain, in Canada, the United States, Japan and India.

In 1954 I began to build up a collection of motorcycles to go alongside the four-wheeled motors. By 1955 they needed the large area of the old kitchen basement all to themselves and we realised that we would have to erect a special building to house future exhibits. Apart from anything else, the house permanently smelt of engine oil. So that year I asked the head forester to fell some trees on the estate and with them we built the first Motor Museum building – little more than a glorified shed but an important landmark in our history. So in 1956, the year of Suez, Lord Brabazon opened the world's first Motorcycle Museum at Beaulieu, attended by Geoff Duke, one time World Champion motorcyclist.

In 1958 Sir Henry Segrave's land speed record breaker, the Golden Arrow, which achieved a speed of 231mph in 1929, arrived at Beaulieu on long-term loan from Castrol. We now had two land speed record cars, as I had previously bought the 150mph Sunbeam of Sir Malcolm Campbell. In years to come we also added Segrave's 200mph Sunbeam and finally Donald Campbell's Bluebird. This collection of land speed record cars, the envy of other collections, is one of the most well-known features of the Museum.

On 5 April 1959 Lord Brabazon of Tara opened our first really serious museum building, built with money specially released from my family trust. This was still only a converted portable school building, which we disguised with stone facings to make it look more attractive. By now we had more than two hundred cars and motorcycles on display. The collection was becoming so large that in 1960 we opened a second museum in the Aquarium building in Brighton and later a satellite museum at the car auction site at Measham, near Burton-on-Trent. That same year we held at Beaulieu the world's first ever old car auction, in conjunction with David Wickins's Southern County Car Auctions, our partners at Measham. This finally recognised that old cars were now genuine 'collectibles'. On the principle that I wanted the Museum to be a 'living' organism, I also began hiring out vehicles for weddings, films like *Chitty Chitty Bang Bang*, and other celebrations. Since the opening of the

Museum I had accumulated 12,000 manuals and almost 30,000 photographs which, added to my father's small personal collection, provided the nucleus from which I created a National Library of Motoring. It has since become one of the world's most important motoring archives and now includes film, video and sound.

The creation of the Motoring Library at Beaulieu gave me a wonderful resource to research the history of motoring. Even before the Montagu Motor Museum was opened in 1959 I had been approached by Brian Gentry of Cassell who suggested I write a book about the Motor Museum. This appeared in 1959, the year the Montagu Motor Museum was opened, as *The Motoring Montagus*. I then produced, in conjunction with Michael Sedgwick, a leading motoring author and Curator of the Museum, a series of books about 'Lost Causes of Motoring' and in particular the first ever biography of Jaguar, when I had the advantage of interviewing Sir William Lyons and hearing his comments about the early days of Jaguar direct from the founder. The book has been updated seven times and even a Japanese edition has been published. In other books I described the history of the Gordon Bennett Races and wrote biographies of Charlie Rolls, the history of the chauffeur and royal motoring. Non-motoring books include *The Gilt and the Gingerbread*, a history of the stately home business, and another comparing the European aristocracy with the British called *More Equal than Others*. Finally I had great pleasure in writing the history of Daimler which was published in 1996 to mark the centenary year of the marque with which my family has so long been associated.

By the mid Sixties we were regularly attracting half a million visitors a year, with thousands coming to special events such as the auctions and our annual cavalcades of motoring, which later evolved into our 'living history' programme. Such was the scale of our success that I decided to turn the Montagu Motor Museum into a genuine National Motor Museum and Charitable Trust, launched in 1969 at the Savoy by Dick Marsh (now Lord Marsh), the Minister of Transport under Harold Wilson. We set about raising three-quarters of a million pounds from the British motor industry and others to build a brand-new state-of-the-art museum complex, designed by Leonard Manasseh and Ian Baker – the foundation stone was laid in 1970. As the day of the opening drew near, frantic work went on amid a builders strike and, determined never to close, by a great effort we moved the entire collection from the old building into the new one overnight, with the aid of a lot of pushing, shoving and towing. We even laid ramps over the garden fountain in order to move the huge World Land Speed Record Breakers. So, on 4 July 1972 the 70,000-square-foot Museum was formally opened by that enthusiastic motorist, HRH The Duke of Kent. This coincided with a new bridge across the Beaulieu river and a village bypass, to be followed later by the new Brabazon Restaurant, the John Montagu administration building and landscaped car parks in the woodlands – all part of an imaginative proposal we commissioned from the landscape planner Elizabeth Chesterton. The Museum even won an award from the Royal Institute of British Architects, which spoke reverentially of its 'cathedral-like atmosphere'. In 1974 we installed a monorail that, uniquely, ran through the roof of the Motor Museum, inspired by a similar one I saw, which ran through the US pavilion at the 1967 Expo in Montreal. We were also thrilled to receive the 'Museum of the Year' Award.

In 1986, to celebrate a hundred years of motoring, we added a new building, the National Motor Museum Trust Centre, which housed its three libraries, offices, a lecture theatre and an extensive stores area, along with a classroom and workshop for the flourishing Education Department. In the Museum the previous year we had created 'Wheels', a Disney-style dark ride through a hundred years of motoring. A most detailed reconstruction of a 1930s country garage was added in 1997. Perhaps the most detailed construction by any museum, the upper floor cunningly conceals a whole array of hands-on exhibits, which graphically illustrate how the motor car works. Our Commercial Vehicles Gallery was revamped as a street scene on the theme of 'Deliveries to your Door'.

In 1967 Michael Ware, the Curator, suggested that we ran an event similar to the great Automobile Swap Meet, which is held annually at Hersey in Pennsylvania. This is a great array of stalls selling spare parts and other material relating to motoring. It was a new event for us to try out and we were well aware that 'swap meet' would mean nothing to anyone in Europe. We therefore invented the 'Autojumble', realising everyone knew what a jumble sale was; hence the word has passed into the English language and is now in modern dictionaries. Later we added another 'jumble' our 'Boatjumble' which together attracts 100,000 visitors a year, and this word, too, is now in common use.

But there has been more to my motoring life than the creation of the National Motor Museum. One of my greatest pleasures has been actually driving the types of car that my father himself would have driven. Rallying of veteran and vintage cars has been an abiding joy.

By the time I took part in my first rally, the 1950 Brighton Run, the cars my father and Charles Rolls had driven in the Thousand Miles Trial had become antiques. They were museum pieces and objects of nostalgic curiosity, as after fifty years the motor car had changed almost beyond recognition. My father and his contemporaries took part in motor rallies in order to demonstrate that the newly invented automobile had the potential to be a serious form of transport. I drove old cars to promote the Museum and as a homage to the past. The great similarity between the two of us was that we both enjoyed the experience and had driven the same car – he when they were new, and I as historic relics.

Most people's ideas about veteran and vintage car rallies are based on *Genevieve*, that charming film of 1954 about the Brighton Run, starring two rival automobiles, a Spyker and a Daracq, with dashing John Gregson and Kenneth More, beautiful Kay Kendall and Dinah Sheridan, and a haunting theme composed and played on his mouth organ by the redoubtable Larry Adler. The film, released in 1955, had a dramatic effect on veteran and vintage motoring the world over, and led to the foundation of many new historic car clubs.

The real thing is rather more prosaic but, for me, rallying has an appeal that is irresistible. In fact, provided you have the time to spare it is the only way to travel – and when I say 'travel' I mean travel as our ancestors experienced it. I have, of course, completed more London to Brighton Runs than I care to remember and rallied around the whole of the British Isles, including the remoter parts of Scotland, Wales and Ireland. I have rattled along the highways and byways of Europe, the USA, Canada, New Zealand, South Africa and India. I have traversed the whole of Australia and experienced the thrill of those vibrant fall colours of New England from the leathery vantage point of a motoring antiquity. I have re-created the thrills and spills of the famed Mille Miglia in Italy and endured the icy hardships of the Monte Carlo Rally itself. My life as a rally driver is a world atlas of motoring.

When the Veteran Car Club of Great Britain was founded in 1930 and the Vintage Sports Car Club in 1934, they consisted of some 200 to 300 enthusiasts who wished not only to preserve our historic cars, but also to protest against the dullness of the utilitarian design of the cars of the 1930s. Who would have thought that seventy years later it would become a worldwide movement with clubs devoted to each sector of historic motor transport in nearly every country?

There are several reasons for collecting old vehicles: first there are those who wish to preserve a particular vehicle, create a collection or build up a museum. Second, another large part of the hobby includes those whose main interests are driving vintage cars – be they in rallies, hill climbs or straightforward racing. It is this active part of the hobby that normally attracts the younger element – getting more adventurous as the years go by. Over the past fifty years, as I was acquiring my collection that eventually became the National Motor Museum, I was very active in rallying and derived an enormous amount of pleasure from driving my veteran and vintage vehicles in various parts of the world. One of the great joys of rallying internationally is that not only do you visit places that would not necessarily be one's first choice for a holiday destination, but travelling at an appropriate speed in an open car and sitting higher than a modern car one can enjoy the countryside with far more ease than the modern vehicle allows, not forgetting the fascinating peeps into others' back gardens. It is flattering to be welcomed with such enthusiasm by local people who not only enjoy the sight and sound of the cars. Often the dignitaries of communities en route lay on elaborate cultural and culinary experiences for the participants as you pass through their districts. I have heard participants discuss rallies entirely in terms of their potential entertainment and culinary value – France, Italy and Spain certainly lead on this front.

Of course, the most famous veteran car rally in the world is the London to Brighton Veteran Car Run, which takes place on the first Sunday in November and commemorates the emancipation of the motor car on 14 November, 1896, when a red flag was symbolically torn up and the motor car received the freedom of the road – albeit with a maximum speed of twelve miles per hour. This date has been regularly commemorated since 1927 and the Run is organised by the RAC. On my first Brighton run in 1950 I drove a 1903 two-seater, 6hp De Dion Bouton accompanied by the model Barbara Goalen. Unfortunately we broke down just outside Brighton. Over the years since, I think I have only twice failed to complete the course. For many years I used to invite as my passengers such people as the reigning world Grand Prix champion or other distinguished motorists and celebrities, and indeed sometimes politicians such as the current Minister for Transport. This has meant that over the years I have taken on the Brighton Run people like Graham Hill, Stirling Moss, Jimmy Clark (whom I had to ask to help push the car over the finishing line in Brighton where we had run out of petrol) and celebrities like Tony Blackburn, two Miss Worlds, five Ministers of Transport, including John Moore and Norman Fowler. In addition, as president of the Historic Commercial Vehicle Society, originally founded at Beaulieu in the late 1950s, I also take part in their London to Brighton Run which is held each May, so by now I should be able to get to Brighton blindfold. Happily, over the years there have certainly been many improvements in the road between London and Brighton, but it is unfortunate now that because of these route changes we have to divert off the old route to face some narrow roads and very steep hills. Of course, all the family have done the Brighton Run.

My first overseas rally was in 1958 when I drove to the Brussels Expo in a 1903 Mercedes, and I later took a 1908 Unic London Taxi to Paris, where we paraded around the around the Circe d'Hiver, frightening the horses. In 1956 I took part in the seventieth anniversary of Daimler and Benz, and paraded through the streets of Stuttgart with engines boiling under the redoubtable command of Alfred Neubaur, the famous Mercedes racing manager. My first historic car race was at Brands Hatch and I won it in a 1915 Prince Henry Vauxhall. A wiser, older friend warned me that you should never win your first race as you are unlikely to win another – he was right.

In 1959, soon after I got married for the first time, my wife Belinda and I, accompanied by two undergraduates, took part in a race organised to celebrate the 1907 flight of Henri Bleriot (the first man to fly the Channel) and since the race was open to every type of transport we did not win. But we were certainly not last! A few years later, the first transatlantic crossing in 1919 by Alcock and Brown was celebrated, but this time no vintage cars were used. I went from the top of the Post Office Tower in London to Heathrow on a motorcycle in twenty-two minutes, flying the Atlantic by Aer Lingus, then travelled by helicopter to New York's West Side and thence to the top of the Empire State Building. Clement Freud won, rather unsportingly I felt, by renting a New York ambulance to get through the traffic, with lights blazing and sirens screeching! Once at the Empire State Building he managed to enlist the help of some friends to block the lifts by sending them all to the top floor, reserving only one for himself. Freud claimed the £2000 prize money!

The first major overseas adventure with Museum cars took place in

1959–60 when Belinda and I sailed on a Union Castle liner from Southampton to Cape Town, accompanied by the 1903 6hp De Dion Bouton (the first car in the Museum), the 1909 8hp Humber and the 1920 350hp Sunbeam (which broke the land speed record at 150mph) and the 1907 TT Norton motorcycle (the first to win the TT), which we had arranged to exhibit in South Africa while visiting the vintage clubs there. Except for the problems of getting the cars into the country, as we were threatened with large customs duty, eventually quashed by the Minister in charge of Customs, we had a splendid time in Cape Town. We then travelled along the Garden Route to Durban in Field Marshal Montgomery's Eighth Army Staff car, a Humber Snipe.

Before we returned home my wife and I spent two weeks in Buganda and visited my old regimental colleague, the Kabaka of Buganda, who showed us his country and took us on an elephant hunt. It is sad to think that only a few years later he was driven out of the country by Milton Obote, escaping with his life, but eventually dying in London.

In the 1960s I did many overseas tours on behalf of the British Tourist Authority to publicise Britain's historic houses and in particular Beaulieu, sometimes with and sometimes without vintage cars. In 1967 I took my 1909 Rolls-Royce to Canada to celebrate the Expo in Montreal. The rally started in Windsor, Ontario and ended in Montreal. To get to Windsor I had to pass through Detroit, which at the time was rather like travelling through a war zone, because serious rioting had recently occurred and fires were still raging in the city. I was eventually reunited with the car at Windsor. It had come through the Great Lakes on a freighter and during the journey had inevitably been robbed by the stevedores. With my friend Tommy Yellowlees we started towards Montreal and, as it was very hot, the wooden wheels of the Rolls began to shrink and were in grave danger of falling off. In desperation we jacked up the car, took off the wheels and put them in a bath in a motel, little knowing how much oil was in the bearings. We had to spend the whole night clearing up. In 1968 I took the same car to Prague, which was celebrating the Prague Spring, short-lived as it was. The Rolls caused a sensation, as the Czechs had never seen one, let alone a 1909 model. I well remember Wenceslas Square filled with hippies strumming guitars, a phenomenon that was very new to Czechoslovakia. During the visit I was shown over a Czech castle which had been a home of the Sternberg family, one of whose members, Diana, I knew very well in London. When I mentioned this to the curators they surreptitiously let my wife and me into the old nursery wing, which had been untouched since the family left in the late 1940s. It was very poignant to see the old school books and other personal belongings that had been left untouched exactly as they had been when the family fled the Communist regime. When I returned to England I told Diana about my visit and eventually she was able to get some personal belongings, including photograph albums, out by a back door.

I particularly enjoyed my rallies in Australia and New Zealand, and found that for veteran car driving the best was the South Island of New Zealand, where the roads were virtually empty and the only other obstruction was wandering flocks of sheep. I won my class in 1964, driving a Prince Henry Vauxhall, when they first opened the Haast Pass in South Island, New Zealand. In the 1960s I had the pleasure of driving Miss World, Anne Sydney, in Tokyo and took the same car to New York in 1964 for the World Fair. With the famous Commander Whitehead it featured in a Schweppes commercial. Unfortunately it did me a great disservice by breaking my wrist while I was cranking it at the World Fair. Driving back to New York with one arm and hand was one of the most perilous journeys I ever undertook. Later in the day I visited a somewhat elderly doctor who remarked that he had not seen a fracture like this for many years, not since the electric starter overtook the hand-cranking of cars.

In 1972 the government body supervising our entry into Europe, known as 'Fanfare for Europe', approved my idea of celebrating the occasion by organising a rally of historic vehicles from London to Brussels. Waved off in the morning of 1 January from Horseguards Parade by the Prime Minister, Edward Heath, by late in the afternoon we found ourselves between Ostend and Brussels, and it was so cold that my carburettor on the 1899 Daimler froze and we had to wait for a trailer to come along to get us to Brussels. The secondary objective of the rally was to impress upon members of the European Parliament and the civil servants the importance of allowing freedom on the roads for older vehicles. Twenty-seven years later, in October 1999, a similar rally comprising over a thousand cars put on a similar demonstration in Strasbourg. In 1994 I, together with the RAC and the Automobile Club of France, organised a rally to commemorate the opening of the Channel tunnel. Led by Prince Michael of Kent in a 1907 Rolls-Royce, and me in the 1899 Daimler, we were the first cars to use the tunnel, and were accompanied by a parade of fifty

French and fifty English cars covering the last century alternately, year by year.

Another long-distance rally of which I have fond memories was the 1988 Bicentennial Rally in Australia, when I drove my 1914 Rolls-Royce Alpine the 2000 miles from Perth to Canberra, again with Prince Michael of Kent. It was very hot and most of the cars boiled, except my Rolls because of an ingenious enlargement of its radiator cap which, when necessary, replaced the famous mascot and gave us a cooler engine. Driving across the Nullabor Plain was very boring, with literally miles of road ahead of us without a bend, littered with dead kangaroos, beer cans and the odd petrol station every hundred miles or so. In fact, we ran out of petrol several times and were saved by the police car shadowing our vehicle. It was a splendid rally – I not only enjoyed visiting the vineyards of Southern Australia but, thanks to Prince Michael, had the privilege of staying with various Lieutenant Governors and finally the Governor General in Canberra where eventually over 1500 cars, driven from five points around Australia, assembled.

As far as long-distance rallying is concerned, the greatest experience for me was the Peking–Paris race in 1997. I entered my 1915 Prince Henry Vauxhall in the 12,000-mile rally organised by the Classic Rally Organisation to commemorate the original challenge ninety years earlier. It took four years to set up with unbelievable complications, particularly those involving Chinese officialdom.

My car was found languishing in a hedge in 1954 and the Museum acquired it four years later. I first drove it in competition at the Brands Hatch August Bank Holiday Edwardian Handicap. We came first with an average of 49mph over four laps, although its maximum speed is about 85mph. At Brooklands in 1913 a single-seat predecessor averaged an astonishing 89.77mph over 500 miles. Although it is a late-Edwardian car it drives more like a vintage model – 'vintage' being defined as one built after 1 January 1919 and before 31 December 1930. In other words it was before its time.

The original Peking to Paris was won by Prince Scipione Borghese in a 7433cc Itala, but we didn't retrace his tyre-prints, not least because roads in the Russian federation had improved to such an extent that they no longer constituted a challenge in comparison with West China, Tibet and Nepal.

All ninety-six entrants were shipped in containers and, despite sailing through a typhoon, arrived in perfect condition and were unpacked by Chinese dockers wearing pristine white gloves. No cars were allowed unless they were built before 1967, and they ranged from a 425cc 1958 Citroën 2CV and a Ford-built 1942 Jeep to a 1907 La France and a 1919 Marmon. There were five Rolls-Royces and three Bentleys.

At 8 a.m. on 6 September we set off from just outside the Great Hall of the People in Peking, urged on our way by a huge crowd, dragon dancers, brass bands and thousands of balloons, not to mention ministerial speeches.

For the first few days there were hordes of well-wishers all along the route. We climbed the Yellow River Valley into Inner Mongolia, skirted the Gobi Desert and passed the Great Wall, which at this point was built entirely of mud. The landscape was a patchwork of rice, sunflowers, maize, melons and sheep, punctuated by the odd brick or cashmere factory.

On the first day, not more than thirty miles from the start, disaster struck when a pin in the Prince Henry's water pump broke and the fan punctured the radiator. In spite of the valiant efforts of our chief engineer, Doug Hill, on the fourth day at Lanzhou, a famous staging post on the old silk route, the poor old car gave up the ghost with a cloud of steam and had to be packed off home. I, on the other hand, luckily managed to cadge a lift in one of the Rolls-Royces, a Phantom V belonging to a Sydney surgeon, John Matheson. The car had formerly been kept for use by the Queen on state visits to Australia.

On we powered along the Roof of the World Yak Track towards Lhasa. We were the first rally to cross China from north to south. It was hard going but, amazingly, when we reached Kathmandu there were still ninety cars operating under their own power. The leaders at this stage were not the glamorous Bentleys and Rolls-Royces, Aston Martins and Mercedes but a Ford Anglia, Citroën 2CV, a Ford Cortina, a Chevrolet Camaro, an Iranian Hillman Hunter and a Rover P5. The two 'Bentley Boys', as we christened Adam Hartley and Jonathan Turner, had to use the hand-throttle and run alongside their vehicle on the steeper climbs. My generous host's Phantom broke a spring and had to continue on a truck until the driver rebelled, on account of the state of the roads, and had to do the final twenty-four kilometres using petrol bought in litre bottles. Luckily a clever Nepalese craftsman was eventually able to forge new springs. The Dutch 2CV, in third place, also broke its suspension, which meant that the co-driver had to stand on the back bumper all the way from the Chinese border to Kathmandu.

By the time we arrived in Pakistan I reckoned I could claim a prize for having the highest number of different rides. After my own Prince Henry and the Australian Phantom, I hitched a lift with a Toyota Landcruiser, a Nepalese-spec Toyota, a Mitsubishi Pajero, a decrepit jeep rented by a *Times* photo-journalist and one of the organisers' Vauxhall Fronteras. Finally, because of the original co-pilot's illness, I ended up as navigator to Jonathan Lux in his V8-powered Rover P5.

There was a false alarm in Nepal when we were warned that we had to negotiate twenty-two bridgeless rivers in a single day. The waves of flood water were capable, we were told, of 'sweeping Morgans and 2CVs down the Ganges'. In the event they turned out to be placid and well-signposted, but the warnings had made us nervous. In Pakistan disaster really did strike when the German Josef Reit collided with a stationary bus in the dark on the outskirts of Quetta. He and his son Rene were killed outright. We were all deeply shocked. Rallies are exciting, sometimes thrilling but, although they are dangerous, they are not like Grand Prix motor races. One does not expect fatalities.

In Iran we were the first rally to cross the country since 1977, in the pre-Ayatollah days of the Shah. This time our female crews had to cover themselves from head to toe, we men had to abandon shorts for long trousers and all food seemed to be accompanied by delicious mint-flavoured yoghurt. On one occasion our convoy was stoned by a gang of youths in the Great Salt Desert. The heat was intense (112°F in the shade one day) but the roads were vastly improved, and the Iranian authorities were efficient and supportive, providing free petrol and servicing. Even so, there was plenty of scope for improvisation. One of the Bentleys, for instance, had a leak in the fuel tank plugged with a packet of Opal fruit gums.

On our arrival in Turkey the girls removed their shawls and the men put on their shorts. Best of all the Dedeman Hotel at Palandoken served beer. We enjoyed the luxury of a motorway between Ankara and Istanbul. In other words we were on the threshold of Europe. In Greece we had our first rain. It was now October. When we spent a night by the Italian lakes, after a visit to the Ferrari factory, there was a snow forecast for the Alps.

In Rimini I met up with a replacement for my abandoned Prince Henry Vauxhall. This was my 1930 Blower Bentley, the fourteenth and final vehicle in which I had driven since Peking. She is a formidable car. She can cover a standing quarter-mile in less than nineteen seconds and can do more than 120mph in top gear and 60mph in first. Naturally, I wished that I could have completed the entire journey in a single car, but this was not to be.

The longest ever motor rally since Prince Borghese won the 1907 event ended in triumph for Phil Surtees's sturdy 1942 Ford-built Jeep, which was generally agreed to be the most uncomfortable car in the rally. As he drove triumphantly down the Champs-Elysées he was just four minutes ahead of another Ford, Ted Thomas's 1950 Club Coupé. I was sad not to be following behind in the Prince Henry, but the Bentley was a magnificent substitute and, after all, I had covered the entire 12,000 miles, even if I had done so mainly as a privileged hitch-hiker.

The Peking–Paris was the true highlight in my rallying career, a climax to a lifetime of adventures which have taken me to every continent on earth. There are few experiences more exhilarating than travelling through exotic landscapes, on testing roads, in classic cars and in the company of like-minded enthusiasts. I have been lucky enough to do it all my life and it has been a huge privilege. No other sensation can quite compare. Unlike modern motoring, this has an elemental appeal. The cars smell and smoke; the upholstery is leather; the headlamps are the size of soup tureens; they vibrate and rumble; the mind knows that they are machines, but the heart is almost convinced they are animals. Handling them requires the sort of skills you associate with riding a horse – or at least a motorbike: you are much closer to your surroundings than in a modern car; you feel the wind in your hair and petrol fumes in your nostrils; you jolt and rattle, coax and cajole, and feel as pleased with life as Kenneth Grahame's Mr Toad in *The Wind in the Willows*.

My mechanical mishaps with the Prince Henry meant that I won no motoring prizes at the end of the Peking–Paris rally. However, my regular despatches to 'Go' and to 'Car 97' in *The Times* were rewarded with a prize for best reporting of the event. This was presented at what *The Times* described as a 'glittering dinner' in Paris by the formal Liberal leader, Lord Steel. David Steel is a long-term rallying companion who was to have taken part in the Peking–Paris, but who had to withdraw because of the Scottish referendum campaign. Such are the penalties of political fame. However, he was determined to compete in the forthcoming London to Cape Town event and was already heavily involved in planning the route.

There are few countries in the world in which I have not exercised my historic cars. One of the most rewarding prizes I won was for a rally to Portugal organised by the Licensed Victuallers Club, which promised all finishers a case of wine nearest to the date of their car. Since I drove a 1925 Bugatti I was rewarded with a case of 1924 La Tour. My outer office at Beaulieu is overcrowded with plaques and cups, all of which bring back many happy memories. I celebrated one of the proudest anniversaries in 1999: the hundredth birthday of a race of my father's second car, an 1899 Daimler. This was the first British car driven by an Englishman to race on the Continent and my father achieved third place in this Paris–Ostend race. In May 1999 I took the same car to Ostend to mark this anniversary. Also, on 4 July 1899, my father was the first Member of Parliament to be allowed to enter and park in the House of Commons yard. He had initially been barred by the police, which led to an appeal to the Speaker of the House for the ancient rights of unobstructed entry for Members of Parliament to Westminster. In 1999 I re-enacted this historic event in the same car with the Speaker of the House of Commons, Betty Boothroyd, the Member of Parliament for the New Forest, Julian Lewis, and Brian McGivern, chairman of the RAC. This time, after a little play-acting, I was courteously received and the police took part in the re-enactment with customary good humour. This was also the car that took King Edward VII, as Prince of Wales, for a drive in the New Forest of which a famous picture was taken, which resulted in the royal family ordering its first car – a 1900 Daimler.

In November 1999 I took delivery of the latest Daimler now made by Jaguar. There can't be many families who can boast they own and drive the same marque after a hundred years. The machine that I now drive is a marvel of modern engineering and electronics – sleek, powerful, comfortable and smooth as silk. I have to admit, however, that with all her sophistication she is definitely not the constant challenge that my father's ancient wagonette is.

Inevitably, as time went on, I became involved in the national and international politics of historic motoring. On the whole, governments in this country have been, and still are, very sympathetic to old cars and I first got involved in securing specific exemptions for them at the time when MOTs were first introduced. This, incidentally, entailed sending several cars from the Museum to the Crystal Palace track where tests were carried out. A special advisory committee representing the historic car movement was set up to liaise with the Government with regard to new legislation and regulations, and this eventually grew into the Federation of British Historic Vehicle Clubs, of which I am president and which today represents over 300,000 enthusiasts in this country. Over the years, often as a result of my raising various subjects in the House of Lords, for instance, exemptions have been obtained for old cars from some of the more stringent regulations: thanks to Kenneth Clarke, when Chancellor of the Exchequer, all cars built before 1973 are now exempt from road tax. I like to feel that I had some direct influence in the introduction of this policy. It was during a fortunate chance encounter with Kenneth Clarke that I was able to put my case to him, as courtesy of the RAC we were sharing a helicopter en route to the Silverstone Grand Prix. I seized the opportunity to try to persuade him to grant the road tax concession for historic vehicles. This, to our great joy, was done in the next budget. Originally granted for vehicles over twenty-five years of age, this concession, unfortunately, is now limited to vehicles built before 1973.

Through my questions in the House of Lords I was able to help ensure the continuing supply of leaded petrol and happily the Beaulieu garage is one of the chosen outlets for this fuel. In addition, assurances were obtained, so that the more draconian regulations directed against old cars by Brussels, forcing them onto the scrap heap, would not apply to vehicles in this country. I even went as far as to defend the Brighton Run against the attack of a Labour peer who thought it caused unnecessary congestion on the roads.

On the international front I was an early proponent of the need for a controlling body for historic motoring. This eventually became known as FIVA (the Fédération Internationale des Voitures Anciennes) and, indeed, I was its president in the early 1980s. Although it has had its ups and downs, it now represents nearly a hundred countries and enjoys a good relationship with FIA (the Fédération Internationale de l'Automobile), which controls motor sport. Every year more countries throughout the world join FIVA, which does much to ensure that the hobby continues into the third millennium and that all vehicles retain the freedom of the road, regardless of their age.

Looking back over the past fifty years I have derived an enormous amount of pleasure, education and friendship attending rallies all over the world. In principle the Museum at Beaulieu is a live museum and I believe should not only attract people to see the cars at Beaulieu but also take the cars out to meet people everywhere.

Because of motoring I have also been able to flex my political muscles through journalism, just as my father did at the beginning of the century. On 28 May 1902 he published the first edition of a new magazine, *Car Illustrated*. Its offices in Shaftesbury Avenue overlooked Piccadilly Circus, which my father rather grandly described as 'the hub of automobilism'. In fact, motoring was still such a novelty that whenever he heard a motor car in the street below he and his staff would rush to the window to marvel at such an unusual sight.

The magazine's title sounds a touch limited, but my father's vision was actually all-embracing as is suggested by the magazine's sub-title, which was 'A Journal of Travel by Land, Sea and Air' – before the Wright brothers' historic flight in 1903.

In 1956, just over half a century after he founded his magazine, I too became a publisher. My publication sounded as limited as his, for its title was *The Veteran and Vintage Magazine*. It succeeded an even more restricted-sounding publication called *The Vintage and Thoroughbred Car*, but like my father I was determined that I should not be confined by narrow specifics. In the very first issue I declared that 'Veteran, Edwardian, Vintage, Thoroughbred and Steam Traction Engines all come within our sphere'. Not only that. I wanted our pages to reflect every aspect of motoring. As motoring touches us all in one way or another this gave me an enviably wide brief. With the innocent bravado of youth I was prepared to tilt at windmills. One well-known reader once took me to task for including an article on a 1937 Hillman Minx and threatened to cancel his subscription – he argued that the Hillman was neither Veteran nor Vintage.

For instance, in a very early issue I thundered forth with a seriousness which would have done credit to *The Times* itself: 'Our roads have been only slightly improved since 1896 and successive Governments have been content to treat the motorist as an excellent source for revenue; they have turned a blind eye to the incontrovertible statistics that our present system of roads is not only the cause of many of the casualties but also is costing the country millions of pounds a year in production and delivery costs.'

This was serious campaigning stuff and in other respects, too, we were far from being a specialist magazine catering for a minority interest. We were, for instance, always international in outlook. From the first we had enthusiastic support from such organisations as the Horseless Carriage Club of America and the Dutch Pionier-Automobilien Club. In an early issue I reported on the opening of Germany's first motorcycle museum (four weeks after ours at Beaulieu), where I rode a 1900 Peugeot and made a speech in German.

Nor were we ponderously serious. I invited three of the twentieth century's most memorable cartoonists, Osbert Lancaster, David Langdon and 'Brockbank', to judge a competition to find a new talent. We carried articles on such subjects as 'The right clothes for rallying' and one by Peter Ustinov on the sex of motor cars ('Alas, most of it today is neuter').

Supervising it all was Ellen Broad, my assistant editor, who for more than twenty years devotedly saw every issue to bed in her own inimitable fashion. Without her the magazine would never have lasted so long.

It was of considerable use to Beaulieu and the Motor Museum, as we used to promote events like Autojumble, the rally to Brussels in 1972, and selling merchandise, publishing directories, and keeping in touch with the Veteran and Vintage movement as it grew bigger and bigger around the world. We employed the best motoring writers, like Michael Sedgwick and Bill Boddy, and although over the years we saw many imitations appear, I think I can claim that *Veteran and Vintage* was the first magazine in the world devoted solely to historic motoring which was not connected to or financed by a car club. So Beaulieu can claim another 'first'. As they say, 'Imitation is the sincerest form of flattery.'

Eventually, however, in May 1979 I sold the magazine to IPC, who assured me that they would look after my baby, and provide a good home and future. In fact, my valedictory editorial was headed 'We pass the baton'. Alas, my optimism was misplaced. I had thought that *Veteran and Vintage* would benefit from the money and power of a big organisation such as IPC, but I was mistaken. It soon became *Collectors Car* edited by Philip Young (who much later ably organised the Peking to Paris event that I enjoyed so much) and then became absorbed into *Classic Cars*, and the older car element that I had fostered just disappeared. Small turned out not to have been beautiful, and in no time at all a quarter of a century of labour and happiness was cast aside as if it were nothing. With little apparent regret and not much evidence of coherent thought, the new owners closed the magazine I had founded and nurtured for so long. At the time it seemed quite needless and a terrible shame, but perhaps in the end they were proved right.

Nevertheless, the Museum continues to flourish, generously supported by a devoted set of trustees, and is today efficiently managed to ensure that it continues to tell the story of the motor industry and recognise its achievements and all of those who have worked in it over the past hundred years. We still get offered many cars each week but, since we go for quality and not quantity, potential new exhibits are very carefully considered by an advisory board. Gradual changes in content and special exhibitions always keep the Museum alive, but I feel very aware that it is a nationally recognised repository portraying the history of motoring on the roads of Britain.

15

House of Lords

Little other than a redtape talking-machine and unhappy Bag of
Parliamentary Eloquence.

Thomas Carlyle

I had only just gone up to Oxford when I made my maiden speech in the
House of Lords. It was not usual for Oxford undergraduates to make their
parliamentary debuts quite so early. Most of my contemporaries were still
cutting their political teeth at university debating societies but I never
even bothered to join the Oxford Union. Instead I simply asked the
Warden for permission to address the House of Lords and went down to
Westminster to exercise my hereditary right. I did so with considerable
trepidation but with the callow confidence of youth it never occurred to
me that some might think I was being a little precocious. It was what one
had to do. There was, of course, a special and pressing reason for making
my maiden speech when I did. After my experiences there I felt pas-
sionately about the Palestine question. Had I not spoken out in the
conveniently timed Palestine debate on the order paper it would have
been a missed opportunity of major importance to me. Had it not been
for Palestine I would have bided my time.

In those far-off 1940s the Lords' noble Lordships met in the King's
Robing Rooms. German incendiary bombs had fallen on several parts of
the Palace of Westminster and the officer in charge of the firefighters was
confronted with the choice of saving the magnificent medieval Westminster hall with its amazing 'hammerbeam' roof or the more modern
and ordinary Victorian Commons Debating Chamber. He opted, quite
rightly, for saving the Hall and letting the House of Commons perish. As
a result of the damage the Commons immediately took over the Lords
Chamber and did not return to its own premises until rebuilding was
completed in 1951.

All my fellow peers were older than me, some of them much older, and

I was certainly the youngest peer to make a speech at the time. Life peers had not yet been conceived so apart from the bishops the Chamber was made up entirely of hereditary peers. This meant that although the post-war government was Labour, the Upper House was overwhelmingly Conservative. For the same reason its procedures were archaic and its language studiously polite in the mannered fashion of the law courts. One had to learn the drill and in the same way that lawyers referred to each other as 'my learned friend' the etiquette of the Lords required that fellow peers were addressed as 'the noble Lord'. It was bad form to be rude to one another or at least overtly so and any sly or impolite remarks were hidden beneath a veneer of icy civility.

This had the effect – as in the law courts – of making rudeness and rebuke far more chilling than they seemed in the coarser and more robust atmosphere of the other House. I remember, early in my parliamentary career, saying something I thought quite uncontentious but which caused great umbrage to the Lord Chancellor, Lord Jowett. I had expressed, said Jowett, 'a monstrous doctrine'. He continued, with magisterial disdain, to tell me that 'I deeply regret that I should have heard it enunciated from such respectable lips'. All I suggested was that the 'verderers' of the New Forest were entitled to financial compensation for the enclosure, in 1851, of 10,000 acres by the Forestry Commission. Lord Jowett's view was that the enclosure had been agreed by the then verderers in return for the Crown removing its deer. He therefore thought it quite wrong to award compensation to the verderers' descendants a hundred years later.

I felt duly chastened.

On the whole, however, the Lords was a friendly place. It felt like a leathery St James's club, peopled almost entirely by one's reactionary uncles. There were a great many retired war leaders – very distinguished ones like Field Marshal Earl Alexander of Tunis, Field Marshal Montgomery of Alamein or Viscount Thurso, better known as Archie Sinclair, leader of the Liberals. Many, however, were unknown backwoodsmen, purple of face and shaggy of eyebrow, gruff, alarming though not unfriendly. In those days there were no expenses paid but one could use the telephones for free local calls – free long-distance calls came in much later – and newspapers were also provided free of charge in the fine library. The restaurant served comforting food of the sort members associated with the nursery and the boarding school: steak and kidney pie and steamed puddings. I was given slightly preferential treatment here because the manageress turned out to be the sister of my ex-governess 'Hopey'. It was a smart and convenient place in which to entertain. There were also some informal clubs within the Lords such as the Motor Club, and the Sailing Club of which I eventually became vice-commodore. All in all I found that it suited my purposes rather better than my other London club, Boodles, and as time went on I used it more and more.

I had learned the rudiments of public speaking at Ridley so I was not as bashful or diffident as I might have been. I could construct an argument and project my voice, and experience at Ridley had also inculcated the importance of meticulous homework and preparation, as well as the unassailable advantages of superior knowledge. The House of Lords liked no one better than the peer who had gone away somewhere and returned as an expert. I resolved, very early in my parliamentary career, that I would try not to emulate those of my peers who had an opinion on everything and were not afraid to voice it. Instead, I would follow the time-honoured House of Lords custom and choose my subjects from areas of which I had first-hand experience and knowledge. Above all, I had been taught to be brief – an injunction which I sometimes felt some of my elders and betters might have heeded, although looking back on it I can see that there were occasions when even I may have been exasperating to some.

So, as I have already described, I delivered my maiden speech on 20 January 1948 on the situation in Palestine. In this I was spurred on by my cousin Michael Cubitt who, as we have seen, had also served in the Middle East. Michael, unlike me, was a thorough-going expert Arabist. He and I believed that the Arab cause was not properly understood in Britain and that the Zionists were winning the propaganda war. Clearly I was in a position to help redress the balance. Not only did I have a platform but I also had the benefits of first-hand knowledge and experience so that I was able to begin my remarks by telling my peers that 'I have just recently returned from Palestine where I have been serving throughout the past year'.

I do not know if, at that time, there was anyone in either of the two Houses of Parliament who could make the same claim but there can't have been very many.

At first my offering was received with respectful silence for it is a parliamentary tradition that maiden speeches are never interrupted. It was unfortunate that on this occasion Lord Harlech, father of David

Ormsby-Gore, later a notable ambassador to the USA in the Kennedy years, forgot himself and tried to intervene. He was sternly rebuked for this rare example of lordly bad manners. I, of course, was simply confused and sat down until the storm had passed.

The gist of my argument was that although 'most fair-minded people would welcome the setting-up of some form of Jewish State', the Arabs in Palestine were basically getting a raw deal. There were two 'main factors' which formed a justifiable basis for Arab objections: 'the illegal immigration of Jews into Palestine and the further territorial ambitions of the Zionists'.

Looking back on it now I am almost surprised to see how vehement I was but one must remember that for the past two years my battalion, the Third BN Grenadiers, had been fighting a war against Jewish terrorists such as Menachem Begin of the IZL and the Stern Gang. Throughout that time we had had to 'endure not only bullets and bombs and kidnappers, but also the endless campaign of lies and abuse which have been levelled against them in the Jewish Press'. I spoke with feeling and conviction; but I also spoke from very recent and heartfelt experience.

The press reaction was friendly. The great Lord Salisbury, 'Bobbity' to his inmates and leader of the Conservative Opposition, congratulated me. A particularly memorable accolade in those early days came from 'Crossbencher' in the *Sunday Express*, author of the most influential parliamentary sketch of the day. The 'Crossbencher' column was written by John Junor, eventually a famous and outspoken editor of the paper and one of the last of the truly great Beaverbrook journalists. He was to become a friend and, over the years, a loyal champion. I later freelanced for the *Express* and became a member of the Institute of Journalists of which its editor, John Gordon, was President Emeritus. Years afterwards, in 2000, I was elected Millennium President of the Institute.

Young as I was, I felt I had begun well although, as I said, 'I am not an expert on foreign affairs' and the only reason I chose to speak on such a subject was that I had special knowledge. This was to be my maxim throughout my active political life in the Lords. I had no desire to emulate hereditary peers such as Alec Douglas-Home and Peter Carrington, active all-round politicians who aspired to – and achieved – high office. I believed that I could develop a few areas in which I could contribute meaningfully to the national debate but I had no political ambitions in the normal sense of the words.

My second contribution, on 9 December 1948, was an altogether more domestic matter. The occasion was the second reading of the New Forest Bill. It was introduced by a Labour peer, Lord Lucas of Chilworth, who owned a garage near me in Southampton. Although the subject might seem more esoteric, possibly even parochial, I spoke again as an interested party. As I told my peers, I was not only 'one of the largest owners of common rights in the New Forest' but also the grandson of a man whose report to the House of Commons in 1876 had been the foundation of the 1877 Act which was generally agreed to be the 'Charter of the New Forest'.

The essentials of the debate are too abstruse to be discussed here in detail but as it carried on into committee and third reading I opposed several of the Government's proposals and did so with a vehemence which in retrospect I find quite surprising. My hostility was couched in the mildly absurd pseudo-polite argot of the House. The Earl of Huntingdon, later to become a Beaulieu resident himself, was the object of my ire and what I actually said was, 'I must say with great respect, that I think the noble Earl's reasons for resisting this Amendment seem to me to be completely nonsensical.' Precisely how one can accuse someone of talking nonsense and do so with 'great respect' would be a mystery to most people but in the House of Lords it was, and at the time of writing still is, par for the course.

In the end I won the day at the third reading and our opposition amendment was carried. The issue may not seem important to many people but, as I said, 'When talking about the New Forest, one is speaking of a district which is completely different from anywhere else in England.' As one of the few peers with lifelong knowledge of the place I was in a position to ensure that its unique character was preserved. This seemed a proper use of my privileged position as a speaking, voting member of Parliament's Upper House. I am glad that I will be able to continue speaking for the New Forest in New Labour's partly reformed House of Lords at least for the foreseeable future.

My first two years of active membership were divided between the situation in Palestine and the New Forest, speaking six times in total. From 1950 my subjects broaden with my expanding public interests. They naturally included historic houses, traffic in London and road construction, the advent of modern tourist transport, air charter services, broadcasting deregulation and the need for local radio stations, and in particular the future of the telecinema (1951) when I urged the Government to preserve London's South Bank, which in fact they did, and it later became the National Film Theatre. Prompted by the many comments during my earlier tour of America, and also the much-publicised clash between English civilians and US servicemen, I raised the issue of the welfare of American servicemen in Britain for debate in the House in August 1953. Unfortunately, earlier that year there had been a number of confrontations, one of which, in Manchester, had been reported on nearly every front page in the US. The speech was more a case of highlighting the work of many of our local community organisations in assisting the US servicemen's integration and relations in our rural communities, but it seemed that the American servicemen were more than able to help themselves. Redressing the balance of bad US press publicity, I pointed this out: 'I can think of no other fact that would better illustrate how well the average American Air Force men get on with the local people than to tell you this most interesting piece of information: that there are an average of 200 marriages a month between American Service personnel and British girls.'

I went on to say – later corrected by the Secretary of State for Air, Lord de L'Isle and Dudley for the underestimating of the statistics – that there were over 35,000 US Air personnel in Britain and 20,000 dependants: 'The chances of a GI returning home single from England are extremely small. Indeed, they should be extremely pleased that, in spite of England having a period of Socialist Government, some sections of the population are still fairly good at private enterprise!'

I make no extravagant claims for these early parliamentary years, but it seemed to me that I was making a decent job of being a responsible, public-spirited member of the House. In my own small way I think I brought something to public debate which it seemed difficult for some elected MPs to do. Naturally, they would bring many other experiences and abilities to bear, but I feel strongly that there are some things into which only an hereditary peer has a privileged insight and to lose this wide forest of knowledge would be a needless shame.

My burgeoning parliamentary career was inevitably curtailed by the events of 1954. I could not be at Westminster to hear the Lord Chancellor, Lord Simmonds, rise to make a brief but chilling statement: 'My Lords, I have to acquaint the House that the Clerk of the Parliaments has received a letter from Mr Justice Ormerod stating that Lord Montagu of Beaulieu, a Member of this House, was on the 24th March, convicted at the Hampshire Winter Assize of certain criminal offences and was sentenced to imprisonment for a term of twelve months.' The language was formal and courteous, but the message was unequivocal. It had the awful finality of an expulsion order, which in a sense it was. Even now, almost half a century later, the words have an awe-inspiring quality, as if one were being rebuked by the headmaster in front of a school assembly. At least, somehow that coy, evasive reference to 'certain criminal offences' was less upsetting than if the reality had been spelt out in full.

It was almost four years before I spoke again in the House as after my release I went to see the then Leader of the House, Lord Salisbury, who was very sage and sympathetic. I remember him mentioning the case of Horatio Bottomley, the MP who had gone rather spectacularly bankrupt in the early years of the century, although his was hardly a comparable situation. His advice to me was simple and so true of many things in life: time heals most wounds. I should allow a decent interval to elapse, return quietly without undue fuss and carry on more or less where I had left off.

This was sound counsel and I had no problem taking it. Other peers like Lord Brabazon of Tara said much the same thing. Lord Brabazon was a famous pioneer of motoring and aviation, he was also the first man in Britain to hold a flying licence and he drove a car with the personalised numberplate FLY 1. He had been a friend of my father and later became a Patron of the Montagu Motor Museum. He was like an honorary godfather to me and I remember once he took me bobsleighing down the Cresta Run, this sport being a passion of his.

I returned to the House of Lords on 23 January 1958 to join the debate on 'the lighting of main roads', before which Lord Brabazon had given me a lunch to which he had invited Frank Longford, another loyal supporter, both of whom had encouraged me to return.

My first speech in the House since my release might, at first glance, seem to have been on a trivial subject that does not usually command headline treatment or the attention of leader writers, columnists, pundits, TV panellists and other experts; but as it happened the subject had a tragic topicality, for there had recently been a fatal accident in Chatham when a bus ran into a column of sea cadets. The cadets, clothed in dark-blue uniforms, were marching along a road in which bright light from erratically positioned street lights alternated with pools of total darkness. This produced the most dangerous conditions imaginable and many were either wounded or killed.

I had the technical knowledge to make a case for saying that 'this system of pools of light and dark is the most treacherous of all types, and one which should certainly be abolished'.

At the end of the 1950s, in February 1958, I was taking Lord Mancroft, Minister without Portfolio and one of the wittiest speakers in the House, to task over the interminable delays, some twenty years, in the building of the Staines bypass. June 1959 was the turn of road accidents, and I found the average person's ignorance incredible and potentially dangerous. My fellow peers were greatly exercised about what they imagined to be an horrific increase in road deaths. In fact, I had to remind them that there were more deaths on the roads in 1929 than 1959 and that half a century earlier there were over 300 deaths annually in London alone as a result of horse-drawn road traffic accidents.

My time in the House of Lords during the 1960s was mainly spent concentrating on the issues of vehicle safety and road accidents, road maintenance and building, and regulation. With further rapid advances in motor engineering, the availability and accessibility of motorised vehicles, the increasing role that they played in the everyday life and business, and the greater demands placed on the country's roads, it was clear that more detailed and thorough legislation was urgently needed. On two separate occasions in 1962 I questioned the Government on the use of flashing vehicle headlamp signals. My suggestion for clarification of their use – 'to indicate the presence of another vehicle on the road to some other road user' – was incorporated into the Highway Code. Unfortunately this advice is still not heeded by some motorists even today.

Among the many new proposals I tried to persuade the Government to encourage the BBC to begin regular radio broadcasts of traffic and weather conditions, after a successful one-day trial on 5 February 1962. However, it was too early on, as very few vehicles had radios and the development of VHF transmission had only just been contemplated. Incidentally, later on that year I raised in the debate on the Pilkington Report on Broadcasting the expansion of sound radio, in particular, VHF radio transmission and more specialised music stations, and the benefits from its possible use to local communities and motorists.

I found in the Pilkington report … that there was little realisation of the tremendous and dramatic change the whole emphasis on sound broadcasting had taken since television came upon us. There seems to be very little looking forward as to what the future of sound broad-casting will be ... Sound radio has an extremely important function to perform ... we badly need good music stations ... and I would urge the BBC to carry out experiments with regard to co-operating with the motoring organisations to give proper information about the roads of this country.

(My later attempt to question the Government on the expansion of VHF radio broadcasts in 1970 got rather bogged down in technical jargon and the diversification of high and low frequencies...)

I also advocated lighter-coloured roads; as the late Sir Henry Segrave, the famous racing driver, once remarked, 'If all roads were white there would be no lighting problems at night.' This was a perfectly serious suggestion, but I confess to a slight flush of embarrassment as I recall the note of special pleading when I mentioned the idea. 'Those who have travelled in the south of Italy on the white limestone roads know how effective white can be on such a surface.' I doubt whether even in the House of Lords there were many of us who had first-hand experience of Calabria's white limestone highways.

My contributions on the questions relating to which shrubs were most suitable for the central reservations of motorways (1965) and the dress of parking meter supervisors (1963) might in retrospect seem trivial, but they were serious matters. At the time the supervisors were not compelled to wear an identifiable uniform and the issue had been remarked upon in a case brought against the Crown. The Government was powerless to act, as it was a scheme controlled by local authorities.

Despite all this I tried, unlike some of the more hysterical opponents of the motor car and motorists, to be constructive. Long before it was introduced I advocated a ban on parking on main roads, a graduated system of motorcycle licences depending on their engine size and the introduction of what were then known as 'safety straps'. I was already using them and another member of the House, the Duke of Richmond, had been saved from almost certain death in a traffic accident because both he and his wife were wearing seat belts. Had Parliament and time allowed, seat belts would have been introduced at least a year earlier than they actually were, but then the idea of making them compulsory was still vastly unpopular, since it was widely considered that the mandatory wearing of seat belts was an infringement of personal liberty. In fact, I was eventually successful in persuading the Government to rethink its policy towards seat belts, but the general election prevented any legislation being passed in the time remaining during that parliamentary session. Later on, in the early 1980s, my own life was saved by seat belts so my faith in them has been doubly rewarded.

During that decade I spoke over thirty-five times in debates on questions and Bills more or less directly related to motoring, but that is not to say that I put aside my concerns and campaigning for the Arts, our heritage and museums, and tourism. These are many of the issues that the average member of the House of Commons would have considered too mundane to be worth contemplating and on which few, if any, would have known what they were talking about. The old House of Lords is frequently portrayed as the last refuge of conservatism and backward thinking, but the truth is that in many matters we were often well ahead of the times: motoring and transport are just two examples.

Another, which we have only recently seen come to fruition in the 1990s, arose during a debate on the Arts in 1967, when due to external circumstances I had to confine my speech to the funding of our museums and the prevention of 'items of historic and artistic interest' being exported abroad. I suggested that a 'National Heritage Fund' be set up, receiving its funding from a 'percentage of Premium Bond prize money each month'. I went on to admit that 'I should like to see a national lottery', but this was not an acceptable idea at the time. There was also the suggestion of an income tax relief scheme similar to what is now called 'Gift Aid', loosely modelled on an American system, where public contributions to museum funds and charities are tax-exempt. Had the Government legislated for this tax provision earlier such works as the Caxton Manuscripts from Magdalene College and the Leonardo Cartoon might have been saved from foreign buyers. In the era of continued nationalisation, and despite the post-war recovering economy, the Government could not see admission charges to our national museums as an additional publicly acceptable source of heritage funding. Even in 1970, when the question of 'free admission' was debated again, there was fierce opposition both 'inside and outside this House'. It was not until the early Eighties that the tide of thought changed towards private and general public funding of our museums and galleries.

A year later, in 1968, I rose again on behalf of the heritage and opened a debate 'to call attention to the difficulties of maintaining Britain's Historic

Large family portrait in front of Palace House in one of my favourite cars, the 1909 Rolls Royce Silver Ghost. (*Left to right*) Jonathan, Mary, Myself, Fiona, Ralph & dogs Scott, Tigger & Sika.

In 1995, for her 100th birthday, I took my mother to Paris on the Eurostar. We stayed and dined at the Ritz accompanied by my stepfather's nephew and his wife, Lord and Lady Radnor.

Fiona and I with our son, Jonathan, for my 70th and his 21st birthday party, October 1996. The theme being, 'If music be the food of love … play on!'

In 1997 I took part in the Paris to Peking Rally. The picture shows me in car number 1 being waved off at the start at the Great Wall of China. Unfortunately we broke down but I completed the route in other cars.

In 1988 I drove a 1914 Rolls Royce, Alpine Eagle, from Perth to Canberra in the Australian Bicentennial Historic Car rally. Accompanied by HRH Prince Michael of Kent we crossed the Nullabor Desert, which was very hot and empty. Note the special radiator attachment to improve engine cooling, in place of the Flying Lady.

HRH Prince Michael of Kent outside Palace House in my 1903 De Dion Bouton – the car that founded the Museum in 1952.

Driving the Speaker of the House of Commons, Betty Boothroyd, accompanied by Julian Lewis, New Forest East MP, celebrating the 100th anniversary of the first car to be allowed into Palace Yard.

Jackie Stewart with Ralph and Mary.

200mph Sunbeam, part of our unique collection of four land-speed record breaking cars.

Cartoon of me from my public relations days, working in London for Voice & Vision in the early 1950s.

In the 1980s I helped found the Wine Guild of the United Kingdom, of which I am Chancellor. This pictures us in Beaulieu Abbey Cloisters, about to attend a blessing for the Grape in the church, October 1996.

'The End of the Peer' show in aid of mencap City Foundation, December 1998. (*Top row, left to right*) Lord Elton, Lord Healey, Lord Gisborough and Lord Rix. (*Middle*) Lord Rae. (*Bottom row, left to right*) Earl of Dundee, Lord Renton, Lord Janner, Lord Montagu of Beaulieu and Earl Alexander of Tunis.

Family conversation piece unusually set in a snow scene, which I commissioned from John Ward RA. The picture rather boldly (with their permission of course) included both wives and our children, as well as my mother, not forgetting the dogs and the horse!

With my daughter
Mary, a keen car
ralliest, in a super-
charged 1930 Bentley.

A week or so after my
horrific car accident I took
part in the Terry Wogan
Radio Show live from
Beaulieu.

In 1978, Lord
Mountbatten asked us
at Beaulieu to assist
and advise him with
regards to opening his
home, Broadlands, to
the public. The actual
opening here is being
performed by Prince
Charles.

My home from home, my beach house today, on the sunny Solent, designed by Sir Hugh and Lady Cusson, where I find great solace.

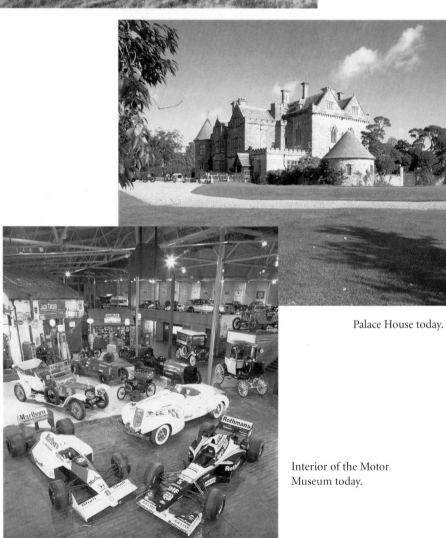

Palace House today.

Interior of the Motor Museum today.

Houses and Castles and to its importance to the balance of payments'. Wary of the issue being clouded with accusations of 'self-indulgence', I promptly pointed out that less than ten per cent of the 883 houses and castles open to the public were owned by members of the Lords and the 300 or so privately owned properties were attracting some five million visitors a year. Again I called for more lenient taxation, especially in respect of repairs and maintenance, and inheritance tax, and my pleas did not fall on entirely deaf ears as Lord Kennet agreed to pass on my concerns to government.

The tourism and leisure industries were becoming major employers and contributors to the national purse, but the government of the day was reluctant to appreciate the full potential of its contribution to the future economy. In 1966 I spoke strongly in favour of further financial support for the British Tourist Authority, whose work in publicising Britain abroad was invaluable. I was able proudly to report to the House that in 1965 my home had received nearly 600,000 visitors. Given my success and the evidence I had gathered of the BTA's work from my many overseas lecture tours, I warned the Government that 'the idea that tourists will come to this country will-nilly, is just not true'. Lord Rhodes, the Government spokesman, gracefully acknowledged my successful work both at Beaulieu and in the House as a member of the working party on tourism to stately homes. During this debate I also raised the question of a fixed date for Easter – this was not to be the first time and, in fact, I have spoken quite regularly over the years on this subject and the benefits that would follow for the tourism industry.

On some occasions I was able to kill two birds with one stone and combine my interests in both transport and heritage, and in particular I was keen to preserve for the National Archives a film record of steam locomotives (1966) made by the BBC and British Transport Films. The steam train was becoming a relic and I believed it was important to record this closing episode in our industrial development which, after all, had begun in the revolutionary age of the nineteenth century. At the end of 1968 I defended the London to Brighton Veteran Car Run, accused by Lord Sorensen of being a 'considerable inconvenience' to other motorists. 'In view of his obvious ignorance', I invited him to come along with me, but although he had already been, he did not share the Government's and my view that the event was well managed by the police and there were very few, if any, complaints.

In the course of this I managed to cause offence to some extremely eminent people, many of whom were, when it came to specialised questions, distressingly ignorant. Even Quentin Hogg (Lord Hailsham), whom I normally much admired, 'utterly failed' to understand me when during the committee stage of the Road Traffic Bill (1961) I suggested that while drunk driving was a serious offence, it should also be realised that some motoring accidents had been caused by drunken pedestrians and cyclists. These people should be subject to the same blood tests as inebriated motorists and I thought the law should recognise this. It still seems a completely common-sense point and I cannot see why such a clever man as Lord Hailsham could not grasp my suggestion, as all that was required to include this in the Bill was an addition to an amendment. I can only conclude that he had been inadequately briefed by his officials and there were political prejudices involved.

On at least one other occasion I found that government ministers did not know the facts and I had to reiterate an obvious suggestion to the Minister concerning night-time access to epileptic prisoners (1963). Clearly unaware that night prison warders did not hold keys to individual cells and that an epileptic, during a fit, is hardly able to ring a bell, Lord Jellicoe was forced to admit that his 'information on this point does not square'. The Minister, embarrassingly, had no idea about either epilepsy or prison regulations and simply did not know what he was talking about.

Although I was not about to become a campaigner for penal reform like Frank Longford, I uniquely intervened in this question because it was something I knew about at first hand and on which I felt strongly. Frank, characteristically, was always urging me to speak in his support on all sorts of penal matters, but I am afraid I disappointed him.

I was not afraid of criticising authority or peers when I knew my subject and had a good reason to do so. Indeed, during the debate on admission charges to public museums and galleries (1970) I remarked to the opponents of this much-needed source of funding that their views were based on little 'experience of employing well-tried commercial methods' in making an 'institution more viable'. The opposition was from, of all people, the curators, directors and trustees – the guardians of the heritage – but there was a desperate need for additional funding, especially for the provincial museums. I concluded, 'I believe the charges will bring about an important change of attitude among museum directors. It will strengthen the Paymaster General's arm with the Treasury, and I am confident that arrangements for students, old-age pensioners ... and so on, will be no problem whatsoever for those who have experience in this matter ... so they can easily be worked out. I believe that museums will emerge stronger both in body and soul.'

In the motoring world 1971 saw the historic nationalisation of Rolls-Royce and in the debate on the Purchase Bill – at second reading – I asked for 'some special consideration to be given to the car division' and sought assurances from the Government 'that the division will in no circumstances be allowed to go out of British control, and ... if necessary', the Government would agree to 'take up shares, such as they have done in British Petroleum'. I believed that this 'modest stake ... in what is a profitable concern will ensure its development and future expansion, an investment which this nation can afford'. Rolls-Royce should 'concentrate more on cars and allow the aero-engine side to be developed in co-operation with European or US partners'. 'Above all,' I said, 'let us keep the Flying Lady, the famous mascot, because she has carried the prestige of Rolls-Royce, and this country, for over 60 years.'

My political inclinations had drawn me to the Conservative side, but I was never hidebound and in some important respects I was decidedly left of centre. Before my enforced departure from the House I had taken the Conservative whip, but during these early years after my return I sat on the cross benches. This was partly because I still harboured resentment against those bigots in the Tory Establishment who had connived at my downfall. I found it hard to sit in the same side of the House as such men as Sir David Maxwell Fyfe, who had been elevated to the peerage as Lord Kilmuir and later became Lord Chancellor, and I just could not bring myself to be part of the same party. Incidentally, Kilmuir was married to the sister of the actor Rex Harrison. On one occasion, in Harrison's company, Kilmuir delivered a lengthy tirade against homosexuality in which he claimed that he was going to 'eradicate' it. Harrison's retort to this was, 'Next I hope you will cure the common cold.' In any case I relished the independence of the cross benches. It suited my temperament and, although after a few years I returned to the Conservative fold, I still retained much of the mind of an independent.

Only once did I help inflict a serious defeat on a Tory government. In 1972 the Labour peer, Lord Shackleton, and I joined forces to prevent my neighbouring town of Lymington being reallocated to Dorset under new local government reforms. The idea was an ill-considered piece of gerrymandering, hugely resented by the honest burghers of Lymington, whose town had been part of Hampshire for hundreds of years. I went into battle in no uncertain terms: 'Over the past two years I have been convinced that the Government have listened diligently to local views ... but, I believe that there is one serious exception. With great respect ... I feel the Government has not been altogether fair and responsible in the treatment of West Hampshire and particularly Lymington borough. I think it is my duty to ensure the Government are well aware of the intense distaste and anger which the people of Lymington feel.' The Government's plan ignored the recommendations of a recent Boundary Commission report. The people of Lymington were given 'three weeks' notice of their impending fate', without any fair explanation. I warned that

> unless some solution can be found to satisfy the people of Lymington I will, together with other Members of your Lordships' House, try to persuade your Lordships ... to accept an Amendment to keep Lymington in Hampshire. I am sure that the Government is anxious to be fair and just, but they must also be seen to be fair and just. Lymington ... is justified in feeling that it has been treated in a rather high-mannered way and subject to horse trading of a rather doubtful character. The Government should at some stage ... recognise that the people of Lymington are trying to use lawful democratic means of persuasion.

I am proud to say we won the day, after a rough, tough tug-of-war with Lord Sandford, a junior Environment Minister, and the concession was in the Report on the Local Government Bill (1972). This result was much appreciated then, as it is today, Lymington remaining proudly part of Hampshire.

Apart from motoring, such interventions in local policies were rare and, in fact, it was not for another eight years that I spoke again on a local issue. Even that was to do with roads: the completion of the M3 and M27 motorway and the A33 Hockley crossroad improvements (1980). Occasionally I took the opportunity to speak on broadcasting matters, another pet subject of mine. Ten years earlier, in the debate on the Pilkington Report, I relished the thought of commercial radio, but in the 1972 debate on the Sound Broadcasting Bill I conceded my position had changed and 'although I was in favour of commercial television (1962), I

felt that the BBC were doing such a wonderful job ... that the introduction of commercial radio would have been a mistake ... but with
considerable heart-searching, I think it is now right to support this Bill
... as there has been such a dramatic change in the role of sound broadcasting'. By 1972 television had taken a major part in most people's daily
lives, providing entertainment, education, news and information, combined with the success of many 'pirate' stations, such as Radio Caroline,
which supplied a broader base of popular music. The time had come to
open up the BBC monopoly. Government plans were to allot about sixty
regional stations and at the time I was involved in a consortium that was
considering bidding for one of these areas. Unfortunately we were not
successful.

My time in public relations, as well as my experiences in the USA,
had given me some useful insights, not shared by all peers, into the
popular development of television and radio. I used to meet regularly
with such luminaries as Lord Bessborough, Norman Collins and Brian
Tesler, all of them key figures in the founding of Independent
Television. Over lunch we planned the campaign to introduce commercial independent television and radio to the country and prepare
both politicians and the public to accept it. By the time ITV was
launched I was not in a position to take advantage of this new
commercial medium.

I also spoke on subjects more peripheral to my central interests: for
instance, on Uganda several times during the Sixties and Seventies. It was
a country I knew quite well, my knowledge and my sympathy stemming
from my friendship with Freddie, the Kabaka of Buganda, who had been
a fellow officer in the Grenadiers. When his children were at school in
England my wife and I helped look after them. I was also chairman, with
David Steel, later the leader of the Liberal party, of a Ugandan friendship
society and with others helped support the Kabaka when he was in exile
here, having fled Uganda, before he was mysteriously found dead in
London. His son, the present Kabaka, has started a charitable trust, known
as the Kabaka Foundation, of which I am a trustee. I also took an interest
in the feasibility of building a Channel tunnel in 1971, a subject that my
father had written about a week before he died in 1929 and on which a
report was due in the following year, 1972. I was concerned with the effects
a tunnel would have on the current ferry services and whether the idea
of such a journey by train would be popular, but a few years later, in 1975,

I questioned the Government on the possibility of seeking Common Market funding, since the tunnel would be of great financial benefit to cross-border trade.

As president of the Disabled Drivers' Motor Club, in 1974 I raised a number of related issues in the House, such as the provision of disabled parking spaces in the new traffic-free precincts of cities and, more notably, the mobility of the physically disabled and the safety of the Model 70 Invalid Tricycle, following a commercially censored report by the Motor Industry Research Association (1975). Given that there had been some 283 turnover accidents in 1973–4, I was dismayed to find that the Government considered them to be cheaper and safer, when 'driven with proper regard for their limitations and special characteristics ... bearing in mind that it is a tricycle and not a car'. In the end Lord Sandford bowed out of answering my further questions, but out of these discussions and the work of Baroness Sharp and the former racing driver Graham Hill, in 1975–6 the Mobility Scheme, and later the orange badge parking permit scheme, was established. The Mobility Scheme allows disabled drivers and passengers to purchase a vehicle with the Mobility portion of their Disability Living Allowance benefit. Over the years this scheme has expanded the range of vehicles to make it more accessible and today, in 2000, Motability Finance is one of the largest fleet vehicles purchasers in the world, providing much-needed and appreciated transport and independence to a vast number of disabled people and their carers.

In all, my non-motoring speeches only amounted to less than a quarter of the total during these years. However, I was beginning to flex my muscles in the areas of the Arts, museums and heritage. As I reminded their Lordships in 1967, I had already founded three museums, so these were subjects I could profess to know pretty well. I had also learned lessons at Beaulieu that I believed had a national relevance and I felt I had a duty to share this experience in the general interest. I was gratified when, in replying to a speech of mine about historic houses in 1968, Lord Kennet, then a junior minister in Housing and Local Government, commented that I had said 'many constructive things which the Government will study at leisure, and take into account and consider'. This was heady stuff. It was one thing to speak and another to be heeded. Kennet's mother, Lady Young, the widow of Captain Scott of the Antarctic, had a cottage on the Beaulieu estate before the war. His half-brother Peter

Scott spent time there and some of his famous wildfowl pictures were painted by the marshes at Beaulieu, and during the war he captained an MTB under the command of my stepfather Ned.

Towards the end of the Seventies I raised an issue that would have far-reaching benefits for many seriously ill people in need of transplant operations. On 8 March 1978 I asked the Government to consider a scheme whereby driving licences could be marked to indicate the holder's consent for the donation of vital organs, upon their death, to hospitals for transplant. Unfortunately, this pioneering life-saving suggestion was not treated with the seriousness it deserved, as during the discussions in the House there were a few flippant remarks from my fellow peers. It seemed a great pity that this attempt to retrieve something good from the tragedy of a serious car accident was to become bogged down by bureaucratic considerations. At the time it was thought that the idea of sending out a donor card with new licences would give the wrong impression – 'driving is dangerous; all drivers will get killed; please give away your kidneys'. It was not until the cause was publicised by Esther Rantzen on her BBC programme *That's Life* that the voluntary carrying of a donor card became publicly acceptable.

As the Seventies closed a new era in the political history of our island began and the Conservatives came to power with Mrs Thatcher at the helm. Before the change of government in 1979 I supported an amendment to the Ancient Monuments and Archaeological Areas Bill to make the possession and use of metal detectors by private individuals, trespassing on land of historical and archaeological interest, a new criminal offence. There was 'great concern felt by museums that many archaeological objects are being found, not reported and ... sold abroad'. Later that year, under the new administration, I initiated a debate on the Drew Report on Museums and Galleries: a report on the implementation of recommendations made in the Wright Report of 1973. The previous government had set up a working party, chaired by Sir Arthur Drew and, needless to say, this was a 'typically British political manoeuvre' to cloud the recommendations of a report which were 'politically or financially embarrassing or inopportune'. Twenty-two of the thirty-nine recommendations could be implemented without 'any new money' and 'I believe it is the Government's duty to encourage ... seek ... and support ways to implement these no-cost recommendations'. It was an opportune time to introduce a new, enterprising way of thinking towards our heritage, and I was keen to test the waters and the commitment of the Tory Government.

The 1980s were by no means any quieter and with my ever-increasing workload my principal preoccupations outside the House – the heritage and motoring – were naturally reflected in my speeches. Consequently the emphasis shifted from the latter to the former so that, for instance, the questions I raised on museums and galleries funding, and VAT concessions on repairs and maintenance of historic buildings (1984), the protection of Stonehenge and the White Horse at Westbury (1985), the gale damage as a result of the October 1987 storms and the fate of the Mappa Mundi (1988), were all English Heritage or tourism related. As were my contributions to the debates on the tourist industry and its contribution to the country's economy (1986), job creation and tourism policy (1983) and the tourist industry and government relations (1988). It was during the last speech that I found myself in the curious position of congratulating my ex-brother-in-law, Earl of Lindsay, on his maiden speech.

In 1987 I supported the Lyndhurst Bypass Bill that was passed at all stages, only to be killed off in the Commons. On that occasion, in February 1987, a bill had been introduced by Lord Boyd-Carpenter, which I supported, but I also pointed out the views of the Verderers of the Forest, a body that my father and grandfather had been members of, and local people alike. Amazingly, this much-needed bypass, started some fifty years ago in 1938, has still to be built and the congestion grows daily. This was not the first rejection, as two years later I attempted to introduce a bill to authorise the building of a rapid transit road for Southampton (1989). This failed, despite the support of Southampton City Council and Hampshire County Council.

There were at least two occasions I can recall, both in 1988, when the Government spokesperson won 'the serve', one being during a question raised by Lord Gridley on the preservation of the old-style red telephone kiosks. I rose to congratulate the Minister on 'the efficiency with which the English Heritage's listing recommendations had been handled by his department [the DoE]' and I was interrupted by mutterings of 'Hear! Hear!' as I was questioning whether he was aware of the contribution of English Heritage in carrying out this listing. The Minister, Lord Caithness, replied, 'I am grateful to my noble friend, and I am sure that the whole House is grateful to him for the work that he has done with English

Heritage in recommending the listing of . . . these boxes!' The second time was later on that year, at the end of a question raised by Lord Sudeley concerning the designation of the sites of Shakespeare's Globe and Rose theatres in Bermondsey as areas of international importance. 'My Lords, is my noble friend aware that in 16th century London that area was better known for its brothels than its theatres?'

Lord Hesketh replied, 'I am very grateful to my noble friend for his ability, yet again, to provide me with an extension to my limited knowledge of 16th century London!' ... Despite this, I had taken a serious interest in the project to preserve and rebuild replicas of these theatres, and with other contributors we donated oak timbers from the Beaulieu estate for the new Globe Theatre and also a flagstone engraved in honour of Shakespeare's patron (and my ancestor) the third Earl of Southampton.

I had not entirely forsaken my motoring interests, however, and during the 1980s and 1990s I spoke on a variety of related issues, such as the control of spray from lorries, and of motorcycle noise (1982 and 1985 respectively), orange badge regulations (1983), motorcycle noise (1985), the clamping of emergency vehicles (1991), the misuse of wheel-clamps on private land (1992) and the increasing problem of car theft (1993). I was particularly concerned with the parking problems and traffic congestion in London, and the consequences of the abolition of leaded petrol for vintage vehicles, issues I had raised periodically since they were first discussed in the 1950s and 1983 respectively. On the latter subject I introduced a debate in 1998, as the general sale of leaded petrol was to cease on 1 January 2000, leaving over 700,000 owners of pre-1980 vehicles with expensive technical conversion costs. British motorists, 'beguiled by a teaser advertising campaign featuring a '20s flapper girl over the headline "Ethyl is coming to give you a thrill"', had been using leaded petrol since 1928. Since the European Union Environment Council had agreed, a year earlier, that leaded petrol was to be subsequently banned, 'poor old Ethyl had been branded a scarlet woman for containing the dreaded poison – lead'. It was eventually agreed upon that 4-star leaded petrol would be available from limited licensed sources, and the following year, accepting the inevitable, I set about quizzing the Government on its provision and the quality of additives in the replacement lead-free petrol. The transition period to unleaded petrol went well but I am glad to say that, as a result of my efforts, the Government have given permission for a good number of garages still to sell leaded petrol to those who need it, particularly for vintage vehicles. In 1999 I asked, not for the first time, about the Government's plans for the eastern end of the M40 at Acton. The Minister, Lord Whitty, told me, very unsatisfactorily, 'I cannot comfort the noble Lord.'

Although my own contributions conformed to a pattern which had been more or less established in the Sixties and Seventies, the composition of the House changed out of all recognition. Some hereditary peers followed the example of Tony Benn – a New College contemporary – who did not wish to inherit his father's title of Lord Stansgate, as he wanted to remain an MP. He renounced his title after challenging the Government in a series of by-elections, which subsequently led to legislation enabling peers to renounce their titles and also to the creation of life peers. Such behaviour was not confined to the Labour party and the best-known example of a Conservative renunciation was that of the fourteenth Earl of Home, Sir Alec, in order to become Prime Minister.

In November 1998 I sat among my fellow peers at the opening of Parliament and heard the Queen announce from the throne the proposed legislation for the next session. This included, not greatly to our surprise, the abolition of the right of hereditary peers to sit in the House of Lords. The Conservative peers sat stoically quiet, but we were all shocked at the 'Hear! Hear!' from some Labour peers. This must have been the first interruption to a royal speech in the House for centuries.

As 1999 progressed and the Bill wound its weary way through the Commons and the Lords, many peers could not bring themselves to believe that it was really going to become law. It dramatically altered the United Kingdom's political constitution and yet outside the House hardly anyone seemed to notice or even care.

A certain unreality pervaded the debate and, of course, one of the main objections, not only from peers but from many outside the House, was that by insisting on abolishing the hereditary element the Government not only unilaterally changed the constitution but utterly failed to provide any thought-out or discussed agreed replacement. This still seems to many of us to be grossly irresponsible and we could not see why the Government could not wait for the Royal Commission's report on the format and powers for a Second Chamber, before abolishing the rights of hereditary peers to sit in the House. Those of us who opposed the manner of the reforms were all unfairly categorised as reactionaries, opposed to all change and reform.

Defeated we were and the House of Lords has already been reformed. Many newly created peers have taken their seats and the institution I have known for over fifty years has changed radically. Some of the more traditional formalities and rituals have been discarded. I welcome a number of these changes. When the Bill received its second reading on 29 March 1999 I reacted with vehemence and conviction, not because I was defending the House of 1948 but the House of the 1990s.

One is always hearing criticisms of the House as being unchanging and unrepresentative, right-wing dominated and hostile to any radical decisions, and when we do defeat governments, we are blamed or praised depending on who is in power. But I should like to point out, as one who has served for over 50 years, that 'unchanging' the House of Lords is certainly not. Since 1947 I have witnessed that small traditional House of the 1940s welcome life Peers, women Peers, trade union Peers, Peers of the Commonwealth origin, showbiz Peers and celebrity Peers. I submit that when its history is written it will conclude that the House has never been better composed or offered more comprehensive expertise or conducted better informed debates than it does today. I doubt it will ever be better, regardless of the Royal Commission – that is, if the Government accepts its recommendations.

All this I honestly believe and I am immeasurably saddened not so much by the House of Lords reform as by the abolition of the hereditary principle. I do not subscribe to an all-hereditary House, but I do defend maintaining a hereditary element, which over the centuries has served the nation effectively. I find very disturbing the vindictiveness with which we were treated. Fair enough, take away the voting rights for hereditary peers if need be, but why deny us the right at least to speak during our lifetime? It has all been so petty and mean-minded: barred like disgraced sportsmen.

I am proud of my record in the House of Lords, of my father's and of the generations from other families who have admirably fulfilled their duty there. I wish that my son could succeed me and carry on what is in every sense a noble tradition.

Mr Blair and his increasingly autocratic New Labour could not wait until the beginning of 2000 for the Commission's recommendations. In June 1999, however, the general debate was dramatically interrupted and changed by the negotiations carried on by Lord Cranborne, leader of the Opposition peers, Lord Weatherill and Lord Marsh with the Prime Minister. These shortly produced a temporary compromise suggestion that ninety-two hereditary peers could remain to assist in the better functioning of the House. This would not only preserve the role and dignity of the Earl Marshal and the Lord Great Chamberlain, but also open the way for the chairmen of committees to continue, all of whom were highly experienced in House procedures and were hereditary peers.

The large majority of Conservative peers accepted this compromise, worked out by three cross-bench peers: Lord Weatherill, past speaker of the House of Commons, Lord Carnarvon, who had great experience in countryside and local government matters, and Lord Marsh, a past Labour Cabinet minister. Unfortunately Lord Cranbourne, for his pains, was unsuccessful in earning the support of the Shadow Cabinet and consequently was sacked by William Hague for apparently exceeding his brief.

Nevertheless, the so-called 'Weatherill' amendment was carried in the Lords, but the Bill did not return to the Commons until the end of the session in early November 1999. In the meantime procedures were set up for every party represented in the House to elect a specific number of hereditary peers according to the strength of each in the House. For example, the hereditary Conservative peers were able to elect forty-two from their ranks to attend the new House of Lords.

I decided that I would throw my hat into the ring but, if elected, I knew it might only be a temporary stay of sentence. In my closing paragraphs of that dismal second reading debate, I said: 'So the final chapters are being written, sadly, without any formal recognition of past work – just "good" old class hatred. How sad, how undignified, and how typical. Naturally I am confident that my fellow Peers will work to the end, when I suppose we will be expected to fold our tents and silently steal away. Perhaps some of us may be a greater nuisance outside the House than we are today. Only time will tell.'

Those peers who wished to contest the election were allowed to produce a seventy-five-word manifesto. Mine read as follows:

Since joining the House aged 21, I have devoted my speeches and Parliamentary questions to issues such as tourism, museums, historic buildings, conservation, motoring, roads and transport, the Historic

Vehicle Movement and the New Forest. If elected, I would strive to contribute my expertise when these subjects are raised. I fear many peers who normally speak on these subjects may be absent. I live in Central London and would be a regular attender.

When we all returned to Parliament in the October 1999, for the last session of the old-style House, the tension was visibly growing. Not knowing whether or not I was going to be elected, and having served the House for fifty-two years, I decided at least to have a last word before I was abolished. By an ironic accidental twist of history I was able to ask a question on the New Forest, thus echoing one of the first speeches I made in 1948. I also spoke in the debate on 4 November, prompted by a question raised by Lord Swinfen on tourism for the disabled, two special interests that I have campaigned for during my time in the House. Unrelentingly, I opened my speech with: 'My Lords, I have spoken in the House on tourism many times in the past five decades. Perhaps I may be forgiven for not declaring my interest. This may well be my swansong, or my dying swansong; I do not know which.'

The New Forest question was listened to by the biggest collection of peers I have ever addressed, as it had been scheduled just before the third reading of the House of Lords Bill and hence there was standing room only.

In the meantime meetings were held to explain to peers the procedures of the vote – mainly to place forty-two peers in order from one to forty-two. The voting was to be held on 3 and 4 November. Since we were all working from an alphabetical list I rather suspected that peers whose names began with 'A' or 'B' would do rather better than those at the bottom of the list in the 'W's.

The result was announced – yet another historic irony – on Guy Fawkes Day. New Labour had managed to do what the Gunpowder Plotters had failed to achieve exactly 394 years before and on 5 November 1999 the results of the election for hereditary peers were read out in the Chamber. This left the House with only ninety-one hereditary peers, removing at a stroke over 500 of them. How Guy Fawkes and his co-conspirators would have revelled in such a triumph!

I decided to watch the results on television at Beaulieu, principally because ITN wished to film my reaction to the news. Consequently, soon after one o'clock I sat down in front of the television set with a camera trained on me as I waited anxiously. In fact, I learned the results before they were due to be displayed on television. Suddenly the ITN reporter came rushing up to me waving a pager in his hand flashing 'Montagu – elected'. At first I thought he was playing a joke on me, but fortunately it turned out to be true and naturally I was delighted to come twenty-seventh out of forty-two.

However, honoured as I was, I felt extremely sorry for all my good friends and colleagues whose dedication and expertise in the House will be sorely missed. The day was further sadly and dramatically complicated when soon after the announcements my good friend and namesake, the newly appointed Labour peer Lord Montague of Oxford, a past chairman of the English Tourist Board, collapsed and died in the Chamber soon after completing a speech. This was announced on the news simply as 'Lord Montague has died', without mention of Beaulieu or Oxford. I think I can modestly claim that I was a better known 'Lord Montagu' than my friend Michael. So the next twenty-four hours caused me great embarrassment explaining that I was still alive – much to the relief of my staff and colleagues – and hopefully my friends and family.

I naturally feel very honoured and privileged that my fellow peers – after all 'peer' means equal – chose me as one of the forty-two. Such is the Government's dithering ineptitude that the length of my parliamentary survival remains a mystery. However, as long as I am allowed to continue serving the country in this newly constituted House I will strive to live up to my manifesto and continue to do my best to represent so many minorities who rarely have the opportunity to have their views expressed or considered by Parliament. Since then, I have continued to speak on heritage, conservation, tourism and motoring-related issues.

I must confess that now, as I go back to the House of Lords, in some senses it is as though I have never left it and I am sometimes overwhelmed by how fortunate I am to have been elected and what a gap would be left in my life if I was no longer a member of the House. I know it has been an agonising wrench for many of my tradition. I have always enjoyed looking up to the windows in the Chamber and seeing my family crest and pointing out to visitors my grandfather and myself in various oil paintings of the House in session. Indeed, for the most recent portrait of the House, painted by Andrew Festing, I was amazed and flattered to find myself depicted on my feet making a speech. When preparing this book I had bound together all my speeches since 1948 and was quite stunned by just how many interventions I have made over the years and on what an enormous variety of subjects. I feel it is very sad that my son, Ralph, will not one day be able to carry on the centuries-old tradition of unpaid service – a service commanding a sense of duty, rather than any other benefit.

In January 2000 we all anxiously waited for the Wakeham Report, produced in a parliamentary record time of a year by a committee representing a diverse range of political opinions. It suggested that at least part of the new House should be elected and an effort be made to equate the party balance of the Commons with that of the Lords – surely an impossible policy to achieve. Many in the Labour party and even some in other parties are deeply apprehensive of creating a Second Chamber which could challenge the will of the Commons. In my opinion the Constitution desperately needs a powerful Second Chamber, as we do not have either a written constitution or a Supreme Court to scrutinise and interpret it. Time will tell what will evolve from the Wakeham Report and how long it will be before the government of the day seeks to legislate for the new Chamber. In the meantime, although the Conservative team inevitably will be smaller, I have every confidence it will be as effective and as well-led an Opposition as ever. But alas for them and others, the future remains uncertain and a great historic institution has passed into history.

16

From Stonehenge to Hetty Pegler's Tump

Fair is our lot and goodly is our heritage.
'A Song of England'

My lifelong interest in the heritage and my experience in transforming Beaulieu into an important British tourist attraction was rewarded in 1983 when I was appointed the first chairman of a brand-new government organisation, the Historic Buildings and Monuments Commission for England, more popularly known as English Heritage. This brought together many of my life's enthusiasms and gave me an unprecedented opportunity to make a lasting contribution to national life. I was surprised and delighted.

In 1978 I handed over to George Howard after five years as president of the Historic Houses Association. At my farewell dinner in the House of Lords I sat between the two most powerful ladies in the historic buildings world: Dame Jennifer Jenkins, chairman of the Historic Buildings Council, and Alma, Lady Birk, the Labour Government's front-bench spokesman on heritage matters in the House of Lords. They told me they had been very impressed with the way I had helped create the HHA and asked me to chair a committee to produce a report, to be commissioned by the British Tourist Authority and the Historic Buildings Council, on the alternative uses of historic buildings and to formulate a policy for their future use.

This was a challenge I had no problem accepting and I duly gathered around me an excellent team of experts, took evidence from a wide range of people and reported in 1980. We urged planning authorities to be much more flexible in encouraging alternative uses of our historic building stock, as we recognised that although the original purpose for which the houses were built was normally residential, when such use was no longer viable, unless they were used in some other way, they were bound to deteriorate. We also urged the Government to carry out a complete review of 'listed' buildings. The then Secretary of State for the Environment, Michael Heseltine, readily agreed to speed up listing and soon produced his own white paper, called 'The Way Forward', in which he envisaged new legislation covering heritage matters which would enable the drive and enterprise of the private sector to be brought to the work of the Department's Ancient Monuments and Historic Buildings Directorate.

In 1982 a Bill was introduced into Parliament which eventually became the National Heritage Act of 1983. While it was in the Lords I was active in speaking in its debates and taking part in the committee stages. On the second reading of the Bill in November 1982 I congratulated the Government on its bold approach, but warned, 'All will fail unless historic buildings are promoted, presented, interpreted and used educationally in the correct way.' I went on to say,

> To succeed, the most modern methods of marketing must be used in order to realise the full potential in co-operation with the tourist authorities and local authorities. It is in the interest of all those concerned with the heritage to make quite sure that this Commission works. Above all, let us remember the interests of the future generations of this country and of many people all over the world. It is for their benefit that museums, historic sites, buildings and gardens must have sufficient resources and should be administered and preserved with imagination, dedication and skill – qualities which we as a nation claim to have pride in possessing.

At the end of all the debates, on third reading, I wished the new commission well and said,

> I am sure it will make a major contribution, and indeed a great impact, on the quality of our heritage, particularly as presented and made available not only to our people but to the world at large. But it must have the right authority and the right resources to do it. That is something which we in this House will make sure of and see that it happens. Our heritage is one of our great assets. We have no sunshine to sell. So far as the private sector is concerned, that has been showing the pioneering spirit of what people in the 20th century really want to see in the heritage. I welcome the fact that the new commission will

combine the expertise of both the private and public sectors to the benefit of all.

The Bill was one of the last to receive Royal Assent in 1984 and just squeezed in before the general election that May.

Knowing that the new Commission would assume its powers in April 1984, everyone was on tenterhooks as to who would be its chairman. The general assumption was that it would be Dame Jennifer Jenkins who had chaired the Historic Buildings Council for several years and it was assumed that she would simply move across to the new body. However, the then Secretary of State for the Environment, Patrick Jenkin MP, was keen on a new approach. In particular, he wanted to encourage a new entrepreneurial spirit in the management of our historic buildings and sites, and to get away from the idea that our heritage had to be permanently dependent on subsidy from the taxpayer.

I hoped I might be lucky enough to become one of the commissioners, but never seriously expected the top job. I was therefore extremely surprised, but very pleased, to receive a letter from Patrick inviting me to become chairman. Unfortunately the letter to Jennifer Jenkins telling her that she was not getting the job went to her London address and she was in the country. I therefore had the embarrassing task of telling her what had happened and went specially to see her in Oxford to discuss the whole business. She was very gracious to me about it, but I understand she was furious with the Department and poor Patrick had a difficult time explaining what had happened.

Years later, Patrick told me that he had asked his department to make suggestions of possible names for the role of chairman, but realised that politically it was impossible to appoint the wife of Roy Jenkins, the Leader of one of the opposition parties, to such a job. The other candidates seemed to him to lack the necessary experience or energy, so he asked his officials to look at those who had been active in the House of Lords during the debates on the Bill and see if they could suggest someone who might be suitable. It was reported at the time that Mrs Thatcher's preferred choice was HRH The Duke of Gloucester, an architect and also the author of an interesting book on London statues. However, Buckingham Palace was against this as it was felt that too much political involvement was inevitable.

The powers that be evidently liked my speeches in the House of Lords and I was duly appointed. I heard that Mrs Thatcher remarked to a mutual friend, 'Why don't they give it to Edward Montagu? He is energetic enough.' As the world knows, the Iron Lady was used to getting her way and English Heritage came into being officially on 1 April 1984 with myself at its head. I suppose they could have chosen a more auspicious date. There was also a certain irony in the choice of location for the launch, which was the Banqueting House in Whitehall. This had been specifically withheld from English Heritage and retained by the Department of the Environment on the grounds that it was a royal palace.

Apart from the Banqueting House party, at which I presented the Secretary of State, Patrick Jenkin, with membership card number one, there was also a reception given by Margaret Thatcher at 10 Downing Street, attended by all the great and good from the heritage world, and I hosted a dinner at the House of Lords. We were not only celebrating the beginning of a new organisation, but the successful winding up of an old one. A smooth transition was essential, while at the same time ensuring that the new organisation had a totally different impetus, direction and identity. Throughout the transitional period the Directorate of Ancient Monuments and Historic Buildings, which was part of the Department of the Environment, retained full responsibility for everything that my new agency was about to inherit.

A nucleus of commissioners was appointed to the new body. This team included Jennifer Jenkins, who gallantly agreed to support me; Sir Arthur Drew, chairman of the Ancient Monuments Board, a wise owl who was a former Permanent Secretary; and the Duke of Gloucester. One of our first tasks was to appoint a chief executive, before getting on with the business of planning the winding up of the old organisation and the creation of the new. Headhunters were appointed to assist the commissioners and myself in the selection of the chief executive. Some assumed that the post would be filled by someone from the private sector, but we chose to appoint Peter Rumble, a senior civil servant, then the director of the Ancient Monuments and Historic Buildings Directorate, and were given appropriate approval by the Secretary of State. As a civil servant, Peter already knew the ropes of central government and his appointment was likely to be more acceptable to the many civil servants on whose secondment we were going to be dependent in the first two years. It would also give the staff a sense of confidence and continuity. In the event, Peter continued as chief executive until retiring aged sixty in

1989. He was succeeded by the energetic Jennie Page, who built brilliantly on the sound foundations Peter laid.

There was a lot of suspicion about the Government's real aims in establishing our new commission (a fear of privatisation and the consequent loss of jobs) although the DoE retained ultimate responsibility for the bulk of the work we were to inherit. The six months from October 1983 to April 1984 were ones of intense activity and the embryo English Heritage, with a tiny staff, moved into the unloved offices of the Department of the Environment in Marsham Street, where the only attraction was a wonderful view from my temporary office on the seventeenth floor.

Five sub-committees were appointed, made up of members drawn from experts from all parts of the heritage world to advise us on the future and matters such as membership, conservation, education and trading policy. I was aided in the delicate task of creating a new organisation by a wide-ranging and enthusiastic team of commissioners which now included not only Jennifer Jenkins, Arthur Drew and the Duke of Gloucester, but Lord Shelburne who was the current president of the Historic Houses Association, Donald Insall the conservation architect, Professor Rosemary Cramp, Professor Colin Renfrew (now Lord Renfrew), Councillor Jeremy Beecham, a powerful figure in both the Local Authorities Association and the Labour party, the late Jeremy Benson who, as an expert on the heritage and taxation, did so much to advise when the Heritage Bill went through Parliament, Peter Burnham, Howard Colvin the architectural historian, Anthony Emery, a director of Reed Publishing, Simon Jenkins, later editor of *The Times*, and Professor William Whitfield the architect and later on, the archaeologist Barry Cunliffe and later Alexander Chancellor the journalist.

The first two working parties dealt with archaeology and ancient monuments and with historical buildings, while the others were involved with marketing and trading, presentation, interpretation and education, all topics on which the Department was glaringly weak. Along with organisational issues, they were matters that I had particular concern for. Peter and his team concentrated on staffing and finance issues. As chairman I always tried to operate on the basis of an agreed consensus, with as few formal votes as possible. This was in marked contrast to the confrontational style adopted by my successor Jocelyn Stevens, but it seemed not only civilised but effective.

In fact, we only ever had one vote in my entire reign and this concerned our title. It had been decided that we were to be called the Historic Buildings and Monuments Commission for England or HBMC(E) for short. This thrillingly catchy title had been devised by the Civil Service and ratified by Parliament – a classic example of *Yes, Minister* in real life. As one of my main briefs was to promote a more vibrant image for what was essentially a handover by the Directorate of Ancient Monuments and Historic Buildings, the designation HBMC(E) was not exactly the start for which I was looking. Although my fellow commissioners agreed readily that we should appoint a design consultancy to create a suitable logo, I had more of a problem over the name. Some of my colleagues gave the impression that they were nervous of being dragged into a world of brash commercialism and catchy populism. I put it to the vote, which mercifully I won quite easily. Thus we became popularly known as English Heritage. Had I been obliged to settle for HBMC(E) we would have been doomed before we began, but English Heritage had a good ring to it and Dick Negus, the designer, came up with a stylish portcullis-type logo which has successfully entered the country's visual vocabulary.

We inherited about four hundred properties and they were an extremely mixed bunch. At the top end came such priceless, if sometimes unpolished, jewels as Stonehenge, Dover Castle, Audley End, Rievaulx Abbey and others capable of attracting hundreds of thousands of visitors. At the other extreme were a ragbag of charming but tiny and sometimes remote monuments, which could never attract significant numbers of visitors and where, indeed, it was not practical to charge an admission fee. These included such oddities as Hetty Pegler's Tump in Gloucestershire, the ruins of Houghton House in Bedfordshire and the de Grey Mausoleum attached to Flitton church in Bedfordshire. A considerable 'mid-list' lay between these two extremes.

All the properties had in common was that they had been judged by the Secretary of State, advised by his department's inspectors, to be, by virtue of public interest, of national archaeological or historic importance. Some of these places had belonged to the government estate, often as part of the defence system. Others had been transferred from private ownership, in which case they were governed by any number of conditions. In almost every case owners had negotiated guardianship deeds under which they retained all sorts of rights, just as the generous donors of the National Trust do. Unfortunately some owners, having spent no money on maintenance for ages, still claimed the entitlement to sell their own brochures or picture postcards on site. This sort of thing was a frustrating restriction when I was trying to impose a coherent unity and image on our new organisation.

Most of the properties had been quite well maintained, although there were some, such as Lulworth Castle in Dorset and Sutton Scarsdale in Derbyshire, which were on the verge of total collapse. Ineffective attempts at restoration coupled with bureaucratic delays and follies had often dragged on for years.

Presentation and marketing were virtually non-existent. The marketing and public relations team was bravely headed for some years by Brian Baylis, who operated as a one-man band. He did his best, not only for the government properties but also to co-operate with the National Trust and private sector. Because of the lack of resources, however, hardly any properties had on-site exhibitions and such guidebooks as existed were dry as dust, academically sound but of little general interest; or unattractive, and sometimes incomprehensible, to the general public. It was patently obvious that the previous regime had regarded such matters as an irrelevance. My thirty years of producing guidebooks for Beaulieu meant I knew what I was talking about.

Personnel could have presented a problem. There was no compulsion on anyone from the previous organisation to join our fledgling ranks and if they did, such recruits were given the right to return to the Civil Service after two years if they were dissatisfied. I need not have worried for I found that many of the old guard were eager to continue in the service of conservation. I inherited a considerable *esprit de corps*, expertise and enthusiasm, which could, I believe, be traced all the way back to the great General Pitt-Rivers, who had become the very first inspector of Ancient Monuments in 1882.

Less satisfactory was the administrative structure, which seemed calculated to produce a condition of chronic inertia. The administrators, who held the purse strings, the inspectors, who did the academic work, and the works staff, who actually looked after the day-to-day running of the properties, sometimes seemed only to have the power of preventing their colleagues from actually doing anything. This was exercised with gusto.

Conservation policy was a much less depressing area. Well-oiled Whitehall bureaucracy had produced a Rolls-Royce structure in response to the demands of the conservation world as a whole. The system of grants to private owners, first recommended by the Gowers Report in 1953, was well established. They were distributed by government almost always on the recommendation of the Historic Buildings Council whose expert membership under a series of excellent and dedicated chairmen nearly always ensured ministerial agreement. It is generally acknowledged as having preserved many important buildings, while the more recent system of financial support for conservation areas within historic towns was well received. The wholesale revision of historic building lists, initiated as a result of my previous report, was proceeding well and approaching the half-million mark. Protected monuments, however, only amounted to about 12,500. As there were an estimated 600,000 monuments in England, this was clearly unsatisfactory.

There was a widespread acceptance of the need for planning restrictions when historic buildings were involved and I use the word 'widespread' advisedly. Whenever one of my friends or acquaintances wanted to carry out work on a listed building they invariably complained to me that English Heritage staff were totally unreasonable, obstinate and elitist. Naturally there was not enough money – there never is. However, I was concerned, as were others, that an articulate owner who knew the ropes was often able to play the system and obtain grant money for a building which really did not need it, or which he or she could well afford to look after without aid.

Finally, I needed to cope with two statutory advisory committees, the Ancient Monuments Board and the Historic Buildings Council. In the old world these two organisations had advised the minister, but now they advised me and my fellow commissioners and we, in turn, advised the minister. This change, along with a concomitant change of title – the Board and the Council both became advisory committees – was a source of grief to a number of stalwarts. Our executive powers were severely limited – we could not, for instance, list a building or schedule a monument ourselves. In practice, therefore, our creation had simply produced a new tier of bureaucracy and some of the committee members felt, understandably, downgraded. The chairpersons of these two committees, Arthur Drew and Jennifer Jenkins, were both commissioners themselves and worked valiantly to establish sensible rules for their committees. But it was not entirely satisfactory.

In certain areas we had to start organising from scratch. Under the old arrangement finance and personnel were dealt with by the Department of the Environment, but now we had to do it ourselves and there were all sort of difficulties. As an example: if there was an underspend at the DoE, they could always allocate it to another of their large number of divisions. We were too small for this, so if there was any financial surplus at the end of March it was lost for ever. There was nowhere else for it to be allocated. Inevitably there were also problems with new technology, and one month early on the computers went completely awry and there was minor chaos in salary payments.

To deal with this I needed staff who were also skilled in management, whether or not they were committed to the cause of conservation. At first this was not easy, because the professional civil servants were sceptical. I held two mass staff meetings, and special ones with the two trades unions, to explain my mission and my vision. The atmosphere was depressingly sceptical, as some people felt the whole initiative was just a way of shedding jobs; others believed that I was about to bring in a crassly commercial expansionist approach that ran contrary to all their traditional practices. To my surprise many people held both views at the same time. It was hard work, but in the end the inspectorate proved loyal to their beliefs, such was the reassuring presence and persuasion of Peter Rumble. For a new organisation such as English Heritage continuity was essential and it owes a great debt to Peter Rumble, who ensured that we got it. Only a negligible number of people decided not to take their chance with us. English Heritage was indeed fortunate to have Peter as its chief executive for the first five years, as he had many years' experience in heritage matters, having helped guide the original Heritage Bill through Parliament. He threw his full effort behind modernising the administration at English Heritage sites and recommended at an early stage that we should have management consultants in to report. The result was that we had a much more efficient organisation based upon inter-disciplinary groups rather than one based on officers all of the same discipline, which hampered communication and contributed to unacceptable delays. I shall never forget the picture of him in one of our first English Heritage T-shirts striding along Hadrian's Wall. For a senior civil servant that was indeed a new look!

Some of our improvements were immediate and simple. For instance, I insisted that each property should have a new sign at its entrance with the word 'welcome' prominent at the top. This had never been done before and visitors were often made to feel positively unwelcome, not least because the custodians who were supposed to do the welcoming were decked out in a uniform more appropriate for prison warders. One we met was so keen for change that he had made his own English Heritage tie with our logo marked in red biro. Needless to say, Peter gave him one of the few official ties, to *sotto voce* mutterings of 'Creep'. To ribald comments in the press, I asked Hardy Amies to design something more suitable. He came up with a much more comfortable style involving corduroys and woollen jumpers, appropriate for our predominantly rural sites. The relaxing effect was immediate and obvious, and I was delighted when the National Trust subsequently copied us.

The custodians who looked after the buildings and monuments, and who acted as the first line of contact with the public were, as one might expect, a highly individual band of people. Some had been soured by years of sitting in their grim little huts and had become so proprietorial about their monuments and the state of the grass they had to mow that they gave off strong negative vibes whenever a visitor came near them. Once they had been fitted into their new outfits (given their physical diversity, this was no easy task) their attitude nearly always softened. However, when I sent round a circular lifting the ban on their talking directly to the press about their monuments many custodians thought it was some sort of joke. But who better than they to speak on the subject?

They needed twentieth-century aids to do their job properly and this meant taking a hard look at our publications. The scholarly handbooks in their distinctive blue covers were much admired by our archaeologist commissioners, Rosemary Cramp and Colin Renfrew, and they were sought after by serious visitors. We therefore kept them in print, but with photographic covers, and augmented them with a comprehensive range of full-colour souvenir guides. Apart from a small booklet at Stonehenge, nothing of the sort had existed before.

Nearly everyone sold literature but most sites had little else to offer but pencils, India rubbers and bookmarks. After we appointed an experienced buyer the range was increased dramatically and while I was chairman many new shops were opened, especially at bigger attractions such as Dover Castle and Stonehenge, which started taking £5000 a day in the summer and making a significant contribution to our coffers. The new shops, as at Rievaulx Abbey and Lindisfarne Priory, were specifically designed to harmonise with their setting. So much for brashness and commercial vulgarity.

Obviously the smaller sites offered less scope, but I was determined that we should have no Cinderellas and that all must be given proper attention. We also began staging special events like battle re-enactments, archery and Roman parades, much to the irritation of the professional sceptics. They need not have worried: the historical re-enactment societies had as high a regard for accuracy and authenticity as the most punctilious inspectors. The Ermine Street Guard, for instance, turned out to be the acknowledged experts on the uniforms of the Roman army. Some events were re-enacted in their original settings – such as the Battle of Hastings at Battle and the Civil War siege of Goodrich Castle. On other occasions we played a little more fast and loose with the past. Part of the American Civil War took place at Audley End! I don't think it mattered too much as the monuments were humanised, and people enjoyed themselves and learned at the same time – all in keeping with the Beaulieu philosophy and for English Heritage bang on the right track.

In our first year the trading income was only £2.3 million. By 1991–2 it had risen to £9.8 million. As at Beaulieu, we were not just commercial and attached much importance to education. We increased the number of education officers from one to five and introduced custom-built education rooms wherever possible, sometimes with commercial backing. The education room at Dover Castle, for instance, was generously sponsored by American Express.

We also began staging exhibitions, the first of which was devoted to the life of the foot soldiers throughout the ages at the old barracks at Berwick-upon-Tweed. It was a marvellous exhibition, but the budget overran and a disgruntled employee made trouble by going to the *Daily Mirror* with the story and with other 'scandals' such as the gift of a River Tweed salmon, a traditional present to VIPs, to Princess Alice, who opened the exhibition. The salmon apparently exceeded the official small Civil Service limit on such gifts. I was not greatly bothered by this, but Peter Rumble was very exercised and devoted a lot of time to compiling a long rebuttal. Copies of this were lodged with the libraries in the House of Commons and the House of Lords, and the row subsided quickly.

*

The one which unfortunately never subsided, and still has not been completely resolved, was Stonehenge. There was some justice in this because Stonehenge, the most famous monument in the country, was and still is a national disgrace, shockingly presented in every sense, with dreadful traffic problems and a drab concrete visitors' centre separated from the main site by a glum subway that ran under the main road.

A few weeks after our foundation in May 1984 I commissioned a Stonehenge study group, chaired, very efficiently and competently, by our new head of secretariat, Francis Golding, with representatives of various local authorities, as well as the National Trust, the English Tourist Board and the Department of Transport. A few years previously a Stonehenge working party had attempted to solve the problem and failed dismally. I was determined that this should be different. After hurrying back from the funeral of my old friend, the film star Diana Dors, I chaired a press conference in Salisbury at which I said that I expected the group's report in six months.

To my satisfaction it came in on time, was endorsed by the Commission and published in January 1985. The chief recommendations were the closure of the main A344 where it passed Stonehenge, almost clipping the Heel Stone, and the erection of a brand-new visitors' centre at Larkhill just to the north of the monument and south of the Royal Artillery's training camp. Most people were in favour, but there was fierce opposition from some local people for whom closure of their main road would have been a minor nuisance. My fellow commissioners, Lord Shelburne, Colin Renfrew, and I had some rough receptions in very cold village halls that winter as we strove to present our case. The local opposition pointed out that there had been a right of way along what was now the A344 since Stonehenge itself was built. Our changes would mean a five-minute longer journey for most of them and I'm afraid the only answer we could give them was that their minor inconvenience would be to the great benefit of the majority. Understandably, they weren't convinced and the chairlady of the local Salisbury planning committee, a doughty fighter with an eye for public relations, threatened to lie down in the middle of the road. I offered to join her, but sadly the event never took place.

Despite previous interest in the issue by Michael Heseltine, then Secretary of State for Defence, opposition also came from the Ministry of Defence. They claimed that our proposals constituted a security risk and protested that they had not been consulted. Prolonged negotiations ensued, at which they always seemed to be represented by a succession of different generals. Unfortunately, in spite of promises, I was never able to get the Stonehenge question taken up at Cabinet level, with the consequence that we were repeatedly fobbed off by an ever-changing succession of junior ministers. Lord Strathclyde was actually visiting Stonehenge for the first time as Junior Minister for the Heritage when he received a telephone call in a nearby car appointing him to the Scottish Office. Indeed, there were few ministers to whom I did not show Stonehenge during my time in office. Jennie Page's dynamism produced some progress but the final solution even eluded the best efforts of my successor, Jocelyn Stevens.

The future now seems brighter, as the Government has approved the plans for diverting the traffic on the A303 by means of a tunnel, the building of a reception centre for the public some way away from Stonehenge and, of course, most important, the closure of the A344. Both Jocelyn and I swore we would resolve the situation during our time in office, but I doubt whether even his successor will be able to write 'finis' under this story.

Until then the way our most famous historic monument is presented remains a national disgrace.

Another intractable problem was that of the Greater London Council's Historic Buildings Division, which had looked after such London adornments as Kenwood on Hampstead Heath, Marble Hill House at Twickenham and Rangers Lodge, Blackheath. The handover to English Heritage was complicated by two factors. First, the break-up of the Labour-controlled GLC was widely regarded as a partisan political act by the Conservative Government and second, it was alleged that I, being an acknowledged Conservative, and my organisation were part of a conspiracy. This was quite untrue, but it was widely believed and was further complicated by the fact that the Historic Buildings Division had been well staffed, funded and admired for its work, and enjoyed considerable power, in comparison with English Heritage. The staff, and in particular their leader, Ashley Barker, were resentful and played the part of martyr with some success. It was resolved in time, but it was a stressful business for all of us. The London properties are still well run and presented, and have earned an ever-increasing reputation for the quality of their special exhibitions.

*

Where protection was concerned the position of ancient monuments was significantly worse than historic buildings, mainly because most of the historic buildings were championed by owners who actually lived inside them, whereas the ancient monuments were, by definition, empty. Urged on by our archaeological commissioners, Colin Renfrew, Rosemary Cramp and David Wilson, we instituted an accelerated Monuments Protection Programme to review all the nation's field monuments as soon as possible and to offer legal protection to an estimated 60,000 of them. I knew it would take longer than I expected or wished, but funds were limited and the inspectors seemed to take for ever establishing criteria for scheduling. However, by 1991–2 we were preparing to schedule annually well over 1000 recommendations, compared with the pitiful handfuls which had been the norm in the early Eighties.

Another minor triumph was in the field of 'rescue archaeology'. Very little work was carried out on virgin or unthreatened sites, but it had become common practice to allow archaeologists to go in ahead of developers where a road or housing scheme effectively would destroy a site of potential archaeological interest. Hitherto this had been funded by the taxpayer or the archaeologists. Under my chairmanship English Heritage achieved a complete switch, so that it became the norm for this sort of archaeology to be funded by the developer. In 1987–8 we even managed, for the first time, to persuade the Department of Transport to allocate £100,000 for 'rescue archaeology in advance of new road schemes'.

Building on the pioneering work of Jennifer Jenkins I published, for the first time, ten separate garden registers in 1984 and a further seven in 1986–7. Garden lobbyists were keen for us to start a scheme of garden grants, but we set our faces against this – at least until the aftermath of the great storm of 1987, when we allocated a quarter of a million pounds to help garden restoration. These were exceptional circumstances, although mercifully English Heritage's own properties for the most part escaped serious damage – the most significant exceptions being Walmer Castle on the Kent coast and Osborne House on the Isle of Wight. We were greatly helped by the fact that we had just published the register of historic gardens and therefore were able to move quickly to assess damage and give grants for replanting. At least the register was there on time.

*

All this was stimulating work that I found challenging and enjoyable. Less so were the necessary bureaucratic reforms of an organisational structure that was cripplingly Byzantine and autocratic. I wanted to devolve as much power as possible and give local and often quite junior people much greater decision-making powers. Our poor organisational structure did not help with this but we made a first-rate start, and in my first annual report I paid tribute to the remarkable job done by senior staff. I wrote, 'The assumption of our responsibilities was achieved with only minor hiccups. That this was so is mainly due to the commitment and effort of our staff, under the management of the Chief Executive and his Management Group of senior officials. Their efforts have been vital. They have done a remarkable job in securing a smooth transition and laying firm foundations for the future.'

Office politics bored me and continued to do so throughout my time in office but we did urgently need change and I initiated two management consultancy reports which were sound, if difficult to implement quickly. This led to the complete reorganisation of the way work was done. The management of the properties was made the responsibility of regional teams, headed by Francis Golding. The conservation work was brought together first under Richard Butt and later by Jane Sharman, who had long experience of the conservation world and eventually took over as chief executive from Chris Green. They all showed great enthusiasm for the work and did their best to cope with my frustration at the time it took to achieve things.

My masters throughout my time in office were a succession of Tory secretaries of state who changed with bewildering speed. In eight and a half years I had to work with no fewer than seven different ones. Actually, there were six individuals but Michael Heseltine held the office on two separate occasions. The other incumbents were Patrick Jenkin, Tom King, Kenneth Baker, Nicholas Ridley and Chris Patten. My relations with them all were perfectly correct and friendly, but I could see, as we changed from one minister to another, that the heritage did not loom very large on their horizons and they were never in the job long enough to get a proper mastery of the brief.

Such a lack of continuity was dispiriting and profoundly inefficient. Junior ministers and civil servants in charge of heritage matters also came and went with alarming rapidity, here today and gone tomorrow. They included high-fliers and dunces, but most of them stayed so briefly that it was difficult to be sure which was which. They included Lord Avon, Neil Macfarlane, Lord Strathclyde, William Waldegrave, Virginia Bottomley, Emily Blatch, Lord Elton, Colin Moynihan and Viscount Astor. As I contemplate that list I really am moved to reflect that Harold Wilson was right when he said that a week was a long time in politics.

The political situation was given an odd twist because, of course, I was myself a member of the Upper House. Realising that my well-known membership of the Conservative party could give rise to accusations of bias, I tried to get all-party support whenever possible and always took care to brief the Labour spokesman, Alma Birk, as fully as possible. There were two parliamentary highlights. One was the long-running and essentially unsuccessful battle to get VAT removed from repairs to all historic buildings – from palaces to historic monuments. This brought home to me the folly of ever embarking on a battle with the Treasury and Inland Revenue.

The other and happy parliamentary involvement was in 1986 when the Heritage Select Committee conducted an investigation into the workings of English Heritage. They were interested in visiting Stonehenge and I combined this with a visit to Beaulieu, where we set up the old lay brothers dormitory in the Abbey as a makeshift parliamentary committee room, complete with clerks and Hansard recorders. Unsurprisingly, the members were muted in their criticisms. I was, of course, a dutiful and – I hope – generous host, and when their findings were made public they made a number of recommendations: deplored the disgraceful state of Stonehenge and praised the work we were doing elsewhere.

The Committee was forthright in its support for English Heritage. Its report – published in February 1987 – made a number of recommendations that would have cut bureaucracy and helped the work of English Heritage, as well as saving money. Based on some of the recommendations in our own substantial evidence, the Committee's report proposed the transfer to English Heritage of responsibility for the non-occupied royal palaces, preservation orders and the determination of applications for listed building and scheduled monument consent. It also raised the probability of a merger with the Royal Commission on Historical Monuments.

None of this was accepted by the Government. But I suppose one shouldn't be too impatient; a mere eleven years later the Department for Culture, Media and Sport announced that the merger with the Royal Commission was to take place. The royal palaces are still not run by English Heritage, as suggested by the Committee, but by their own separate agency; although English Heritage did manage to acquire the management of Osborne House on the grounds it was not a royal palace but a private royal family home, a principle firmly established by Queen Victoria and Prince Albert when they built it.

Events like that make one wonder more and more how much importance Parliament will have in the twenty-first century in relation to the executive. A sober, non-partisan examination of the facts came up with proposals which were certainly sensible as far as the practitioners and experts were concerned, but the administration ignored them. For those of us closely involved this was profoundly dispiriting and frustrating.

A more immediate threat to Parliament occurred in 1987 when a proposal for a vast new Westminster Pier for a new ferry landing complex attached to Westminster Bridge, with two layers of shops, appeared to be in serious danger of acquiring planning permission. It would have intruded into the setting of the Palace of Westminster and wrecked the view from the bridge, but for some reason no one but English Heritage seemed to realise the extent of the threat. We stood firm against it, and I rallied support by personally writing to every Member of Parliament and making a fuss in the press. I am delighted to say that the proposal was defeated, albeit only after a public inquiry, and my standing among the staff of English Heritage was greatly enhanced.

Where the day-to-day business of conservation is concerned, local government is of more importance than national government and the local authorities were probably the most important partner for English Heritage in carrying forward its work. In size, resources and attitudes to conservation they were a terribly mixed bunch, and this made it difficult to deal with them on a consistent basis. At the one extreme were authorities like my own county of Hampshire. Led by Freddie Emery-Wallis, they clearly understood the importance of maintaining their historic buildings and archaeological resources, and realised what a contribution they could make to economic well-being. In places like that there was enthusiasm for joint working – for example, on schemes for small grants to help improve buildings in conservation areas – and a willingness to spend wisely as much grant as we could make available. At the other extreme were authorities who saw the heritage as an unwanted burden, an obstacle to development, or a symbol of the past they wanted to forget. In such cases there was sometimes an unwillingness to employ a single conservation officer and an attitude of resentment towards any 'interference' from London. In these circumstances we decided that we had, to some extent, to starve the good authorities and to focus our attention on the bad ones. Inevitably this caused complaints from both.

We were helped in our relationships with local authorities by having excellent commissioners from that world, first Jeremy Beecham, for long the Labour Leader of Newcastle-upon-Tyne, then by Patricia Hollis, formerly Leader of Norwich, and now a colleague in the House of Lords and a member of the Blair Government. We also made it our business to get out and about every year as a commission and make a tour of a different part of the country, visiting some of our own properties and spending plenty of time in discussion with members and officers of the local authorities.

The first of these trips was a rather amateurish affair concentrating on Hadrian's Wall and involving considerable hiking, at least as far as the local press were concerned. Accommodation can be somewhat spartan in that part of the world and I particularly remember the Duke of Gloucester joining the queue for a bath in the morning. This he did with the good humour and lack of self-importance that marked his attitude to his work in English Heritage at all times. The tour I remember with most pleasure, however, was the one to Hampshire and the Isle of Wight, where we celebrated our takeover of responsibility for Osborne House by entertaining the local authorities and others to a dinner in the Durbar Hall, probably the first held there since the death of Queen Victoria. I threw myself into the task of re-creating a menu such as the Queen herself might have eaten. I modelled the meal on early menus kept in the Library at Windsor. It was cooked for us by the students at Newport College, who received a round of applause from the guests, and was accompanied by suitable wines, which I managed to obtain by way of sponsorship. These included an Indian-made sparkling wine called Omar Khayyam, which I felt Queen Victoria would have approved, even though it wasn't available when she was alive.

That visit was also enlivened by the presence of the s.s. *Osborne*, the steam launch used as a tender by Queen Victoria, which English Heritage bought from an island resident who had lovingly restored her over many years. It seemed particularly appropriate to me that she should join Queen Victoria's bathing machine and the Swiss Cottage to show the more domestic side of life at Osborne.

In the course of my chairmanship these visits took us to every part of the country. They were useful in enabling commissioners and members of staff to get to know one another, as well as in building up our relations with local authorities. They also brought home to members of the Commission the importance of certain problems in a way that nothing else could have done. Examples I remember are the potential cost of repairs to the wonderful churches in Norfolk and Suffolk, and the extent of dereliction affecting disused farm buildings in several parts of the country.

I am particularly proud of the initiative I took to set up an industrial archaeology committee under the expert chairmanship of Sir Neil Cossons, now the chairman of English Heritage. He had done pioneering work at industrial museums like Ironbridge and the Maritime Museum at Greenwich, and as director of the Science Museum he was just the person to inspire the Committee to ensure that the monuments of our industrial revolution were preserved, if possible still in working order. One of our better successes was the steam-driven Queen Street Wool Mill in Burnley and I was pleased to have listed some of the historic buildings relating to the car industry – in particular the old Morris Garage in Oxford from which came the MG. Other listings of which I was proud were the Cavalry and Guards Club in Piccadilly, which by upgrading its status prevented it becoming an hotel, the Penguin House at London Zoo, the original red telephone kiosks designed by Sir Gilbert Scott, the Commonwealth Institute in Kensington High Street, Jodrell Bank Telescope, the *Economist* and *Time* and *Life* Buildings, the Royal Festival Hall, and a million pounds to the Ribblehead railway viaduct.

Relations with the press and broadcasting media were also vital. The Department of the Environment had a policy of not allowing anyone to talk to the press in any circumstances, so openness was a totally alien concept, although it was clearly necessary if we were to establish the right kind of image for English Heritage. This was not only a matter of my being prepared to be photographed in funny hats, but of custodians at the individual properties talking to local newspapers to answer questions, publicise events or gain good publicity in some way. Once they had realised that attitudes had changed, some turned out to be excellent publicists for their properties. I also ensured a degree of professionalism; media experts were called in to provide a series of training days to assist the staff in giving television or radio interviews.

Nationally, we were lucky that we were set up when more media space and attention was being given to conservation matters, which were suddenly becoming fashionable. We enjoyed lots of good coverage. Any press release headed 'Stonehenge' was guaranteed coverage in the national press, even if it only related to opening times.

The bad publicity was of three kinds. First there was 'Who do they think they are?'. In this category were reports that I had installed a jacuzzi in my office at the taxpayers' expense, which I hadn't – although I had installed a toilet and shower down the passage in a room in which executives could change for formal occasions. There was also, rather more seriously, the big story in the *Daily Mirror* alleging all kinds of extravagance.

The second sort of bad publicity was 'Why don't they leave it alone?'. This was most common in London, where the defenders of the former Greater London Council had a field day in opposing every proposal we made to improve the historic house museums. At Kenwood, although the curator, John Jacob, was a friend of mine he made no secret of his distaste for the new regime and refused even to come and meet me to discuss the matter. His closeness to the editor of the *Hampstead and Highgate Express* meant that there were several hurdles thrown in the way of new proposals by English Heritage. Holding receptions in Kenwood and allowing a motor car to be displayed at the time of a Kenwood concert in exchange for generous sponsorship was even worse – just the sort of thing to be expected from Lord Montagu (hear! hear!). Worst of all, we proposed to clear away some of the dense scrubby undergrowth of rhododendron which was increasingly threatening to choke all the Kenwood part of Hampstead Heath, thanks to inadequate and poorly planned maintenance during the whole post-war period. This produced such a frenzy of opposition, despite the careful historical research on which it was based and a well thought-out programme of public consultation, that the whole project was delayed by several years and considerably watered down.

At Marble Hill in Twickenham we achieved the remarkable feat of being attacked for proposing to plant trees rather than cut them down. The setting of this beautiful Thames-side villa had been destroyed and it was surrounded by a municipal array of sports fields and tennis courts with nondescript shrubbery at the sides of the park. Again, careful research showed that it was possible, by moving some of the sports pitches, to recreate paths on historic routes and plant trees which would give the house a more suitable setting than goalposts. This led to a huge campaign in the local and national press, and accusations of fascism from a famous professor of Italian history. Of course, the resited tennis courts were moving closer to his garden.

The third sort of bad press coverage was 'Why don't they?'. Much the best example of this was the Rose Theatre saga. In the course of excavations in Southwark in advance of building an office block in 1989 the foundations of the Rose Theatre, where Shakespeare undoubtedly trod the boards, were discovered in a reasonable state of preservation. This immediately gave rise to a campaign for the building work to be halted and the remains to be opened to the public. The theatrical profession, led by Dame Peggy Ashcroft and Sir Ian McKellen, were the leaders of the campaign, which included marches and rallies as well as innumerable media appearances. Practical arguments were useless and the fact that the foundations would not survive if they were exposed, and at best would have to be entirely rebuilt and hence destroyed, was brushed aside as a quibble. The fact that English Heritage did not have the legal powers to do what they wanted was also a quibble. The deeply unappealing nature of the flimsy foundations as a spectacle to all but a handful of people was an irrelevance. Eventually, thanks to the generosity of the developers and our persistence in reasoning, there was a solution in which the preservation of the historic artefacts was ensured without the need for rebuilding, and the sad long-term fate that has befallen the Temple of Mithras in the City of London – moved, rebuilt and then more or less forgotten – has been avoided.

The single most important institutional relationship of English Heritage was probably the one with the National Trust. It was a difficult one for several reasons. In the first place the Trust, understandably, saw the creation of English Heritage as producing a rival organisation, particularly in the case of opening up to the public when we launched our membership scheme. On the building-grant side we were their major contributor, allocating a significant share of our budget to their properties, in spite of their public claim that they received no government support. We did sometimes refuse what we thought unreasonable and we certainly did not accept uncritically the bills presented for repair work on their properties. This produced an atmosphere of competition that was occasionally damaging.

Second, in English Heritage we had inherited certain arrangements made by governments over the years, which were highly advantageous to the Trust and expensive for English Heritage. For instance, a number of houses run by the Trust were known as 'maintenance deficit grant' properties. Effectively, English Heritage footed the bill for any losses and the bigger the loss could be made to appear the bigger the grant entitlement. Similarly, we were obliged to pay to the Trust and its tenants the full cost of clearing up the aftermath of the illegal Stonehenge festivals. In certain places we were responsible for the difficult and expensive bits of properties, while the Trust looked after the glamorous parts. Hardwick Old Hall, the ruin of the house abandoned by Bess when she built the famous Hall alongside it, was one example of this; and at Fountains Abbey English Heritage is still responsible for all the difficult and expensive work of repairing the monastic ruins, while the National Trust controls the whole site and looks after the Studley Royal Estate. Here the Trust absolutely refused to allow free entry or concessions to English Heritage members, a position which was understandable in commercial terms, but deeply frustrating, too.

A comical aspect of this rivalry was that to the outside world the two organisations were largely indistinguishable. To foster the sense of common understanding and purpose among the staff, Peter Rumble and Angus Stirling got together to arrange an annual joint day out at one of the properties for any of the staff who cared to go, and this worked well as a way of bringing people together. It also helped to have Jennifer Jenkins, who had resigned from English Heritage to take up the post of chairman of the National Trust. She was resolute in defending the Trust's position and in making the case for grants, but she also had a good understanding of the pressures on us. Before she handed over to her successor, Lord Chorley, we had established much improved relations, especially with regard to our joint responsibility for Stonehenge.

The same could not always be said for the many other interest groups that made up our constituency. The historic house owners, the dirt archaeologists, the area conservationists and the churches all believed that their interest was paramount and that they deserved a large share of any public funds that were going. Each of them tended to have at least one advocate as a commissioner, eager to plead their cause. Of course, the upshot of this was that the percentage of funds going to different activities changed rather little from year to year since the one thing no one would accept was a weakening of his or her position vis-à-vis one of the other groups.

As a previous chairman of the Historic Houses Association, I found it extremely difficult to be too vocal when grants to private houses were discussed. It would naturally be thought that I had an axe to grind. However, I did feel it necessary to establish the principle that historic houses that desperately needed repairs and maintenance should have priority over others. Consequently, during my time in office, I was able to endorse a million-pound grant for Wilton House, not forgetting large grants to enable the National Trust to take over Belton, Calke Abbey and Castleton.

I was also really proud about the introduction of a brand-new grant scheme for cathedrals in 1991, which started with an extra £11.5 million over its first three years of operation. This met a need which had been growing rapidly, as cathedrals found it increasingly hard to raise the funds for urgently needed repairs. In this second – Jennie Page – part of my reign we also brought historic ships into our remit. A less successful venture was creating a Friends of English Heritage in America. It only ran for a few years. More useful was the scheme for the Japanese association, to whom we sent acorns from the Boscobel Oak where Charles II hid from Cromwell's troops. They have now been planted on a Japanese golf course.

Another area in which I was much involved was the great expansion of music at our sites. After my experiences with the Beaulieu Jazz and Folk Festivals it was wonderful to have the opportunity to become a musical impresario on a much wider scale. English Heritage was still in its infancy when I decided to bring in music of all kinds, a concept originally started by the GLC at Kenwood but expanded by us to many other sites. I put Michael Webber in charge and he did a wonderful job.

The first open-air concert season in 1986 was in the concert bowl by the lake in the grounds of Kenwood when Norman del Mar conducted the London Philharmonic Orchestra. Among the other artists in that first season were Sir Edward Heath conducting the Philharmonia Orchestra, two of the great brass bands in the Grimethorpe Colliery Band and the Sun Life Band, and three of the great names in British jazz: Chris Barber, Acker Bilk and Humphrey Lyttelton, all old friends from the Beaulieu Jazz Festivals.

Such was the success of that first season that it was decided to arrange at short notice a concert by the London Mozart Players in the grounds of Marble Hill House by the River Thames. It proved sufficiently popular to justify a full season in the next and subsequent years.

A third venue was introduced in 1989 when more than 12,000 people attended a concert at Audley End, Essex. In later years concerts were to be held in such venues as Wrest Park, Portchester and Pevensey Castles. In 1989 we decided to go into grand opera and our debut and highlight of the year was undoubtedly the performance given in July by the full company of the Royal Opera, Covent Garden in the concert bowl at Kenwood. On that occasion 8000 people in the arena and thousands more on the 'free terraces' enjoyed splendid performances of *Cavalleria Rusticana* and *I Pagliacci* conducted by Robin Stapleton with, among others, Ghena Dimitrova, Piero Cappuccilli and Vladimir Atlantov in the casts. That concert resulted in universal praise. In 1990 the Royal Opera was back at Kenwood with a concert performance of Puccini's *La Bohème*, superbly conducted by the man who is now the Musical Director of the Royal Opera, Antonio Pappano, born not far from Kenwood yet educated and trained in the USA. The young Italian tenor Vincenzo la Scola, flown in at the very last minute to replace the ailing Jerry Hadley, sang in his mac as the weather was so cold. I remember too Sir Jeremy Isaacs, the then Director of the Royal Opera House, saying what great satisfaction it had given him to see a mother sitting on the grass and feeding her baby while listening to grand opera. In 1991, not only did we present Verdi's *Attila* but also a splendid *Tosca* starring Placido Domingo and Maria Ewing. Finally, we were able to put on the English National Opera's *Madame Butterfly* at Marble Hill.

I was determined to celebrate the contribution of English Heritage and my retirement as chairman with a wide range of music. One concert, conducted by Sir Alexander Gibson, included only music by British composers and the first performance of a work specially commissioned for the occasion – *Solent Forts* by Arthur Butterworth, chosen to commemorate the proximity and historic connections between those forts and Beaulieu. For the first time since the dissolution of the monasteries Beaulieu and all its offshoots were under the same control. The daughter abbeys of Netley and Hailes are both Heritage properties, as are Calshot and Hurst Castle, which are built from Beaulieu stone. My retirement was also marked at Marble Hill in September when Sir Edward Heath conducted a 'Last Night of the Proms'-type programme that included a splendid performance of the Triple Concerto by Beethoven.

From the first we felt that English Heritage should perform music by both well-known and lesser-known English composers. This included works by Delius, Elgar, Holst, Walton, Sir Malcolm Arnold and Malcolm Williamson, Master of the Queen's Music. I was delighted that so many fine musicians were able to contribute to these performances.

Since I left I am sorry to hear that the concerts are no longer undertaken internally but put out to a concert organiser. I regret this as we always tried to relate programmes to English Heritage or a particular monument and I fear this may no longer be the case.

Apart from these concerts I was very much part of the new development of the Royal Opera House and all the problems that had to be solved at that time. I would like to think that we influenced beneficially the long-term completion of what is a magnificent result, especially the use of Floral Hall, with which English Heritage was particularly involved.

I also especially enjoyed being associated with the erection of blue plaques, renamed English Heritage plaques, for distinguished people who had lived in London. During my time we had the honour of having The Queen Mother unveil a plaque for P. G. Wodehouse and Simon Callow, for Charles Laughton, as well as plaques for the author Charles Morgan and for Amy Johnson.

The final area of work I want to mention is international activity. Apart from an endless stream of foreign visitors, who shook hands and listened in mystification as we explained the difference between English Heritage and the National Trust, this didn't originally amount to much more than attendance at a few committee meetings in Strasbourg by junior officials. I decided that it was absurd for us to make no real effort to put our skills of tourism management and archaeological investigation to work to benefit countries that really needed them. Apart from the American and Japanese schemes to which I have already referred, I also led a delegation to China in 1986 to meet officials and look at their situation at first hand. Professor Rosemary Cramp, Andrew Saunders (Chief Inspector of Ancient Monuments), Francis Golding and I had a most interesting visit looking at historic sites and discussing common problems. We were astonished by the scale of the task for archaeology and by the need for tourist management to prevent important sites, such as the gardens of Soochow and the Great Wall, from being destroyed by the sheer weight of visitors. Our attempts to arrange for the direct transfer of skills all foundered, but we did form a strong friendship with Mr Guo Zhan who guided us on our visits. He has since become a senior figure in the Cultural Relics Bureau and has come to England several times, so our influence has spread, albeit more slowly than I had hoped. As well as the experience of the obvious cultural sites – the Great Wall, the Terra Cotta Army, the Ming Tombs and so on – the trip was memorable for the wonderful food we were given – eating Imperial recipes in the Summer Palace, for example – and the thoughtfulness with which we were treated. This led to such curiosities as an attempt to eat fried eggs with chopsticks on a wobbly railway train and an evening listening to the famous jazz band in the Peace Hotel, Shanghai. Food also provided the theme for the limericks which Francis Golding showed a regrettable facility for improvising on this trip. The only memorable one referred to the sea slug we were given to eat as a sign of great honour wherever we went:

> At a banquet in distant Cathay
> Edward said, 'Sea slug twice in one day
> Is not only offensive,
> It's frightfully expensive;
> Thank goodness we don't have to pay.'

When a return delegation came from China I did my best to provide a similar level of entertainment, with a fifteen-course banquet at Beaulieu and a dinner in Kenwood, probably the first meal in the house since it became a museum, with the Rembrandt self-portrait and the Vermeer looking on.

This account can only give a faint flavour of my eight and a half years at

English Heritage (my second term of office prolonged at the end of 1991 by the extraordinary difficulty the Government found in making up its mind about my successor). I have tried to stress the breadth of responsibilities and the range of relationships with different interest groups, but when I look back at the organisation taken over by Jocelyn Stevens and compare it with the one I encountered in 1984 it is the transformation of the properties and the way they are presented that really strikes me.

At Osborne, for example, the visitor experience was improved in many ways. The route was reversed, so that it didn't start with the last bit of the house to be built. The Royal Nurseries were restored to a scrupulously high standard and opened to the public for the first time with a visit from the Duchess of York, which led directly to her book about royal children. Access to the terrace was no longer only the prerogative of residents in the convalescent home which shared the building and Queen Victoria's bathing hut was put back in sound working order. I was delighted to welcome both Her Majesty the Queen and the Princess Margaret to Osborne on separate occasions. My old friend Princess Margaret wondered, incidentally, whether it was *lèse-majesté* for visitors to tramp through Queen Victoria's bathroom and toilet.

At Dover Castle, too, there were huge improvements. A new restaurant and shop were opened and the magnificent Second World War tunnels in the cliffs were inaugurated as Hell Fire Corner by no less a person than Dame Vera Lynn. Elsewhere on the Kent coast Walmer Castle, the Duke of Wellington's last home, was finally turned into a residence, which could be occupied by Queen Elizabeth the Queen Mother as Lord Warden of the Cinque Ports, and the gardens improved. At Deal Castle the Governor, General Harrison of the Marines, was for a long time frustrated in his ambition to have a bathroom so that he could actually occupy his rooms there. The reason was that when the post was re-established after being in abeyance, Sir Edward Heath had said that it must not create expenditure for the public purse and Peter Rumble, a stickler for propriety, reminded the General of this every time he repeated his request, which was quite often. This led to some hilarious correspondence.

It wasn't only the well-known monuments that had improved, as in my own backyard at Southampton the Merchant's House at 58 French Street was opened for the first time, equipped with thoroughly researched copies of textiles and appropriate furniture in a way quite different from the sterile 'Ministry of Works' approach. Because of its use by a medieval wine merchant we even sold our own-labelled wine.

The English Heritage estate had both grown and shrunk. For example, we had formally acquired control of Stokesay Castle, a magical place which we restored so gently that the work was all but invisible. We also took over Brodsworth Hall, a wonderfully intact nineteenth-century house near Doncaster, where we set about an understated programme of repair and restoration. On the other hand we began a programme of transferring certain properties into the hands of those who could give them good management locally: Conisborough Castle was an early example of this and started an excellent trend for the future. Of course there were disappointments and frustrations too: the eventual decision to demolish Number One Poultry, the refusal of the National Heritage Memorial Fund to provide any grant for the acquisition of Monkton House, Edward James's surrealist bolt-hole on the West Dean Estate, and many others. But overwhelmingly my memories are positive and I believe that the task of creating a successful institution was achieved with considerable success.

Peter Rumble retired on his sixtieth birthday and we employed headhunters to find his successor. Most applicants were from the civil service or the museum world, even from the Natural Trust. I was particularly attracted to Jennie Page, who had a distinguished career in government before she moved into private sector banking. She more than justified my expectations that she would continue to build on the excellent foundations laid by Peter Rumble and significantly expand the horizons of English Heritage. An important new dialogue most publicly epitomised by the discovery of the Rose Theatre was developed with property developers, who we persuaded to recognise the need for more balance between conservation and essential development. A warm relationship was developed with the churches, labouring under heavy repair burdens, and the array of bodies concerned with the rural and urban policy from which protection of the built environment could be separated. With considerable bravery, English Heritage persuaded the government to embark on the highly controversial post-war listing programme. Certainly in the last three years of my chairmanship, we began to make headway with the intractable problem of Stonehenge. Jennie's great ability was networking, not only around the civil service, but also in the real world.

The proof of my judgement of Jennie's worth was well illustrated by the fact that she was appointed chief executive of the Millennium

Commission, and then of the Dome itself which she magnificently completed in time. The unfortunate events of the first night of the Dome was not the shambles that the press made it out to be. As one who attended, I had a wonderful evening and it was an experience I would not have missed for anything. The fault lay with security, and following an IRA bomb scare, the police insisted that all people disembarking at Stratford station must be scanned first, but they only provided one scanner. After the opening, a disgraceful campaign of scapegoating resulted, and both Jennie Page and Ken Robinson, my ex-director at Beaulieu, were forced out. I felt very hurt and angry on their behalf, and it is a good example of when politicians interfere with operations on such a scale – they end up doing more harm than good.

By the time I was due to retire I felt that the organisation I had helped create was one in which I could take great pride. Unfortunately the manoeuvring surrounding the appointment of my successor resulted in a second reappointment for myself. What happened was that I should have retired in September 1991, and all plans to do so were in place, but because of their inability to chose a suitable person to take over, they asked me to stay on for a further six months, which I reluctantly agreed to do, as my retirement in the end was overwhelmed by the more pressing government matter of the general election campaign.

Various appropriate names such as Lord St John of Fawsley and Simon Hornby of W. H. Smith were mooted and eventually Simon Jenkins, who was a commissioner and at that time editor of *The Times*, agreed with me that Jocelyn Stevens, who had made such a success at the Royal College of Art, would be an ideal chairman. I was asked to sound him out and when shooting with him at Stype, near Hungerford, asked him whether he would be interested in the position. I doubt whether he knew very much about English Heritage at the time, but it obviously opened great horizons for him.

With the run-up to the general election, decisions by government were hard to come by, although Michael Heseltine, the then Secretary for the Environment, was keen to get the matter settled and had, of course, known Jocelyn for many years.

Needless to say the story was leaked and I was exasperated when articles began to appear in various journals saying what a terrible mess English Heritage was in and that Jocelyn had been sent to clear it up. I do not for a moment suggest that he instigated these stories, but certainly somebody did on his behalf. As for shaking up English Heritage, it had twice been shaken up during my time by management consultants and the last thing the staff wanted was another shaking.

There is no doubt that Jocelyn has done a good job at English Heritage, and I am particularly pleased that some of the ideas I initiated have been expanded and improved upon. As chairmen I am aware that we were very different in style, as I believe in delegating and trusting people to get on with the job whereas he is much more hands-on. When he in turn retired he was quoted as having made some less than gracious remarks about the structure he inherited and I felt obliged to write to the national press to put the record straight. The comments were not only mildly wounding to me personally but also gratuitously hurtful to the many dedicated public servants who helped both of us in our successful efforts.

My last few weeks at English Heritage were made even more disturbing because the country was in the middle of a general election campaign with most people thinking that Neil Kinnock would be victorious. The outgoing government gave a special reception at Lancaster House for both myself and Lord Charteris, who was about to hand over the chair of the National Heritage Memorial Fund to Lord Rothschild, and the senior staff presented me with a lovely silver pen tray. I had several dinners with Jocelyn and tried to pass on as much information as I possibly could about the job he was taking on. I promised him, and myself, that once I ceased to be chairman I would 'let him get on with it' without any comment or criticism – a promise I have always kept. Except, on one occasion when English Heritage was being accused of selling the 'family silver', I always spoke up for the organisation in the House of Lords.

The new Conservative Government appointed David Mellor as Secretary of State for Environment and Heritage, and the Government instructions to me, two years earlier, to arrange to transfer the English Heritage offices to Nottingham were reversed, much to the relief of the staff.

During my time as chairman I had the privilege of recommending honours for lots of people who had contributed positively to heritage matters, not only senior people from English Heritage and the outside world, but also the hard-working custodians and members of the direct labour force, who were the backbone of English Heritage and without whom it could not have existed.

After I retired several staff told me how concerned they were that I had not received any recognition in the subsequent honours list after eight years of service. I responded by saying I was already a Baron, so I could hardly expect to be made a Viscount! In any case, I was content to be judged and remembered by my record. Certainly I think I can take pride and comfort from helping to create, with the assistance of my fellow commissioners, solid foundations for English Heritage that placed it on a firm basis for the future. I think that I can fairly claim that the prestigious position it holds today owes much to all the hard work and future planning that went on during its first years of existence. I watched with barely qualified admiration as Jocelyn Stevens picked up the torch and ran with it so successfully for the next eight years, and I now look forward with great confidence to the success of the new chairman, my old friend, Sir Neil Cossons.

Many people wrote to me at the end of my term of office, but the letter that gave me the greatest comfort was from Virginia Bottomly MP, one of my favourite past ministers from the Department of Environment, and the one who took the most sympathetic interest in our work. She wrote:

You have been superb! English Heritage is firmly established and much respected. For all the solid work and sound reputation of the Historic Buildings and Monuments Commission, the transformation of style, activity and reputation is down to you. I write, on behalf of a wide circle of admirers and friends, to proclaim the country's debt to you.

With the team of Commissioners who served and English Heritage's professional staff, you have carried forward the conservation, preservation and improvement of our buildings and monuments. The greatest tribute is that English Heritage is recognised as a firmly established part of our nation's future, present and past: that is a splendid achievement delivered during the time you led the English Heritage team.

I well remember the day you took me by launch to Beaulieu. It matched the tour of Queen Victoria's Osborne on the Isle of Wight. I well recall your attention to detail and the campaign to ensure that our magnificent heritage buildings looked like homes rather than museums. You were a pioneer in identifying the huge potential for the tourism and hospitality industry that our magnificently built heritage offered.

When I was the Heritage Under-Secretary, I valued your experience, enthusiasm and commercial acumen, in combination with my respect for your responsibilities and for the proper way you worked with the civil servants and Ministers.

Thank you for nearly 10 years of effective work for the Nation as the first Chairman of English Heritage.

17

Wine, Women and Song

If music be the food of love, play on . . .
William Shakespeare

Such was the theme of my seventieth birthday fancy dress ball in October 1996.

Music has always dominated my life. It has been a solace in times of sadness and distress, and in moments of joy and happiness it has inspired me and enhanced my pleasure in life. It has been a bond that has brought me enduring friendships; it has taken me to beautiful places at home and abroad. I have always enjoyed the company of musical people, whether they be singers, musicians, composers or impresarios. As a child I had a good treble voice and sang in choirs at school, but after puberty I never developed a good singing voice. Although I would never pretend to professional standards, as I have said, I have frequently sung Noël Coward's 'Stately Homes of England' in all manner of places: with the Duke of Bedford, on the BBC *Tonight* programme; with the late Marquess of Bath; at a concert at Wakefield Prison in 1954; on the *Bernard Braden Show*; and in 1999 at the 'End of the Peer Show' with the new Lord Bath and the Lords Gisborough and Oxfuird, which raised money for Mencap and marked the impending demise of the hereditary House of Lords. My performances have always been charitably received and the song has become a sort of signature tune for me.

I don't believe I inherited a special love of music from my parents nor was I brought up in a particularly musical house. The wind-up gramophone records in the nursery included 'The Teddy Bears' Picnic', Rossini and Wagner overtures, 'One Night of Love' sung by Grace Moore and 'The Lion and Albert' by Stanley Holloway, which, as I have said already, I can still recite today.

As a child I first became conscious of such BBC signature tunes as 'The Teddy Bears' Picnic' for *Children's Hour*, Eric Coates's 'Knightsbridge

March' for *In Town Tonight* followed by its great 'Stop the roar of London's traffic'; and Henry Hall's 'Here's to the Next Time'.

At St Peter's Court, as a member of the choir under the doughty watch of the choirmistress Miss Kingsford, I not only became fully grounded in Church of England hymns and descants, but also tutored in musical appreciation. The tunes were mostly thumped out by Miss Kingsford on the piano, 'thump' being the operative word. But although she was no Myra Hess, she was knowledgeable and, above all, enthusiastic. When it came to learning to play the piano myself, trying to read music proved difficult. However, I seemed to have the ability to play by ear, which I found much more satisfying, and I spent hours at the piano developing this talent.

The most musical member of the family was my half-sister Elizabeth. Her love of music came from her mother's family, the Kerrs, who were very musical, and the six daughters and two sons of the Marquess of Lothian, who formed their own orchestra. Similarly, Elizabeth's elder sister Helen played beautifully by ear but, after trying to be an actress in London, ran off to America to become a chorus girl. Elizabeth also trained to be an actress at the Royal Academy of Dramatic Art, being a contemporary of Vivien Leigh, and appeared successfully on the West End stage. Before the war she became very friendly with Toscanini's daughter, Wally, and often stayed with them in their house in Venice where she met some of the leading musicians of the day like Horowitz, who later married Wally. When Toscanini came to London before the war to record all the Beethoven symphonies she acted as his personal assistant. I still remember how jealous I was when she took my sister Caroline to a Toscanini rehearsal in London. She gathered around her a particularly musical circle of friends. Two special ones, Etienne Amyot and his wife Robin, were our neighbours at Littlemarsh, a house on the Beaulieu foreshore. Robin was one of England's earliest woman conductors working as far afield as India. Etienne, from South Africa, had been a successful concert pianist and at the end of the war was co-opted, together with Sir George Barnes and Leslie Stokes, as part of the triumvirate to create the BBC Third Programme, arguably the most important cultural and broadcasting landmark of the Forties and Fifties.

A great friend of Robin and Etienne was the pianist Renata Borgatti whose father was the original Cavaradossi in Puccini's *Tosca*. Her god-parents were Toscanini and Busoni. Renata was a wonderful teacher and musician, and had a great influence on Elizabeth and Etienne before and after the war. When she was dying she asked that the Verdi Requiem should be played on the gramophone . . . what a way to go!

Elizabeth became my musical mentor – a distinct advantage on my wind-up gramophone – particularly on her return from Switzerland after the war and my arrival in London after leaving Oxford.

My evacuation to Canada in 1940 and my enrolment at Ridley College further extended my musical range. Dr Betts, the organist, was a great disciplinarian and rigidly trained us not only to learn the school song but also football songs that we had to sing at matches to encourage the Ridley teams. He wrote annual musicals for the school and, as I have said, in 1941 staged a production of Gilbert and Sullivan's *HMS Pinafore* in which I was given the role of 'The Admiral' – Sir Joseph Porter KCB – with my friend Henry Bathurst playing 'The Captain'. The English contingent rather dominated that production, with several others in less prominent roles. I shall always treasure this unforgettable introduction to Gilbert and Sullivan and, although I know that some music buffs are snobbish about them, I think Sullivan was a composer of merit and originality, and Gilbert's lyrics had wit and topicality.

Ridley is near the Canada–US border, so it was easy to receive American radio. Not only did I tune in to NBC concerts from New York, but also I discovered the delights of jazz. Listening on my 'cat's whisker' radio under the blankets after lights out, I first heard artists such as Tommy Dorsey, Artie Shaw, Harry James, Duke Ellington and Glenn Miller. This youthful enthusiasm for jazz later bore fruit at Beaulieu in a way that was not far short of sensational.

On my way back to England via New York in September 1942 I made a point of going to the Radio City Music Hall to hear a concert by the NBC Symphony Orchestra and was very excited when I got a ticket. However, my joy was rather dashed, as not only was Toscanini not conducting that day, but also the programme was devoted to Carl Nielsen, the Danish composer, whose music I now admire but whom, at fifteen, I found rather difficult to listen to.

Happily, wartime Eton continued to offer opportunities for live orchestral music and I have several contemporaries who were not only very musical but also much more knowledgeable than I was. Robert Ponsonby, later Director of Music at the BBC, was notable in this respect, but other friends in my house, David Gibbs and Robin Warrender, were too and we spent many hours discussing concerts we had heard and what music we would like to hear when the war was over. At Eton I regularly listened to the wartime promenade concerts, which were broadcast from the Albert Hall until there was an air raid warning, when they were faded out, as it was suspected that the German bombers might use the radio waves for navigation purposes. Fortunately, the school concerts at Eton by visiting orchestras still went on and I particularly remember hearing Mendelssohn's Violin Concerto for the first time played by Eda Kersey, who I believe was killed by a flying bomb during a German air raid.

At Beaulieu, during holidays, I played our wind-up gramophone and discovered all the Beethoven symphonies and the New World Symphony by Dvořák, which I noted in my diary had been sent to us by the Czech squadron – who were flying Liberators for Coastal Command, stationed at the Beaulieu aerodrome – as a token of their gratitude for the frequent entertainment we provided for them. At the other end of the scale was the ever-popular *Warsaw Concerto* which featured in the film *Dangerous Moonlight*, starring Anton Walbrook and directed by Brian Desmond Hurst, who later became a good friend and who had asked the composer, Richard Addinsell, to write the film music in the style of a Rachmaninov piano concerto.

During my last year at Eton we were promised by our housemaster, W. N. Roe, that we would get a much-needed piano for boys to play in the house if we won a music competition. This we achieved in the interhouse choir competition, singing a Chorale from Bach's *St Matthew Passion* and clinching the first prize by a spirited version of 'Uncle Tom Cobley and All'. Although we won we did not get the piano, which we thought mean on the part of the housemaster. One of my most abiding memories was singing in the tenor chorus of *The Messiah* in the School Chapel. I have loved *The Messiah* ever since and always try to catch broadcasts of it at Christmas.

My three years with the Army deprived me of access to professional music and I was forced to rely on my own resources. During my army training days I played the piano in the NAAFI and led sing-songs of all the popular songs of the day like 'This Is a Lovely Way to Spend an Evening', 'Long Ago and Far Away', 'It Had To Be You' and all the favourites like 'Clementine', 'There Is a Tavern in the Town' and always, of course, 'Auld Lang Syne' at the end. The worst music starvation was in Palestine, as we slept in tents with no electric power to play a gramophone.

Before leaving for the Middle East I was stationed for some time in Wellington Barracks in London, where one of my fellow officers was Richard Buckle, the ballet critic. He introduced me to the prima ballerinas of the day such as Margot Fonteyn, Pamela May and Moira Shearer – who later became famous for her film *The Red Shoes* and married my friend Ludovic Kennedy, later a contemporary of mine at Oxford – and also to distinguished choreographers like Frederick Ashton. One memorable occasion was the first performance of Frederick Ashton's new ballet based on César Franck's *Symphonic Variations*. The dancing by the six principals was beautiful but unusual, as it was pure dancing and there was no storyline; but the ballet caused a sensation in post-war Britain.

Oxford provided many opportunities for the music lover and I took a great interest in the Oxford University Operatic Society. I was not good enough to sing but enjoyed being their official photographer, covering performances of such operas as *Dido and Aeneas* and *Iphigenia in Aulis*. The splendid concerts in the Sheldonian included a memorable one by Sir Thomas Beecham; memorable for the way he conducted 'God Save the King', when he faced the audience instead of the orchestra. It was now that I became very friendly with Andrew Porter, then an aspiring young South African pianist, but later the distinguished music critic on the *New Yorker* and *Observer*, and the first successful translator of Wagner's *Ring* Cycle into English. Another friend, Anthony Besch, who produced *Dido and Aeneas*, was destined to become a well-known opera producer. Aeneas was sung by the young Thomas Hemsley, later to become a renowned singer. For years Anthony remained closely connected with the presentation of opera in Great Britain and all over the world.

Meanwhile, at Beaulieu, the newly fledged Arts Council was presenting its annual concerts by the Bournemouth Symphony Orchestra under the baton of Sir Charles Groves in the Cloisters of the Abbey – an association with this fine orchestra that we still enjoy today with our annual promenade concerts.

I think one of the most significant of my steps on the road to musical education and appreciation on an international scale was my visit to the Salzburg Festival in 1949. I drove there in my trusty Hillman Minx with my old school friend Mark Chinnery, spending three weeks in that magnificent place. Admittedly, it rained most of the time, but I fell in love with the city and its surroundings, particularly its lakes and mountains. We stayed in a humble guesthouse and daily went down to scrounge tickets. Fortunately we had a good contact in the director of the Festival, Baron Puthon, whose daughter Marechi was married to our MP for the New Forest, Sir Oliver Crossthwaite-Eyre. It was a fascinating time to be in Austria, as many of the aristocracy were beginning to emerge after the war, and open up their *Schlosses* and entertain. Musically Salzburg was brilliant at that time, with Wilhelm Furtwängler conducting *Fidelio*, featuring the magnificent voice of Kirsten Flagstad who was singing Leonora, with Julius Patzak as Florestan.

In 1949 I enjoyed the Verdi Requiem conducted by Karajan and my first *Rosenkavalier* conducted by Georg Szell and starring Maria Reining, Hilde Gueden, Jarmila Novotná and Helge Roswaenge, the last two being legends from the pre-war era. The most unpleasant experience, however, was the new one-act opera by Carl Orff (whose famous *Carmina Burana* was not yet well known) called *Antigone*, which was scored entirely for percussion instruments. As we left the theatre after this terrible trial I heard an American lady say to another, 'I like the way they do it here in Salzburg. They give it to you all at once and then you can go out and eat.'

Most moving was, on 21 August 1949, hearing Kathleen Ferrier and Julius Patzak singing *Das Lied von der Erde* with the Vienna Philharmonic conducted by Bruno Walter, who did so much for her career. It was a tragedy that Ferrier died so young, because hers was one of the great voices of the century, which Walter, her patron, father figure and teacher, helped to bring to the attention of the world.

Two emerging stars of those Salzburg days were the conductor Herbert von Karajan and the soprano Elisabeth Schwarzkopf. Years later when von Karajan was in London, shopping for equipment for his beloved yacht, I was asked to entertain his wife Anita for the afternoon. She asked to go to Madame Tussaud's. Going through the Chamber of Horrors we came across a tableau of the leading Nazi hierarchy, some of whom, it was alleged, Anita had known very well. That day at Madame Tussaud's she took a close look at them all, then turned to me and said: 'You know, it doesn't look like them at all.'

Salzburg made such an impression upon me that I continued to go to the Festival regularly afterwards and I became very friendly with the Walderdorf family, who ran the famous hotel the Goldener Hirsch. I was introduced to a lot of interesting people by my sister Elizabeth and her close friend Ernst Lothar, who produced the famous *Jedermann* Miracle Play performed outside the south façade of the cathedral. In 1952 I was very proud to have been at the first night of the world première of Richard Strauss's last opera, *Die Liebe der Danae*, starring Paul Schöffler and Joseph Gostic, and conducted by Clemens Krauss. This opera was intended to have been premièred in July 1944, but coincided with the attempt on Hitler's life and so was cancelled and not performed until after Strauss's death. Fifty years later I had the pleasure of hearing it again at its first performance in England at Garsington, a splendid new opera festival run by Leonard Ingram, which I have warmly supported since its inception.

My proudest musical moment was the first European performance of *School for Wives* by Rolf Liebermann, commissioned by the Music Society at Louisville, Kentucky. Liebermann asked my sister Elizabeth, who was fluent in German and English, to write the libretto. I well remember staying in Vienna with her in the spring of 1955. Each day she worked frantically on the words and then every night we rushed them to the Post Office to telegraph them to Liebermann in Zurich. After the première in Louisville it was performed in New York, then in Salzburg and later all over Europe, and in England.

Looking back at Salzburg after all those years I am reminded not only of the incomparable music, but also the Austrian food and drink: the Wiener Schnitzel, blaue Forelle (steamed trout), Salzburger Nockerl (a sort of baked Alaska without the ice cream), Erdbeeren mit Schlag (wild strawberries with clotted cream) and the great cream desserts from the famed patisserie Tomaselli. Also the Weinheber, a splendid way of dispensing wine at a large party, where wine is poured into an inverted carafe, which has a metal valve at its neck that lets the wine pour out into your glass, everybody being able to help themselves without passing the bottle around. I am grateful that I was able to fall in love with and enjoy Salzburg before *The Sound of Music* was filmed there.

As a 'Wagnerian' the Bayreuth Festival is, of course, very important to me and it did not take me long to fall under its spell. I was delighted to make my first visit with Andrew Porter and learn all the customs and problems of attending that festival. For instance, one has to change into a DJ at about four in the afternoon and sit quietly on what were then very uncomfortable seats. After the performances the wine bars and beer cellars become a hive of activity and are full of Wagnerians discussing the merits and demerits of that performance and ones remembered from the past. In recent years the English have made a big contribution to performances, particularly John Tomlinson, probably, today, the world's most renowned Wagnerian bass, Graham Clark and Anne Evans.

One of the strangest incidents at Bayreuth involved an accident on the autobahn which caused such a traffic jam that I, and many other opera goers, failed to arrive at the appointed time. What we didn't then realise was that half the orchestra was similarly delayed. *Rheingold*, which is the first of the four great operas of the *Ring*, is two and a half hours long, without an interval, so we were all getting very impatient to reach the Bayreuth exit on the motorway as it was completely blocked. Eventually I followed some other cars, took to the fields beside the motorway and made an unofficial diversion through muddy farmland. Arriving twenty minutes late for the opera, we assumed we would not be let in but because the orchestra also arrived late they delayed the start by half an hour – unheard of in Bayreuth – so we squeezed in just in time, without changing. I am glad to say that subsequent festivals have been more tranquil.

The subject of Wagner reminds me that, when I came to live in London in 1950, musical life was experiencing a great post-war renaissance. I attended my first *Ring* at Covent Garden and was swiftly seduced by Flagstad's great Wagnerian voice. For me, one of my most historic moments was attending the world première in the Albert Hall of Strauss's Four Last Songs, performed after he had died by Kirsten Flagstad. These songs were then, of course, unknown, but are now one of the great virtuosic showpieces for dramatic sopranos. The genius who organised these concerts was Walter Legge, then Head of Music for Columbia Records, who later married Elisabeth Schwarzkopf. He did more for music in Britain after the war than any other person.

The concert was one of the series of Mysore concerts, subsidised by the Maharaja of Mysore, who was a great collector of gramophone records. My sister Elizabeth was on the Philharmonia Society Board which was responsible for putting on the series. Incidentally, the Maharaja never attended any of these very popular concerts.

Elizabeth was also on the committee of the English Opera Society and therefore I was in a good position to hear performances of Benjamin Britten's work and visit the Aldeburgh Festival. We got to know Ben and Peter Pears very well, and I remember meeting them unexpectedly in Cannes one evening after one of their concerts. During dinner I asked Ben which composers he most admired and who had most influenced him. I was surprised when he answered Purcell and Tchaikovsky – the first for his purity of sound and the second for his orchestration.

Britten's early death was a great loss to this country, although I confess that *Gloriana*, his opera especially written for the coronation in 1953, was to my mind a disappointment. But I much admired *Peter Grimes*, *The Turn of the Screw* and *Billy Budd*.

I became much more closely involved with Flagstad when she agreed to sing in *Dido and Aeneas* for the opening of the Mermaid Theatre, the brainchild of Bernard Miles, which started in the grounds of his house in St John's Wood. Bernard was a celebrated actor, but also an idealist. It was an extraordinary venture for a single individual to set up in his back garden and build, as nearly as possible, a replica of the original Elizabethan Mermaid Theatre.

Bernard planned two productions, Shakespeare's *Tempest* and Purcell's *Dido.* The latter was to play twice nightly on the evenings it was given. The cast was exceptional with Flagstad, a very intimate friend of Bernard, as Dido, and Maggie Teyte as Belinda. Although in her early sixties, Maggie Teyte had been a very famous singer in her day and was especially known for Mélisande, a role she had studied with Debussy himself.

Bernard was very skilled at getting people to help him for nothing. I met him at a theatrical party and when he heard that I was in public relations he prevailed upon me to come and help. We used to sit once a week on the floor at Acacia Road, eating sandwiches and discussing the promotion of this new venture. I eventually summoned up courage to tell my managing director, John Metcalf, what I was doing, as I knew we would not get paid, but he fully supported my involvement. I also persuaded Robin Howard of the Gore Hotel to set up the bar where I entertained the press in the interval.

I suppose the height of my own musical career as a performer was the Concerto for Motor Car and Orchestra concocted by Fritz Spiegl, a flautist with the Hallé Orchestra, and Anthony Hopkins and performed at the Albert Hall in one of the many Gerard Hoffnung concerts. The Concerto consists of two movements in which various car horns accompany the orchestra. I played the horns. It was a splendid success and I have performed it three times since, twice at Beaulieu and once at the Winter Gardens in Bournemouth. No two performances are exactly alike as, quite frankly, I make it up as I go along, armed with bulb horns, klaxon and a testaphone, a special motor horn that plays a sequence of notes. I more or less do what I like. I have recently found the music score, so next time

I play it, it will be more like the composer's original intentions.

In recent years I have been involved with organising all sorts of musical events, in particular as chairman of the committee for a charity performance in the Albert Hall of the Verdi Requiem following the earthquake disaster in Mexico City. I also arranged a performance by the English National Opera of *The Magic Flute*, for the Queen Mother, who is patron of the Museums Association, on the occasion of the International Museums Conference in London.

For the most part my musical life has been spent as a member of the audience. I have often been privileged to enjoy a seat in the front row of the stalls, but I have seldom ventured over the footlights. In one case, however, I was very closely involved with what was going on. It was an extraordinary episode in my life, containing as it did the seeds of both triumph and disaster. On the one hand it was extraordinarily enjoyable, if nerve-racking, on the other it was as depressing as almost anything I have experienced. It was the Beaulieu Jazz Festival which at one time I had hoped to establish as the Glyndebourne of jazz.

Its beginnings were modest. In the middle of July 1956 I was approached by a group of young men from the Yellow Dog Jazz Club in Southampton. At the time jazz was going through one of its periodic revivals in the UK. I had long been a fan myself and when they asked if I would let them use the front lawn to stage a concert I was more than happy. They were a pleasant group, patently keen on jazz, not interested in exploiting anyone or anything for profit. As a jazz enthusiast I welcomed their proposal.

Their plans were modest. They wanted only a few bands, of whom the best known was the now sadly forgotten Avon City Jazz Band from Bristol. As we closed for the day we handed over the grounds and ticket office to the Jazz Club and left them to get on with it. A few cushions were scattered on the grass and a basic square stand was erected at the far end of the lawn, but anyone who turned up was free to wander round the garden or sit on the grass. We agreed to split the receipts which, as only 400 people turned up, were comparatively small. It was a thoroughly enjoyable evening. The Avon City Jazz Band was fine and so was the supporting cast. The audience was enthusiastic but well-behaved, and nobody could drink because there was no bar. With the benefit of hindsight, perhaps we should have left it at that.

I was too hungry and eager in those days. Quiet, agreeable jazz concerts for 400 people were simply not enough and I resolved to expand. I had enjoyed a minor success and I therefore decided to turn it into a major one. The resurgence in traditional jazz was becoming a craze and I was determined to capitalise on it. The following year I engaged a small staff. We launched a modest publicity offensive, erected a scaffold stage and booked the then famous trad bandleader Mick Mulligan. Having done this we attracted a crowd five times bigger than in the inaugural Yellow Dog Jazz Club year. The *Observer* gave us a full page and I sensed the start of something big.

By the fourth year the attendance had doubled to 4000. We were on the map. The 'festival', as it had then become known, had acquired a national status: the Beaulieu Jazz Festival. For 1959 we set up a serious and independent administration system, and planned an elaborate and sophisticated promotional campaign. We bought a nineteenth-century fairground merry-go-round with magnificent galloping horses to become our special stage. Queen Victoria herself was said to have ridden upon it.

This time we had a crowd of 5000 and apart from attempts to climb over the wall into the grounds things went off reasonably well. Unfortunately my opinion was not shared by some of my conservative neighbours and there was muttering in the village. The complaints mainly focused on the noise and the mess. In my opinion the first of these was melodious and comparatively short-lived. The second was minimal and my staff cleaned up what there was quickly and efficiently. After all, it was not in my interests to have Beaulieu looking littered.

Actually, the complainants were the sort of older people who often exhibit a knee-jerk grudge against anyone younger than themselves. As I was still in my early thirties, this included me too. I take some pride, incidentally, in the fact that now that I am over seventy I bear absolutely no resentment whatever against the young. The sort of person who disliked 'youth' in the late Fifties also tended to disapprove of my other commercial activities. They seemed not to realise that, without the money generated by the Motor Museum, the opening of Palace House and events like the Jazz Festival, the estate was in danger of being broken up. Its essential character, which was what they claimed to enjoy so much, would have been destroyed. Despite this they persisted in thinking that what I was doing was inherently 'vulgar'. I don't think I am being unduly paranoid when I also suggest that there were some – and this included one or two senior members of the county police force – who remembered my prosecution and who believed, rather eccentrically, that I had 'got off lightly'. Sexual tolerance in a certain section of middle Britain was, by the standards of today, quite unheard of. This was to change in the Sixties, but at the time of what became known as the Battle of Beaulieu the Sixties had barely begun.

The fifth festival was scheduled for August Bank Holiday, 1960 and was spread over the entire holiday with three evening sessions each of which began at 7.30 and continued until midnight. We provided a campsight and a caravan site under the command of two specially recruited sergeants from the Irish Guards. Caravan and camping both cost 5s. a night. Our marketing and sales were much more sophisticated than hitherto. We offered special concessions for parties and our poster campaign was so cosmopolitan that they even went up in Paris. The cast list included the cream of British jazz – Acker Bilk, Johnny Dankworth and Cleo Laine, Tubby Hayes, Nat Gonella, Ronnie Scott and Humphrey Lyttelton. We even had two Americans, Memphis Slim and Little Brother Montgomery. Riches indeed!

I have always been catholic in my tastes and I have no problem in accommodating all sorts of music. I have never had much sympathy with people who say they are addicted to 'classical' music but can't stand jazz. I have even less sympathy for Wagnerians who hate Mozart and vice versa. I have least sympathy of all for those who profess enthusiasm for one sort of jazz while loathing another. Unfortunately, there were many who did not share my catholicity over jazz and hundreds of them flocked to Beaulieu in 1960 to represent both factions – trad and modern.

We predicted an audience of around 10,000 to listen to more than a hundred musicians from twenty-one bands. Special trains and buses were laid on, beer and refreshment tents erected. We built a barbecue big enough for an ox. BBC TV were doing live broadcasts on the Saturday and Monday.

The one person who did not seem to appreciate the magnitude of the event was the Chief Constable. At the time I was naive enough to be baffled by his apparent lack of interest. With the benefit of hindsight, however, I believe that he was deliberately trying to wreck the Jazz Festival. Temperamentally he was on the side of the local mutterers.

Three weeks earlier the Newport Jazz Festival in Rhode Island, USA had erupted in an orgy of tear gas and disorder, with fans and riot police attacking each other. From the very first I had said that my ambition was to make Beaulieu the European equivalent of Newport, but I was talking about the music not the mayhem. I suspect that some of our so-called fans thought it would be fun to emulate the riots in Newport. Naturally we took our own precautions, but we simply did not have the resources or the expertise to control thousands of overexcited jazz fanatics. The sergeants from the Irish Guards were all very well, but there were only two of them. If the Chief Constable had not been so uncooperative he would have drafted in at least the same sort of police presence that I saw two days later at the non-combustible local event, the New Forest Agricultural Show. Not much chance of a riot there! Despite all our entreaties, the Chief Constable refused to give us any extra police. Later, John Freeman, writing in the *New Statesman*, said he thought the Chief Constable's behaviour should be formally investigated. Needless to say, nothing happened.

The trouble really began on the Saturday night during Johnny Dankworth's performance. His 'modern' jazz was not appreciated by the large numbers of 'trad' fans present. Troublemakers climbed under the ropes around the stage and gathered under the scaffolding supporting the television arc lights. A little later they started to climb the scaffolding for a better view. Alan Dell, the compère, twice interrupted the music and tried to persuade them to climb down. He failed.

Somehow Dankworth and his orchestra, accompanied by his lovely singer wife Cleo Laine, managed to complete their performance. After this there was supposed to be a fifteen-minute interval before the advent of the 'trad' jazz hero, Acker Bilk. This was a mistake. Over that weekend the landlord of the Montagu Arms in Beaulieu village claimed to have sold 330 gallons of draught beer and 24,000 bottles. To judge from the general air of inebriation, most of it had been imbibed by the time the Dankworth orchestra were preparing to leave the stage. Half the crowd was chanting 'We want Acker'. The other half obviously didn't want Acker, but wanted Dankworth to finish his programme and started throwing bottles to show their disapproval.

A number of 'fans' climbed on to the horses on the roundabout behind the stage and refused to move. A girl with a lighted candle in her hat appeared high on the scaffolding. A shadowy figure suddenly came out on to the roof of Palace House – a remarkable climb even for a professional cat burglar. This prompted more bottle throwing and yet the few police provided still remained resolutely outside the grounds. My own staff were powerless and before long the crowd had invaded the stage itself.

Finally Acker Bilk and his band arrived, proceeding through the mêlée with extreme difficulty in a Model T Ford bus from the Museum. Soon after his band started playing the bedlam and bottles got worse and, without warning, the BBC scaffolding suddenly collapsed. I was on stage at the time, trying to evade the bottles being thrown and making an attempt to pacify the crowd.

Amazingly, despite the powerful arc lights and the cables attached to them, no one was electrocuted. One of the BBC's cameras was already out of action and this further disruption reduced their commentator, Derek Jones, to complete speechlessness. The BBC producer, foolishly in my view, stopped the transmission, thus blacking out what would have been one of the Corporation's most dramatic live broadcasts. Acker and his band were forced to retreat, his banjoist's instrument crushed to bits, and a long way after the nick of time the police finally arrived, accompanied by twenty ambulances and five fire engines.

My favourite moment in this alarming, though oddly exhilarating, episode concerned the Queen's cousin, the Hon. Gerald Lascelles, younger son of The Princess Royal, my annual guest and a well-known jazz lover, who was valiantly battling alongside the stewards in a vain attempt to keep order. At the height of the confusion my dignified butler, Fox, sailed into the crowd, dropped on one knee immediately in front of the battling Gerald and announced: 'Sir, Her Royal Highness the Princess Royal has phoned.' I think Gerald found time to say that he was otherwise engaged.

Almost immediately after this surreal moment I heard Gerald, some-what peremptorily, ordering a man off the roof of the merry-go-round. He had a rather fruity, patrician voice and the man objected. 'Come down,' said Gerald.

'No,' said the man, 'not until you say please.'

'Come down,' repeated Gerald.

'Say please,' said the man.

'Oh, all right,' said Gerald, 'please.' The man came down and, despite the general disorder, I couldn't help feeling a tiny bit proud to be British.

Astonishingly, some sort of calm was restored. The ambulances took away thirty injured but, mercifully, they were only slightly hurt. Many of the audience stayed on, rather shamefaced, to listen to a final hour of music played without interruption or incident. In the village itself there was some bottle throwing and windows were broken. Some straw in a lean-to garden shed was set on fire and an unrestored 1922 charabanc was singed. Humphrey Lyttelton's trumpet was found abandoned in the car park and clothing attributed to George Melly halfway up a tree. It could have been a lot worse.

Immediately afterwards I held an impromptu press conference at which I said that this was the end of Beaulieu Jazz Festivals. There would be no performances on Sunday and Monday, and no Festival the following year. By morning I had changed my mind, as I was comforted that 200 remorseful fans had come to help with the clearing-up. We rewarded them with free tickets and I decided to carry on the programme. I did not want to disappoint the thousands of bona fide fans who had made long journeys to attend the Festival and I was greatly influenced by the courage of Peter Bale, the BBC Bristol producer, who said he wanted to go ahead with the Monday evening broadcast. So we did and the last two days passed off without further incident, except that just before the BBC's Monday broadcast they were again blacked out, this time by an unexplained power failure. Poor Auntie, she too had a miserable Festival in 1960, as did one tragic taxi driver who was killed for his money by a fan.

The press comments were predictably unpleasant. The *News of the World* ran banner headlines, an Italian newspaper wrote about the '*Pandemonio di 8000 giovani*' and in the *New Statesman* John Freeman pompously took me to task for not providing good enough lavatories. Some moralised and upbraided me for my role in the disorders. I was particularly irritated by a comment in an Irish paper deploring 'the deliberate exploitation of the young by avaricious men who lust after their ever-rising earnings and who care little if, in the process of relieving the teenagers of their money, they are set on the road to ruin'. Needless to say, I did not recognise myself in this stricture and despite a petition from forty-one protesting villagers I decided to go ahead with a 1961 Festival.

This time we were scrupulously careful, as we instituted a total ban on alcohol and a limit of 6000 advance tickets per performance, with no admission at the door. We brought the date forward from the August Bank Holiday to the preceding weekend and we engaged twenty-two stewards from the Boxing Section of the Eastleigh Youth Club, five Alsatians and fifteen policemen whom we had to pay ourselves. We also replaced the vulnerable old merry-go-round with a state-of-the-art modern stage protected by a palisade of spiked hurdles worthy of a medieval battlefield like Agincourt.

The cast list was the best ever. Chris Barber came for the first time; Johnny Dankworth returned. So did Kenny Ball, Mick Mulligan and George Melly. From the States we had Anita O'Day, who had created a sensation with her 'Tea for Two' as sung at the Newport Jazz Festival, and from Germany the saxophonist Hans Kroller. 'Trad' and 'Mod' were kept well apart and my only regret was that Acker Bilk was not on the bill. We all agreed that his presence would be too provocative.

The Festival was a huge success and so orderly that even the most lurid sections of the press conceded that it was more like a Sunday school outing than a jazz festival. Unfortunately, our writ did not run beyond the Festival grounds and the situation in the village was very different. An estimated 20,000 visitors crowded in for the weekend, markedly unpoliced. The visitors were generally described as 'beatniks', although this seemed unfair on beatniks. They were no more than hooligans who had come for a spot of good old-fashioned bother. They fought in the streets, copulated in front gardens, disrupted the traffic, defecated in garages and urinated in gutters. In fairness to the constabulary, it would have taken a battalion of the SAS to keep them under control. The situation was intolerable and I knew in my heart that I could never risk a repeat. Accordingly, at midnight, I called all seven bandleaders on stages and asked them to blow a final combined version of 'When the Saints Go Marching In'. It was our Last Post. Immediately afterwards I announced with deepest regret that there would be no more Jazz Festivals at Beaulieu. It had become, I thought, like trying to hold a test match on a village green. Sadly the Festival was a victim of its own popularity, destroyed by its own success.

George Melly, who had performed at every one of the Festivals, wrote a moving obituary: 'Somehow Beaulieu had become a part of how we live now. It gave one a chance to see what was happening to the young, and most of that was for the better; they are more tolerant than they were, mentally tougher, and more vivid and lively. There have been several really magic moments. There have been a lot of giggles. Beaulieu, like Aldermaston, had become one of the secular festivals of the atheists' year.'

Time's passing can be harsh, but at the time George was surely right. The Campaign for Nuclear Disarmament's Aldermaston March and the Beaulieu Jazz Festival were foremost among the high days of the alternative society. Now they have been consigned to history. Still, in a small way I can claim that the Beaulieu Jazz Festivals helped make that history, and it is some comfort for the ultimate defeat by a handful of hooligans and by an equally hostile reactionary local 'Establishment'. Even now I still receive nostalgic letters from people who enjoyed the Jazz Festivals. There are men and women in their late thirties and early forties who claim they were almost certainly conceived in the rhododendrons.

After our last Jazz Festival in 1961 such music was rapidly being overtaken by rock 'n' roll. This was reflected when we tried one more Festival in 1962 in Bellevue, Manchester, which was not a success, although we had hired a band called The Swinging Blue Jeans from Liverpool – they were very much in the new mood – a rock band not a jazz group. Jazz was falling out of fashion. The post-jazz period in Beaulieu was a difficult one, but I tried to revive the idea of outdoor concerts with a Folk Festival in 1966, starring Julie Felix. Unfortunately we were deluged with rain and we reluctantly decided not to try again.

However, in 1977, on the twenty-first anniversary of the first jazz concert in 1956, we decided to put on a big reunion of classical music and jazz, which included performances by Dizzy Gillespie, Major Holley, Joe Venuti, Humphrey Lyttleton and the Bournemouth Symphony Orchestra, with whom I played the Concerto for Motor Car and Orchestra. The seating, staging, lighting and so on were all excellent, but we still lost money on the event. On the whole, however, I have left it to others to continue the music festival tradition originally established at Beaulieu. Such annual fixtures as Glastonbury, Reading and Knebworth were, I believe, Beaulieu's natural descendants.

As my direct interest in jazz faded I became keen on the new popular music of the Beatles, the Beach Boys and particularly the Rolling Stones. I got to know Mick Jagger well because we lived close to one another in Marylebone. As we shared a garage, his Aston Martin 'slept with' my Mini, and we often used to see each other when I was fetching my car. In talking to him one day I discovered that he had never seen *Hair*, then the great hit musical in London, in which his name was mentioned. So I got some tickets for the show and, as was the custom, the audience ended up dancing on the stage – one of the leading roles was performed by our good friend Oliver Tobias. Now a famous actor, Oliver is the son of the distinguished Swiss actress Maria Becker, who was a great friend of Elizabeth, and he used to come to Beaulieu when he was a child. After dinner we went back to Mick's house in Cheyne Walk where a certain amount of smoking of 'exotic substances' was going on. Everybody was feeling very relaxed when the front doorbell rang and it was reported that there was a policeman at the door. Panic ensued and a large amount of 'substances' were thrown on to the fire. The door was opened and the policeman asked about a car which had been improperly parked outside, but actually did not belong to anyone in the house – rather an anticlimax and very much to the chagrin of the party.

A year or so later Mick Jagger was arrested for possession of marijuana and was due to come up at the Lewes Assizes. At that time the Lord Mayor gave a welcome home luncheon at the Mansion House to Sir Francis Chichester to mark his epic round-the-world voyage at which he was made a Freeman of the City of London. As an old friend of Sir Francis, I was invited and sat opposite William Rees-Mogg, then the editor of *The Times*. We found ourselves engaged in a heated discussion about marijuana and the persecution that the government of the day was employing against many virtually innocent people. I suggested to Rees-Mogg that alcohol and tobacco were the cause of more deaths than 'drugs'. I was delighted to see the next day that the leading article in *The Times*, by William Rees-Mogg, was headed WHY BREAK A BUTTERFLY ON A WHEEL?. A few days before his attendance at Lewes I met Mick and asked him where he was going after the trial. Knowing he would like some peace and quiet in order to avoid the attention of the press, I invited him and Marianne Faithfull to the Beach House. They duly turned up and spent two days there and in spite of frantic press searching nobody ever found out where they had been.

So successful was the visit that, about a year later, when Brian Jones was had up on a similar charge he too came down to Beaulieu for a few days to hide. His efforts not to be noticed were somewhat spoiled by his arriving in an enormous hired Rolls-Royce and asking at the Montagu Arms Hotel in the village how to get into the grounds of Palace House. Nevertheless, the next day we all went to the Isle of Wight in my motor yacht and he was able to unwind a bit. Another group whom we got to know well was the Seekers, whom my wife heard perform in Brisbane when they were virtually unknown. We became very good friends with Keith Potger and, although he lives in Australia, we still keep in touch.

Another international singer, Roy Orbison, came to see me, because he collected historic cars. I took him out on the Solent in my yacht. Next time he came to England he was due to visit Beaulieu again, but during one of his concerts at Bournemouth there was a terrific fire at his home in the USA. All his cars were destroyed but, far worse, his two sons perished in the blaze. I never saw him again.

I have always tried to introduce a musical element into my own events. One memorable occasion was the arrival at Buckler's Hard of Sir Francis Chichester from his round-the-world voyage. Buckler's Hard was the home port of *Gipsy Moth* and Neville Mariner, whom I first met at the Mermaid Theatre, brought his orchestra down and conducted the *Royal Fireworks Music*, with real fireworks and *Gipsy Moth* lit up in the foreground.

When I became chairman of English Heritage in 1984 I was very keen to expand the cultural side of the organisation and gave an undertaking in the House of Lords that the GLC-organised Kenwood concerts would be continued. I was greatly assisted by the initiatives and devoted work of Michael Webber of the English Heritage staff, who was also responsible for souvenirs and marketing. I soon relieved him of these tasks and made him concentrate full-time on running musical events for us. The results were splendid and, as I have mentioned in my chapter on English Heritage, the activities were greatly increased to include jazz, brass bands and even poetry readings.

Although music has played a very big part in my life I have been equally interested in theatre and film. I attended my first theatre when I was five and I remember going to see *Peter Pan* starring Jean Forbes-Robertson, staged at the Empire theatre in Southampton, now called the Mayflower. I got so frightened when Captain Hook, bathed in a green light, was trying to poison Tinkerbell, that I covered my face with my hands and asked my mother to tell me when Captain Hook had left the stage. My next theatrical experience was much more exciting and rewarding. I saw Ivor Novello playing Henry V in the Theatre Royal Drury Lane and the chorus was played by my sister's great friend Gwen Ffrangcon-Davies, and with great excitement I was taken backstage to meet her and Ivor, who showed me his sword. Late on in life, I became quite a 'Stage Door Johnny' when visiting my friends in the theatre, once even picking up Peter Ustinov in a vintage sports Mercedes and taking him out to dinner.

We had regular Shakespeare and other plays performed in the Cloisters of Beaulieu Abbey, and I was very pleased to bring about a performance of *King John*, its founder.

And so to film. My early diaries seem to consist of little else but listing the films I had seen and my comments on them. Post-war Britain was full of good theatre and I encouraged local amateur companies to Beaulieu to perform shows in the Cloisters. As Beaulieu became more famous we also attracted a lot of film companies, continuing the tradition of when *A Gipsy Cavalier* was filmed here in 1922, starring the then famous boxer George Carpentier and Marie Claire, who had to be rescued from being drowned when a scene they were shooting on the river got out of hand. Later in the same year we had none other than Lady Diana Cooper making *The Virgin Queen.*

One of the greatest films shot at Beaulieu was *A Man for All Seasons* in 1966, with Paul Scofield, Robert Shaw, Orson Welles, Leo McKern, Susannah York and John Hurt. The location was chosen because the Beaulieu river was the only one in the country which still resembles the Thames in the sixteenth century. It seemed almost ironic that Thomas Cromwell and Henry VIII should be debating the reformation and the dissolution of the monasteries on a site which their real namesakes had destroyed. Most days I would join the unit for lunch and one day Mrs Zimmermann, wife of the director Fred Zimmermann, remarked on the wonderful singing she had heard in our church that morning. I realised at once that she had heard our haunting and not the Beaulieu choir which, excellent as it was, cannot aspire to Gregorian chant. She got quite upset at the thought of what she had heard but accepted it with good grace as it was after all a well-known haunting. Indeed, Beaulieu was used for *The Stately Ghosts of England*, a film for NBC Television starring Margaret Rutherford. It was shown throughout the network on the day after Churchill died and I went to New York especially for the transmission.

Other programmes which have been made at Beaulieu include *The Avengers*, Anneka Rice's *Treasure Hunt* and *The Two Ronnies*, as well as numerous documentaries and TV commercials. In 1997 we had a great Christmas Concert there with Montserrat Caballé and Cher, which was broadcast on Christmas Eve and, as a double bill, the BBC broadcast its Christmas Day *Songs of Praise* from Beaulieu. The final accolade was eight half-hour television programmes made for Meridian television by Mike Mansfield Television Ltd, which gave a wonderful overview of the whole estate and all its various activities, and which will be a permanent record of the estate in the last year of the twentieth century.

*

I can hardly write an autobiography without mentioning my famous fancy dress balls. My first, in 1963, held to mark the opening of the Maritime Museum, was an eighteenth-century naval ball attended by Lord Mountbatten, who later opened the Museum. This was followed in 1967 by a 'Kings and Queens' party to celebrate the centenary of the presentation of the estate to my father, as a wedding present from his father. In 1974, when I married again, we celebrated with 'The Great Gatsby Ball'. My wife can pride herself that she can still get into her lovely white suit, but I am afraid mine has shrunk. Among the guests were Lord Mountbatten, Diana Dors and Lord Bath. For my fiftieth birthday in 1976 we returned to the nostalgia of World War Two and everyone was encouraged to come in 1940s clothes or uniform. We served Brown Windsor Soup out of tin mugs. Before the ball I gave a special dinner party for my old army friends and some were even able to turn up in their original uniforms. RSM Britain, the famous 'voice' of the Brigade, announced the guests but the star of the evening was Dame Vera Lynn, whom we kept hidden until midnight and who came down the stairs singing 'We'll Meet Again'. There was hardly a dry eye in the hall.

On my sixtieth birthday in 1986, the hundredth anniversary of the first cars produced by both Benz and Daimler in 1886, we had a great ball in the Motor Museum. Guests came dressed as everything from Belisha beacons to pedestrian crossings and, of course, wearing splendid Edwardian coats. I started off wearing a tweed knickerbocker suit and ended up in mechanic's overalls. Our entertainer there was Lynsey de Paul and I am glad to say no cars were damaged by over-exuberant guests, although one or two back seats were used.

The most recent fancy dress ball was my seventieth birthday, the theme for which, as I mentioned at the beginning of this chapter, was 'If Music be the Food of Love, Play On'. It was held in an enormous marquee, erected on the lawn, and over a thousand guests came, including a whole group of young people, as it was my son Jonathan's twenty-first birthday too. At midnight I appeared in a cloud of smoke, sitting in my 1909 Rolls-Royce Silver Ghost. We were then entertained by our good friends Diana Montague and David Rendall, two great international operatic singers who live nearby.

Apart from giving parties, I enjoy going to them and I remember memorable balls at Buckingham Palace; Jimmy Goldsmith's election night party in 1983 at Cliveden when Mrs Thatcher swept the boards; as well as occasions at Kensington Palace, Castle Howard, Longleat and the Royal Yacht Squadron at Cowes, among others. The most amusing incident happened when I was returning to Beaulieu from a Roman fancy dress party near Portsmouth and the car ran out of petrol within two miles of Palace House. Dressed as a Roman centurion and leaving my wife, dressed as a Roman maiden, in the car I started striding back to the house to fetch another car or some petrol to get home. A car coming in the opposite direction caught me in its headlights and there was a screech of brakes as it nearly drove into the ditch. The two policemen in the car were very glad that it was me and not a ghost ... for which Beaulieu is well known. They kindly drove me back home enabling me to rescue the car.

Over the years we have had many concerts at Beaulieu. Latterly we established our annual Palace House Proms, performed by the Bournemouth Symphony Orchestra, and these have been enormously successful. There is a great atmosphere, with people picnicking on the grass, and the concert ends with fireworks. Long may such occasions continue.

Nowadays some of the best music at Beaulieu is heard monthly in the church, organised by Music at Beaulieu Abbey, with distinguished soloists – both professional and amateur – and bands, orchestras and singers of all sorts. These concerts raise much-needed money for the restoration of the church. Recent productions have included performances by the celebrated US soprano Joanna Porackova, and the choral scholars of King's College Cambridge, the London Welsh Male Voice Choir and the Tallis Chamber Orchestra.

I still enjoy music of all kinds, although I must confess that now most of my music listening is done in the car either from the BBC, Classic FM or CDs. One's CD library grows apace and one never has enough time to listen to them all. At least I take comfort from the fact that the British public are getting more musical each year and the Proms continue to be well attended.

I feel very fortunate that I have been able to experience and enjoy such a wide range of music – from Acker Bilk to Wagner. I still enjoy music of all kinds, although, as I grow older, I find some pop music, such as Rap, does get on my nerves. Nevertheless, music, drama and films have been a wonderful solace to me in times of stress and have given me enormous inspiration, excitement and emotion throughout my life. They have also introduced me to a fascinating and stimulating stream of good friends.

Of course, good music sounds even better if one has a glass of wine in one's hand. Since I was a small boy I have always been fascinated with wine, even before I was able to drink it. During the war, when I was a teenager, I cannot remember wine other than rather warm sherry being drunk at home. My interest was very much aroused and stimulated during my time at Voice and Vision, when we were charged with publicising wines from Bordeaux and Madeira, which required the organisation of wine tastings in London and the sending of journalists to Madeira to report on their vineyards.

In immediate post-war Britain Beaujolais and Mateus Rosé became the firm favourites, as did Blue Nun Liebfraumilch, but as people gradually began to travel more and more, they returned from continental holidays with an improved knowledge of wine and demanded better quality.

I had long wished to re-create the ancient vineyard which the monks had planted at Beaulieu in the thirteenth century. This dream came true through the splendid initiative of Colonel Robert and Mrs Margaret Gore-Browne who bought the house at Beaulieu called The Vineyard overlooking the ancient site and replanted a vineyard in 1959. I took real interest from the beginning and assisted as the first wines were produced. It was managed by an Italian called Lanza, who claimed to be a cousin of Mario, and he brought typical Italian customs to the business. After Robert Gore-Browne died Margaret approached us to ask whether we would take over the day-to-day management, which we were delighted to do and, when she died, she very generously left the vineyard in her will to my son Ralph. So the vineyard is now again part of the estate. Since 1959 we have won several medals. Our first wine was a rosé, but this has been largely discontinued and we now concentrate on white wine and our Beaulieu Bubbly sparkling white wine, which has real merit. At the moment we are contemplating renewing the vineyard, using different varieties, and are confident that we can further improve our quality.

My connection with English wine led me eventually to succeed Sir Guy Salisbury-Jones, who started the famous Hambledon Vineyard in Hampshire, as president of the English Vineyards Association. Some forty years after its foundation, the Association has over 400 members and its vineyards produce three million bottles of mostly white wine a year. English wine is now seriously considered by masters of wine and we have an annual awards ceremony in the House of Lords, where a full tasting of the best wines takes place. Initially very few varieties, like Müller-Thurgau and Seyval Blanc, were being planted, but now many new varieties are providing successful and people even make a red wine. Fundamentally, most of our grape varieties come from northern Europe, primarily the Riesling grape. It seems to us that it is very unfair that we have to pay such a high tax on English-grown wine compared with similar wine growers in the rest of Europe. However, I hope that a future Chancellor will relent one day.

About twenty years ago, together with Brian Hope of IPC and with the help of Sir Alex Alexander of Allied Breweries, we formed the Wine Guild of the UK, which is an official chapter of the Fédération Internationale des Confréries Bachiques. Our first international congress was in Nantes and our special robes, which we had made for the Guild, were splendidly received by the crowds on the way to the cathedral. Since then the Guild has gone from strength to strength and consists of many distinguished people from the wine industry and elsewhere. Bi-annually we have a Harvest Thanksgiving at Beaulieu and in alternate years we have overseas trips to such places as Saint-Emilion, Spain, Hungary and elsewhere on the Continent. Dedicated as we are to wine education, awards are given to journalists for their contribution to wine knowledge. Our most sought-after events are our tastings, conducted by the owners of some of the great vineyards of France like Château Palmer and Pichon Longueville. I certainly subscribe to the view that wine is very good for you and I have not drunk spirits for years.

For me music and drama have indeed been the foods of love and even now I am happy to say . . . play on!

Epilogue
Family matters

This above all, to thine own self be true...
William Shakespeare

As I end the writing of this book I contemplate the now closed chapters with a mixture of regret and pride. I am reluctant to say goodbye to them and so, for one final time, I am going to cast an eye over them. As I do I cannot help but wonder what the verdict will be of those whose opinions have meant most to me. What would my mother and father think? Actually, I have a shrewd idea of what my mother would think but my father I never knew and I have little or no way of knowing what sort of mark he would give me. I suppose this is what concerns all of us who attain mature years and look back over the lives we have led.

I am essentially a believer when it comes to religion and I have a respect and fear of the Last Judgement. I cannot help feeling that when the final moment comes and I enter the pearly gates there will be a censorious figure – a strange combination, perhaps, of my parents, Mr Ridgeway of St Peter's Court, the headmaster of Eton, the lieutenant-colonel of the Grenadiers, the Dean of New College, the Lord Chancellor, or one of the seven secretaries of state to whom I was responsible at English Heritage – all those, in short, who at one stage or another have stood in authority in my life. They will be there to deliver a verdict: not perhaps to send me to heaven or hell but at least to grade my performance according to the standards to which I was educated, on a classically based scale of marks ranging from the excellence of an alpha plus to the ignominy of a delta minus.

There have been a number of alphas and deltas in my life for, like most, mine has had its ups and downs as well as its wheels within wheels. This happened from the very beginning when, from the comfort and security of my nursery I was deposited in the next from bottom class of my prep school, homesick, scared and a natural prey to bullies of all kinds.

After five years or so of climbing up the ladder of prep school with a modicum of social, academic and athletic success, I was sent sliding down the slippery snake by having to become, once again, a frightened new boy in a new school's lower form. I had a double adolescent experience of this because of leaving Ridley and moving on to Eton in my mid-teens at a time when most of my contemporaries had been *in situ* for at least two years. After ascending Eton's greasy pole there was another rapid fall from grace with my military training. It was quite a shock to go from being a senior at Eton to being shouted at by a regimental sergeant major from the Brigade of Guards. After a year or so with my regiment I had climbed once more, only to be reduced to the ranks as a callow freshman at Oxford.

And so throughout life I seem to have experienced the relentless seasonal shift through summer, autumn and winter to the unfailing miracle of spring. Office boy to director in just four years; company director to prison inmate in a matter of months; and so on through the years until now I hope that I may have seen my last trough before the final inevitable winter and the ultimate spring of life after death where, doubtless, one will have, yet again, to climb through the ranks before being allowed to sit with the angels.

As I conclude these autobiographical musings I am also intrigued by the inevitable question all of us ask ourselves in moments of reflection: 'What if . . .?' Birth itself is often described as an accident. We live in a world that has become more envious since I was born and when the idea of being 'born with a silver spoon in your mouth' is widely considered unfair. Perhaps so. As I have been at pains to point out, the inheritance of an ancient title and estate implies obligations as well as privileges, but I cannot pretend that in my case the benefits of being a baron and a landowner have not outweighed enormously the penalties. I admit it: I was born lucky. But what if I had been born unlucky? Would I have surmounted handicaps? Do I owe my good fortune to the circumstances of my birth? Would I have been fulfilled if I had not been a Montagu of Beaulieu?

What if my father had not died when he was only sixty-two but had lived on into his eighties? I would then have been in my teens. I do not believe that I am being ungrateful if I say that I view my earliest years with a degree of ambivalence. The early death of my father was a blow to all concerned and although I am eternally grateful to a variety of male influences, most notably my stepfather Ned, I cannot pretend that never really knowing my father has been other than a great deprivation. My mother did her level best to make up for this, striving to take his place, but there is no denying that his death left a void which could never be filled. And devoted though I am to my sisters, I do regret that I had no male siblings of comparable age. My early prayers for a brother were finally answered in 1937 with the arrival of my half brother Robin, who is, of course, ten years my junior. Robin has always been a great friend but he arrived, alas, too late, to diminish the feminine character of my nursery years. I often wonder if this female dominance affected my own sexuality for, in early childhood, my gender was something of a mystery to me.

Despite slightly more than my fair share of illness and a reputation for being a fragile plant, I enjoyed those earliest years as much as possible. The creature comforts were considerable, I had a doting family and friends, and Beaulieu was a special place. However, I think it fair to say that those earliest chapters in my life's story do not quite live up to the heady optimism of my arrival as the long-awaited heir.

What if I had not gone to St Peter's Court? For the first time in my life I was in an all-male society. The school itself gave me a sound grounding in academic subjects and increased a catholic love of music which had already begun. Above all, however, this was a period when I made friends, and friends for life. I know that many people, for any number of reasons, never hang on to childhood friends but I count myself incomparably blessed to have a number of people who have remained close to me for more than sixty years. These are the friends that I first made at St Peter's Court. What if I had never been there? What if I had gone to the Beaulieu village school instead?

What if I had never been to Canada and been exposed to North American culture for two years? War and the consequent disruption were a blow. This is in no way to denigrate my Canadian friends and benefactors, nor Ridley College, which was a fine establishment where I and my other British evacuee friends were as happy as could be. North America gave me self-confidence and opened my eyes to a different sort of life. I have loved it ever since. Yet at the same time I was homesick and at the back of my mind there was always the feeling – unjustified I think, but nonetheless real – that I had somehow funked it and run away from the danger of Britain at war.

And what if I had gone to Eton straight from prep school? I make no complaint about the school, about the education it afforded, about the opportunity for forging yet more enduring friendships, about the beauty of the historic setting. I had moments of great happiness there – messing about on the river, experiencing the first tremors of romantic love, joining in jazz 'jam' sessions and even sharing in the perils and privations of wartime England – but my Canadian exile exacted a penalty. Despite the many bonuses of life at Eton I felt that I never quite caught up with my contemporaries and that consequently I never felt entirely at home and never completely entered into that special fraternity peculiar to those many friends for whom their Eton schooldays were truly the happiest days of their life. I almost feel as if I only ever had 'half' an Eton. What if I had been granted a 'whole' Eton? Or stayed at Ridley and had none at all?

I enjoyed the Army more but what if I had been just a little older? I would certainly have seen action in World War Two; seen friends killed; perhaps been killed myself. Those early days of London soldiering were fascinating and revealing, and huge fun even if my socialising sometimes took precedence over the rigours of military training. I still feel slightly hurt, incidentally, that my adjutant considered that my social activities interfered with my duties as a soldier. And when I was ordered to join the battalion in strife-stricken Palestine I in no way regarded it as the punishment which I think my CO intended. Palestine, in fact, provided my first real taste of adult life – and death – of commanding men, of sexual intercourse, of shots fired in anger, of being, in a word, 'grown-up'. It also gave me a lifelong interest in the Middle East. But once more, I have to ask myself 'What if . . .?'

After that heady experience I suppose my Oxford chapter was always going to be something of an anticlimax. In different circumstances it could have been the idyll that others obviously enjoyed. But as with Eton, I never felt entirely at ease. It was partly that I was not fundamentally suited to the academic life, partly that I was torn to an extent between what one might describe as my high social and aesthetic leanings. I saw no conflict here but others did – on both sides of the divide. Worst of all, however, was that after soldiering in an overseas war zone conflict, Oxford with its petty rules and regulations seemed like a step back into childhood. I regret this. It should have been a memorable chapter in the book of my life but it came several pages too late. Perhaps it was partly my fault. Once more I forged new friendships and revelled in experiences involving

photography, motoring, music, theatre, public speaking (although significantly in adult London rather than adolescent Oxford) and even
lectures by such luminaries as A. J. P. Taylor. But what if I had never been
there? What if I had gone straight into a London career or concentrated
exclusively on Beaulieu? Would I have acquired the love of music, the
Arts, politics and travel which Oxford nurtured? And would I have
become more or less confused about my sexuality? My attraction to both
sexes neither changed nor diminished at university and it was comforting
to find that I was not the only person faced with such a predicament. I
agonised less than my contemporaries for I was reconciled to my bisexuality, but I was still nervous about being exposed as I ultimately was.

What if I had stayed on and got a degree instead of sending myself
down?

My time in public relations was another matter altogether. These racy,
unfettered moments were some of the best of my life. I loved the raffish
bohemianism of this world and I believe I was suited to the job. My Voice
and Vision accounts, from the launch of the children's weekly *The Eagle*
to the social promotion of Cadbury's Drinking Chocolate, all had a touch
of glamour. I myself was good-looking, well-connected, tolerably well off
as well as having a title which had and still has an irresistible ring to it.
'Montagu of Beaulieu' has a resonance which everyone found attractive.
It sounds impressive and, I would be the first to admit, looked equally
impressive in such gossip columns as the *Daily Express*'s 'William Hickey'
and the *Daily Mail*'s 'Paul Tanfield'. Besides these magical metropolitan
moments I was also sowing the seeds of success at Beaulieu with the
first beginnings of what was to become the great Motor Museum – an
enterprise which was greatly helped by the experiences gained during
four years at Voice and Vision. I discovered a natural flair for PR and
learned how to work with the media, and what were the tricks of the
trade. I particularly learned never to make an 'off-the-record' remark
unless I really wanted it to be printed. Above all, I learned not to compete.
In a war of words with the press you can never win.

So what if that fatal weekend in August 1953 had never happened? It
certainly changed my life dramatically, caused me deep physical and
mental shock, and exposed and labelled me as a person that I was not. I
found myself vilified in the very newspaper columns in which I had once
been favourably featured; in the dock and – the ultimate humiliation –
condemned to prison itself. The Montagu Case must rate as the worst

time of my life. The whole affair caused great grief and unhappiness to family and friends wide and far. I learned that some 'friends' are like rocks while others melt like the spring snow. Realising that I was a victim and a political scapegoat made me bitter and paranoid. I felt not just unfairly prosecuted but positively persecuted. I was particularly upset by the apparent manifest dishonesty and inhumanity of the police and the Director of Public Prosecutions.

Fortunately, when the darkness seemed impenetrable there were shafts of sunlight to relieve the gloom. The support not only of my family and friends, but also of complete strangers, did much to revive my faith in human nature. Later I had the triumphant revenge of knowing that the trials and tribulations of myself and my friends and co-defendants Peter Wildeblood and Michael Pitt-Rivers had not been in vain. It is no small thing to have been one of those who helped change the law of the land and especially so when it concerns the rights of adult men and women to love each other as they wish. It did not seem so at the time but in retrospect I have the satisfaction of knowing that the three of us, however unwillingly and unwittingly, struck a crucial blow on behalf of civilised society. I do not wish to make myself out a martyr but the knowledge is a fine consolation for what was otherwise a bleak and forlorn few paragraphs of my existence. I would like to believe that our suffering has brought peace of mind and contentment to many people who now lead happy lives.

What if, once I was released, I had fled abroad and tried to live on a sunny beach in exile? Or become an active campaigner for homosexual law reform? I resolved to do neither but to fight back by building up a number of successful careers and generally leading a fruitful, constructive and productive life. Our sentence was supposed to act as a deterrent. I doubt if it deterred a single person's desires or actions and it certainly did not change mine. My sexuality has not altered, although as with us all the desire for companionship becomes more important as one's sex drive fades away. Significantly and most important, I still enjoy the affection and love of my first wife and my second wife as well as my three children.

I have, in this book, used the aftermath of the Montagu Case as an opportunity for taking stock, a pause for reflection and a deliberate change of pace and emphasis. I believe this accurately reflects the pattern and tenor of my life, which was afterwards never quite the same. How could it be? Those experiences not only seared my soul, they transformed me into a household word. From being moderately famous, for mostly the right reasons, I had suddenly become extremely notorious for most of the wrong ones. Now the wheels within wheels have gone several full circles and I like to think that I am known for the right reasons once again.

Rehabilitation was a long road but the most important first step was to return to my beloved Beaulieu and to make it clear to everyone involved with the estate that I was returning, unashamed, to the helm. This, after all, was my heritage and I was responsible for its future.

When I succeeded in 1951 I had no ideas as to how I was going to be able to preserve it. To suggest that I foresaw that the opening of Palace House and the assembling of a motor collection would be successful enough to achieve my objectives is stretching the truth. Now, almost fifty years later, Beaulieu is one of Britain's leading tourist attractions and the National Motor Museum is an established institution of international repute. What if I had never founded it? Beaulieu has international acclaim and direction because of its identification with the history of the motor car in its widest sense. This has been the main achievement of my life.

I feel satisfaction at my past achievements and also I have no doubt that in the coming decades, under the wise guidance of its trustees and staff, the Museum's reputation will continue to grow – possibly in directions and areas at present undreamed of.

What if I had not accepted the challenge of championing our heritage in more general terms than those offered by Beaulieu alone?

As a founder of the Historic Houses Association and the establishment of English Heritage, I have led from the front and by example, so that the cause of all who have a concern for Historic Britain has benefited from my example and from the pioneering work that I have been privileged to undertake. I hope that in any number of ways I have carried the flag forward. Because my love of motoring has an important historical emphasis I feel that my championship of heritage in the broadest possible sense is importantly allied to that of the motor car. I hope that I have served both to the best of my ability, especially in Parliament in which I have come to take a great interest.

Reading this story of my life I realise that although those nearest and dearest to me are a constant presence I have not devoted a separate section to my family. This is not because my family is not important to me – quite the reverse. I have tried not to embarrass them with too much mention but I feel that I ought, before I end, say just a few words about what 'family' has meant to me.

Some might consider being Head of the Family a privilege to be envied, others might think it a burden. In Britain it is rarely sought after or contrived, as it is normally ordained by primogeniture. Certainly at the age of two and a half I was unaware of my future role. From the time my father died in 1929 to my succession to the estate in 1951 in this respect my mother fulfilled the role with great success and devotion. To the outside world primogeniture might seem unfair, particularly to younger children, but it has in fact been instrumental in the conservation of our historic estates and over the centuries has enabled them and their contents to be handed down from generation to generation virtually intact, at least until the introduction of death duties at the end of the last century, which started the relentless destruction of our heritage.

In essence what remained was by custom left outright to the eldest son and heir or heiress unless specifically diverted to another branch of the family. A very different situation existed in Europe under the Code Napoléon, as by law each child can claim a part of the inheritance, which meant that the death of the head of a family often resulted in the selling of ever-increasing amounts of land and the contents of the house. That is why, today, so many French chateaux are denuded of valuable pictures, furniture and carpets, and often stand magnificently alone in a park with all the surrounding land sold. Historically, one of the great benefits of primogeniture for the UK was that the younger sons and daughters did not hang around like their continental contemporaries waiting for their father to die, but went into the armed services, the Church, or politics and, as far as the girls were concerned, sought to marry well. More important, many younger sons went overseas where they re-created their own estates in the fashion of the ones they left at home, bringing to them all that is best in the British way of life which can be seen so clearly in the English-speaking world today. Thus was the foundation laid of the British Empire and the domination of the widespread use of English as a language in the world today.

As a child I do not ever remember being told that I was the head of the family, nor did I ever assume that it would be my responsibility to act as one. However, it gradually dawned on me, particularly at weddings and christenings, that I had a special part to play, for instance in frequently 'giving away' one or other of my five sisters when they got married – a job I got very used to. I felt rather thrown in at the deep end in 1951 when my stepfather Ned, who had acted as a temporary head of the family, died. From the time he married my mother in 1936, until he died tragically young in 1951, he had been involved in two world wars, been Commander of the Royal Yacht in between, and on retiring from the Navy threw himself into local politics and other local associations. Taking the place of a father I never knew, he was very understanding with me and taught me a lot about country sports and gardening. He also foresaw much about the future of Beaulieu and the benefits that would accrue after the war when it would be forced to become more commercial. I remember he persuaded the agent to put up the entrance fee to the Abbey Ruins up from 6d. to 1s. As a trustee, he certainly made a substantial and constructive contribution to planning the estate and its future. Ned died a few months before I succeeded, which could be said to be a blessing in disguise as my mother stayed at Beaulieu, moving out of Palace House to The Lodge, where she lived for the next forty-six years. After Ned died it was left to me as a responsible older brother to comfort and help my stepbrother Robin who was only fifteen and try to teach him those things that Ned had taught me. Meanwhile my elder sister Anne, who had served in the Red Cross during the war, faced tragedy when her husband Major Howell Moore-Gwyn, whom she married in 1946, contracted leukaemia as a result of wounds suffered in the Guards Chapel bombing of 1944 and died quite young, leaving a little boy. Anne was magnificent in the last months, even flying Howell to the USA for treatment, unfortunately to no avail. Their son David is now a director of Sotheby's, looking after English pictures.

My second sister Caroline, who was in Canada with me during the war and then served in the Wrens, married in 1950 Grainger Weston, eldest son of Garfield Weston the Canadian entrepreneur who built up a worldwide empire in bread, biscuits and supermarkets – not forgetting Ryvita and Fortnum & Mason. Grainger was studying at Harvard and the young couple went first to Massachusetts and from there to Texas, where the family owned cookie factories. She has been there ever since and I am very proud of my Texan family, not forgetting my Texan nephews and nieces, and great-nephews and great-nieces. Caroline and Grainger had their tragedy when their ranch was burned down and one of their sons died as a result. Grainger owns a hotel in the Caribbean, indeed one of the oldest in Jamaica situated at Frenchman's Cover near Port Antonio.

Unfortunately it was severely damaged by a hurricane some years ago but is now making a good recovery.

My younger sister Mary Clare married David, Viscount Garnock, eldest son of the Earl of Lindsay. David was in the same house as me at Eton and I knew and liked him. He was a director of Crossley Carpets and they started their married life in Yorkshire. Sadly the marriage did not flourish as we had hoped but it resulted in two children. My nephew James, now Lord Lindsay, made a very encouraging start prior to the 1997 election as a junior minister in the House of Lords and Caroline is married to Sir George Wrey and is herself a great expert on drapes and curtains, having written books and lectured in the USA on the subject. Mary Clare is now happily married to Tim Horn, who is a business consultant, and they live in Wales.

I was brought up with the knowledge that I had two half-sisters. The elder, Helen, born in 1890, was always considered something of a 'black sheep'. She ran away and went on the stage in London and from there to New York where she became a chorus girl in shows like the *Ziegfeld Follies*, shocking my father as would be expected. In fact, when my father went to New York in 1916 on a military mission he felt it his duty to see his daughter on stage. Noting that she was rather scantily clad, he felt it was better not to visit her at the stage door but left a message for her to come and have supper with him at his hotel. When Helen arrived the receptionist firmly refused to allow her entry as he suspected that neither my father nor she was up to any good. After violent protests from my father that she really was his daughter and not just someone pretending to be she was let in, with the further enquiry whether he wanted champagne too. Later she married a reprobate from Scotland called Arthur Clark-Kennedy. Both thought the other had money but discovered on their wedding night that neither had. After the war my father paid for an expensive express divorce in Scotland and no sooner had it been granted than Arthur Clark-Kennedy died. Helen was a lovely person and played the piano well by ear. At the time of writing only she and Ned have died in the immediate family and, of course, my mother, aged 101. In the 1960s it was a great joy and the fulfilment of a dream to discover the existence of an unknown half-sister. On reading my father's will on my succession I became aware that one particular clause could only refer to a trust set up for a natural child but there was no clue as regards the existence, name or whereabouts of such a child. My mother told me that it was a girl and she was the result of my father's great love affair with Eleanor Thornton, his personal assistant on his magazine *Car Illustrated* and the model for the Rolls-Royce mascot Spirit of Ecstasy. Although her life ended when she was tragically drowned in 1915 when the S.S. *Persia* was torpedoed, the child, Joan, born in 1903, had been sent for adoption, indeed immediately from the moment of birth. This might seem callous and unfeeling but Eleanor Thornton had to make the agonising choice of continuing her great love affair with my father and involving herself in the work he did or making a clean break. Later I found out that she was well provided for by my father throughout her life and my half-sister Elizabeth suspected that she got better Christmas presents than she did. So, except for knowing that she probably existed somewhere, I had no idea where and often prayed to find her as I wanted to discover more about the great love of my father. My prayers were wonderfully answered and came about this way.

My sister Elizabeth went to live in Devonshire in the 1960s and after a few years was approached one day by a friend in a queue in a fishmonger, who pointed out to her a lady and said, 'Do you know who that is? She is your sister.' Elizabeth was thrilled but her hopes were dashed when the friend told her that the lady did not want to meet her. I was greatly frustrated and determined to bring about a meeting. My plot involved sending her, through the mutual friend, not only a guidebook of Beaulieu but also photocopies of an amazing letter that her mother had sent to Cis, my father's first wife, before her fateful voyage, in which she prophesied her own death assuring Cis that, whatever happened, she would care for my father to the death. The ruse worked, she contacted me and so, with great excitement, I agreed to meet her the following week in London. I thought it would be apt to meet her in an Edwardian atmosphere and for this I booked a table at the Ritz, a place I rarely visited. Upon sitting down and ordering oysters as a first course, she said to me, 'You know, our father always used to bring me here and always made me order oysters but ate most of them himself.' We got on famously and she explained that she had not wanted us to meet so as not to be an embarrassment and burden, although she had sneaked in at the back of the Beaulieu church at my father's funeral in 1929. She had married a naval surgeon and had two sons, one of whom coincidentally worked for Rolls-Royce and, indeed, looked exactly like his grandfather. I was thrilled with this family reunion and arranged as soon as possible for her not only to meet the family at Beaulieu but also for us to go down to see her in her house in Devonshire. She told me, too, that there was some money which would be due to me on her death, which I quickly renounced in order that she could leave it to her children. Sadly, she died in 1979 and her ashes were duly scattered in our family graveyard in the Abbey, as they should be, to parallel the action of my father who in 1916 put up a bronze plate in Beaulieu church in memory of Eleanor after the sinking of the *Persia*. It was a rather bold move in those days for someone in my father's position to put up a memorial to his lover by the family pew but his wife and family accepted it. Both boys are married with children but I have made our family's recognition of them clear to all concerned by putting them and their mother in *Burke's Peerage*, confirming that they are fully recognised as members of the family. I know my father would have approved of what I have done but in those faraway Edwardian days such matters were inclined to be more complicated.

So what about myself and my two marriages and children? After Anne Gage quite understandably broke off our engagement in 1954 I somewhat naturally got it into my head that I was now so notorious and undesirable that nobody would want to marry me. Consequently I swiftly embarked on a series of love affairs that were pleasurable and educational; one who later married a famous photographer, another a lovely fashion model who died, a lady technical journalist, and the daughter of a family friend – the romance of which rather swiftly died on the ski slopes when I broke my leg.

One of the most difficult situations was when I made a young girl pregnant. Her father was a distinguished peer and scientist, and it was in the days when abortions were illegal but my girlfriend's father used his powerful influence to have the child aborted with the excuse that any child of mine would have bad blood in his veins. Hardly a very scientific approach but nevertheless, reluctantly, the girl agreed. Finally I got unofficially engaged to Lyndall Hopkinson, daughter of the famous editor of *Picture Post* and his wife Antonia White, the well-known novelist. Needless to say they did not approve but until we were forced to admit defeat we had very happy times together, especially in Italy where Lyndall worked in the Food and Agriculture Organisation. She eventually married Count Passarini and is now widowed and living in Italy.

In 1958 I rediscovered Belinda Crossley who lived locally and whose mother was a Drummond and a close neighbour. In the week she lived off Fulham Road and was trying to eke out a living as an artist and illustrator. Of course, our two families had been neighbours and close friends for years, and Belinda's Great-uncle Maldwin was one of my father's best friends who died only a few days before him. This led to a strange incident two days after Maldwin's death when my father, who was also dying, saw him come into the room and sat bolt upright in bed and said: 'Hello, Maldwin, old boy, come and sit down and talk to me.'

Belinda and I hit it off very well and I was very happy, as were all the family, when she accepted me. No sooner was our engagement announced than I competed in the Monte Carlo Rally in a Ford with *Sunday Express* Motoring Correspondent Bob Glenton, starting from Stockholm. On our arrival in Monte Carlo we were all shocked to hear that Mike Hawthorn had been killed on the Guildford bypass. Mike was a great loss to British motor racing and was, in fact, on his way to London to sign a large new contract with a motoring organisation. He was a classic example of an English amateur racing driver and would have been at home at Brooklands, just as his father was. It was particularly sad for me as I had just taken delivery from his garage in Farnham of a new red 3.4 Jaguar with black upholstery and wire wheels, a colour combination which had been an obsessive dream of mine since I was a child and I had to get it out of my system.

It was then back to Beaulieu to plan the wedding but more important, to win a court case in order to be allowed to use trust funds to construct a special building for the Montagu Motor Museum. The case went to the High Court under jurisdiction of Mr Justice Wilberforce who approved the variation of the trust and in giving the judgment gave the opinion that in modern times a De Dion Bouton veteran car could be as much of an heirloom as a Toulouse Lautrec, a truly prophetic judgment which made it possible for me to start to build what has over the years become one of the best Motor Museums in Europe. We decided to have a party to open the new building on Sunday, 5 April, one week before our wedding on Saturday the eleventh, which gave us an ideal opportunity to welcome many friends who would normally not have come. Lord Brabazon of Tara did the honours and was supported by various old racing drivers like George Eyston and Raymond Mays, and new ones like Stirling Moss and Tony Brooks. Fortunately Southern Television decided to cover the event live and it was the first time that I really appreciated the power of television, as people started driving to Beaulieu before the outside broadcast was finished.

The wedding went off well and although it rained Belinda looked wonderful in a beautiful dress adorned by the family jewels. She came from her home near Fawley in the Museum's 1906 Renault which, because of the rather relaxed attitude of her brother John, unfortunately arrived agonisingly late but that is the bride's privilege. We went to Rhodes and Greece for our honeymoon, having been lent a Humber Hawk by the Rootes dealer in Athens, and visited Olympus and Delphi. After a hectic summer when we saw the attendance figures at Beaulieu leap up to over 300,000 as a result of the new Museum, we sailed, as mentioned previously, on a Union Castle liner for Cape Town complete with four cars, the 1903 6hp De Dion Bouton, 1909 8hp Humber, 1920 350hp Sunbeam – the first car to go at 150mph – and Field Marshal Montgomery's 1941 26.9hp Humber Snipe staff car which we planned to exhibit in South Africa and Rhodesia. The first exhibitions were in Cape Town, Durban and Johannesburg, although we had problems importing the cars under South African customs regulations and great difficulty in moving them from one city to another as we were not allowed to use road transport and had to send them by rail. We travelled from one location to another in Monty's staff car which did us well but constantly overheated. The first part of the journey took us along the so-called Garden Route from Cape Town to Durban and we particularly made a point of visiting Richmond in Natal, which had been founded in 1848 by my great-grandfather; the first settlers coming from Beaulieu. It was indeed called Beaulieu to begin with but then altered to Richmond to avoid confusion to the inhabitants, although today a Beaulieu farm still exists. I took part in its centenary celebrations in 1948 and look forward to future celebrations. Having spent Christmas in Southern Rhodesia, we visited the legendary house of Shiwa in Northern Rhodesia, built by Sir Stuart Gore-Browne who was nephew of Dame Ethel Locke King on whose husband's land Brooklands, the famous racing circuit, was built. Shiwa could be described as a Scottish baronial estate and house in the middle of Africa where Sir Stuart still dressed for dinner and served the best champagnes and ports. He was indeed one of the legends of Africa. His brother Robert came to live in Beaulieu and restarted the vineyard which had been originally founded in monastic times. Then we visited Kenya where Belinda's brother farmed, and she and I both had many relations.

I love Kenya, although there was then still considerable tension resulting from the Mau Mau crisis. We went on to Uganda where we saw the Kabaka of Buganda, who had been a fellow Officer in the Grenadiers with me, and his fellow King Omukama of Toro. We finally ended up in the Sudan and went shooting sand grouse with the British Ambassador and so back home on a British Airways Comet, my first flight on a jet plane.

One great advantage was that Belinda knew Beaulieu well, having been brought up there, and our families were old friends. She was therefore able to involve herself in local activities without problems, and I was much aided by her cultivated tastes in redecorating the house, and before long preparing the nursery for new arrivals. She was enormously supportive in the early days of the museum.

We both liked travelling and in the first few years of our marriage we covered much of the world. We collected around ourselves a wide circle of friends from all walks of life and her artistic abilities were frequently used for the commercial activities of the estate and museum. There is no doubt that she made a great contribution to Beaulieu while she was there – and I pay great tribute to her for that.

After a time, when children were not appearing as we had hoped and after consulting the famous gynaecologist Mr T. Stallworthy in Oxford, Belinda found out that she had to have a cyst removed from her ovaries. This happily resulted in her becoming pregnant so we were in Oxford by 1961 under the care of Stallworthy for the birth of our first child. I stayed with my old friend from Oxford, Teddy Hall, who had found fame in scientifically dating the Piltdown Skull and later the Turin Shroud. In those days it was not done for fathers to be present at births but I remember that at three in the morning Teddy walked into my room and said, 'Congratulations, Edward, you have a son.' I was overjoyed as were all the family and I reflected on how agonising it must have been for my father to wait thirty-six years to have a son. Beaulieu was rejoicing and a blue flag flew on the mast of Palace House – but I don't know what the swans did! At a party for all staff I announced that his name would be Ralph, after the great eighteenth-century Ralph, Duke of Montagu. In 1964 daughter Mary was born in London so my happiness was complete. We had a good, if rather possessive, nanny, which was essential since Belinda and I were travelling all over the world – including Australia where, incidentally, Mary was conceived while on a car rally in the Blue

Mountains of New South Wales. Wherever we went I gave lectures, met veteran and vintage car clubs, gave press, television and radio interviews, and did all I could to interest potential overseas visitors in Britain's historic houses and, of course, the Motor Museum.

Meanwhile the estate and Museum were developing fast in the competent hands of Brian Hubbard, the resident agent appointed by Strutt and Parker, who minded the shop very well while I was away. At home I became more absorbed in building up the new Montagu Motor Museum and editing the monthly *Veteran and Vintage* magazine in London. I embarked upon long lecture tours to promote stately homes, and Beaulieu in particular, generally for the British Tourist Authority. These were very tiring and time-consuming, but I certainly covered a lot of the United States in those years and spread the message about Beaulieu and Britain.

In retrospect I now realise that my long periods away from home were damaging our marriage and were not helped by various charming, if rather indeterminate, people turning up at Beaulieu as a consequence of invitations I had casually extended while I was overseas. There is no doubt that Belinda started feeling overwhelmed and wanted to fulfil her own chosen career as an embroiderer and artist. She felt the commercial operation at Beaulieu was suffocating her, giving her no freedom to relax and develop her considerable talents. Ralph and Mary by this time had gone to boarding school, which meant her presence at Beaulieu was less necessary. I desperately tried to save the situation, even converting a small building for her on the Mill Dam into a studio. Unfortunately other people began to exert undue destructive influence on our day-to-day lives so inevitably we found ourselves going down a road that could only lead to divorce. Fortunately Belinda had her own house nearby, inherited from her mother, so she moved there with Mary, while Ralph spent more time at Beaulieu. Divorces are always painful to all concerned. Personally, I did not want one and had hoped we could work things out. Nevertheless as far as our divorce was concerned we kept it non-adversarial as we were both determined to remain as friendly as possible for the sake of the children and the future. Some conditions laid down irked me, such as not taking the children abroad without permission, but I understand how important such a clause could be in some divorce proceedings. Christmas was a difficult time as Beaulieu Christmases were very traditional and Ralph was always very upset by changes in routine. It was indeed sad that we started to drift apart at a time when I felt that perhaps a little more understanding and patience would have saved the marriage, particularly for the sake of the children. Notwithstanding, I look back with gratitude for Belinda's contribution over the years.

But time is a great healer – it was not long before matters settled down, especially after my second marriage to Fiona. Today we could almost be called one big happy family. Belinda joins us on all family occasions, goes in and out of Palace House at will and agreed to be painted as part of a large family portrait that I commissioned from John Ward, which depicts three children, one wife and one ex-wife, my mother, one horse and five dogs, which I am delighted was shown at the Royal Academy. I felt it only fair that my older children should have their mother in the picture. The final accolade to the women in my life is that Fiona was happy that Belinda should be invited to our Silver Wedding dinner on 26 September 1999. In the past twenty-five years Belinda has lived happily nearby and established herself as an expert embroiderer, having created the famous New Forest Embroidery and a series of embroidered wall hangings I commissioned on the history of the Abbey, which are on display to the public in the Domus.

During the drawn-out period after the divorce my brother Robin asked me to join him and his girlfriend on a trip to the theatre and she brought along a friend of hers to make up the party. That girl was Fiona Herbert who worked in the film industry in Wardour Street. We got on very well and began to see more and more of each other. Admittedly I was on the rebound but as matters developed we four went to Turkey on a vintage car rally for the opening of the new Bosphorus Bridge that joined Europe to Asia for the first time. We had an uproarious time and we called the two girls our 'night mechanics'. I discovered that Fiona was a great swimmer and I used to get very worried when she would disappear for hours off the beach.

Back home it became more and more apparent to us that we were in love but neither wanted to rush things. Fiona's parents had recently returned from Rhodesia where she was born and were living near Arundel. Before we got married we decided to visit Africa to see her many relations and were generously looked after by Anton Rupert, the great South African entrepreneur who owned a lovely house in the Cape called Fleur de Cap, after which some of his wines were named. We finally agreed on 26 September as the date of our wedding – the same day as my sister Elizabeth's sixty-fifth birthday. There was the usual problem about divorced couples being married in church but we went to a register office in Lymington and from there direct to Winchester, where we had a blessing by John Taylor, the Bishop of Winchester, at a special service in the private chapel at his residence Wolesey Palace. We were loaned a lovely house in the South of France for our honeymoon, then returned to Beaulieu where Fiona started learning about the stately home business and produced a second son for me.

Fiona did not have such an easy time because she was basically a town girl. Brought up in Rhodesia, and educated in Switzerland, she was now working in London for a film production company. Nevertheless, she was fascinated by Beaulieu and wisely felt she could not compete with my mother's deep involvement in many of Beaulieu's organisations and activities – the Women's Institute for example – and decided to concentrate instead on activities closer to her heart, including the Countryside Education Trust, the Beaulieu school, ensuring that the public parts of the house were full of flowers, running Christmas fairs, and, most of all, lavishing her attention on our son, Jonathan. As an expert skier, she reintroduced me to the sport. I had given skiing up after breaking my leg in a serious accident in 1957 at Klosters, but now we enjoy being part of the Parliamentary Skiing Week at Davos each January. One of my greatest achievements was to introduce to her a love for opera, which we now both try to attend as regularly as possible.

I must admit that both wives sometimes found it extremely difficult to keep up with me and my various activities and interests, and both wives have found it necessary to get away from it all, from time to time – just as I enjoy being at the beach house by myself.

Since its construction, and during the summer months, the beach house has remained the centre of my entertaining activities. Hardly a weekend goes by without my playing host to large and varied groups of friends – occasions which allow me to indulge my culinary skills and Nature's bounty, using our own game, fish and special fare – seakale, sea spinach and samphire – not forgetting the wonderful gull's eggs that come from the mouth of the river. The house's proximity to the sea, some thirty yards, makes it ideal for all sorts of water sports – windsurfing and water skiing, and even swimming as the Solent gets much warmer than people think. However, if it is too cold I have a small sauna and jacuzzi to warm people up.

To me the beach house is a magical place, a much needed sanctuary when the pressures at Beaulieu and the rest of the estate get too demanding. Next door, my daughter has built a similar house, on the site that was originally the club house of a golf course created by my father in 1912, and for many years the residence of Ewen Montagu. Not far away are the romantic coastguard cottages where many of my close friends have weekend cottages, and where Sir Hugh Casson and family lived for many years. It is also where Dirk Bogarde's brother, Gareth, lives, and whose wife, Lucilla, I have known since I was a child.

Looking back from my mid-seventies I have been especially blessed by becoming a father to three splendid children, all very different but compatible with each other and following well-chosen careers. Ralph is first and, although he looks like me, is very much more of a Crossley like his mother and grandmother. From an early age he wanted to have a well-planned day and developed special likes and dislikes. From the start he was a great home lover and never expressed any desire to be anywhere else but Beaulieu – a significant pointer to his later life. It took some time before we realised he was a bit dyslexic, as is his mother, and found school work difficult – particularly learning from the printed word. However, in all artistic and design matters he excelled and, like my father, started taking a great interest in steam railways and signal boxes. Of course, boarding school proved a problem, coinciding with his nanny leaving, but luckily Walhampton was only 5 miles away from Beaulieu and not too academically strict and demanding. It soon became apparent that he would never get into Eton, which of course I would have liked, but in the end he went to Millfield, which he just about tolerated, because a master there understood his difficulties and let him do creative things with his hands. His happiest school period was when he came to live at home and went to the Sixth Form College at Brockenhurst, where he started to flourish. Always being a great believer that to survive an estate must have continuity of succession, I took great trouble to involve Ralph in estate matters from an early age and very soon started making plans to hand over to him as soon as was practicable and live out the requisite number of years. Although dangers existed, it did seem a prudent thing to do. The process was gradual and has now worked out very well, and by my seventieth birthday most of it had been handed over and at the same time Ralph was able to gain experience of estate administration. Meanwhile he graduated from the Central School in graphics and design, and got a job with the BBC, a great love of his, where he has been especially successful in reconstructing *Dr Who* programmes, recordings of which the BBC failed to keep. His greatest success has been the building of new social housing in the village for local people. For years we were frustrated in this aim because the village had no main drainage. After two decades of wanting new houses they are now a reality and have made a great contribution to its architectural appearance and the life of its inhabitants. Very many young working parents, who probably would have left, now have an opportunity to remain. I am confident that Ralph will carry on all the policies that my family has, for the past 150 years, tried to practise as good, benevolent, practical and progressive landlords who believe in the future prosperity of estates like Beaulieu.

In November 1964 a pink flag flew over Palace House to denote the birth of a daughter – the first since 1928. Mary always showed much more independence of character than her brother, being very resolute, not to say stubborn. When she firmly refused to go to the dentist I told her she could have no more sweets, to which she agreed without demurring and, in fact, did not for many years, which probably did her teeth more good than if she had gone to the dentist. I like to think that, although she looks like her mother, she has more of my character. She likes travel, new things and graduated with a theatre design degree from the Central School. Unfortunately there is very little money in that profession and she is now a very successful interior designer, her most recent commission being the home of the Earl and Countess of Wessex at Bagshot. Other commissions have been a golf club in Japan, restaurants in London and she is, of course, a great help to me at Beaulieu from time to time, having recently supervised the refurbishment of our hotel, the Master Builder's at Buckler's Hard. I am delighted that in June 1997 Mary got married to Rupert Scott, a distant cousin of ours from the Scottish Borders, having just completed the building of a new beach house on the Solent where she and her husband have become expert windsurfers, a sport which I discovered for the family in the 1970s. Mary was determined not to have a traditional wedding and settled for the tiny chapel in Buckler's Hard, arriving in my motor launch *Cygnet* and going away in an amphicar. The whole wedding had a very nautical theme to it and certainly was different. I am sure she will have a very successful life with her husband, who is an up-and-coming publisher.

Finally in 1975, a year or so after our marriage, I was blessed by Fiona having a son. This time I actually watched his birth in Southampton General Hospital, and was very inspired and wished I had seen the births of my other two children. It appeared that Jonathan was destined to be a scientist, always displaying a keen enquiring mind as to how things worked and very stubbornly doing his own thing. Initially, I was disappointed with how little interest he appeared to take in the estate and the Museum as a boy but he was always into something worthwhile and his life changed, I think, when I bought him his first computer, which he took to like a duck to water. As a young boy he was the first to explain to me all about the Internet and later e-mail. School was a mixed success – he excelled in science and maths but he hated games, which he thought were a waste of time, as was standing in a wood waiting for pheasants to fly over. His prep school was Hawtreys, founded by Dorian Williams, the show jumper commentator, and the school used to play against my school, St Peter's Court, before the war but had been evacuated to Wiltshire in 1940. After winning a science prize at school Jonathan embarked on a very successful career at Eton, becoming an Oppidan scholar and winning a scholarship to Cold Spring Harbour, the magnificent laboratory set up in Long Island by Professor Jim Watson who, together with his colleague Francis Crick, discovered DNA. Then to New College, my old college, to read chemistry, achieving a first-class degree, redeeming the family honour as neither his father nor grandfather had managed a degree at all. In 1998 he also helped organise the New College Ball, as did my father who installed electric light for the first time at such an occasion. Sadly chemistry graduates find it difficult to get well-paid jobs and so finally he decided on management consultancy as a stepping stone to an entrepreneurial career which one day will surely benefit him and hopefully Beaulieu in some as yet unforeseen way. It is very fortunate that he gets on so well with his half-brother and half-sister, and all three of them love Beaulieu. Like me, he is gregarious, enjoys travel and new experiences and is showing promising signs of having a good eye for business, and he may yet use his considerable scientific skills at some point in the future.

I must mention one other member of the family who has been a great support and friend through good and bad times, and that is my half-brother Robin Pleydell-Bouverie. He too had a difficult school period but all turned out well and he has become very successful in London in property development. In the 1950s I asked him to become a trustee of the estate, as was his father who died in 1951. Robin made a great contribution and had a very constructive attitude to problems that I believe we have overcome. Beaulieu has always been his home since he was born, although his family estates are in fact near Salisbury. His first marriage sadly failed but his present wife, Flickie, herself an interior designer, and their two children are hard-working, charming and successful, especially Nicholas who is excellent at rowing. I will always be extremely grateful to Robin for all he did over the years to foster the estate and encourage its development.

So what does all this say about me? Dare I give myself an alpha? Surely I deserve better than a second-class degree in life – even if I have to admit to moments of gamma and delta?

The titular head of my family is the Duke of Buccleuch and the present duke's father told me that one of the distinctive traits of the family is that we are all slow developers. This is undoubtedly true in my case. I must have inherited the genes through my grandfather, the second son of the Duke of Buccleuch, born Lord Henry Montagu Douglas Scott, but who changed his name to Douglas Scott Montagu on being made a peer in 1885, taking the title Lord Montagu of Beaulieu.

There is some evidence that the Scotts and the Montagus seem to grow up at a measured pace and fortunately keep their much-envied youthful looks. Additionally I feel that my personality has been influenced by being a Libran and feel I can sometimes cope with crises and dramas with better equanimity than most. Indeed, some people sometimes describe Librans as controlled schizophrenics. Nevertheless, I am a typical Libran, agonising sometimes on what decision to take or which shirt or tie to wear. Although we give the impression of uncertainty we are really just weighing things up and I was accused at school of expressing other people's opinions while pondering the issues until I had formed my own view. Nevertheless, it is accepted that Librans have charm, with peaceful, harmonious personalities, and will avoid at all cost all disruption or unpleasantness in their lives or anyone else's.

Self-analysis can be a trap and readers will be amused, I think, to hear that I was desperately shy and withdrawn as a child, especially when I had to meet other people. I have known myself stand in a bar for hours not daring to open a conversation with a person, even one drinking alongside me. If I were introduced I would undergo a complete turnabout of personality and immediately become the friendliest most outgoing person imaginable. It was just breaking the ice that I found difficult. I am full of imaginative ideas, but I then become desperately impatient if they are implemented slowly. I spend much time thinking of the future, thereby inheriting some of my father's skill and foresight, when he prophesied so accurately the effect that the internal combustion engine would have on the world. He subtitled his weekly magazine 'A Journal of Travel, by Land, Sea and Air' (founded in 1902) a year before the Wright brothers flew. In the same way, when in Canada in the 1940s, I was obsessively drawing rocket ships, which look today remarkably like the modern space ships.

I am proud to be a neophile for I love to experiment with new ideas, explore new places, new discoveries and experiences, new music, new food and wines ... and new friends. I am sorry for neophobes as they miss out on so much in life. I always adored travelling, and am rarely happier than when I am sightseeing in some exotic land and meeting its people. In all, there are few countries that I have not visited as I have covered most of Africa, America from the southern tip to Alaska; I have travelled from Peking to Paris via Nepal, one of my favourite countries. My most fulfilling experiences were my three treks in the Himalayas in Nepal with a group of friends and family. I shall never forget the emotions I felt at about 12,000 feet up in the mountains watching the moon glistening on the snow-covered peaks and listening to Mahler's Second Symphony, the 'Resurrection', on my Walkman. I was high on life in more ways than one and felt I was on the verge of paradise. Hard physical exercise like trekking up mountains is something that did not come entirely naturally, although I thoroughly appreciated the inspiring views and wild flora and fauna. Looking back on my life, I have been involved in all sorts of sports, from school soccer, rugby and squash to cricket. As an adult I went through a phase of loving water skiing, which was followed by windsurfing, jogging round Hyde Park every morning and cycling. My body needs exercise and I feel much better for it.

My worst battle was to defeat my shyness and it took many years. I was only too well aware that so many of my contemporaries were much more mature than I was. When I was only eighteen, I remember the embarrassment of being taken to the Bag of Nails, a Soho nightclub, which was the traditional place for young Guards officers to lose their virginity. I was impressed with the great sang-froid displayed by my friend, who with all the confidence of a twenty-five-year-old soon abandoned me and went upstairs with a girl, leaving me struggling to keep the conversation going with one of her friends.

Over the years I have taught myself to be more courageous both physically and mentally, and never was this more important than in 1954 when I had to face almost daily shocks and public shame.

I have not shrunk from describing the Montagu Case, even though I would much rather have maintained my long silence on the matter. I felt that I had to do so before it was too late. I do not regret having done so but I still feel, as I did then, that sex between consenting adults is a purely private and personal matter. If that miserable period in my life helped to make that a possibility then I am satisfied. As the Canadian statesman Pierre Trudeau memorably proclaimed: 'The State has no place in the bedrooms of its citizens.'

That publicity was unwelcome and in fact I did not at first enjoy being the centre of attention but to promote Beaulieu well I eventually taught myself to be more extrovert and to speak definitively on many subjects both in public and in the House of Lords. I am gregarious, trusting and generous to a fault, some would say too much so and more than I safely should be. I am proud to hold in major regard the importance of loyalty. However stung or hurt, I find it hard to desert a friendship and I am indeed proud that I am still on close terms with all the most important friends of both sexes in my life. I have never lost one by default and I cherish their loyalty to me.

Perhaps it is a desire to be liked, and I confess I like to be thanked, but I find accepting gifts and praise very difficult. My bad faults are numerous and I am aware that I am very impatient, which sometimes leads to being accused of being uncaring to those around me. I find it hard to show my emotions outwardly but they burst out when moved by theatre, films or music. I fear I do not always listen to what people say to me as I am probably thinking of something else instead. I am a fast worker and a natural delegator. This has its merits as I leave administrative work to my devoted staff who fill in the details while I have already moved on to the next task in hand.

That events in my life may have taken an all together different turn was sharply brought home to me in the early 1980s when I was involved in a traumatic car accident in the New Forest, just on the edge of the Beaulieu estate. My car collided head-on with another car which was overtaking on the brow of a hill. Regrettably, the man in the other car was killed outright. I was knocked unconscious, as was our good family friend, Richard Vessey, who was travelling with me. Fortunately, he only suffered a broken collar bone while I got away with a broken nose and crushed vertebrae from the whiplash. I am convinced our lives were spared because we were both wearing seat belts and my car, a Jaguar saloon, was built on a solid chassis. Although the impact of the accident tore the engine out of the frame, amazingly, the windscreen was not broken or cracked in any way. The staff at the Southampton General Hospital did us proud and I was well enough within ten days to appear on the Wogan morning radio programme, broadcast live from Beaulieu.

In the end, however, I recognise that, like any mere mortal, I can be no more than a cog helping to drive the wheels of progress. 'Forward, forward let us range,' wrote Tennyson. 'Let the great world spin for ever down the ringing grooves of change.' I like to think that in however small a way I have helped the world forward on the wheels of change.

Finally, however, I always return to the part of me which is forever England: Beaulieu itself. The key to the long-term survival and integrity of estates like Beaulieu is the continuity of succession. What constitutes the Beaulieu Estate today has been owned by the family since it was bought from Henry VIII in 1538. I have every confidence that my three children, Ralph, Mary and Jonathan, will continue to safeguard Beaulieu as a sacred trust, the ownership and management of which is to be enjoyed as a lifetime privilege, but which entails the handing down of the estate as intact as possible for future generations to enjoy. I know I can be confident that my children and their children will honour and cherish it, bearing in mind that our family belongs to Beaulieu and not Beaulieu to us. The next generation, the son of my daughter Mary and her husband Rupert Scott, born on 1 June 2000, symbolises my faith in the future. He will always belong to Beaulieu wherever he chooses to live.

That will be true of my children and their grandchildren just as it has been true of me.

There is still one question I ask myself and it is this: what if I had not written this book? I have done so to ensure that an accurate account of my life is presented and not one by an enterprising writer who sensationalises the facts and allows excessive rein to his imagination. I want my family and friends to understand my side of the story. This is a 'thank you' letter to them all: an appreciation of their understanding and sympathy over the years. I am what I am. And although I have many regrets I believe that I have reached this stage in my life as a more resilient and sympathetic person than I once was.

My life can certainly be described as 'Wheels Within Wheels': unconventional I may be but I am always positive and constructive in my outlook on life. I can blame only myself for the difficult paths I took, but nevertheless I am inwardly content and I am glad, at last, to have abandoned fear and told my honest and unusual tale. Meanwhile the swans and cygnets will still be on the river silently witnessing our family's future unfold.

Above all, I and the family have endeavoured to live according to our family motto:

SPECTEMUR AGENDO – May we be judged by our actions

INDEX

Ermine Street Guard, 236
Esdaile, Alfred, 87
Essex, Earl of, 8
Eton College, 47, 51–3, 55–9, 77, 80, 260–1, 283, 284–5
Evans, Anne, 265
Ewing, Maria, 249
Exbury, 173
Eyston, George, 294

Faithfull, Marianne, 275
Faiza, Princess, 65
Farouk, King, 65
Fearnley-Whittingstall, Bill, 111, 113, 137
Fearnley-Whittingstall, Bob, 111
Featherstonhaugh, David, 31, 35
Federation of British Historic Vehicle Clubs, 197
Federation Internationale de l'Automobile (FIA), 197
Federation Internationale des Voitures Anciennes (FIVA), 197
Felix, Julie, 274
Ferrier, Kathleen, 263
Festing, Andrew, 224
Ffrangcon-Davies, Gwen, 276
Fiat, 86
Fishlock, Trevor, 166, 172, 173
Flagstad, Kirsten, 263, 265, 266
Fletcher, Cyril, 35
Fonteyn, Margot, 262
Forbes, Patrick, 123
Forbes-Robertson, Jean, 276
Ford: Club Coupé (1950), 195; Jeep (1942), 195; Model T, 271
Ford, John, 93
Forster, Lord and Lady (uncle and aunt), 20, 35
Fortescue, Lord, 94
Fountains Abbey, 247
Fowler, Norman, 189
Fox-Andrews, James, 108
Fox-Andrews, Roy, 108
Fraser, Lady Antonia, 131, 134
Freeman, John, 270, 272
Freud, Clement, 189
Fuchs, Klaus, 128
Fürtwangler, Wilhelm, 263

Gage, Anne, 100, 101, 109, 125–6, 129–30, 293
Gaitskell, Hugh, 131
Garbett, Archbishop Cyril, 78, 122, 127
Garbo, Greta, 90
garden registers, 239
Garnock, David, Viscount, 291
Garsington Festival, 264
Genevieve, 187
George I, 9
George III, 9
George V, 21, 77
George VI, 33, 36, 58, 62, 63, 79–80
George, Prince Regent (George IV), 60
Gibbs, David, 260
Gibson, Sir Alexander, 249
Gielgud, Sir John, 122
Gift Aid legislation, 210
Gillespie, Dizzy, 274
Gilmour, Sir Ian, 94, 133
Gilpin, John, 88
Gilt and the Gingerbread, The (Montagu), 145, 153, 185
Gipsy Cavalier, A, 277
Gisborough, Lord, 258
Glen, Sir Alexander, 154, 161
Glenconnor, Lord, 84
Glenton, Bob, 294
Gloucester, HRH Prince Henry, Duke of, 29
Gloucester, HRH Prince Richard, Duke of, 228, 229, 230, 243
Glubb, Lt. General Sir John (Glubb Pasha), 66
Goalen, Barbara, 131, 188
Goddard, Lord, 98
Goering, Hermann, 104
Golan Heights, 75
Golden Arrow (Segrave land speed record breaker), 184
Golding, Francis, 237, 240, 251
Goldsmith, Jimmy, 278
Gollancz, Victor, 131
Gonella, Nat, 269
Goodall, Dr, 21
Goodman, Arnold, Lord, 160, 161
Goodman, Benny, 46
Goodrich Castle, 236
Goodwood House, 158
Gordon, John, 120–1, 122, 204
Gordon Bennett Races, 185